EYEWITNESS TRAVEL

FAMILY GUIDE

LONDON

LONDON, NEW YORK,
MELBOURNE, MUNICH AND DELHI
WWW.DK.COM

PUBLISHER
Vivien Antwi

LIST MANAGER
Christine Stroyan

MANAGING ART EDITOR
Mabel Chan

SENIOR EDITOR
Michelle Crane

EDITORS
Vicki Allen, Hugh Thompson,
Alexandra Whittleton

DESIGNERS
Louise Dick, Marisa Renzullo

PICTURE RESEARCH
Ellen Root

SENIOR DTP DESIGNER
Jason Little

SENIOR CARTOGRAPHIC MANAGER
Casper Morris

PRODUCTION CONTROLLER
Rebecca Short

PHOTOGRAPHY
Max Alexander

CARTOONS
Tom Morgan-Jones

OTHER ILLUSTRATIONS
Arun Pottirayil, Brian Delf, Trevor
Hill, Robbie Polley

DESIGN CONCEPT
Keith Hagan at www.
greenwichdesign.co.uk

Printed and bound in China by South
China Printing Co. Ltd., China

First published in the United States in
2012 by Dorling Kindersley Publishing,
Inc., 375 Hudson Street, New York 10014.
A Penguin Company

12 13 14 15 10 9 8 7 6 5 4 3 2 1

**Copyright 2012 © Dorling
Kindersley Limited, London**

Contents

*Colourful soft toys in Eric Snook's toy
shop, Covent Garden*

EYEWITNESS TRAVEL

FAMILY GUIDE

LONDON

Getting hands-on in a helicopter cockpit at the Royal Air Force Museum, Hendon

How to Use this Guide

This guide is designed to help families to get the most from a visit to London, providing expert recommendations for sightseeing with kids along with detailed practical information.

The opening section contains an introduction to London and its highlights, as well as all the essentials required to plan a family holiday (including how to get there, getting around, health, insurance, money and communications), a guide to family-friendly festivals and a brief historical overview.

The main sightseeing section is divided into areas. A "best of" feature is followed by the key sights and other attractions in the area, as well as options for where to eat, drink and play and have more fun. At the back of the book are detailed maps of London.

INTRODUCING THE AREA

Each area chapter is opened by a double-page spread setting it in context, with a short introduction, locator map and a selection of highlights.

Locator map locates the region.

Brief highlights give a flavour of what to see in the area.

THE BEST OF...

A planner to show at a glance the best things for families to see and do in each area, with themed suggestions ranging from history, art and culture to gardens and games.

Themed suggestions for the best things to see and do with kids.

WHERE TO STAY

Our expert authors have compiled a wide range of recommendations for places to stay with families, from hotels and B&Bs that welcome children to self-catering apartments.

Easy-to-use symbols show the key family-friendly features of places to stay.

Price Guide box gives details of the price categories for a family of four.

SIGHTSEEING IN LONDON

Each area features a number of "hub" sights (see below): pragmatic and enjoyable plans for a morning, afternoon or day's visit. These give adults and children a real insight into the destination, focusing on the key sights and what makes them

interesting to kids. The sights are balanced by places to let off steam, "take cover" options for rainy days, suggestions for where to eat, drink and shop with kids, ideas for where to continue sightseeing, and all the practicalities, including transport.

Introductory text focuses on the practical aspects of the area, from the best time of day to visit to how to get around using public transport.

The hub map identifies the sights featured in the chapter, as well as restaurants, shops, places to stay, transport, and the nearest playgrounds, supermarkets and pharmacies.

The Lowdown gives all the practical information you need to visit the area. The key to the symbols is on the back jacket flap.

The hub sights are the best places to visit in each area, and use lively and informative text to engage and entertain both adults and children.

Key Features uses illustrated artworks to show the most interesting features of each sight, highlighting elements likely to appeal to children.

Kids' Corner is featured on all sightseeing pages (see below).

Find out more gives suggestions for downloads, games, apps or films to enthuse children about a place and help them to learn more about it.

Eat and drink lists recommendations for family-friendly places to eat and drink, from picnic options and snacks to proper meals and gourmet dining.

The Lowdown provides comprehensive practical information, including transport, opening times, costs, activities, age range suitability and how long to allow for a visit.

Letting off steam suggests a place to take children to play freely following a cultural visit.

Next stop... suggests other places to visit, either near the key sight, thematically linked to the sight or a complete change of pace for the rest of the day.

Further sights around each hub, selected to appeal to both adults and children, are given on the following pages.

Places of interest are recommended, with an emphasis on the aspects most likely to attract children, and incorporating quirky stories and unusual facts. Each one includes a suggestion for letting off steam or taking cover.

Kids' Corners are designed to involve children with the sight, with things to look out for, games to play, cartoons and fun facts. Answers to quizzes are given at the bottom of the panel.

The Lowdown provides the usual comprehensive practical and transport information for each sight.

Colourful Union Jack balloons floating in front of Big Ben

Introducing
LONDON

The Best of London

A city with a rich history, impressive architecture, world-class museums, lush parks, superb shops and incomparable theatre, London is a treasure chest for visitors and has a wide choice of family-friendly activities. Explore famous monuments, then relax on a river cruise or in a park. Attend an art workshop, take part in an exciting sport, then find time to witness the spectacle of one of London's traditional ceremonies, full of heritage, pomp and colour.

For culture vultures

Start the day at **Tate Britain** (see p69) and try out the Art Trolley. Continue to **Westminster Abbey** (see pp66–7), where you can follow the Children's Trail, and then dress up as monks in the museum. Spend the afternoon with exciting games, map-making and clue-matching in **Tate Modern** (see p148).

Another day, take a family tour at the **National Portrait Gallery** (see pp82–3). Break for lunch in Chinatown, near Leicester Square, then follow one of the children's audio tours or printed trails at the **National Gallery** (see pp80–81).

Alternatively, climb up to the Whispering Gallery at **St Paul's Cathedral** (see pp130–31), and then explore the fascinating **Museum of**

Right Toys from the past on display at the Museum of London
Below Soldiers taking part in the Changing the Guard

Children in colourful costumes taking part in the annual celebrations of the Notting Hill Carnival

London *(see pp136–7)*. Hop on the Tube to the **V&A Museum of Childhood** *(see pp208–9)* and spend the afternoon doing a gallery trail.

In three days

Take an open-top bus tour *(see p22)* and hop off at the Queen's London residence, **Buckingham Palace** *(see pp74-5)*, to watch the Changing the Guard. Spend the afternoon in the **Science** and **Natural History museums** *(see pp180–3)*, then let off steam in the **Diana Princess of Wales Memorial Playground** *(see p177)*.

Next day, arrive early for a morning at that castle of castles, the **Tower of London** *(see pp122–3)*, followed by lunch in picturesque **St Katharine's Dock** *(see pp126–7)*. Go by river bus to the South Bank for a trip on the **London Eye** *(see pp160–1)* and a 3D movie at the Imax.

On the last day, spend the morning at **Madame Tussauds** *(see pp112–13)*. Enjoy lunch in Marylebone High Street, then visit a classic attraction – **London Zoo** *(see pp110–11)* or the **British Museum** *(see pp102–3)*.

By season

In spring, visit **Kew Gardens** *(see pp228–9)* to see spectacular carpets of bluebells and yellow daffodils, and stunning blossom. Take part in free, fun activities, such as the chocolate workshop and Easter egg hunt.

Book tickets in advance for a summer concert at glorious **Kenwood House** *(see pp216–17)*; pack a rug and delicious picnic (or pre-order one). Dress up in something colourful for the lively, late August Notting Hill Carnival.

Go for an autumnal walk on **Hampstead Heath** *(see pp216–17)* to see the glorious leaf colours, and, if it's one of those clear, sunny, autumn days, take a trip on the London Eye.

Do some Christmas shopping in **Harrods** *(see p185)* and visit Santa's Grotto. Go skating on the large outdoor rink at Hyde Park's Winter Wonderland *(see p16)*, then warm up afterwards with traditional tea at Brown's Hotel *(see p248)*.

Outdoors

After a morning at **Battersea Park Children's Zoo** *(see pp188–9)*, hire bikes and cycle round the park. Take a train to Waterloo and have lunch in Gabriel's Wharf, before visiting **Shakespeare's Globe** *(see pp146–7)*.

Let the kids loose in **Coram's Fields** *(see p52)*, then explore the canals from Little Venice to **London Zoo** *(see pp110–11)*. After visiting the zoo, go for a row on the boating lake in **Regent's Park** *(see pp110)* and finish with a play at Regent's Park Open-Air Theatre.

Visit **Kew Gardens** *(see pp228–9)* to clamber inside a giant badger sett and along the Xstrata Treetop Walkway. Or take a river cruise to **Hampton Court Palace** *(see pp236–7)* and get lost in the 300-year-old maze.

Costumed chefs rustle up historical delicacies in the Tudor kitchens at Hampton Court Palace

Left *Youngsters having fun in one of London's many free playgrounds.* **Right** *Running around and letting off steam in the grounds outside the British Museum*

On a budget

Entry is free to the permanent collections of London's major museums and galleries. Many also offer complimentary or inexpensive children's tours, trails, storytelling and workshops. The capital's parks (*see pp52–3*) also provide plenty of free family entertainment, including some playgrounds. And the city's excellent urban farms, such as **Vauxhall** (*www.vauxhallcityfarm. org*) and **Mudchute** (*www.mudchute.org*), do not charge for admission – although a donation of some kind is appreciated.

A great way to get to know the city is on foot, as London and its fascinating, historic architecture is like a living walk-through museum. **Transport for London** (*www.tfl.gov. uk/tfl/gettingaround/walkfinder*) suggests routes, or simply follow the river and watch the boats as you walk. A stroll around **Covent Garden** (*see pp88–9*) guarantees hours of amusement from the street performers.

For discount theatre tickets, visit the **tkts** booth in Leicester Square (*www.tkts.co.uk*), or one of the internet sites: **www. discounttheatre.com** or **www.lastminute. com**. The cheapest places to eat (*see pp36–9*), apart from a do-it-yourself picnic in a park, are often local cafés or ethnic restaurants outside of the central touristy areas – sometimes only a few streets away from the main drag.

Stage and screen

A number of London theatres are dedicated to performances for children (*see pp46–7*). Other theatres stage plays for younger audiences, particularly during school holidays, among them, the **Tricycle** (*www.tricycle.co.uk*), **Chickenshed** (*www.chickenshed.org.uk*), **Rose Theatre** (*www.rosetheatrekingston.org*), **New Wimbledon Theatre and Studio** (*www. ambassadortickets.com/Wimbledon*) and **Hackney Empire** (*www.hackneyempire.co.uk*).

A pantomime is a Christmas holiday highlight – for adults as well as children: among the best are those at the **Old Vic** (*www.oldvictheatre.com*) and **Richmond Theatre** (*www.ambassadortickets.com/ Richmond-Theatre*). Also at Christmas, there are ballets for children at the **Coliseum** (*www.ballet.org.uk*) and the **Royal Opera House** (*see p90*), and throughout the year at Sadler's Wells' **Peacock Theatre** and **Lilian Baylis Studio** (*www.sadlerswells.com*).

London's principal cinemas are **Odeon** (*www.odeon.co.uk*), **Vue** (*www.myvue.com*) and **Cineworld** (*www.cineworld.co.uk*). These and the independent **Clapham Picture House** (*www.picturehouses.co.uk/cinema/Clapham_ Picturehouse*) and **Electric Cinema** (*www. electriccinema.co.uk*), have regular kids' clubs.

Active London

Sports-mad families will find plenty going on in London to keep their heart rates up, whether they want to be participants or spectators (*see pp50–51*). Other activities that should appeal to energetic kids are climbing, go-karting, bowling, inline skating and even dry skiing.

Westway Sports Centre has a terrific beginners' climbing wall and a junior programme that includes family sessions (www.westwaysportscentre.org.uk/climbing). The best places for budding racing drivers (aged 8+) to go karting are **Playscape** (www.playscape.co.uk) and **Daytona** (www.daytona.co.uk), while children's bowling is offered at **Hollywood Bowl** (www.hollywoodbowl.co.uk/surreyquays.php), with special lightweight bowls, and **Bloomsbury Bowling** (www.bloomsburybowling.com). There are inline skating programmes for children in Kensington Gardens, run by **Roller Star** (www.rollerstar.co.uk), **LondonSkaters** (www.londonskaters.com) and **Citiskate** (www.citiskate.co.uk), which also operates elsewhere. For dry skiing within the M25, try **Sandown Ski Centre** (www.sandownsports.co.uk/ski-centre.htm) and **Bromley Ski & Snow Board Centre** (www.bromleyski.co.uk).

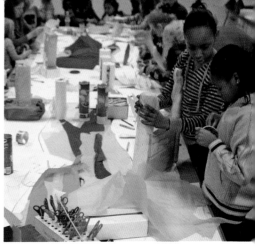

Above Children trying their hands at the arts and crafts on offer at Somerset House

Behind the scenes

London museums – big and small – often host highly imaginative workshops for families. Some of the best are at the **Geffrye Museum** (see p210), where the creative emphasis is on making or decorating objects. Workshops at the **Imperial War Museum** (see p164) can introduce children to storytelling through art and handle the difficult subject of war in a sensitive and involving way. At the small and slightly eccentric **Horniman Museum** (see pp222–3), children can find their imagination fired by being able to handle some of the extraordinary objects from the collection. As you would imagine, the **British Museum** (see pp102–3) puts on some excellent workshops, using technology to create fun, sometimes gruesome animations about mummification, fantastical creatures or the Aztec gods.

Going behind the scenes at a theatre can be fascinating for children, offering a glimpse into the hidden worlds of costumes, lighting, scenery shifting and even technical wizardry. Of all London's backstage tours, the most impressive are those organised by the **National Theatre** (see p162), **Royal Opera House** (see p90), **Shakespeare's Globe** (see pp144–7) and **Theatre Royal Drury Lane** (see pp90–91).

Below Enjoying a rollerblading lesson from a member of the Roller Star team in leafy Kensington Gardens

London Through the Year

The best time for a trip to London depends on what your family likes to do. The late spring, summer and early autumn will appeal to families who like being outdoors, while those who are happiest visiting museums and galleries might prefer to come in the winter, when the city is quieter and activities are not so dependent on the weather. Regardless of the elements, every season in London has plenty to recommend it.

Spring

Springtime in London, when the blossom is out, can be wonderful for a visit. Although London is among the most temperate parts of the UK and spring is often pleasant, the weather can be unpredictable, chilly and wet, so warm clothes and waterproofs are sensible precautions. From March onwards, outdoor sporting (see p50–51) and social events are fun for all the family and there is plenty in the calendar around Easter, especially for children.

A charming **Oranges and Lemons Service** is usually held on the third Thursday in March in St Clement Danes church. Pupils from the local primary school recite the well-known nursery rhyme, and each child is given an orange and a lemon after the service. On 21 March, the **Spring Equinox**, the first day of the solar New Year, is celebrated at Tower Hill in a historic pagan ceremony with contemporary druids dressed in long white robes.

On Good Friday, after an 11am service held at St Bartholomew the Great, Smithfield, hot-cross buns and coins are distributed to local children by the **Butterworth Charity**. Over the Easter weekend, there are **Easter egg hunts** at Battersea Park Zoo, Kenwood House, Fenton House, Handel House Museum and Kew Gardens. There is egg painting and rolling at Ham House, and, suitable for older children, the London Bridge Experience stages a gruesome treasure hunt for missing severed heads. There are traditional Easter **funfairs** on Hampstead Heath and the green opposite Hampton Court, and **Easter Eggstravaganza** is a four-day family street-skating event in Hyde Park, aimed at skaters of all levels.

Over the May Day bank holiday weekend, **Canalway Cavalcade** is a colourful occasion in Little Venice, featuring a boat rally, puppet shows and street entertainers. May is traditionally the month of fairs, and on the second Sunday there is a **May Fayre and Puppet Festival** in Covent Garden. A 10:30am procession is followed by a service at 11:30am in St Paul's Church, and until 5:30pm there are performances of Punch and Judy shows on the site where, in 1662, Samuel Pepys watched the first ever show staged in England. Over four days at the end of May, gardeners can enjoy the creative gardens at the **Chelsea Flower Show** at the Royal Hospital Chelsea.

Summer

Although never entirely reliable, the weather in summer is usually fine and sunny, with long days and light

Below left Children taking part in the Easter egg hunt at Fenton House in Hampstead. *Below right* A colourful and energetic performance of Crazy for You at Regent's Park Open Air Theatre evenings. People picnic in the parks; restaurants and cafés move their tables outside; and the city takes on an almost Mediterranean feel. There is always plenty to entertain families, from ceremonies (see pp18–9) and sporting events (see p50–1) to open-air theatre and concerts. The downside is that London can be very hot and crowded during July and August.

Summer has arrived when the **Royal Academy Summer Exhibition** opens in early June. It continues until mid-August and has a reputation as the art world's most eclectic show. Also on throughout the summer is the **City of London Festival**, an extensive programme of music, art, films and talks all over the city, and there are open-air plays (some specifically for children) at the **Regent's Park Open Air Theatre** and **Shakespeare's Globe**, operas (some for children) in **Holland Park**, and picnic concerts at **Kenwood House**. One of the first outdoor events is the **London Green Fair** in Regent's Park on the first Sunday in June, with eco-friendly attractions such as a mini farm, willow weaving, sewing classes and wigwam building.

Blackheath Bike and Kite Festival, in mid-June, features synchronized kite ballets, breath-taking mountain-bike stunts and

BMX racing, plus art workshops, bike skills and a funfair for under-12s. From mid- to late June, the streets of East London are filled with classical, jazz and contemporary music at the **Spitalfields Festival**, which includes toddlers' concerts, guided walks and musical picnics. There is more lively outdoor music, plus dancing and processions at the week-long **Greenwich & Docklands International Festival**.

In early July, the five-day **Hampton Court Flower Show** rivals Chelsea for its colour and variety, but is not as crowded. Mid-July sees the start of the ever-popular, two-month-long **BBC Promenade Concerts** (the "Proms") at the Royal Albert Hall, founded to bring both classical and modern music to a wider audience. Also in mid-July, **Doggett's Coat and Badge Race** dates from 1714 and sees apprentice Watermen of the River Thames in bright costumes rowing single sculls from London Bridge to Chelsea Pier. The summer season culminates with the Caribbean **Notting Hill Carnival** over August bank-holiday weekend. Europe's largest carnival, it is musical, vibrant and colourful, with a procession of eye-catching floats and costumes, steel bands and food stalls. Sunday is children's day.

Autumn

Once the summer crowds have gone, new shows open in the theatres, the shops restock and autumn days can still be blue-skied and sunny. In early September the **Mayor's Thames Festival** combines carnival, street art, music and river events between Westminster and Tower bridges. The highlight is Sunday's Night Carnival, when performers take to the streets, followed by fireworks on the river. The next Saturday, spectators return to the river to watch as some 300 boats, ranging from Hawaiian canoes to Viking longboats, row the **Great River Race**. The course is usually from Docklands to Ham in Surrey, and competitors often dress in flamboyant costumes.

On the first Saturday in October, the **Punch and Judy Festival** is staged in Covent Garden Piazza, with shows from 10:30am–5:30pm. The following day, the **Pearly Harvest Festival** at St Martin-in-the-Fields church is the flagship event of the Pearly calendar, attended by traditional Cockney pearly kings and queens.

Visit London between the end of October and the beginning of November and find piles of leaves to kick in the parks and the festivals of Halloween and Bonfire Night.

Below left Vibrant costumes and floats take centre stage at the Notting Hill Carnival. *Below right* Tucking into a feast on Southwark Bridge, part of the Mayor's Thames Festival

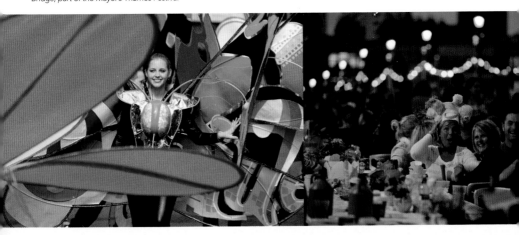

A terrific way to occupy the kids over half term is the **London Children's Film Festival**, with nine days of films, animations and workshops; it is based at the Barbican Centre but has events elsewhere too. For **Halloween**, there are always hair-raising shows at the London Dungeon and London Bridge Experience, and a spine-tingling tunnel ride on a narrowboat, courtesy of the London Canal Museum. Wrap up warm to watch the fireworks celebrating **Bonfire Night** on or near 5 November. Among the best are those in Bishop's Park, Ravenscourt Park, Battersea Park and on Blackheath.

If yours is a family of early birds, between sunrise and 8:30am on the first Sunday in November, a splendid collection of vintage, pre-1905 cars leave Hyde Park on the **London to Brighton Veteran Car Run**. Sleepy heads might prefer to catch the cars as they parade down Regent's Street the day before, from 1–4pm.

As evidence that winter is on its way, mid-November sees the switching on of the **Regent Street Christmas Lights** and the arrival of **Winter Wonderland** in Hyde Park (until early Jan), with the city's largest outdoor ice rink, a circus, toboggan slide and a host of other rides.

Winter

From early December, Christmas lights twinkle in the streets, decorations transform shops and public places, and Santa mans his grottoes. Skaters flock to outdoor rinks (see p50–1) and carol singing and the scent of roasting chestnuts spread through the streets. For families who enjoy culture, there are exhibitions, plays and ballets, and for those who prefer to shop, there are the sales. When it snows, children gather in the parks to toboggan and make snowmen. The downside is that transport tends to grind to a halt, and the snow quickly turns to slush.

If your children are aching for a glimpse of Father Christmas, take them to visit him in one of **Santa's Grottoes** in Harrods, Selfridges, Hamleys, Kew Gardens or Canary Wharf. On the first Thursday in December, there is a **Christmas Tree Lighting ceremony** to switch on the 500 lights that decorate the gigantic Norwegian spruce in Trafalgar Square. The event kicks off at 6pm with carol singing, and the lights are switched on at 6:30pm. Carols are sung beneath the tree most evenings in the run-up to Christmas, and there are also **carol concerts** at the Royal Albert Hall and the Horniman Museum

and **carol services** at many London churches. Magical candlelit services are held at St Mary-at-Hill, Southwark Cathedral and All Hallows-by-the-Tower.

A pre-Christmas treat for horse and dog lovers, the week-long **London International Horse Show** is held at Olympia in mid-December. Highlights include show jumping and dressage competitions, a Shetland pony race and dog agility and jumping events. Christmas Day is quiet in London, but there is a tremendous celebration on **New Year's Eve** with midnight fireworks at the London Eye (shown on giant screens in Trafalgar and Parliament Squares). The following day, more than 10,000 performers take part in the **New Year's Day Parade** from Piccadilly to Parliament Square from noon–3pm. There is a carnival atmosphere, with steel and marching bands, clowns, jugglers and classic cars and motorbikes.

Gasp at the impressive speed and skills of the sculptors at the **London Ice Sculpting Festival** in Canada Square Park in mid-January. In late January or early February, **Chinese New Year** is a wonderfully colourful and noisy Chinatown event, accompanied by dancing dragons, lanterns, flags, torches, food and firecrackers.

Below left A horse and rider taking part in an event at the Olympia London International Horse Show. *Below right* One of the sculptors at work on his ice sculpture at the London Ice Sculpture Festival, held at Canary Wharf.

The Lowdown

Spring

Battersea Park Zoo www.batterseaparkzoo.co.uk

Butterworth Charity www.greatstbarts.com

Canalway Cavalcade www.waterways.org.uk/events_festivals

Chelsea Flower Show www.rhs.org.uk

Easter Eggstravaganza www.lfns.co.uk

Fenton House www.nationaltrust.org.uk

Ham House www.nationaltrust.org.uk

Hampstead Heath funfair www.hampsteadheath.net

Hampton Court funfair www.hamptoncourtfunfair.co.uk

Handel House Museum www.handelhouse.org

Kenwood House www.english-heritage.org.uk

Kew Gardens www.kew.org

London Bridge Experience www.thelondonbridgeexperience.com

May Fayre & Puppet Festival www.coventgardenlondonuk.com

Oranges and Lemons Service www.raf.mod.uk/stclementdanes

Spring Equinox calendarcustoms.com/articles/druid-spring-equinox

Summer

BBC Promenade Concerts www.bbc.co.uk/proms

Blackheath Bike and Kite Festival www.lewisham.gov.uk/inmyarea

City of London Festival www.colf.org

Doggett's Coat and Badge Race www.watermenshall.org

Greenwich & Docklands International Festival www.festival.org

Hampton Court Flower Show www.rhs.org.uk

Kenwood House www.picnicconcerts.com

London Green Fair www.londongreenfair.org

Notting Hill Carnival www.thenottinghillcarnival.com

Regent's Park Open Air Theatre www.openairtheatre.org

Royal Academy Summer Exhibition www.royalacademy.org.uk

Shakespeare's Globe www.shakespearesglobe.com

Spitalfields Festival www.spitalfieldsfestival.org.uk

Autumn

Battersea Park www.wandsworth.gov.uk

Bishop's Park & Ravenscourt Park www.lbhf.gov.uk/Directory/News/Time_for_Bonfire_night.asp

Blackheath www.lewisham.gov.uk/NewsAndEvents/Events/Fireworks

Great River Race www.greatriverrace.co.uk

London Bridge Experience www.thelondonbridgeexperience.com

London Canal Museum www.canalmuseum.org.uk

London Children's Film Festival www.londonchildrenfilm.org.uk

London Dungeon www.the-dungeons.co.uk/london/en/index.htm

London to Brighton Veteran Car Run www.lbvcr.com

Mayor's Thames Festival www.thamesfestival.org

Pearly Harvest Festival www.pearlysociety.co.uk

Punch & Judy Festival www.thepjf.com

Regent's Street Christmas Lights www.regentstreetonline.com

Winter Wonderland www.hydeparkwinterwonderland.com

Winter

Carol services: All Hallows-by-the-Tower www.ahbtt.org.uk; Horniman Museum www.horniman.ac.uk; Royal Albert Hall www.royalalberthall.com; St Mary-at-Hill www.stmary-at-hill.org; Southwark Cathedral cathedral.southwark.anglican.org

Chinese New Year www.chinatownlondon.org

London Ice Sculpting Festival www.londonicesculptingfestival.co.uk

London International Horse Show www.olympiahorseshow.com

New Year's Day Parade www.londonparade.co.uk

Santa's Grottoes: Canary Wharf www.mycanarywharf.com; Hamleys www.hamleys.com; Harrods www.harrods.com; Kew Gardens www.kew.org; Selfridges www.selfridges.com; Christmas Tree Lighting www.london.gov.uk/trafalgarsquare/events/xmas.jsp

Public holidays

New Year's Day 1 Jan

Good Friday Mar/Apr

Easter Monday Mar/Apr

May Day first Mon in May

Spring Bank Holiday last Mon in May

August Bank Holiday last Mon in Aug

Christmas Day 25 Dec

Boxing Day 26 Dec

Below left Performers in lion costumes dance on podiums in Trafalgar Square to celebrate Chinese New Year. *Below right* A young enthusiast inspects a display of vintage cars; part of the London to Brighton Veteran Car Run.

London's Ceremonies

London has a full calendar of ceremonial events, occasions and customs, most of them connected with the royal family and many dating back to the Middle Ages or beyond. Not only are these colourful ceremonies historically important, but they are also bursting with spectacular costumes and pageantry, making them thrilling to watch for the whole family.

Trooping the Colour

Combining pageantry, military precision and music, this splendid ceremony in Horse Guards Parade honours the Queen's official birthday on a Saturday in mid-June. The Queen inspects a Guards' regiment from the Household Division, resplendent in their scarlet tunics and bearskins or plumed helmets and carrying the "colour" (their regimental flag). Afterwards, the Queen is escorted to Buckingham Palace to appear on the balcony.

Changing the Guard

Troops from the Household Division have been guarding the monarch since 1660, and a colourful ceremony marks the handover of duty from the old guard to a new one, usually with the Foot Guards in their full-dress uniform. Accompanied by a Guards' band, it takes place at Buckingham Palace daily from May–July and on alternate days throughout the rest of the year, starting soon after 11am. Children will enjoy the colour and spectacle.

State Opening of Parliament

The Queen opens the new session of Parliament each year, usually in November or December, with this historic ceremony. Although the actual ceremony – in which the Queen announces a programme of proposed legislation on behalf of her government – is closed to the public, it is televised and the royal procession from Buckingham Palace to Westminster can be seen along The Mall and Whitehall. The Queen travels in a state coach, while the Imperial State Crown has its own carriage.

Remembrance Day

Through this solemn ceremony in Whitehall on the second Sunday in November, the nation commemorates those who died in the two world wars and other more recent conflicts. The Queen and the royal family, political leaders and representatives of the armed forces observe a two-minute silence at 11am and, after the sounding of the last post, lay wreaths of poppies at the foot of the Cenotaph. Once the Queen has left, war veterans march past the Cenotaph to pay their respects.

Gun Salutes

The custom of firing a cannon was once a sign of respect or welcome, an unloaded gun indicating friendly intent. Today, gun salutes at the Tower of London and in Hyde Park mark royal occasions, such as

Below left The magnificent state coach taking part in the celebrations and pageantry of the Lord Mayor's Show
Below right Wreaths of poppies laid at the foot of the Cenotaph as part of the Remembrance Day ceremonies.

birthdays or anniversaries, and in Green Park, state visits, the State Opening of Parliament and the Queen's birthday parade. The basic royal salute is 21 rounds, but 20 extra rounds are included if it is fired in a royal park, palace or fortress. Salutes usually take place at 11am or noon.

Ceremony of the Keys

Yeoman Warders, or "Beefeaters", have performed this ceremony, which is open to the public, to secure the Tower of London every night for 700 years. The gates are locked at around 9:50pm by the Chief Yeoman Warder, escorted by four armed guards. He is challenged by a sentry, who then allows him to pass, acknowledging that he is the bearer of the Queen's keys. The ceremony ends with the Chief Warder taking the keys to safety while a trumpeter sounds the last post.

Lord Mayor's Show

This procession occurs on the second Saturday in November, taking the newly elected Lord Mayor in a state coach from the Guildhall to the Royal Courts of Justice, where he/she pledges allegiance to the Crown, and then comes back again. The custom,

---

The Lowdown

Beating Retreat www. guardsbeatingretreat.com
Beating the Bounds www.ahbtt.org. uk/history/beating-the-bounds
Ceremony of the Keys www.hrp.org. uk/toweroflondon/whatson/ ceremonyofthekeys.aspx
Lord Mayor's Show www. lordmayorsshow.org

Oak Apple Day www.chelsea-pensioners.co.uk/founders-day
Royal Ceremonies (Trooping the Colour; Changing the Guard; State Opening of Parliament; Remembrance Day; Gun Salutes) www.royal.gov.uk/ RoyalEventsandCeremonies/ Overview.aspx

---

which is almost 800 years old, starts at 11am, includes floats, military bands and City guildsmen, and culminates in fireworks at 5pm.

Beating Retreat

In a spectacular show, the massed bands of the Household Division perform this ceremony on two consecutive June evenings. It dates back to the time when a drum was used to communicate on the battlefield. Beating a retreat signalled the soldiers to stop fighting and return to camp. Rousing tunes are played by 300 musicians and the Queen usually takes the salute.

Oak Apple Day

Celebrated on 29 May, Oak Apple Day commemorates the lucky escape of the future Charles II from

Parliamentary forces by hiding in a hollow oak tree. The date was both Charles's birthday and the day in 1660 when he returned to London to claim the throne. Today, it is celebrated by Chelsea Pensioners, who decorate the statue of Charles II, their founder, at the Royal Hospital, and parade before royalty.

Beating the Bounds

Dating back to a time when there were few maps and boundaries were constantly in dispute, this custom involves walking around parish boundaries, whacking them with a stick and praying for protection. It is still observed on Ascension Day at All-Hallows-by-the-Tower, where the parish's southern boundary is in the middle of the Thames. Members of the party must board a boat to beat the boundary mark in the water.

Below left The Queen making her speech in the House of Lords during the State Opening of Parliament *Below right* Gun salute outside the Tower of London, marking a Royal occasion or celebration.

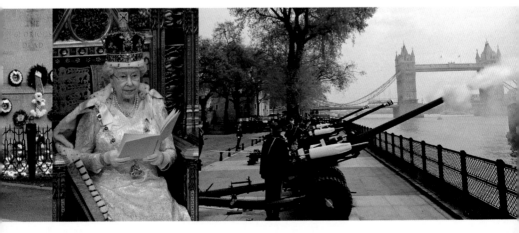

Getting to London

London is a major European transport hub, and there are many ways to reach it. By air, there is a huge choice of carriers from all over the world, and competition and budget airlines have driven down prices. Eurostar links the UK to Europe, and ferries, jetfoils and catamarans cross the English Channel and North Sea. Coaches to London from Europe are often the cheapest option.

Arriving by air

Five airports serve London: Heathrow, Gatwick, Stansted, Luton and City.

FROM HEATHROW

Heathrow is 24 km (15 miles) west of Central London. The quickest way in is by the **Heathrow Express**, a 15–20-minute non-stop train to Paddington Station. Trains depart every 15 minutes 5am–11:40pm. Tickets are cheaper for **Heathrow Connect**'s 25–35-minute stopping trains to Paddington, departing every 30 minutes 5am–11pm. Three stations link Heathrow to **London Underground**'s Piccadilly line, which takes around 50 minutes to the reach the West End. At night, the N9 bus runs to Aldwych, central London, leaving every 10–20 minutes.

The journey into London on the busy M4 motorway takes around 1 hour. **National Express** runs a good-value coach service to Victoria from Heathrow's bus station from 5:20am–9:40pm. A shuttle bus service to various London hotels is provided by **Heathrow Shuttle** and **SkyShuttle**, a cheaper alternative to taxis, which cost £45–75.

FROM GATWICK

London's second airport is 50 km (31 miles) south of the city and has two terminals. The fastest way into the city is on the **Gatwick Express**. Trains leave the South Terminal every 15 minutes from 4:35am–1:35am and take 30–35 minutes to get to Victoria Station. National Express coaches leave for Victoria every 30–60 minutes from 5:15am–9:45pm. Departing every 15 minutes from 4:25am to 1:10am, **easyBus** runs coaches to Earl's Court/ West Brompton. There are coach pick-up points in both terminals and the journey takes 60–90 minutes. Taxis to central London cost £50–60.

FROM STANSTED

The quickest way to travel the 56 km (35 miles) southwest to London from Stansted is on the **Stansted Express**. Trains run to Liverpool Street every 15 minutes from 5:30–1am, and take about 45 minutes. National Express provides 24-hour coaches to Victoria (every 20–30 minutes) and Stratford (every 30 minutes). **Terravision** coaches leave every 30 minutes for Victoria (7:15–1am) and Liverpool Street (6–1am). The 24-hour easyBus runs coaches to Baker Street every 20–30 minutes. Coaches to East London take 45–55 minutes and to the centre, 60–90 minutes. Taxis to the centre of town cost £70–80.

FROM LUTON

From Luton, 50 km (31 miles) north of London, a 5–10-minute shuttle bus runs from 5am–midnight to Luton Airport Parkway station (price included in rail tickets). From there,

Below left Ferry leaving the port of Dover, heading for France. *Below centre* The Docklands Light Railway station at London City Airport, from where the DLR takes passengers directly into Central London trains to St Pancras International are run by **First Capital Connect** (24 hours, every 10–30 minutes, taking 25–50 minutes) and **East Midlands Trains** (6am–10:30pm, every hour, taking 25–35 minutes). **Green Line 757** and easyBus both have a 24-hour coach link to Victoria. The journey usually takes slightly over 1 hour. Green Line coaches leave every 20 minutes–1 hour; easyBus ones leave every 15–30 minutes.

FROM LONDON CITY
London City Airport is in Docklands, 14 km (9 miles) from the centre. From the **Docklands Light Railway** (DLR) station, trains leave every 8–15 minutes to Canning Town and Bank, both also on the Underground. Bus number 473 goes to Stratford and the 474 goes to Canning Town. **LCYShuttle** operates a well-priced bus to Canary Wharf and central London. Taxis cost from £25 to the City and from £30 to the West End.

Arriving by train

St Pancras International is the London terminus for the **Eurostar**, the high-speed train linking the UK and Europe. From King's Cross St Pancras Underground station, it is possible to travel almost anywhere in the city via six Underground lines.

The city's other main stations and the areas they serve are **Liverpool Street**, East Anglia; **King's Cross**, the northeast; **Euston**, the northwest; **Paddington**, the west; **Waterloo**, the southwest; **Charing Cross** and **Victoria**, the southeast. All have Underground stations. Buy tickets in advance from **National Rail**.

Arriving by sea

The UK's ferry ports all have good rail links. Trains arrive at St Pancras International from **Dover**, which serves Calais and Ostend, and **Folkestone** (Calais and Boulogne), which is also the terminus for the **Eurotunnel**, the drive-on-drive-off rail service for cars. From **Newhaven**, which serves Dieppe, trains arrive at Victoria. Trains from **Portsmouth**, which serves Cherbourg, arrive at Waterloo, and from **Harwich**, which serves the Hook of Holland, they arrive at Liverpool Street.

Arriving by coach

Coaches from European and UK destinations arrive at **Victoria Coach Station**, often stopping at other London drop-off points. The biggest operator within the UK is National Express, with **Eurolines** serving as its European arm.

The Lowdown

Airports
Heathrow *www.heathrowairport.com*; Gatwick *www.gatwickairport.com*; Luton *www.london-luton.co.uk*; London City *www.londoncityairport.com*; Stansted *www.stanstedairport.com*

Underground/Buses/DLR
Transport for London *www.tfl.gov.uk*

Buses/Shuttle buses
easyBus *www.easybus.co.uk*; Green Line 757 *www.greenline.co.uk*; Heathrow Shuttle *www.heathrowshuttle.com*; LCYShuttle *www.lcyshuttle.co.uk*; National Express *www.nationalexpress.com*; SkyShuttle *www.skyshuttle.co.uk*; Terravision *www.terravision.eu*

Trains/Stations
Charing Cross *www.networkrail.co.uk/aspx/795.aspx*; East Midlands Trains *www.eastmidlandstrains.co.uk*; Eurostar *www.eurostar.com*; Euston *www.networkrail.co.uk/aspx/819.aspx*; First Capital Connect *www.firstcapitalconnect.co.uk*; Gatwick Express *www.gatwickexpress.com*; Heathrow Connect *www.heathrowconnect.com*; Heathrow Express *www.heathrowexpress.com*; King's Cross *www.networkrail.co.uk/aspx/867.aspx*; Liverpool Street *www.networkrail.co.uk/aspx/897.aspx*; National Rail *www.nationalrail.co.uk*; Paddington *www.networkrail.co.uk/aspx/935.aspx*; Stansted Express *www.stanstedexpress.com*; St Pancras International *www.stpancras.com*; Victoria *www.networkrail.co.uk/aspx/947.aspx*; Waterloo *www.networkrail.co.uk/aspx/959.aspx*

Ports
Dover *www.doverport.co.uk*; Eurotunnel *www.eurotunnel.com*; Folkestone *www.directferries.co.uk/folkestone.htm*; Harwich *www.harwich.co.uk*; Newhaven *www.newhavenferryport.co.uk*; Portsmouth *www.portsmouth-port.co.uk*

Coach
Eurolines *www.eurolines.com*; Victoria Coach Station *www.tfl.gov.uk/gettingaround/1210.aspx*

Below left A British Airways plane on the tarmac at London City Airport. Below right One of Eurolines' fleet of coaches, which serve the rest of the UK and much of Europe

Getting Around London

London has an excellent, comprehensive and busy public transport system. Transport for London (TfL) is responsible for buses, the Underground, Docklands Light Railway (DLR), London Overground, Barclays Cycle Hire and River Buses. The worst times to travel are during the morning and afternoon rush hours – 8–9:30am and 4:30–6:30pm from Monday to Friday. Possibly the most pleasant way to travel in London is by river bus.

By bus

London buses provide a cheap and enjoyable way of seeing the city as you travel. They generally run from 5am to 12:30am (7:30am–11:30pm Sun), with night buses, recognizable by the prefix N before the number, providing a less frequent service on many popular routes. Sometimes slow, particularly during rush hours, buses have dedicated lanes on most main roads and cover parts of the city that the Underground does not.

The traditional double-decker Routemaster, now only in service on two heritage routes, has been replaced by modern double-decker, single-decker and articulated or "bendy" buses, which have low-floor access for wheelchairs and buggies. Routes are displayed at bus stops and on the **Transport for London** (TfL) website. The destination is indicated on the front of the bus.

Make sure you are heading in the right direction and, if in doubt, ask the driver.

There are two types of bus stop: a normal stop, where all buses stop, and a request stop, with the same logo and the word "Request" beneath it. Buses only stop at request stops if you raise your hand at the stop or ring the bell on the bus. Night buses only stop on request.

Routemaster heritage buses Nos 9 and 15 are particularly good for sightseeing, but if the weather is fine, an even better way to see the city is from an open-topped double-decker. Guided bus tours are offered by **Big Bus Tours** and **Original London Sightseeing Tours**, which provide commentaries specially designed for children. Tickets are valid for 24 hours, and routes include most major landmarks, the service is hop-on-hop-off.

By Underground, DLR and train

Although perhaps not as pleasant or interesting as travelling by bus, the London Underground (the "Tube") is the fastest and easiest way to get around the city. It operates daily, except for 25 December, from approximately 5am to 12:30am and from 7:30am to 11:30pm Sun. If planning a journey late at night with several connections, be sure to set off in good time. The service is prone to delays and disruption, particularly at weekends, and trains can be very crowded during rush hours.

Stations are easily recognized by the TfL logo – a blue horizontal line across a red circle. There are 11 colour-coded lines, making it simple to plan journeys and changes. Maps are displayed in Tube stations and on trains. Some lines are straightforward single

Below left An iconic red double-decker London bus travelling through Central London. *Below right* London Underground sign showing where to pick up the different lines routes; others have several branches. The Circle line operates in a continuous loop around the centre, with one recent extension.

Once you are through the ticket barrier (see Tickets below), follow the signs to the platform for the line and direction you need. Check the front of the train and the platform's electronic indicator for the final destination and to make sure it's not branching off or terminating early. On leaving the train, there are well-signed exits, as well as connections to other lines.

Supporting London Underground, are the **Docklands Light Railway** (DLR), an automated, driver-less light rail system linking the City of London with the redeveloped Docklands area, including City Airport, and **London Overground**, a rail overground network serving suburban boroughs. The suburbs are also served by **National Rail** (visit its website). DLR trains run from 5:30am–12:30am Mon–Sat and 6:30am–11:30pm Sun. Overground train timetables are available on the TfL website.

With the exception of new stations, few Underground stations have a lift. The Transport for London website has a map marked with wheelchair symbols indicating Tube stations that have disabled access.

Travelling on the Underground with a pram or pushchair can be awkward, particularly during the rush hours.

Tickets

TfL divides the city into six charging zones for Tube, DLR, London Overground and National Rail services, radiating out from the most central Zone 1 to Zone 6, which includes the outer suburbs. Zones 7–9 extend beyond Greater London. Tube and rail fares are expensive, especially individual tickets for each separate journey. The most economical tickets that can be used on all forms of transport, including National Rail to Zone 9, are **Travelcards** – paper tickets available for one or seven days and in various combinations of zones – and **Visitor Oyster cards** – "smartcards" that store credit to pay for journeys. Both are available from the TfL website, Tube stations and **Travel Information Centres**. Oyster cards are also available from the many **Oyster Ticket Stops** (mostly newsagents) across London and can be charged up here, at Travel Information Centres and at Tube stations – but not National Rail stations. There is a small charge for the card, but it never expires so you can use it on your next visit.

Oyster cards are valid across all zones and automatically calculate the cheapest fare for the journeys you make in a day. To use your Oyster card, touch it on the yellow reader when you enter a bus and at the start and end of every Tube or train journey. Travelcards must be shown to the bus driver and placed into the ticket machine at the start and end of Tube or train journeys.

Children under 11 travel free on buses and up to four under-11s travel free on the Tube, DLR, London Overground and National Rail services when accompanied by an adult. Under-16s are also eligible for free bus and discounted Tube travel provided they have an 11–15 Oyster photocard, which must be ordered for a fee from the TfL website at least three weeks in advance. A simpler option, the child Travelcard gives 11–15 year-olds half-price travel on all Tube and rail networks.

Cash fares are not accepted on any central London buses. For those without a Travelcard or Oyster card, it may be possible to buy a ticket from a machine at the bus stop, but these are sometimes not working and only take exact change, so consider using a card. For buses outside the centre, it is possible to pay on the bus, but keep plenty of change handy.

Below left The red, blue and white London Underground logo, which can be found at every Tube station throughout the city.
Below right Platform in one of London's bustling overground stations.

By taxi

London's distinctive "black" cabs (although some now sport different colours) have drivers who must pass a tough test to prove their familiarity with the city before being licensed. Cabs can be hailed in the street if their yellow "taxi" light is illuminated. They can also be found at ranks outside airports, stations and some major hotels and stores, as well as various other locations throughout the capital. Once they have stopped, taxis are obliged to take you to your destination, provided it is within 9.6 km (6 miles) of the pick-up point and inside the Metropolitan area. The fare is shown on the meter, which will start ticking as soon as the driver accepts your custom, but there are additional charges for extra passengers, baggage, and if it is after 8pm. It is common practice to tip the driver 10–15 per cent of the fare. Cabs can also be ordered online or by phone from **Radio Taxis** and **Dial-a-Cab**.

By mini-cab

Mini-cabs are not governed by the same strict regulations as black cabs and the drivers are not as well qualified. Order a mini-cab by phone, or email or by visiting a mini-cab office, and agree the fare in advance. Do not hail one in the street as it is illegal for mini-cab drivers to take customers without a booking. For names of local mini-cab firms, enter your location into **Findaride** on the TfL website. **Lady Minicabs** only employs women drivers.

By car

Expensive parking and congestion charging are designed to deter people from driving in Central London, and traffic, particularly on arterial roads outside the congestion zone, can be very heavy during rush hours. The charge for driving in the congestion zone, which covers the area to the east of Park Lane, south of Marylebone/Euston Road, west of Tower Hamlets and north of Elephant and Castle, is £10 per day (7am–6pm, Mon–Fri), payable on the day, or £12 if paid by midnight the following day. It costs £9 if you register online for **Congestion Charging Auto Pay**. Payments can be made online, by phone, by text or at shops across London (visit Shop locator on the TfL website). If you fail to pay in time, you will be fined £120, reduced to £60 if you then pay within 14 days.

Parking in Central London, usually in pay-and-display bays with payment by mobile or text, can be scarce and restrictions need to be observed. Be careful not to park in a residents-only bay during the designated hours. There is also no parking on red routes or on double yellow lines. You can park on single yellow lines in the evenings and on Sundays. Parking illegally or overstaying the time limit in a pay-and-display bay can result in a fine and/or your car being wheel-clamped or towed away. A notice should be displayed informing drivers of where to go to pay their fine and collect their vehicle.

There are plenty of car-hire firms in London, including **Avis**, **Budget**, **Europcar**, **Hertz** and **Thrifty**, which have offices at airports and other locations throughout the city, but the best rates are through comparison websites such as **travelsupermarket.com**. For large families, **5th Gear** has 7- and 9-seaters, plus child and booster seats to rent. Most firms offer a car delivery and collection service. All drivers need to study the UK **Highway Code** and familiarize themselves with the traffic signs used in London.

By river

Regular river services are operated by TfL's **River Bus**, which operates four lines between Putney in the

Below left A London "black" cab travelling through the streets of Central London. *Below right* A cyclist picking up one of the Barclays Cycle Hire bikes from one of the many ranks located throughout the city.

west and Woolwich Arsenal in the east. Timetables, which change according to the season, and maps are available on the TfL website. For river tours and cruises, see p28.

By bicycle

Barclays Cycle Hire is a public bicycle-sharing scheme, sponsored by Barclays bank and launched in 2010. Its distinctive blue-and-grey bikes are now available from ranks at locations throughout Zone 1 (shown on a map on the TfL website). Register with TfL, or pay by card at machines on the spot, borrow a bike and drop it off at any docking station in the scheme. The bikes have three gears and adjustable seats. They are quite heavy though, so maybe not ideal for long rides. Bikes suitable for all the family can be rented from the **London Bicycle Tour Company**, which also arranges cycle tours, and **Go Pedal**, which offers child seats and trailers. If you are cycling with children, TfL promotes **Greenways** – safe, family-friendly routes running through parks, forests, and quiet streets and along waterways. It is always advisable to wear reflective clothing and a helmet when cycling and to use a strong lock to deter thieves.

The Lowdown

By bus
Big Bus Tours www.bigbustours.com
Original London Sightseeing Tours www.theoriginaltour.com
Transport for London www.tfl.gov.uk

By Underground, DLR & train
Docklands Light Railway www.tfl.gov.uk/modalpages/2632.aspx
London Overground www.tfl.gov.uk/modalpages/2688.aspx
National Rail Enquiries www.nationalrail.co.uk
Oyster Ticket Stops ticketstoplocator.tfl.gov.uk
Travel Information Centres www.tfl.gov.uk/tickets/14432.aspx

By taxi and mini-cab
Dial-a-Cab www.dialacab.co.uk
Findaride www.tfl.gov.uk/tfl/gettingaround/findaride/default.aspx
Lady Minicabs www.ladyminicabs.co.uk
Radio Taxis www.radiotaxis.co.uk

By car
5th Gear www.5th-gear.net
Avis www.avis.co.uk

Budget www.budget.co.uk
Congestion Charging Auto Pay www.tfl.gov.uk/roadusers/congestioncharging/17096.aspx
Europcar www.europcar.co.uk
Hertz www.hertz.co.uk
Highway Code www.direct.gov.uk/en/TravelAndTransport/Highwaycode/index.htm
Thrifty www.thrifty.com
travelsupermarket.com www.travelsupermarket.com

By river
River Bus www.tfl.gov.uk/modalpages/15547.aspx

By bicycle
Barclays Cycle Hire https://web.barclayscyclehire.tfl.gov.uk/maps
Go Pedal www.gopedal.co.uk
Greenways www.tfl.gov.uk/roadusers/cycling/11673.aspx
London Bicycle Tour Company www.londonbicycle.com

On foot
London Walks www.walks.com
Transport for London www.tfl.gov.uk/gettingaround/walking

On foot

Although it is large, London is still a great city to explore on foot, whether it's a stroll around the back streets of Covent Garden or the City or a more serious ramble through the green spaces of Richmond Park or over Hampstead Heath. The TfL website has a walking route planner. A number of companies arrange themed walks, from Ghosts of the Old City to Harry Potter Film Locations. The most established operator is **London Walks**.

Below left A river bus cruising along the Thames, past Cleopatra's Needle on the Embankment. *Below right* A family walking across Westminster Bridge, leaving the Houses of Parliament and Big Ben behind them.

London by River
Westminster Bridge to Blackfriars Bridge

The Thames has always been at the heart of London life. Today, its banks are lined with important, historic buildings and monuments, from the medieval Tower to the Houses of Parliament. Although commercial ships no longer ply the Thames as they did until the 1950s, the river now has a role as an attraction. Whether you take a river cruise or a commuter shuttle, a boat trip is a fascinating way to see the city. For most cruises, children must be at least 5 years old.

Westminster Bridge to Blackfriars Bridge

see next page

South Bank

① Big Ben *(see p68)* is the nickname of the huge bell inside the Palace of Westminster's clock tower, and is also used to describe the tower itself, one of the city's most recognizable symbols.

② Watch fish swim beneath your feet at the wonderful Sea Life London Aquarium *(see p164)*, home to more than 500 different marine species, in the former seat of London's council.

③ Take a "flight" on the London Eye, a giant Ferris wheel *(see pp160–61)*, for one of the capital's best views. The pods allow you to see for miles in every direction (as long as the weather is clear).

Temple

Waterloo Bridge

Savoy Pier

Charing Cross

Festival Pier

Embankment

Embankment Pier

Hungerford Railway and Golden Jubilee Footbridges

Waterloo Millennium Pier

Westminster Pier

Westminster

Westminster Bridge

④ Rejuvenated during the 1951 Festival of Britain, the South Bank boasts London's most important arts complex, as well as many other sights, including Shakespeare's Globe, Tate Modern and the BFI Southbank *(see pp140–46)*.

⑤ Buried in the pedestal of Cleopatra's Needle *(see p81)*, the ancient Egyptian obelisk presented to Britain in 1819, is a Victorian "time capsule" containing such everyday items as hairpins, a baby's bottle, a railway guide and a map of London.

⑥ Britain's first luxury hotel, the Savoy, was built in 1881 by Richard D'Oyly Carte, who produced Gilbert and Sullivan operas at his adjacent theatre. The hotel reopened in 2010 after a three-year renovation, and though it is lovely to look at, it's more of an adult treat to visit.

⑪ Christopher Wren's masterwork, St Paul's *(see p130)* once dominated the city skyline.

⑦ In winter, head to 18th-century Somerset House *(see p93)* to skate on its central courtyard's open-air ice rink; in summer enjoy one of the concerts or outdoor movies held there. Inside is the superb Courtauld Gallery art collection.

⑧ A landmark building, the OXO Tower was owned by a company that makes beef stock. As advertisements were banned, the windows were designed to spell out the name of the famous brand. The top-floor restaurant and public gallery have terrific views.

⑨ The capital's showcase for significant international modern art, Tate Modern has 88 light and airy galleries in the former Bankside power station.

⑩ When the Millennium Bridge opened in 2000, pedestrians were unnerved to feel it swaying. The "Wobbly Bridge", closed for two years while the wobble was eliminated, connects Tate Modern *(see p148)* to St Paul's *(see pp130– 31)*.

The Lowdown

Big Ben www.parliament.uk/about/living-heritage/building/palace/big-ben

London Eye www.londoneye.com

OXO Tower Barge House Street, SE1 9PH; www.harveynichols.com/oxo-tower-london

Savoy Hotel Strand, WC2R 0EU; www.fairmont.com/savoy

Sea Life London Aquarium www.visitsealife.com/London

Somerset House Strand, WC2R 1LA; www.somersethouse.org.uk

South Bank www.southbanklondon.com & www.southbankcentre.co.uk

Tate Modern Bankside, SE1 9TG; www.tate.org.uk/modern

London by River continued ➤

London by River (continued)
Southwark Bridge to St Katharine's Dock

Southwark Bridge
to St Katharine's Dock

see previous
page

City

Southwark

⑬ This grand church became Southwark Cathedral (see p150) in 1905. Don't miss the memorials to Shakespeare or the beautiful Great Screen (see detail, right).

⑭ One of the fascinating artifacts in the fine building of Fishmongers' Hall (1834) is the dagger used by Lord Mayor Walworth, to kill Wat Tyler, leader of the 1381 Peasants' Revolt.

⑮ Climb the 311 steps to the top of Christopher Wren's Monument (see p124) to the Great Fire of 1666 for a superb panorama. It stands 62 m (205 ft) high, the same as the distance to the Pudding Lane bakery where the fire started.

Canon Street

Bankside Pier

Southwark Bridge

Monument ⑮

⑫

Cannon Street Railway Bridge

London Bridge

London Bridge City Pier

⑫ Audiences at Shakespeare's Globe (see p144–5) are meant to heckle, just like they did in the Bard's day. The original theatre burnt down in 1613, but this is a fantastic replica made from brick, oak and thatch.

⑬

London Bridge

⑯

⑯ Known as the "Larder of London" in the 19th century, when it handled most of the city's imported dry goods, Hay's Galleria is a former wharf converted into a smart shopping arcade.

The Lowdown

Design Museum Shad Thames, SE1 2YD; www. designmuseum.org

Fishmongers' Hall London Bridge, EC4R 9EL; www.fishhall.org.uk

Hay's Galleria London Bridge City, Tooley Street, SE1 2HD; www.haysgalleria.co.uk

HMS Belfast Morgan's Lane, Tooley Street, SE1 2JH; hmsbelfast.iwm.org.uk

The Monument www. themonument.info

St Katharine's Dock www. skdocks.co.uk

Shakespeare's Globe 21 New Globe Walk, Bankside, SE1 9DT; www.shakespearesglobe.com

Southwark Cathedral London Bridge, SE1 9DA; cathedral. southwark.anglican.org

Tower Bridge www.towerbridge. org.uk

Tower of London www.hrp.org. uk/toweroflondon

Thames Cruises, Taxi Services and River Buses Bateaux London 020 7695 1800; www.bateauxlondon.com

City Cruises (Westminster to Greenwich) 020 7740 0400; www.citycruises.com

Thames Clippers (London Eye to Greenwich) 020 7001 2222; www.thamesclippers.com

Thames Executive Private Charters & River Taxi 01342 820605; www. thamesexecutivecharters.com

Thames River Services (Greenwich, Thames Barrier) 020 7930 4097; www. thamesriverservices.co.uk

Transport for London River Bus and River Tours Information www.tfl.gov.uk/river

Turks (Kingston, Richmond & Hampton Court) 020 8546 2434; www.turks.co.uk

Westminster Passenger Services Association (Kew, Richmond & Hampton Court) 020 7930 2062; www.wpsa.co.uk

⑰ Kids can clamber up ladders, duck through hatches and let their imagination run riot on the navigation deck of HMS *Belfast (see pp154–5)*, a World War II warship that played a crucial role in the Normandy landings of 1944.

⑱ Britain's most famous medieval fortress, the Tower of London *(see pp122–3)* is steeped in gory history. Prisoners were brought by boat through the notorious Traitors' Gate for execution. The Tower contains a superb collection of arms and armour as well as the priceless Crown Jewels.

Fishy fact: Jaws!

In February 2004, a recently dead red-bellied piranha, a native of the Amazon, was discovered on the deck of a boat in the Thames. The mystery was that this razor-toothed killer fish with short powerful jaws, which, in a group, can devour large prey in seconds, is unable to survive in cold temperatures. It appeared to have been dropped by a seagull onto the deck. But how had the seagull got hold of it? It is likely that it was a pet that grew too big and was set free by its owner. It died in the cold water and floated to the surface, where it was picked up by a gull, but the bird must have decided it had bitten off more than it could chew!

⑲ A London icon, Tower Bridge is still raised to let ships pass, but not as often as it was in the days of tall-masted cargo vessels. Visit the exhibition to see the hydraulic machinery that operated the bridge before electrification in the 1970s.

Tower Millennium Pier

⑰

Tower Bridge ⑲

St Katharine's Pier

⑳

㉑

⑳ Now a lively marina, St Katharine's Dock *(see p126–7)* was built on a site with over 1,000 years of history. This was London's first and most successful Docklands' redevelopment in the 1970s.

㉑ Play vintage video games or glimpse the styles of the future at the Design Museum *(see p157)*, which opened in this white 1930s-style building in 1989.

Practical Information

London has an impressive range of useful facilities for visitors, many of which are available 24 hours a day. Among them are cashpoint machines (ATM), bureaux de change, pharmacies and the health advice and information service, NHS Direct. To make the most of a visit – and to ensure everything goes as smoothly as possible – it is essential to have some inside knowledge of the city.

Passports, visas and customs

Visitors from outside the European Economic Area (EEA) and Switzerland need a valid passport to enter the UK; EEA and Swiss nationals can use identity cards instead. Most countries now require children (under the age of 18) to have individual passports, and children travelling to the UK must have their own or be included on an accompanying parent's passport.

Visitors from European Union (EU) states do not need a visa. Neither do visitors from the USA, Canada, South Africa, Australia and New Zealand who are in the UK for less than six months. Visitors from other countries should visit the **Home Office UK Border Agency** website to check whether a visa is required and, if so, how to apply. Visitors from EU states can bring unlimited quantities of most goods into the UK for personal use without paying duty. For information about allowances from outside the EU, visit the **HM Revenue & Customs** website.

Insurance

It is advisable to take out travel insurance to cover the cancellation or curtailment of your trip, the theft or loss of money and other personal property, and any necessary medical treatment. If you are planning to drive in London, take out fully comprehensive driving insurance and carry a valid driver's licence. Keep all car receipts and police reports in case of an insurance claim.

The UK has reciprocal health care agreements with all EEA states, Australia, New Zealand and a number of other countries listed on the **National Health Service** (NHS) website. Visitors from these countries, are entitled to free treatment under the NHS. However, there are exceptions for certain kinds of treatment, which is why taking out medical insurance is always advisable. Ensure you bring all documentation with you, such as the **European Health Insurance Card** (EHIC).

Visitors from a country without a reciprocal health agreement, such as the US, are only covered for treatment received in a hospital Accident and Emergency (A&E) department, so insurance is particularly important.

Health

In a medical emergency, dial 999 for an ambulance. They are on call 24 hours a day. There are a number of London hospitals with 24-hour A&E

Below left Some of the coins currently in circulation in the UK. **Below right** London police officers on duty in the busy area surrounding Piccadilly Circus.

departments, but not all treat children. **Chelsea and Westminster**, the **Royal London** and **St Mary's** have specialist paediatric departments. To find a General Practitioner (GP), or to check out symptoms online or by phone, use **NHS Direct**, which has a website and a 24-hour telephone advice line staffed by nurses.

For minor injuries or ailments, consult a pharmacist. Search for your nearest pharmacy on the NHS Direct website. Most have the same opening hours as other shops, although some stay open later. **Zafash** is open 24 hours daily; pharmacies that open till midnight include **Pharmacentre, Bliss, Boots Victoria Station** (9pm Sun) and **Boots Piccadilly Circus** (6pm Sun). Although it is possible to buy many medicines over the counter, some are only available on prescription. Pack any prescription drugs your family is likely to need, including allergy medication. There is now a keen awareness of serious food allergies and intolerances and items in shops are usually clearly labelled. If you have an intolerance, check the ingredients of dishes served in hotels and restaurants. The UK sun can be surprisingly hot and burning, especially for young children, so it is wise to use a good sunscreen.

Personal safety

Crowded shopping areas such as Oxford Street, busy markets, and Tube stations and bus stops are popular with thieves, who sometimes work in teams. Carry a handbag that closes effectively and keep it near you. Don't carry large amounts of money, or valuables, around with you, and avoid badly lit areas at night.

Never leave a bag or suitcase unattended on the Tube, at a station or in any other public place. It may be treated as a suspect package and cause a security alert.

In an emergency, dial 999 or 112. Report serious crimes at a Police Station (the **Metropolitan Police** website lists station addresses). For non-emergency crimes you can complete a form (available on the website) or dial 101. If you lose something on public transport, report it via the TfL website or visit the **TfL Lost Property Office**.

When out, arrange a safe meeting place with your children in case you become separated. Make sure they know where you are staying and the best people to ask for help (a police officer or security guard) if they get lost. Remind your children that cars in the UK drive on the left, and to always use pedestrian crossings or underpasses to cross the road.

Money

The unit of currency in the UK is the pound sterling (£), divided into 100 pence (p). There are coins in circulation for 1p, 2p, 5p, 10p, 20p, 50p, £1 and £2, and notes for £5, £10, £20 and £50. There is no limit to the amount of cash you can bring into the UK, but a pre-paid cash passport, used like a debit card, or traveller's cheques are more secure alternatives. Keep a separate note of the cheques' serial numbers. Visa and MasterCard are the most widely accepted, followed by American Express, Diners Club and JCB.

High street banks, such as **HSBC, Barclays** and **NatWest**, and **post offices** will change money and traveller's cheques at better rates than bureaux de change, whose advantage is longer opening hours. **Thomas Cook** and **Chequepoint** have numerous London offices, and Chequepoint in Gloucester Road is open 24 hours. **Travelex** and **American Express** cash traveller's cheques (remember your passport). Cashpoint machines (ATMs) are also widely available, but beware of ATM crime. Only use an ATM where and when you feel comfortable. Never accept help from strangers while using the ATM, don't be distracted and always cover your hand when you enter your PIN.

Below left The Boots pharmacy in Piccadilly Circus. *Below centre* Transport for London officers patrolling a busy platform in one of London's many Tube stations

Communications

The UK telephone country code is +44 and the area code for London is 020. To phone abroad, dial 00, followed by the country code. If you have problems with a number, call the operator on 100 or the international operator on 155. The main mobile phone network providers are **Orange**, **O2**, **T-Mobile** and **Vodaphone**. To save money, consider buying a UK SIM card. Most public phones are operated by coins, credit cards and **British Telecom Calling Cards**, available through the BT website. Some are Internet phones, from which you can send emails and texts.

WiFi is available in most hotels, often for a fee, and for free in many cafés, parks and other public places. Public libraries offer free Internet access on their computers, although you might have to queue. **Visit London** features a list of Internet cafés.

Apart from numerous satellite and cable channels, UK television has a number of digital stations, of which two, BBC1 and BBC2, are public service; the rest, including ITV1, Channel 4 and Channel 5, are commercial. Ceefax and Teletext give travel and weather news. London's radio stations, BBC London Live (94.9FM), Capital FM (95.8FM) and LBC (97.3FM), have regular news and travel bulletins. For news plus entertainment listings, the daily *Evening Standard* newspaper is free. The magazine *Time Out* is also excellent for listings. The *International Herald Tribune* is available on the day of issue, and European publications usually appear a day or so later. **Gray's Inn News** in Theobalds Road stocks a range of foreign newspapers and magazines.

Opening hours

Shops are generally open 9:30am–6pm Mon–Sat and 11am–5pm Sun, with late-night shopping until 8pm on Wed or Thu in central areas. Official banking hours are 9:30am– 3:30pm Mon–Fri, although most banks stay open until 5pm and many are open 9:30am– noon Sat. In general, museums and galleries open daily 10am–5:30pm or 6pm; some stay open later one night a week, usually Friday. Tourist attractions often open at 9am or 9:30am; last admission is 30 minutes before closing time. Always check times before setting out.

Visitor information

The Visit London website provides information on popular attractions and places to stay and lists what's on. Another website, **Young London**, suggests events for kids. The main Tourist Information Centres are **Britain and London Visitor Centre (BLVC)** and **The City of London Information Centre**.

Disabled facilities

Most of London's major sights are wheelchair accessible. Before a visit, phone to check that your needs can be met. Websites for accessible attractions are **Artsline**, **Disability Now** and Visit London (which also features hotels). For accessibility on public transport, visit the **TfL** website. There are an increasing number of adapted toilets; many are part of the National Key Scheme (NKS), unlocked by a key from the **Royal Association for Disability and Rehabilitation** (RADAR), which also produces a guide to their locations.

Time

London operates on Greenwich Mean Time (GMT) in winter, 5 hours ahead of Eastern Standard Time, and from late March to late October, changes to British Summer Time, 1 hour ahead of GMT. You can check the exact time by phoning the BT Speaking Clock on 123.

Below left The internet café area of The Hoxton hotel. *Below centre* Child playing with a Nintendo DS – be sure to pack a variety of games and activities to keep youngsters occupied.

Electricity

UK voltage is 240V AC, and plugs have three square pins and take 3-, 5- or 13-amp fuses. Visitors will need an adaptor for appliances.

What to pack

If you forget something, don't worry unless it is your child's much-loved toy or blanket. You can buy almost awnything else in London, but bring particular brands if your children have strong preferences. Let the children choose some of their favourite clothes and toys. Be super-organized and order nappies and wipes through **Amazon** to be delivered to your hotel or apartment.

Be prepared for changeable weather: raincoats and umbrellas are essential, even in summer, when you will also need sunscreen. In winter, bring warm clothes and shoes with non-slip soles. Always pack comfy shoes. For young children, a compact buggy might be handy.

Bring toys for the journey that will keep the kids occupied but won't disturb other passengers. If it's a long flight, buy a few new toys and hand them out at intervals. Include books, puzzles, crayons, paper, colouring and sticker books and cards. If your children have Game Boys, bring headphones and mains chargers.

The Lowdown

Visas and customs
Home Office UK Border Agency www.ukba.homeoffice.gov.uk
HM Revenue & Customs www.hmrc. gov.uk

Insurance
European Health Insurance Card ec.europa.eu
NHS www.nhs.uk/NHSEngland/ Healthcareabroad/Pages/ Healthcareabroad.aspx

Health
Bliss 5–6 Marble Arch, W1H 7EL; 020 7723 6116
Boots Victoria Station; 44–6 Regent St, W1B 5RA; www.boots.com
Chelsea and Westminster Hospital 369 Fulham Rd, SW10 9NH; 020 8746 8000; www.chelwest.nhs.uk
NHS Direct www.nhsdirect.nhs.uk
Pharmacentre 149 Edgware Rd, W2 2HU; 0207 7723 2336; www. pharmacentre.com
Royal London Hospital Whitechapel Rd, E1 1BB; 020 7377 7000; www. bartsandthelondon.nhs.uk/about-us/ how-to-find-us/the-royal-london
St Mary's Hospital Praed St, W2 1NY; 020 3312 6666; www.imperial.nhs.uk/ stmarys
Zafash 233–5 Old Brompton Rd, SW5 0EA; 020 7373 2798; www.zafash.com

Personal safety
Metropolitan Police www.met.police.uk
TfL Lost Property Office 200 Baker Street, NW1 5RZ; 0845 330 9882; www.tfl.gov.uk/contact/871.aspx

Money
American Express www. americanexpress.com/uk
Barclays www.barclays.co.uk
Chequepoint www.chequepoint.com
HSBC www.hsbc.co.uk
NatWest www.natwest.com
Post Office www.postoffice.co.uk
Thomas Cook www. thomascookmoney.com
Travelex www.travelex.com

Communications
British Telecom Calling Cards www. payphones.bt.com
Gray's Inn News graysinnnews.com
O2 www.o2.co.uk
Orange www.orange.co.uk
T-Mobile www.t-mobile.co.uk
Vodaphone www.vodafone.co.uk

Visitor information
Britain and London Visitor Centre 1 Regent St, SW1Y 4XT; 0870 156 6366; www.visitlondon.com
The City of London Information Centre Guildhall, EC2P 2EJ; 020 7606 3030; www.cityoflondon.gov.uk
Young London www.london.gov.uk/ young-london/kids/index.jsp

Disabled Facilities
Artsline www.artsline.org.uk
Disability Now www.disabilitynow.org.uk
RADAR www.radar.org.uk
TfL www.tfl.gov.uk/gettingaround/ transportaccessibility/1167.aspx

What to pack
Amazon www.amazon.com

Below left A huge selection of tourist brochures and leaflets on display at Allen House apartments. *Below centre* The main desk at the City of London Information Centre

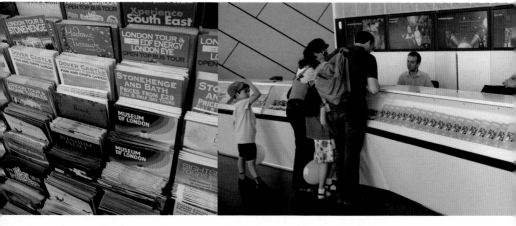

Where to Stay

Staying in London is expensive, but there are plenty of family options among the hotels, B&Bs and apartments. Some hotels and B&Bs provide rooms for four, or suites of connected rooms. Some can provide camp beds or sofa beds, but typical rooms are not large and will be a squeeze for four. Apartments can be more flexible. The best family accommodation provides cots, high-chairs and even babysitting services. Check what is on offer before you book. For information on accommodation options, go to the Visit London website.

Hotels

London hotels once had a reputation for being unfriendly places for families, where children were rarely seen, and if they were, they should certainly not be heard. But times have changed and most welcome children now. Many have special children's rates or allow kids to stay free in their parents' room and provide them with complimentary or half-price breakfast. Some also have flexible meal times. Expensive West End hotels are now among the most child-friendly. Many employ kids' concierges, who can suggest fun outings and make reservations for shows and attractions. They also keep collections of story books, toys and suitable DVDs, arrange special meals, and provide a host of things to tempt tinies, from fun bed linen to cookery sessions.

Hip designer hotels are not often so family friendly, but in the same price bracket there is a core of charming, family-run establishments with genial staff prepared to go the extra mile for their younger guests.

Chain hotels can be an excellent choice for families. What they lack in character and location, they make up for in value for money and children's facilities. Among the family-friendliest chains are **Apex**, **Crowne Plaza**, **Marriott**, and **Park Plaza** at the upper end of the market, and **All Seasons**, **Novotel** and **Premier Inn** at the budget end.

Bed & breakfast

There are two types of B&B: a simple hotel with no restaurant, and a private home where bedrooms are let out to guests. At their best

clean, comfortable and friendly, the former offer a less expensive alternative to hotels and a base from which to explore the city (most have limited public areas and are not places for lingering). The breakfast is usually a full English and included in the price.

If the owners are welcoming and amenable, staying in a home can be remarkably successful, and you might even make friends for life. But success is not guaranteed: most private houses only have a few rooms to let and it can be tricky to find one with suitable family accommodation. Using a specialist home stay agency is advisable (see p242), or try the **Bed & Breakfast and Homestay Association**, an affiliation of several reputable agencies whose properties are inspected regularly.

Below left Stylish bedroom at The Hoxton hotel in Shoreditch. **Below right** The kitchen and living area of one of the self-catering SACO – Holborn apartments located in Central London.

Self-catering

Staying in an apartment is probably the most relaxing option for families, especially if you are in London for more than a few days. Most apartments have a minimum stay of two nights to one week. Jet-lagged children, on the go from dawn, can have the run of the apartment without disturbing others. It also means you don't always have to eat out. You can cook your children's favourite meals (particularly useful for fussy eaters) and save money. Another alternative, is a home swap. This is best arranged through an established agency such as **Home Base Holidays**, **Home Link**, **Intervac** or the US-based **Home Exchange**.

The choice of apartments is between serviced and privately owned. Most London apartments are serviced, with a concierge and a cleaner. **BridgeStreet**, **Cheval Residences**, **Citadines**, **Fraser Place**, **MiNC** and **SACO** all have several buildings in good locations for families. Other apartments are attached to a hotel, where guests can still have breakfast and use the facilities. Privately owned apartments are less expensive, but harder to find. Some agencies have them on their books (see p242). Most are in the suburbs.

The Lowdown

Apex www.apexhotels.co.uk
All Seasons www.all-seasons-hotels.com
Bed & Breakfast and Homestay Association www.bbha.org.uk
BridgeStreet www.bridgestreet.com
Cheval Residences www.chevalresidences.com
Citadines www.citadines.com
Crowne Plaza www.ichotelsgroup.com/crowneplaza
Expedia www.expedia.co.uk
Fraser Place www.frasershospitality.com
Home Base Holidays www.homebase-hols.com
Home Exchange www.homeexchange.com
Home Link www.homelink.org
Intervac www.intervac.co.uk
lastminute.com www.lastminute.com
Late Rooms www.laterooms.com
Marriott www.marriott.co.uk
MiNC www.mincapartments.com
Novotel www.novotel.com
Park Plaza www.parkplaza.com
Premier Inn www.premierinn.com
SACO www.sacoapartments.co.uk
Travelocity www.travelocity.co.uk
Visit London www.visitlondon.com

Rates

London hotels usually quote room rates rather than prices per person and include VAT, but not always breakfast (double check before booking). Rates tend to remain high throughout the year, although it is possible to find reductions through special offers and weekend breaks, often on a minimum two-night stay. Generally, the longer you stay, the better the rate, and the best-value deals are available by booking in advance online. If they are not fully booked, some hotels offer last-minute discounts on their published "rack rates". Some of the best deals are available through websites such as **Late Rooms** and, for city breaks as well as accommodation, **Expedia**, **lastminute.com** and **Travelocity**.

Price categories

The three price categories in this guide are based on accommodation for a family of four for one night during high season, inclusive of service charges and any additional taxes. The inexpensive category is under £120; moderate is £120–200; and expensive is over £200. Inexpensive accommodation is extremely hard to find in London, where hotels are notoriously costly.

Below left The elegant exterior of the Arosfa B&B near Regent's Park. *Below right* The smart lobby of the Grange City hotel, located minutes from the Tower of London.

Where to Eat

Once hushed and barely tolerant of children, London's restaurants have become more accommodating towards families, and dining has grown more informal. Noisy children will not be welcome in any restaurant, but even upmarket establishments will be happy to see well-behaved ones, and often provide high chairs, colouring books and crayons. The choice of cuisines is enormous, offering dishes from all over the world. Prices given in this guide allow for a two-course lunch for a family of four, excluding wine but including soft drinks.

Chinese

The obvious place to go for Chinese food is Chinatown in the West End. Its pulsing heart, pedestrian-only Gerrard Street, is lined with exotic aroma-filled supermarkets and restaurants that range from plain eateries with bare tables and rows of glazed ducks in the windows to elegant places with wide-ranging menus. Chinese families eat out regularly and the restaurants are all geared to cater for children. Many have high chairs, and all will provide small portions – try dim sum, which only comes in small servings. Most children love the delicate flavours, from rice, noodles and dim sum dumplings to spring rolls and crispy aromatic duck (a fun dish for children as they can construct their own pancake parcels).

Indian

Indian curries are among the UK's favourite dishes. For truly authentic dishes, head to the Indian communities of Southall in west London or Brick Lane and Bethnal Green in the east, where you will also find Bangladeshi and Pakistani restaurants. Although many dishes are likely to be too hot and spicy for young taste buds, there are many gentle versions that older children might relish, such as tandoori, tikka masala, korma and pasanda. Mild curries are often made with coconut milk. If the dish is too hot, a little yogurt will calm it down (water provides only temporary relief). Curries are served with rice or flat breads, such as naan or chapati, and crisp poppadoms. Vindaloo, madras and jalfrezi are among the spiciest. Two family-friendly Indian

restaurants with kids' menus are **Imli**, which has a vibrant dining room, and the Covent Garden **Masala Zone**, with many Rajasthani puppets suspended from the ceiling.

Thai

Kensington and Fulham have a choice of Thai restaurants, including the well-established **Blue Elephant**, which has a stunning garden-style interior. Children will be entranced by its carp ponds crossed by little bridges, waterfall and bar that is a replica of the Royal Barge. There are also plenty of modest local restaurants and pubs and cafés that serve Thai food. Although some dishes are incredibly fiery (ask the waiter if unsure), Thai menus always contain milder ones, often inspired by Chinese cuisine. Satay (made with

Below left Indian restaurants and curry houses line Brick Lane in East London *Below right* The interior of a Chinese restaurant in Chinatown, in the heart of the West End.

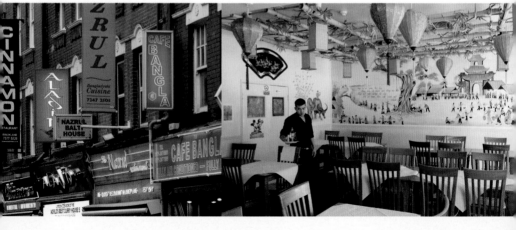

peanuts), noodle recipes such as pad Thai, sweet and sour dishes and spare ribs usually appeal to children.

Greek and Turkish

The food is very similar to that of the Middle East, with mezze (small bites and dips) being an integral part of the meal. Greek specialities include tzatziki (yogurt, garlic and cucumber dip), dolmadakia (vine leaves stuffed with rice, herbs and sometimes meat), spanakotyropita (filo pastry parcels filled with spinach and feta cheese), keftedes (meatballs with mint and shallots), moussaka (layers of potatoes, aubergines, courgettes and minced lamb topped with béchamel sauce and cheese), lamb and chicken kebabs and simply grilled meat and fish.

Similar Turkish dishes have slightly different names: for instance, cacik is a version of tzatziki and dolma of dolmadakia. It is traditional to start a meal with soup, and then children might enjoy kuzu tandir (oven cooked-lamb), eksili köfte (meatballs in a lemon sauce) or iskender (mixed grill with yogurt and tomato sauce served over pitta bread). In both cuisines, desserts such as baklava are very sweet and syrupy. The restaurants are concentrated in central and north London, and

dinner is often accompanied by music and dancing, and sometimes plate smashing in Greek restaurants. For Greek food, try the traditional tavernas **The Four Lanterns** and **Konaki**, and for Turkish, try **Sofra**.

Indonesian and Malaysian

If your children have adventurous tastes, seek out London's Indonesian and Malaysian restaurants: most are in the centre, including **Melati** and **Bali Bali**, which serve dishes from both countries. They don't have children's menus, but obliging staff will be happy to bring children's portions. Both cuisines have been influenced by Thailand, China, India and the Middle East. Rice and noodles are staples, and satay chicken and beef kebabs appear regularly on menus. Some dishes contain hot chilli peppers, but Indonesian specialities that might tempt children include gado-gado, (vegetable salad with peanut dressing) and nasi uduk (rice in coconut milk). Milder Malaysian dishes include Hainanese chicken and noodle dishes such as hokkien mee and konloh mee. Finish with fragrant purple mangosteen (fruit) or goreng pisang (banana fritters).

Below left The outside seating area of The Real Greek restaurant on the South Bank
Below right The buffet at Young Cheng, Chinatown

The Lowdown

Al Waha 75 Westbourne Grove, W2 4UL; 020 7229 0806; www. alwaharestaurant.com

Ask www.askrestaurants.com

Bali Bali 150 Shaftesbury Avenue, WC2H 8HL; 020 7836 2644; www. balibalirestaurant.com

Benihana www.benihana.com

Blue Elephant 3–6 Fulham Broadway, SW6 1AA; 020 7385 6595; www.blueelephant.com

Brasserie Gérard www. brasseriegerard.co.uk

Café Rouge www.caferouge.co.uk

Carluccio's www.carluccios.com

Chicago Rib Shack 145 Knightsbridge, SW1X 7PA; 020 7591 4664; www.thechicagoribshack.co.uk

Ed's Easy Diner www.edseasydiner. com

The Four Lanterns 96 Cleveland St, W1T 6NP; 020 7387 0704; www. the4lanterns.com

Giraffe www.giraffe.net

Gourmet Burger Kitchen www.gbk. co.uk

The Real Greek www.therealgreek. com

Hard Rock Café 150 Old Park Lane, W1K 1QZ; 020 7514 1700; www. hardrock.com

Imli 167–9 Wardour St, W1F 8WR; 020 7287 4243; www.imli.co.uk

Konaki 5 Coptic St, WC1A 1NH; 020 7580 9730; www.konaki.co.uk

Nando's www.nandos.co.uk

Noura www.noura.co.uk

Maroush www.maroush.com

Masala Zone 48 Floral St, WC2E 9DA; 020 7379 0101; www. masalazone.com

McDonald's www.mcdonalds.co.uk

Melati 30–31 Peter St, W1F 0AR; 020 7437 2011; www.melati- restaurant.co.uk

Ping Pong www.pingpongdimsum. com

Pizza Express www.pizzaexpress. com

Roast The Floral Hall, Stoney St, SE1 1TL; 0845 034 7300; www. roast-restaurant.com

Sofra 36 Tavistock St, WC2E 7PB; 020 7240 3773; www.sofra.co.uk/ sofra_coventgarden.htm

Spaghetti House www. spaghettihouse.co.uk

Strada www.strada.co.uk

Tas www.tasrestaurant.com

The Diner www.goodlifediner.com

Wagamama www.wagamama.com

Zizzi www.zizzi.co.uk

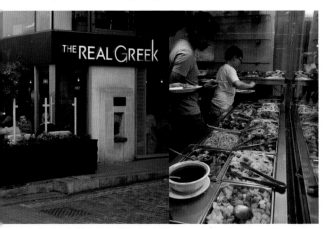

Middle Eastern

It is easy to overlook Middle Eastern food as a family option, but the selections of little hot and cold dishes – mezze – particularly suit children. Most kids are familiar with hummus (a smooth, mild chickpea dip), but there are plenty of new dishes to try: samboussek (a pastry triangle filled with meat, cheese or vegetables), tabbouleh (a salad of bulgur wheat, chopped mint, parsley, tomato and spring onion, with lemon juice and olive oil) and fatoush (a lemon-flavoured salad with parsley, mint and thin, crisp pieces of toasted flatbread), as well as larger dishes of marinated chicken and lamb. At their best, these dishes are bursting with fragrant flavours without being too spicy. There is a cluster of Middle Eastern restaurants in and around Edgware Road, most of which specialize in Lebanese food, among them are several in the **Maroush** chain and, slightly further west, **Al Waha**.

British

Once burdened with a reputation for being tasteless and stodgy, British cuisine was unpopular with other nationalities. But times have changed and a clutch of high-profile chefs, such as Jamie Oliver, Heston Blumenthal and Gordon Ramsay, have transformed it, borrowing from other nations while never forgetting their roots.

Some British restaurants make a great effort to appeal to families: one such is **Roast** in the foodie paradise of Borough Market. Here, you will find high chairs, colouring books and a children's menu, as well as excellent traditional British cooking using locally sourced, free range and organic ingredients. Excellent food is also available in a number of the city's gastropubs – pub-restaurants that opened in the 1990s and serve good-quality food in pleasant surroundings, most of which welcome children.

Italian

Of all the world's cuisines, Italian food has to be the most child-friendly, at least in the form of pizza, pasta and ice cream. Children will also be welcomed and fussed over by the friendly staff in Italian restaurants, trattorie and pizzerias. The best places tend to be family-run and unpretentious, serving classic, reasonably priced dishes, with a special menu for children, perhaps including pasta with a simple sauce such as pesto (basil and cheese), pomodoro (tomato), bolognese (meat) or carbonara (eggs, cheese and ham or bacon), home-made pizza or simply cooked meat. There will usually be a choice of different flavoured ice creams to follow.

Spanish

The growing popularity of tapas restaurants and bars has raised the profile of Spanish cuisine in London. Like the Italians, the Spanish are well-disposed to children, and their tapas meals (small portions of different dishes) allow kids to try out new flavours and ingredients without having to order a whole course. The restaurants are usually informal and meals relaxed. Some have children's menus, but tapas such as jamón Serrano and jamón Ibérico (both dry-cured hams), calamares fritos (fried squid), gambas al ajillo (garlic prawns), tortilla (Spanish omelette) and croquetas (croquettes) are tasty without being too sophisticated.

French

The French, whose cuisine is considered one of the finest in the world, have been influencing British cooking ever since the Norman Conquest, and in London today

Below left A branch of the popular Italian chain Carluccio's *Below right* A serving of the classic British dish, fish and chips, best eaten straight from the paper wrapping it comes in there are plenty of good French restaurants serving high-grade food. As people have become more health-conscious, the once typical rich cream- and butter-based sauces have been replaced by lighter, more delicate dishes. Brasseries and bistros are more likely to have children's menus than upmarket restaurants, and feature such favourites as steak or steak haché (burger) and frites (fries), chicken, omelettes and salade Niçoise, with plenty of choice for dessert, from apple or lemon tart to chocolate mousse and ice cream.

North American

Londoners have had a love affair with North American food since the **Hard Rock Café** opened in 1971. With its juicy burgers and fries, hot dogs, barbecued chicken and ribs, creamy milkshakes, American-style decor and rock'n'roll music, the hard Rock Cafe is a piece of the States transported to Old Park Lane. Other restaurants appeared in its wake, including the authentic and child-friendly **Chicago Rib Shack** in Knightsbridge, and a number of replica diners. The food is hearty, the setting is fun and children couldn't be better catered for.

Chain restaurants

They may not be the most imaginative choice, but chain restaurants are guaranteed to be a safe option for families, with high chairs, easy-wipe surfaces, suitable, good-value food, and no complicated dishes, pristine linen, snooty staff or exorbitant prices. And it doesn't have to be the ubiquitous but universally popular burger and chips at **McDonald's**. For North American food, try **Ed's Easy Diner** and **The Diner**, replicas of a 1950s original; for good-quality burgers try the **Gourmet Burger Kitchen**. Another popular chain, **Nando's**, specializes in chicken dishes with Portuguese flavours. For Chinese food, the **Ping Pong** chain serves up dim sum-style dumplings, and Pan-Asian dishes are staples at **Wagamama**. Although Japanese food is not usually popular with children, at **Benihana**, meals are theatre, with all the ingredients cooked sizzlingly before your eyes. **Maroush** and **Noura** are Lebanese chains; the **Real Greek** really is Greek; **Tas** is Turkish; and **Brasserie Gérard** and **Café Rouge** are French. Among the most family-friendly Italian chains are **Ask**, **Carluccio's**, **Pizza Express**, **Spaghetti House**, **Strada** and **Zizzi**. And for good-value international food that kids all love, there's **Giraffe**.

Below left Tucking into a meal at Giraffe Below right A delicious selection of cakes and pastries on display at Paul

Shopping

Whether it's in a shiny modern mall, a famous traditional department store, a distinctive independent shop or a lively street market, shopping in London is an exciting experience. It is one of the world's great commercial cities, with thousands of stores selling everything anyone in the family could want. Although luxury items are expensive here, dedicated hunters can find bargains in year-round sales, street markets and cut-price shops.

Shopping streets

OXFORD STREET, W1

London's main shopping street is lined with more than 500 shops, from major department stores such as **Selfridges, John Lewis** (see *Department Stores and Shopping Malls for both*) and **Debenhams** (nos. 334–348), to the flagship stores of world-famous brands, including **Nike** (no. 236), **Topshop** (no. 216) and **Gap** (nos. 223–225), along with a generous smattering of tacky tourist shops. At the western end, the Marble Arch **Marks & Spencer** (no. 458) is the company's largest and best-stocked store. Busy and brash, Oxford Street heaves with crowds at weekends, during the January and June sales and before Christmas, when it is decked with festive lights. When it's busy, using Oxford Street Tube station can be a disconcerting experience for anyone with children.

It's easier to use Bond Street Tube station, which is a little further west along Oxford Street, close to John Lewis, Selfridges and Debenhams.

KING'S ROAD, SW3

Chelsea's King's Road had its heyday in the "Swinging Sixties" when it was at the heart of bohemian London. Though not so trendsetting today, it remains popular for its upmarket High Street clothes, jewellery and accessories shops. On Sloane Square, **Peter Jones** is the department store west Londoners find indispensable. Other useful shops include **Trotters** (no. 34) and **Igloo** (no. 227) for children's clothes and a few toys; **Paperchase** (no. 289) for stationery, art supplies and gifts; and **Bluebird** (no. 350), a smart restaurant, chilled café with courtyard and food store rolled into one.

KENSINGTON HIGH STREET, W8

Favoured by fashion-conscious hippies in the 1960s and 70s, "High Street Ken", as it is affectionately known, is not as crowded as Oxford Street and is possibly more functional than the King's Road. As for shops, it has all the usual suspects: **Trotters** (no. 127), **Topshop** (nos. 42–44), for fashion-conscious children's clothes, **Russell & Bromley** (no. 151) for good-quality shoes, **Waterstone's** (no. 193) for books and magazines, and **TK Maxx** (nos. 26–40), which sells designer clothes at knock-down prices. There is also a huge branch of the American organic grocery store, **Whole Foods Market** (nos. 63–97). The best thing is that it's easy to escape to nearby Hyde Park or Kensington Gardens (*see pp170–73*) when the children start to droop and need an energizing runaround.

Below left The children's clothing store Trotters, on the King's Road in Chelsea *Below right* Meeting a shop's mascot outside one of the many gift shops located on Oxford Street

Department stores and shopping malls

HARRODS see p181

The UK's biggest shop will wow children and adults alike. It sells high-end clothes, beauty products, electronic goods, sports equipment, toys and has a fabulous food hall.

SELFRIDGES

One of London's most popular stores, Selfridges opened in 1909 in the Oxford Street building it still occupies today. It was founded by American magnate Harry Gordon Selfridge, who wanted to transform shopping from a chore into something fun. More recently it has become known for its bold window displays, which are almost as much of an attraction as the award-winning store itself. It has an excellent range of adult and kids' fashion, a superb food hall and a new toy department.

JOHN LEWIS

"Never knowingly undersold" is the motto of the John Lewis Partnership, which has a chain of practical, upmarket department stores in the UK, including Peter Jones. Its Oxford Street branch, opened in 1864 as a draper's shop, is the flagship store. It still has a particularly good range of fabrics, and holds a Royal Warrant as a supplier of haberdashery and household goods to the Queen. You'll also find everything you could possibly need for a baby, from rattles to a pushchair. Shoppers love the store's no-quibble returns policy and two-year guarantee on electrical goods.

WESTFIELD

This West London shopping mall, which opened in 2008, is so huge that it could comfortably hold 30 football pitches. It has plenty to occupy families who are happy to shop till they drop, with more than 250 shops over several levels, 50 restaurants and cafés, a "soft" play space and a multiplex cinema. Among the most child-oriented shops are the **Early Learning Centre**, **Mamas & Papas**, **LEGO**, **Build-A-Bear Workshop** and the **Disney Store**. "The Village" is an area devoted to the most sought-after designers, including **Versace, Miu Miu** and **Tiffany & Co**.

Clothing

GAP

The American clothing giant Gap arrived in London from San Francisco in 1987. Out of the 20 branches in London, a number specialize in kids' and baby clothes. The style is informal, preppy American – jeans, khakis, track suits and sweat pants and button-down-, polo- and T- shirts, all practical, good quality and reasonably priced. It's great for children's socks, hats and other accessories, too.

LA STUPENDERIA

If you're looking for something special for your children to wear, try the Italian label La Stupenderia, which has a swanky Knightsbridge store. The collection caters for boys and girls from newborn to 12 years old. The superb quality of the fabrics is typically Italian, and the look is classic and elegant: tweed jackets combined with shorts and waistcoats for boys; full skirts and dresses for girls. There are also plenty of well-cut casual styles, though even these come with a high price tag.

OH BABY LONDON

New Zealand-born designer Hannah McHalick was so uninspired by the choice of dull, pastel-coloured baby clothes on the market when she was pregnant, that she started creating her own fun, original designs. She sells her cool clothes for kids aged 0–8, including T-shirts and playsuits with clever captions, from her shop in buzzing, fashionable Brick Lane.

Below left Main concourse of the vast Westfield Centre in White City *Below right* Playtime in the Toy Kingdom area of the enormous Harrods department store in Knightsbridge

Books

GOLDEN TREASURY

London's largest independent children's bookshop has an excellent selection of books that should whet the appetite of even the most reluctant reader, but, the best thing about the shop is the helpful staff and their recommendations and advice. The shop also stocks cookery and childcare books, hand-picked adult titles and book-character toys like the Hungry Caterpillar.

THE LION AND UNICORN

So enticing are the window displays of this specialist Richmond bookshop that it's almost impossible not to go inside. Hidden down a lane off the green, it is full of appealing titles and has a friendly atmosphere. The enthusiastic and knowledgeable staff are always happy to offer guidance, and they encourage their young customers to browse.

Toys and games

BENJAMIN POLLOCK'S TOYSHOP

If you think toys were better in the past than they are today, this is the place to confirm your belief. Pollock's sells all kinds of traditional toys, from spinning tops and music boxes to rag dolls and tiny tea sets. The original shop in Shoreditch was run by Benjamin Pollock, who produced toy theatres. The Covent Garden shop still stocks a wonderful array of these, along with puppets – finger, glove and on strings.

DAVENPORT'S MAGIC SHOP

Tucked away in an arcade, this shop is a must for all aspiring members of the Magic Circle. It was established in 1898 by Lewis Davenport, a magician and music hall entertainer, and is the oldest family-run magic shop in the world. Whether you're a novice or a pro, it's a treasure trove of ingenious tricks and illusions, some simple, others sophisticated. There are cards, books, DVDs and accessories, including handkerchiefs, miracle rings, balls and beakers.

DISNEY STORE

For children besotted with Jack Sparrow or Hannah Montana, this US import will be a hit. The Covent Garden store is one of two in central London. Kids might be tempted by a *Toy Story* Zurg's Blaster or 3-D puzzle, a pair of pink cowboy boots just like Hannah Montana's or an iconic Mickey Mouse T-shirt.

EARLY LEARNING CENTRE

A British chain specializing in toys for very young children, the Early Learning Centre has six London stores, with the most central in Kensington High Street (*see p40*). Colourful and well-made, the indoor and outdoor toys are designed not only for play, but also to encourage mental and physical development. Tough, hard-wearing materials range from wood to plastic, and toys include puzzles and activity centres. The stores are child friendly, with toys to try out.

HAMLEYS see p85

This is the kind of shop that Santa Claus shops at – floor after floor of every type of toy and game.

LITTLE STINKIES

For children who hate having their hair cut, Little Stinkies is the answer, being both a toyshop and a kids' hair salon. It even offers makeovers. Don't be put off by the name – it's a terrific place, jam-packed with animals, dolls, puppets, fancy-dress costumes, games, books, stationery, and a host of other affordable toys guaranteed to entrance your little ones. The only tears you're likely to see are when it's time to leave.

PLAYLOUNGE

A little shop with big ideas, Playlounge is crammed with arty, design-conscious toys that appeal to both children and grown-ups.

Below left A stall selling freshly baked bread, pastries and savoury treats at Borough Market. *Below right* A member of staff welcoming customers to the jam-packed Hamleys toy store

Refreshingly different, it shuns bland, mainstream toys and only stocks creative, stimulating ones. It has a remarkable collection of vinyl figures, including some imaginative Tim Burton characters and Moomins for nostalgic parents. Soft toys, books, stationery, games and T-shirts are packed in too.

Markets

BOROUGH see p151

Open Thursday to Saturday, Borough Market is foodie heaven, with top-quality (and top-dollar) global treats as well as the best of British produce.

CAMDEN LOCK MARKET

This rambling weekend market has a fun mix of junk and wonderful finds, including antiques, books, music, crafts and new and second-hand street fashion. It started in a small way in 1974, since when it has spread along Chalk Farm Road. With a hippy-punk vibe, the main market is down beside Regent's Canal and makes a great family outing on a Saturday; Sundays can be a crush.

PETTICOAT LANE

An East End institution, this Sunday street market spills over from Petticoat Lane (whose real location

is Middlesex Street) into the maze of roads that surrounds it, and is where you might catch traders chatting in Cockney rhyming slang. If your children are extremely early risers, come with the serious bargain hunters at 4am. The more touristy part isn't in full swing till 9am, although it gets very crowded by 11am. Bargains are likely to be elusive, but there's an impressive range of leather goods, clothes, jewellery and toys, plus fast food.

PORTOBELLO ROAD

Follow the Saturday crowd from Notting Hill Gate Tube station swarming to this vibrant street, lined with stalls, arcades and funky shops. Several markets rolled into one, it has more than 1,000 stalls, from upmarket antiques, jewellery and silverware as it heads north, to bric-a-brac, crafts, food, clothes and music. Dodge into Portobello Green covered market, just north of the Westway, for original youth fashion.

The Lowdown

Benjamin Pollock's Toyshop 44 The Market, Covent Garden, WC2E 8RF; www.pollocks-coventgarden.co.uk

Camden Lock Market www.camdenlockmarket.com

Davenport's Magic Shop 7 Charing Cross Underground Arcade, The Strand, WC2N 4HZ; www.davenportsmagic.co.uk

Disney Store Unit 10 The Piazza, WC2E 8HD; www.disneystore.co.uk

Early Learning Centre 174 High Street Kensington, W8 7RG; www.elc.co.uk

Gap www.gap.eu

Golden Treasury 29 Replingham Road, SW18 5LT; www.thegoldentreasury.co.uk

John Lewis 300 Oxford Street, W1A 1EX; www.johnlewis.com

King's Road kingsroad.co.uk

Little Stinkies 15 Victoria Grove, W8 5RW; 020 7052 0077

The Lion and Unicorn 19 King Street, Richmond, TW9 1ND; www.lionunicornbooks.co.uk

Oh Baby London 162 Brick Lane, E1 6RU; www.ohbabylondon.com

Oxford Street www.oxfordstreet.co.uk

Petticoat Lane petticoatlanemarket.net

Playlounge 19 Beak Street, W1F 9RP; www.playlounge.co.uk

Portobello Road www.portobelloroad.co.uk

Selfridges 400 Oxford Street, W1A 1AB; www.selfridges.com

La Stupenderia 16 Motcomb Street, SW1X 8LB; www.lastupenderia.com

Westfield uk.westfield.com/london

Below left Storytime at the Golden Treasury bookshop. *Below right* A second-hand stall at Camden Lock Market, bursting with collectibles – books, magazines, toys and much more

Entertainment

London's theatre *(see pp46–7)*, music and cinema scene is one of the very best in the world – and there's plenty for families to enjoy. There are children's festivals, notably LolliBop for under-10s, in Regent's Park in August; and Imagine, on the South Bank in February. To find out what's coming up, register for a free bulletin at *www.officiallondontheatre.co.uk*, and check the listings on *www.timeout.com/london/kids* or *www.visitlondon.com/attractions/family*.

Music

London's smartest music venues are keen to woo families: the **Royal Opera House** *(see p90)* puts on Christmas shows, Sounding Out workshops and a Summer Screens season, which beams live opera and ballet from Covent Garden onto big screens in Trafalgar Square and Canary Wharf. Nearby, at the London Coliseum, the **English National Opera's** kids' music-making sessions are pitched at ages six months and up – while the grown-ups get to sneak off and enjoy a matinee. There are Saturday afternoon classical concerts for families at **St Martin-in-the-Fields Church** on Trafalgar Square, and regular Discovery Concerts for ages 7–12 from the **London Symphony Orchestra**. There are also strong children's programmes at **Wigmore Hall** in the West End (mostly chamber music), **Lauderdale House** *(see p218)* in Highgate (comedy, cabaret and classical) and the **Southbank Centre's** *(see p162)* Royal Festival Hall (jazz, world and classical). Summer brings free outdoor music and theatre to **The Scoop**, beside Tower Bridge.

A popular outdoor concert venue is Hampstead's **Kenwood House** *(see pp216–17)*. London's grandest alfresco venue, however, must be **Somerset House** *(see p93)*, which invites pop stars to its courtyard in August. The **Underage** rock festival – for 13–18-year-olds only – blasts into Hackney's Victoria Park in August.

Cinema

London's West End cinemas, such as the **Odeon Leicester Square**, show mostly mainstream Hollywood fare. For more eclectic movies, try the Barbican Centre's *(see p138)* Family Film Club or its London Children's Film Festival week, in November, when kids get to make films as well as watch them. The Southbank Centre's **British Film Institute's (BFI)** *(see p162)* programme of children's film focuses on the BFI IMAX – book ahead for its Film Funday gatherings. Family clubs run at cinemas across the city, including **Clapham Picture House**, the **Electric Cinema** in Portobello Road and the **Renoir** in Bloomsbury; while summer heralds 12 days of screenings in the courtyard at Somerset House.

Arts and crafts

There is always something creative afoot for families at the city's art goliaths, such as the **National Gallery** *(see pp80–81)*, **Tate Modern**

Below left Children watching the interactive "bubbles bubbles bubbles" show at the Science Museum *Below right* A child learning how to weave with characters dressed in Tudor costume at Sutton House (see p148), the **British Museum** (see pp102–3) and the **National Portrait Gallery** (see pp82–3).

Elsewhere, stand-out venues include the **Whitechapel Gallery** (see p127) in the East End, which boasts family workshops most weekends in its dedicated children's studio; and the distinctly more traditional **Dulwich Picture Gallery** (see p224), whose twice-monthly "Artplay" sessions spill out into the grounds on Wednesdays in summer: bring a picnic. Bloomsbury's **Cartoon Museum** has a permanent art room for kids, and monthly doodling drop-ins for families. In summer, don't miss the outdoor season at the **Serpentine Galleries** (see pp176–7), set in its landmark pavilion on the lawns of Kensington Gardens. An art-themed "playscape" is in the offing at the Serpentine's new satellite gallery nearby.

The **V&A Museum** (see p184) offers "Drop-in Design" sessions on Sundays and Saturday workshops in applied arts for older children, and masterminds the **London Design Festival** every September.

The best of the rest

Little bookworms are well looked after in London, with free family storytelling events at nearly all the major museums across the city (covered in the sightseeing part of this guide). So, too, are budding scientists, with the plethora of live science demonstrations, shows and hands-on sessions that take place regularly: kids can get to grips with rocket-launching at the **Science Museum** (see pp180–81) and "speed surgery" at the **Old Operating Theatre** (see p151). Entertaining "Nature Live" shows run more or less daily at the **Natural History Museum** (pp182-82) , while there are dedicated space shows for children at the **Royal Observatory**'s (see pp198-99) planetarium in Greenwich. Finally, no family should miss the world-class clowning, magic and pop-opera on the streets of Covent Garden. If all else fails, head for Funland Trocadero, with its many floors of arcade games, dodgem cars and tenpin bowling.

The Lowdown

Cartoon Museum 35 Little Russell Street, WC1A 2HH; 020 7580 8155; www.cartoonmuseum.org

Clapham Picture House 76 Venn Street, SW4 0AT; 0871 902572; www.picturehouses.co.uk

Electric Cinema 191 Portobello Road, W11 2ED; 020 7908 9696; www.electriccinema.co.uk

English National Opera London Coliseum, St. Martin's Lane, WC2N 4ES; 020 7836 0111; www.eno.org

Funland Trocadero 7–14 Coventry Street, W1D 7DH; www.funland.co.uk

Imagine Children's Festival Southbank Centre, Belvedere Road, London, SE1 8XX; 020 7960 4200; www.southbankcentre.co.uk/imagine-childrens-festival

LolliBop Festival 0844 844 0440; www.lollibopfestival.co.uk

London Symphony Orchestra Barbican Centre, Silk Street, EC2Y 8DS; 020 7588 1116; www.lso.co.uk

London Design Festival 020 7734 6444; www.londondesignfestival.com

Odeon Leicester Square 0871 224 4007; www.odeon.co.uk

Renoir Cinema Brunswick Square, WC1N 1AW; 020 7837 8402; www.curzoncinemas.com

Royal Observatory Blackheath Avenue, SE10 8XJ; www.nmm.ac.uk/places/royal-observatory

St Martin-in-the-Fields Church Trafalgar Square, WC2N 4JJ; 020 7766 1100; www.smitf.org

The Scoop 2a More London Riverside, SE1 2DB; 020 7403 4866; www.morelondon.co.uk/scoop.html

Underage Festival www.underagefestivals.com

Wigmore Hall 36 Wigmore Street, W1U 2BP; 020 7935 2141; www.wigmore-hall.org.uk

Below left Getting creative during the Saturday Film Club at the Barbican Centre *Below right* Enthralled children at a Sounding Out workshop at the Royal Opera House

Best Theatres and Shows

One of the major centres of theatre in the world, London offers a remarkable range of superb, high-quality drama. Across the different categories of theatre – subsidized, West End and fringe – there is always a choice of plays to entertain and engage children of all ages, as well as their parents. Alongside new productions, there are also plenty of old favourites to choose from.

Best theatres

HALF MOON YOUNG PEOPLE'S THEATRE

Founded in the 1980s in East London, Half Moon produces theatre for and with young people. The company uses drama to teach, inspire and engage children from all backgrounds and with all abilities. Plays are often by promising new playwrights. The London season runs from October to April.

LITTLE ANGEL THEATRE

This 100-seat puppet theatre, in a former Temperance Hall in Islington, puts on plays and runs workshops, during which a production is developed and the puppets made. The Little Angel Theatre tours world-wide and showcases performances by visiting companies. Various cultures inspire productions, which include firm favourites *The Secret Garden* and *The Sleeping Beauty*.

The theatre also runs creative family Fun Days to coincide with shows.

LYRIC THEATRE HAMMERSMITH

It is not specifically a children's theatre, but the Lyric often puts on wonderful shows for children in its two superb performance spaces. The theatre also offers a lively pantomime at Christmas, as well as imaginative hands-on activities, usually geared to under-7s, such as "Messy Play" workshops.

NATIONAL THEATRE

Each year, London's main publicly funded theatre stages a number of productions for children, mostly during the holidays. It has three auditoriums, ranging from the grand Olivier to the tiny Cottesloe (to be renamed the Dorfman in 2013). The summer Watch this Space Festival, which celebrates outdoor theatre, offers children's performance classes.

POLKA THEATRE

More than 100,000 children visit this Wimbledon theatre every year. Its aim is to entertain, inspire and stimulate, both with brand-new plays and adaptations of much-loved classics. The plays, shown in two auditoriums, are chosen not only to spark kids' imaginations, but to be accessible and relevant. Its Early Years programme embraces simple, visual stories for children between ages 6 months and 6 years.

PUPPET BARGE

A unique concept, this floating puppet theatre makes a terrific family outing. The 55-seat barge has a regular mooring in Little Venice from April–July, but tours each summer, with a mooring in Richmond August–September. The company, Movingstage, is known for its inventive productions and traditional stories with a modern twist.

Below left A performance of The Tempest by puppets at the Puppet Barge, moored in Little Venice *Below right* Actors and puppets take to the stage in a vibrant performance of The Lion King

UNICORN THEATRE

From a mobile theatre operating out of an old truck, the Unicorn has grown into one of the UK's flagship children's companies, with an airy, purpose-built South Bank building. Here, it stages more than 600 performances a year. Family workshops complement the shows by exploring their various themes.

Best family shows

THE LION KING

Since 1999, this joyful screen-to-stage musical has been delighting audiences at the Lyceum Theatre with its magical evocation of the Serengeti Plain, re-created through movement and puppetry. Visually, it is spectacular: the stage is packed with dancers sporting fabulous costumes and masks, and there is rousing African-inspired music.

SHREK THE MUSICAL

The bad-tempered yet lovable green ogre, who won hearts in the hit DreamWorks movie, translates smoothly to the theatre. The lively show follows the improbable hero and his trusty donkey on a mission to rescue the beautiful but feisty Princess Fiona. Mixing spectacle and humour, it is an ironic fairy tale for today's clued-up kids (and adults).

WICKED

The stage prequel to *The Wizard of Oz*, *Wicked* delves into the past of two Oz witches reinvented as university students – the good Glinda and the Wicked Witch of the West, Elphaba. It premiered in London at the Apollo Victoria Theatre in 2006, and has been showing there ever since. It can be appreciated on different levels by adults and children alike.

Tickets

London's West End theatreland is the place for blockbusting shows. Visit *www.thisistheatre.com* for the latest listings. Calls to a theatre box office will usually be redirected to ticketing giant **Ticketmaster**, which has an online family section (*www. ticketmaster.co.uk*). For discounted seats, visit **Tkts** (Leicester Square; open 10am–7pm Mon–Fri, 11am–4pm Sun); the website lists bargains (*www.tkts.co.uk*), but does not sell tickets. Prime time for theatre-loving families is **Kids Week**, a fortnight of shows and workshops in August. Watch out for the Child's Play sessions at **Shakespeare's Globe** (*see pp146–7*), timed so that kids act up while their parents take in a play. The **Theatre Royal Drury Lane** has London's child-friendliest

The Lowdown

Half Moon Young People's Theatre 43 White Horse Road, E1 0ND; 020 7709 8900; *www.halfmoon.org.uk*

Kids Week *www.kidsweek.co.uk*

Little Angel Theatre 14 Dagmar Passage, N1 2DN; 020 7226 1787; *www.littleangeltheatre.com*

Lyric Theatre Hammersmith Lyric Square, King Street, W6 0QL; 0871 221 1729; *www.lyric.co.uk*

National Theatre South Bank, SE1 9PX; 020 7452 3000; *www. nationaltheatre.org.uk*

Polka Theatre 240 The Broadway, SW19 1SB; 0202 8543 4888; *www.polkatheatre.com*

Puppet Barge opposite 35 Blomfield Road, W9 2PF; 020 7249 6876; *www.puppetbarge.com*

Shrek The Musical *www. shrekthemusical.co.uk*

Theatre Royal Drury Lane Catherine Street, WC2B; 0844 412 2955; *www.reallyuseful.com/ theatres*

The Lion King *www.disney.co.uk/ MusicalTheatre/TheLionKing/home/ index.jsp*

Unicorn Theatre 147 Tooley Street, SE1 2HZ; 020 7645 0560; *www. unicorntheatre.com*

Wicked *www.wickedthemusical. co.uk*

backstage tour (book the costumed version) and those at the **National Theatre** and **Regent's Park Open-Air Theatre** (*see p112*) are fun, too.

Below left The interior of the Unicorn Theatre near London's South Bank Below right An imaginative and interactive session of storytelling at Wimbledon's renowned Polka Theatre

London at Play

A visit to a theme park, playground or fun zone can be the highlight of a family holiday, but it's always best to plan ahead. Buy tickets in advance online and try to go on a weekday to avoid the biggest queues. Check with theme parks and fun zones for height restrictions – minimum and maximum – so if your children are too small or tall, they won't be disappointed. Fun zones can close to the public when hired for private parties, so check they're open before setting out.

Best theme parks

CHESSINGTON WORLD OF ADVENTURES

A mix of amusement park and zoo, Chessington and its themed lands will keep everyone entertained for the day. Older kids will be keen to try white-knuckle rides, such as Dragon's Fury, a spinning roller coaster, and Runaway Train, which careers along at speed, while the tamer Bubbleworks and Toytown rides are perfect for little ones. Take the Safari Skyway to spy the zoo's big cats, gorillas and sea lions.

THORPE PARK

Smaller than Chessington, Thorpe Park nevertheless features record-breaking rides including Stealth, Europe's fastest roller coaster and Tidal Wave, a terrifyingly high water ride, as well as the Colossus and Nemesis Inferno roller coasters. There are calmer alternatives exclusively for families with young children, such as the scenic Canada Creek Railway and the Wet Wet Wet water slide.

Best playgrounds

BATTERSEA PARK ADVENTURE PLAYGROUND

A host of fun things to climb up, slide down, swing on, scramble over and explore make this wooden adventure playground a great place for 5–16 year-olds. Staff are on hand to supervise children playing on the zip wires and climbing walls and the nearby toddlers' playground is full of colourful structures to play on.

CORAM'S FIELDS

This Bloomsbury playground was built on the site of a children's hospital founded by 18th-century philanthropist Thomas Coram. There are grassy areas and equipment for all ages, including climbing frames, slides and a zip wire. The big draw for toddlers, apart from the sandpits and paddling pool, is pets' corner, with its sheep, goats, rabbits and other animals.

DIANA, PRINCESS OF WALES MEMORIAL PLAYGROUND see p177

HOLLAND PARK ADVENTURE PLAYGROUND

For any would-be Tarzan aged 5 plus, this playground is perfect. It contains swinging ropes, an aerial runway, a zip wire, climbing frames and a tower, as well as swings, a giant tyre and slides. Conveniently placed next door, is an enclosed play area for tots, with swings, slides and a seesaw.

Best fun zones

BRAMLEY'S BIG ADVENTURE

Kids up to age 11 play happily and safely in this indoor playground. It consists of a colourful three-level

Below left Riding the excellent bowl at Camden's Cantelowe Skate Park *Below centre* All the fun of the fair on a carousel at Gambado Chelsea *Below right* Feeding time at the squirrel monkey enclosure, Chessington World of Adventures

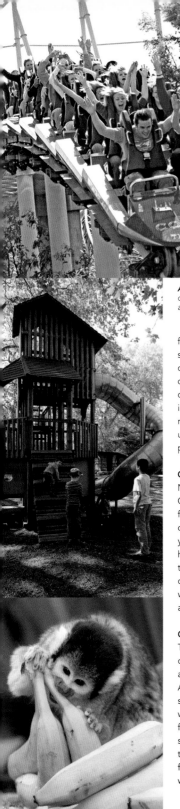

Above *The exciting Colossus roller coaster at Thorpe Park* Left *Imaginative adventure park, Coram's Fields*

frame, a maze of slides, ball pools, swings, ladders and a "spook den" complete with sound effects. It is all designed to build confidence by challenging children physically and intellectually as they work out their routes. There are separate areas for under 5s and babies, and a café for parents if the noise gets too much.

CLOWNTOWN
North London's version of Bramley's, ClownTown has a similar activity frame with slides, runways, rope climbs and "spook room" to keep young adventurers entertained. It has an area for crawlers and one for toddlers, with a ball pool, bouncy castle and climbing zone. On some weekdays, craft sessions are held and there is also an on-site café.

GAMBADO, CHELSEA
This large indoor adventure play centre holds a carousel, dodgems and a huge multi-level play frame. Although more expensive than some fun zones, it's worth it. Kids will cheerfully spend all day on the fairground rides or trampolines, sliding, climbing and squeezing through tunnels, or having their faces painted. There's a climbing wall for budding mountaineers; a

soft play area for tots; and a room with free WiFi and newpapers for adults, while hands-on staff supervise.

Best BMX & skate parks
BAY SIXTY6
Tucked under the Westway in Notting Hill, this concrete street park is practical, well equipped and under cover if it rains. It has a bowl, jump and fun boxes, a handrail, transitions, ramps and pipes. The park suits beginners as well as experienced BMX riders and skate boarders. There are sessions for novice boarders on Sat and Sun mornings, and set times for BMXers.

CANTELOWES SKATEPARK
One of the best BMX/skateparks in London, this has a cradle, concrete bowl, mini and vertical ramps, skid rails, practice pavements, a fun box and performance platform. There are separate areas for beginners and experts. The park is supervised and floodlit after dark.

The Lowdown

Battersea Park Adventure Playground *www.batterseapark.org/ html/playgrounds.html*
Bay Sixty6 65 Acklam Rd, W10 5YU; 020 8969 4669; *www.baysixty6.com*
Bramley's Big Adventure 136 Bramley Rd, W10 6TJ; 020 8960 1515; *www.bramleysbig.co.uk*
Cantelowes Skatepark Cantelowes Gardens, Camden Rd, NW1 9HG; *www.cantelowesskatepark.co.uk*
Chessington World of Adventures Leatherhead Rd, Chessington, Surrey KT9 2NE; 0871 663 4477; *www.chessington.com*
ClownTown The Coppetts Centre, N12 0SH; 020 8361 6600; *clowntown.co.uk*
Coram's Fields *www.coramsfields. org*
Gambado, Chelsea 7 Station Court, Townmead Rd, SW6 2PY; 020 7384 1635; *www.gambado.com/chelsea*
Holland Park Adventure Playground *www.rbkc.gov.uk/ leisureandlibraries/parksandgardens/ yourlocalpark/hollandpark.aspx*
Thorpe Park Staines Rd, Chertsey, Surrey KT16 8PN; 0871 663 1673; *www.thorpepark.com*

Sporting London

London has an impressive variety of sports on offer, to be enjoyed both as a spectator and a player – below are some of the most popular. Enthusiastic young fans might enjoy a behind-the-scenes glimpse of their favourite sports stadium. Most of these, including Wembley (football), Twickenham (rugby) and Lord's (cricket), organize regular tours.

Athletics

Most major track and field events are held at **Crystal Palace National Sports Centre**, but one of the most fun events of the year is the **Virgin London Marathon**, with a course from Blackheath to the Mall through central London. Runners will find tracks at **Battersea Park Millennium Arena** and **Linford Christie Stadium**. For more casual running, there's a track in **Regent's Park**.

Cricket

An integral part of an English summer, amateur cricket matches are played throughout London at the weekends. Among the more central are those in **Regent's Park** and on **Barnes Common**. To watch first-class professional cricket, try **Lord's**, home of the famous MCC (Marylebone Cricket Club) and Middlesex, or Surrey's **Kia Oval**.

Football

Football is the UK's most popular spectator sport. The season runs from Aug–May, and fans flock to cup finals and international games at **Wembley Stadium**. London's top clubs are **Arsenal**, which is based at the Emirates Stadium, and **Chelsea**, based at Stamford Bridge. However, it is easier to come by tickets to see less high-profile teams, such as west London's **Queens Park Rangers**, and **Crystal Palace** in south London.

Horse-riding

Stables are located near a number of London parks. **Ross Nye** and **Hyde Park Stables** are on Hyde Park's doorstep. **Stag Lodge Stables** are just outside Richmond Park's Robin Hood Gate, and **Ridgway** and **Wimbledon Village Stables** are both within easy reach of Richmond Park and Wimbledon Common.

Ice-skating

London's major permanent covered rinks are **Queen's Ice and Bowl**, and **Streatham Ice Arena**. During winter months, outdoor temporary ice rinks crop up across the city. Popular ones are at **Broadgate, Hampton Court, Hyde Park,** the **Natural History Museum, Somerset House** and the **Tower of London**. All are floodlit, many run until 10pm.

Rowing

Of the regular races on the Thames, the highlight is the **Oxford and Cambridge Boat Race** from Putney to Mortlake. Supporters line the river to watch the "eights" of these rival universities battle it out on the river in April. Rowing is also a fun family activity, and there are boats for hire on the **Serpentine** (Easter–Oct) and the lakes in **Greenwich** (Feb–Oct) and **Regent's parks** (Apr–Sep).

Below left Skating on the outdoor ice rink at the Natural History Museum. *Below centre* Enjoying a riding lesson at Hyde Park Stables. *Below right* Fans celebrating in the stands at Wembley Stadium.

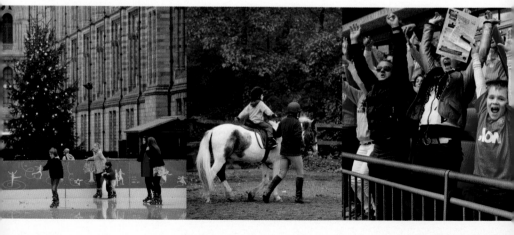

Rugby

A 15-a-side sport, rugby union has certain similarities to American Football. International and major matches are played at **Twickenham Stadium**, the sport's headquarters. London-based clubs include **Harlequins, London Welsh, London Scottish** and **Rosslyn Park**. Matches can be watched most Saturday afternoons (Sep–Apr).

Swimming

Although there are many pools in London, surprisingly few are geared towards children. For kid's pools, try **Brentford Fountain, Newham** and **Woolwich Waterfront Leisure Centres**, which all have water slides. **Finchley Lido Leisure Centre** has indoor and outdoor pools and is popular with families. **Chelsea Sports Centre, Oasis** and **Porchester Centre** are not so family-friendly, but more central. For outdoor pools, try **Oasis** or the **Parliament Hill** or **Serpentine lidos**.

Tennis

There are quite a few municipal tennis courts around London, and these can usually be booked on the day. Bring your own tennis racket and balls. Good local courts include **Holland Park** and **Battersea Park**. When it comes to watching tennis, June–July brings the grass court **AEGON Championships** at Queens and, of course, **Wimbledon**, the home of the sport – a must for any tennis or strawberry enthusiast.

Water sports

Sailing, canoeing and kayaking courses and more are on offer for kids aged 8+ at **Thames Young Mariners, Docklands Sailing and Watersports Centre, Surrey Docks Watersports Centre** and **Royal Victoria Dock Watersports Centre**. For less complicated water sports, there is a children's pond in **Regent's Park** with mini pedal boats (over 5s).

The Lowdown

Athletics

Battersea Park Millennium Arena www.wandsworth.gov.uk/info/644/sports_facilities/381/battersea_park_millennium_arena/1

Crystal Palace National Sports Centre www.gll.org/centre/crystal-palace-national-sports-centre.asp

Linford Christie Stadium www.lbhf.gov.uk/Directory/Leisure_and_Culture/Sports_and_leisure/Leisure_centres/37548_Linford_Christie_Outdoor_Sports_Centre.asp

Regent's Park www.royalparks.org.uk/parks/regents_park/sport.cfm

Virgin London Marathon www.virginlondonmarathon.com

Cricket

Barnes Common Cricket Club www.barnescommoncc.co.uk

Kia Oval www.kiaoval.com

Lord's www.lords.org

Regent's Park Cricket Club www.regentspark.play-cricket.com

Football

Arsenal www.arsenal.com

Chelsea www.chelseafc.com

Crystal Palace www.cpfc.co.uk

Queens Park Rangers www.qpr.co.uk

Wembley www.wembleystadium.com

Horse-riding

Hyde Park Stables www.hydeparkstables.com

Ross Nye Stables www.rossnyestables.co.uk

Ridgway Stables www.ridgwaystables.co.uk

Stag Lodge Stables www.ridinginlondon.com

Wimbledon Village Stables www.wvstables.com

Ice-skating

Broadgate www.broadgateinfo.net

Hampton Court www.hamptoncourticerink.com

Hyde Park www.hydeparkwinterwonderland.com/rink.html

Natural History Museum www.nhm.ac.uk/visit-us/whats-on/ice-rink/index.html

Queen's Ice and Bowl www.queensiceandbowl.co.uk

Somerset House www.somersethouse.org.uk/ice_rink/default.asp

Streatham Ice Arena streathamicearena.co.uk

Tower of London www.toweroflondonicerink.com

Rowing

Greenwich www.royalparks.org.uk/parks/greenwich_park/facilities.cfm

Oxford and Cambridge Boat Race www.theboatrace.org

Regent's Park www.royalparks.org.uk/parks/regents_park/facilities.cfm

Serpentine www.royalparks.org.uk/parks/hyde_park/facilities.cfm

Rugby

Harlequins www.quins.co.uk

London Scottish www.londonscottish.com

London Welsh www.london-welsh.co.uk

Rosslyn Park www.rosslynpark.co.uk

Twickenham Stadium www.rfu.com/TwickenhamStadium

Swimming

Brentford Fountain Leisure Centre www.fusion-lifestyle.com/centres/Brentford_Fountain_Leisure_Centre

Chelsea Sports Centre www.gll.org/centre/chelsea-sports-centre.asp

Finchley Lido Leisure Centre www.gll.org/centre/finchley-lido-leisure-centre.asp

Newham Leisure Centre www.gll.org/centre/newham-leisure-centre.asp

Oasis www.camden.gov.uk/ccm/navigation/leisure/sport-and-physical-activity/sports-centres/oasis-sports-centre

Parliament Hill Lido www.camden.gov.uk/ccm/content/contacts/non-council-contacts/contact-parliament-hill-lido.en

Porchester Centre www.gll.org/centre/porchester-centre.asp

Serpentine Lido www.royalparks.org.uk/parks/hyde_park/sport.cfm

Woolwich Waterfront Leisure Centre www.gll.org/centre/waterfront-leisure-centre.asp

Tennis

AEGON Championships www.lta.org.uk/fans-major-events/AEGON-British-Tennis-Series/AEGON-Championships

Battersea Park www.batterseapark.org/html/tennis.html

Holland Park www.rbkc.gov.uk/leisureandlibraries/sportsandleisure/sportsfacilitiesinparks/tennis.aspx

Wimbledon www.wimbledon.com

Water sports

Docklands Sailing and Watersports Centre www.dswc.org

Royal Victoria Dock Watersports Centre www.royaldockstrust.org.uk/summerwatersports.htm

Surrey Docks Watersports Centre www.fusion-lifestyle.com/centres/Surrey_Docks_Watersports_Centre

Thames Young Mariners www.surreycc.gov.uk/outdoorlearning

Outdoor London

Celebrated for its many beautiful parks, London even manages to cram green spaces into its bustling centre. Most of these larger expanses – and some of the small ones – date from the Middle Ages: some were always common land, others were preserved for the exclusive use of royalty as hunting grounds, and only later opened to the public. As a result, wherever you are in London, you are only minutes away from historic open spaces.

Battersea Park

With a boating lake, a small zoo and an adventure playground, this is an all-action destination (see pp186–9).

Blackheath

Once covered by thick gorse, which made it popular with highwaymen, Blackheath has long been a rallying point, from Wat Tyler's rebellious peasants in 1381 to suffragette marches in the early 20th century. It also has a sporting heritage: James I introduced the Scottish game of golf to England here, and it is the start of the London Marathon (see p50). The most popular pastime here is kite-flying.

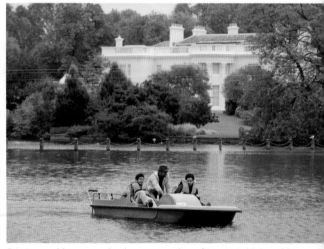

Enjoying a pedalo session in the glorious surroundings of Regent's Park boating lake

Coram's Fields

This space has enough to keep kids happy: a paddling pool, a farmyard, a playground, sports pitches and play sessions (see p48 and p101).

Green Park

With mature trees and grassy lawns, Green Park (see p77) is perfect for walks and picnics. In spring, carpets of daffodils turn the grass yellow. A royal hunting ground until Charles II enclosed it in 1668, it was turned into a pleasure garden in the early 18th century, with temples and pools (now long gone). Later, it became a favourite spot for duels.

Greenwich Park

You can see most of London on a clear day from this park. On its eastern side, excavations have unearthed evidence of a Roman temple. On one of the hills that crown it, stands the Royal Observatory, where east meets west at the Meridian Line (see p198).

Hampstead Heath

"The Heath", as locals call it, is a stunning area of hills, ponds, woods and glades. There is plenty for families, from outdoor swimming, model boating or the adventure playground. Nearby, Golders Hill Park has a children's zoo and putting green, and there's a great view from Parliament Hill (see p214).

Holland Park

Although bombs destroyed most of the Jacobean Holland House in 1941, its glorious park survived, with paths that wind through woods, and a wildlife enclosure that is home to peacocks and other exotic birds. A peaceful Japanese and formal flower garden, an adventure playground and play area, and space to kick a football make it a park for all ages.

Hyde Park and Kensington Gardens

One of the finest royal parks in London, this is also close to many must-see sights (see pp174–5).

Primrose Hill

A good place to come when it snows, this 78-m (256-ft) hill (see p113), just north of Regent's Park, is perfect for tobogganing. In the 16th century, Henry VIII appropriated it for hunting, and it was not until 1841

Above Panoramic view over London from Primrose Hill **Below** A fine 12-pointer red deer stag and small female in Richmond Park

that the public were allowed in. It can be very windy at the top, which makes it popular with kite-flyers. From here, the view includes the O2 Arena and the Post Office Tower.

Regent's Park

Run around in open spaces to the sound of lions from nearby London Zoo, walk along the canal or enjoy the boating lake (see p112).

Richmond Park

Charles I's personal hunting ground, Richmond (see p232) is the largest and most wild of the royal parks. Its heath and woods are home to a large variety of native plants, birds and animals, including herds of red and fallow deer that roam freely.

Royal Botanic Gardens, Kew

No longer a stuffy Victorian botany collection, there are lots of exciting things for kids at the Royal Botanic Gardens (see pp228–9).

St James's Park

The oldest of the royal parks, this is close to Buckingham Palace and boasts lovely flower beds (see p72).

Wimbledon and Putney Commons

Once popular for duels, these commons form London's largest expanse of heath and woodland. They are used for activities ranging

from golf and horse riding to model boating and blackberry picking. Don't miss the 1817 windmill, now the Windmill Museum (open Apr–Oct: 2–5pm Sat, 11am–5pm Sun & public hols), with displays of models, machinery and tools, and a nearby Nature Trail.

WWT London Wetland Centre

More than 180 species of birds and animals shelter in this lovely nature reserve (see p230).

The Lowdown

Blackheath www.lewisham.gov.uk/ inmyarea/openspaces/Pages/ default.aspx

Green Park www.royalparks.gov.uk/ Green-Park.aspx

Greenwich Park www.royalparks. gov.uk/Greenwich-Park.aspx

Hampstead Heath www. cityoflondon.gov.uk/Corporation/ LGNL_Services/Environment_and_ planning/Parks_and_open_spaces

Holland Park www.rbkc.gov.uk/ leisureandlibraries/parksandgardens/ yourlocalpark/hollandpark.aspx

Primrose Hill www.royalparks.gov. uk/the-regents-park.aspx

Richmond Park www.royalparks.gov. uk/Richmond-Park.aspx

St James's Park www.royalparks. gov.uk/St-Jamess-Park.aspx

Wimbledon and Putney Commons www.wpcc.org.uk

The History of London

Although there was only a small collection of huts beside the River Thames at the time of the first Roman invasion in 55 BC, some 100 years later, a small port and trading community had been established, which the Romans called "Londinium". Growing rapidly, London was the obvious choice for the capital by the time of the Norman Conquest in 1066. Over the next 1,000 years, the city grew in size and importance, becoming one of the major cities of the world.

The Romans

In AD 43, rampaging Romans under the Emperor Claudius defeated the unruly Celtic tribes of southeastern Britain and, in AD 50, founded "Londinium", building a bridge across the River Thames close to the site of the later London Bridge.

Early Roman London became a flourishing port and settlement at the centre of the network of straight roads that the Romans were so fond of building. In AD 60–61, a revolt by the Iceni tribe from Norfolk, led by the fierce warrior Queen Boudicca, ended with London being burnt to the ground. Like a phoenix, the city rose from the ashes to become capital of England, a prosperous financial and trading centre, and headquarters of Britain's Roman governor, with a market and its own mint. By 200, the Romans had fortified the city with a defensive wall, but the Roman Empire was already in decline. At the end of the 3rd century, the Romans had to use ferocious Germanic mercenaries to help them repel Saxon raiders. Roman rule ended in AD 410.

The Anglo-Saxons

The Romans' fine houses were left to decline, and the city remained mostly uninhabited for some 400 years. When the Anglo-Saxon warrior kings eventually arrived, they settled an area just to the west of the old Roman city. Anglo-Saxon London was not as developed as Roman London had been, becoming instead a simple farming town. During the early 9th century, however, London's importance grew as a market town. England reunited under the Kings of Wessex from Winchester (including King Alfred), Christianity was reintroduced and with it came education.

The Vikings

In 836 London was sacked by the Vikings, who continued their attacks throughout the 9th century. After Alfred the Great's victory over the Vikings in 878, London was returned to the Anglo-Saxons and there was a brief period of calm, during which the inhabitants moved east, back to the more secure area within the

A 10th-century vellum depicting Vikings arriving in England

rebuilt Roman walls. The raids started again in 994, until a final battle in 1014. Legend has it that in a fine strategic move, Olaf, an ally of the Anglo-Saxons, tied his boats to London Bridge and pulled it down – possibly the basis for the song, *London Bridge is Falling Down*.

The Normans

The year 1066 saw the Norman invasion of England. After the death of the Anglo-Saxon king, Edward

Timeline

AD 200	410	836	1070	1176–1209	1259	1348
Roman invaders build a bridge across the Thames and found "Londinium", fortifying it with a defensive wall		London sacked by Vikings; later the Anglo-Saxons regain control under Alfred the Great		First stone London Bridge constructed. Lined with houses and shops, it survives for more than 600 years		The Black Death ravages the city wiping out half of all Londoners
	The Romans withdraw from Britain. London declines, becoming an Anglo-Saxon market town		Tower of London begun by William I to consolidate power after the Norman Conquest		"Provisions of Westminster" signed by Henry III, laying foundations for parliament	

the Confessor, his warlike cousin, William of Normandy, claimed the throne, but found that Edward's brother-in-law Harold had been crowned in his place. William defeated Harold at Hastings, but didn't want to attack well-fortified London. Instead, he razed the fields around it and the city swiftly accepted William the Conqueror as king. He was crowned in Westminster Abbey on Christmas Day 1066.

Under the Normans, London thrived and in 1070 William started work on the Tower of London, where he lived until he moved to the Palace of Westminster, built alongside Westminster Abbey by Edward the Confessor in the mid-11th century.

The Middle Ages

In 1215, angered by heavy taxes, London supported the barons in drafting the Magna Carta to limit the powers of King John. The 13th century saw a building boom in the city, with the construction of Henry III's abbey at Westminster (1269) and the first St Paul's Cathedral (1280) – half as tall as the current version.

In 1338 Edward III made Westminster the place for regular Parliamentary sessions, but there was trouble ahead. In 1348, the Black Death struck the city, killing half its 60,000 inhabitants. In 1381, the peasants revolted: an army of serfs led by Wat Tyler took over London for two days, but the revolt ended when Tyler was killed by the mayor. The early 15th century saw

the rise of a wealthy class of former soldiers and tradesmen, threatening the feudal aristocracy. By 1461 London's support was crucial to Edward IV, who won the Wars of the Roses, to restore stability to England.

The Tudors

During the 16th-century rule of the Tudors, England was transformed from a minor state into a major world power, London's economy boomed and its population quadrupled. The downside was that slums developed on its outskirts. In Henry VIII's Reformation of 1533, the new gentry acquired the land freed by the dissolution of the monasteries (half of the city was occupied by religious buildings). After Henry's death, "Bloody Mary" reinstated Catholicism and martyred hundreds of Protestants at Smithfield from 1553–8. On Mary's death, Protestant Elizabeth I came to the throne. She was supported by the people of London for her 45-year reign, during which the city flourished as a centre of European trade, exploration and discovery.

A painting of Henry VIII with his third wife, Jane Seymour, and their son, Prince Edward, circa 1545.

The "Princes in the Tower", 12-year-old Edward V and his brother Richard, disappear. Their uncle becomes King Richard III

Globe Theatre built by William Shakespeare's theatre company, the Chamberlain's Men

1381	1483	1533	1597

Rebels storm the Tower of London to demand an end to serfdom, in the failed Peasants' Revolt

Henry VIII breaks with the Vatican and forms the Church of England

The Stuarts

In the 17th century a new generation of moneyed gentry expanded the city's boundaries westwards by building on land in Piccadilly and Leicester Square. Puritanism increased as a reaction against the high-handed Stuart kings, James I and Charles I, and in the ensuing English Civil War (1642–9), London merchants put their finances behind Parliament. The war ended when Charles I was beheaded in London in 1649 and England became a Commonwealth republic under Oliver Cromwell. After Cromwell's death, there were numerous quick-fire changes of government and, fed up with the Puritan restrictions on simple pleasures such as dancing and theatre, Londoners vigorously supported the restoration of Charles II to the throne in 1660.

Illustration showing residents fleeing the Great Fire of London in 1666

Plague and fire

The Black Death broke out in 1665. Although there had been earlier outbreaks, this was the last and the worst, in which nearly 100,000 people died. Pits were dug and cartloads of bodies thrown into them. The following year, the Great Fire of London swept through the medieval city, after a blaze that started in a bakery in Pudding Lane spread to the surrounding streets. The fire destroyed 60 per cent of London, including St Paul's Cathedral. Reconstruction in the late 17th century saw stone buildings replace wooden ones and narrow streets swapped for broad ones. Sir Christopher Wren built 52 churches, including his masterpiece, the new St Paul's. The fire also cleansed the city of the plague and led to the dispersal of the population over a wider area.

Georgian London

In the early 18th century, the population exploded again, with an increase in the poor as well as the rich. By 1750 London had 675,000 inhabitants. The villages of Kensington, Knightsbridge and Marylebone were incorporated into the city, building started in Greenwich, and stylish St James's and Mayfair were developed for the elite. There were also slums to the east and south, where the poor drank too much gin and only one child in four lived beyond the age of five. In 1750 Westminster Bridge was opened – only the second over the Thames. The 1780 Gordon Riots, a violent Protestant uprising against Roman Catholic freedoms, led eventually to the establishment of the Metropolitan Police force in 1829. The policemen were known as "Bobbies" or "Peelers" after their founder, Robert Peel. Between 1820 and 1838, the foppish Prince Regent (later George IV) and architect John Nash developed Regent Street, Regent's Park, Buckingham Palace and The Mall.

The Victorian era

During the 19th century, London became the largest city in the world and the rich, powerful capital of the British Empire. But as its wealth increased, so did its poverty. The overcrowding and foul, insanitary conditions of London's slums preoccupied Charles Dickens and

Timeline

Guy Fawkes and his Catholic conspirators make an abortive attempt to blow up Parliament in the Gunpowder Plot	The Great Fire destroys the city, clearing the way for Sir Christopher Wren's city of stone, including St Paul's.	Queen Victoria ascends the throne, and Buckingham Palace becomes the monarch's official residence	The Representation of th People Act grants votes all men over 21 and som women over 30
1605	**1649**	**1666**	**1721**	**1837**	**1863**	**191**
	Charles I beheaded at the Banqueting House, as Oliver Cromwell's Parliamentarians triumph in the English Civil War		Robert Walpole is named First Lord of the Treasury, effectively Britain's first prime minister		The first line opens on th London Underground; a comprehensive sewerag network follows later	

other writers. In 1832–66 cholera killed thousands, and in the summer of 1858, the smell in London grew so bad it was called the "Great Stink" and Parliament had to stop work. But not everything was bad, Victorian successes included Crystal Palace's 1851 Great Exhibition, celebrating British dominance in trade, science and industry; Charles Barry's Gothic Palace of Westminster (1840); the UK's railway network; London's first Underground line (1863); and Joseph Bazalgette's sewage system (1875). The quality of life improved with more mobility and progress in public health and education. In 1897, the normally rather reserved Victorians joyfully celebrated Queen Victoria's Diamond Jubilee with street parties.

Model Twiggy on the King's Road during the "Swinging"1960s

The 20th century

In the early years of the 20th century, public transport expanded and so did the sprawling suburbs. During World War I (1914–18), women took over many of London's public services, and in 1918 the suffragettes won the vote for women. In 1920–30 immigration increased and the capital quadrupled in size, reaching an all-time population peak in 1939.

In World War II, London was bombed heavily during the 1940–41 Blitz, with the City and East End being worst affected. The post-war years saw the Olympics at Wembley in 1948, the Festival of Britain (1951) and a property boom from 1955–65. After the Great Smog of 1952, the 1956 Clean Air Act put a stop to London's famous "pea-soupers" and marked the end of industrial London.

In the 1960s, the city became known as "Swinging London", a centre of fashionable youth culture. There was conflict in the 1970s, when "The Troubles" in Northern Ireland made London a target of terrorist attacks by the Provisional IRA, and again in the early 1980s when racial tension surfaced in the Brixton Riots. A boom in the 1980s was followed by bust in the 1990s.

The 21st century...

In 2000, Tony Blair's government created the Greater London Authority, led by an elected mayor. On 6 July 2005 London won the bid for the 2012 Olympics, but celebrations were short lived; terrorists bombed the London Underground and a bus the next day. As a global recession loomed, the first coalition government since World War II was formed (of Conservatives and Liberal Democrats) in May 2010. In April 2011, London held jubilant celebrations in honour of the wedding of Prince William and Kate Middleton.

HEROES & VILLAINS

Boudicca
She burnt London to the ground in AD 60, but this warrior queen is a heroine to many because she almost beat the Roman invaders. Look for her on Westminster Bridge *(see p69)* and at All Hallows by the Tower *(see p125)*.

Dick Whittington
This 14th-century merchant became Lord Mayor of London four times. He was much loved – but nobody knows if he really owned a cat! Look for him at Westminster Abbey *(see pp66–7)* and The Guildhall *(see p133)*.

Guy Fawkes
In 1605 Fawkes tried to wipe out King James I by stacking gunpowder under the Houses of Parliament. He is remembered on Bonfire Night (5 Nov). Look for him at the Museum of London *(see pp136–7)*.

Christopher Wren
London's greatest architect helped the city rise from the ashes after the Great Fire of 1666, building 51 churches and St Paul's Cathedral. Look for him there *(see pp130–31)*, and at The Monument *(see p124)*.

Colonel Thomas Blood
This Irishman is famous for plotting to steal the Crown Jewels in 1671, disguised as a priest. His gang stuffed some of the gems down their trousers – but were captured while fleeing. Look for him at the Tower of London *(see pp122–3)*.

Charles Dickens
This famous writer created Oliver Twist and Mr Scrooge, and campaigned against the cruel treatment of poor children and orphans in London. Look for him at the Charles Dickens Museum *(see pp106–7)*.

	"Swinging London" is the world's trendiest city; stars include singer Mick Jagger and actor Michael Caine		The Olympic Games come to London for the third time	
1940–1	**1965**	**1991**	**2012**	
The Blitz destroys or damages 1 million London homes, and kills more than 20,000 civilians		Canary Wharf, Britain's tallest building, spearheads the regeneration of the Docklands as a business quarter		

The Queen's Household Cavalry
Mounted Regiment outside
Buckingham Palace

Exploring
LONDON

Westminster
and the West End

Only two things stand still in the thumping heart of central London: the "living statues" in their fabulous costumes in Covent Garden, and the stony-faced sentries standing like toy soldiers outside Buckingham Palace. Everything else seems in perpetual motion, and there is enough to keep families fulfilled for weeks, including 40 theatres, a dozen cinemas and some of the world's greatest museums and galleries.

Bloomsbury and
Regent's Park

The City and
the East End

Westminster
and the
West End

Southwark and
the South Bank

Kensington,
Chelsea and
Battersea

Highlights

Guards Museum
Watch the Foot Guards leave Wellington Barracks, then don a bearskin in the museum and take home a soldier or two from the shop *(see p76)*.

St James's Park
Say hello to squirrels and see the famous pelicans near Duck Island in this lush green wedge between Westminster and the West End. It's picnic paradise *(see p74)*.

London Transport Museum
Step back in time in this giant "play barn" full of classic buses to board and vintage trains to ride. All aboard! *(see p92)*.

Royal Opera House
Peeking into a rehearsal on a backstage tour of the opera house feels like a great privilege, while the family Christmas shows are amazing spectacles *(see p90)*.

Somerset House
Pack your beach wear and brave the water jets in the Neo-Classical Fountain Court. In winter, it hosts one of the most glamorous ice rinks in London *(see p93)*.

The National Gallery
This place cleverly brings painting alive with "Teach Your Grown-ups About Art" trails, where the kids lead the tour *(see pp80–81)*.

Left *Panoramic view of Westminster showing part of the London Eye, Big Ben and Westminster Abbey*
Above *The Young Dancer (1988), by Enzo Plazzotta, is a fitting statue for the theatrical area of Covent Garden*

The Best of
Westminster & the West End

From Big Ben to Buckingham Palace, Nelson's Column to the National Gallery, this is picture-postcard London, squeezing scores of museums and monuments into 5 square kilometres (2 square miles) on the north bank of the Thames. Visiting families can be in the House of Commons one minute, pretending to be the prime minister, and wander through the Queen's throne room the next – but please don't sit on Her Majesty's chair!

Pomp and circumstance

Soaking up the full majesty of royal London takes careful planning. The State Rooms at **Buckingham Palace** (*see p74–5*) are open in summer only: book ahead online for the first tour of the day at 9:45am. There's just enough time to tour the palace and get to Wellington Barracks by 11am, when the troops line up for the **Changing the Guard** (*see p76*) – it gets less crowded here than on the Palace forecourt.

Visit the tombs of former monarchs at **Westminster Abbey** (*see pp66–7*) – resting place of 16 kings and queens – and be sure to follow the engaging children's trail. Admire, too, Big Ben and the impressive **Houses of Parliament** (*see p68*). After lunch by the lake in **St James's Park** (*see p74*), watch the pelicans get theirs – the daily feed takes place at 2:30pm. Finish the day with a horsey treat: either a tour of The Royal Mews (Mar–Dec – *see p76*) or a close-up look at the sentries at **Horse Guards Parade** (*see p70*), where kids can dress up as guardsmen at the museum.

Seasonal festivities

Spring makes a colourful splash here, from the St Patrick's Day Parade that musters in Green Park in March to the London Marathon on The Mall in April. Children will love the twirling ribbons and dancing strings of the Covent Garden May Fayre & Puppet Festival (May).

In summer, Trooping the Colour at **Horse Guards Parade** celebrates the Queen's official birthday in June. It's a great time to take a riverboat cruise along the Thames. In the West End meanwhile, children can get free theatre tickets to a host of shows during Kids' Week (*p46*), which runs for a fortnight in August.

London puts on a good Christmas, too. Enjoy carols round the Norwegian Christmas tree in

Above *Covent Garden May Fayre & Puppet Festival*
Below *Spectacular New Year's Eve fireworks display*

Crowds gathered outside Buckingham Palace on The Mall, the finishing line for the London Marathon

Trafalgar Square (*see p82*), the bright lights of **Hamleys** toy shop in Regent Street (*see p85*), or the fairy-tale ice rink at **Somerset House** (*see p93*). There are two New Year celebrations to choose from: the fireworks show along the Thames on 31 December, or the dragons dancing through Chinatown for Chinese New Year about a month later.

Backstage West End

Begin a starry day out in Theatreland at the **Royal Opera House** (*see p90*) in Covent Garden. If it's Monday, be at the box office for 10am to get tickets for the free lunchtime recital. Failing that, sign up for the 10:30am backstage tour – a glimpse behind the scenes at the Royal Ballet, to see where the principal dancers practise their *pas de deux*. Next, explore the smart boutiques and busy lunch spots around **Covent Garden** (*see pp88–9*), where there's always a mix of performers to see on the streets.

If it's Wednesday or Saturday, take in a matinée of a musical at Britain's oldest working playhouse, the **Theatre Royal Drury Lane** (*see p91*). For star-struck youngsters, the stage door is in Russell Street. This theatre, too, offers family-friendly daily tours. As night falls, head for **Leicester Square** (*see p84*) and hunt for film-star handprints in the pavement, grab cut-price tickets for a show, or choose from dozens of films at the cinemas on every corner.

Art versus Science

It may be best known for shows and shopping, but the West End offers plenty to stimulate young minds, too. The galleries beside Trafalgar Square are the perfect introduction to fine art: the **National Gallery** (*see pp80–81*) has three audio-trails just for families, plus drawing and daubing workshops. Next door, the **National Portrait Gallery** (*see p82*) has artist-led "tour and draw" events. Tiny geniuses may prefer **Tate Britain** (*see pp68-9*), which dispenses free build-it-yourself art boxes to children.

For children unmoved by Van Gogh and Van Eyck, how about the fascinating Faraday and Franklin? Both men have museums dedicated to them here. **The Royal Institution** (*see p77*) has restored the lab where Michael Faraday tamed electricity, and kids get to explore using a cool console packed with puzzles and games. The **Benjamin Franklin House** (*see p83*) uses a sound and light show to tell the great statesman's story.

Buckingham Palace guards in traditional red tunics and bearskin hats during the Changing the Guard

Westminster Abbey and around

Ever since Christmas Day 1066, when William the Conqueror was crowned here, Westminster Abbey has been the coronation site of monarchs – and the resting place of many too, including Henry V and Elizabeth I. Outside, the pomp of Parliament Square is dented a little by traffic, so save the surrounding sights for a Sunday, when it's quieter. St James's Park and the attractions along Whitehall can be comfortably tackled on foot, but hop on a bus (number 87 or 88) to visit the Tate Britain gallery.

Westminster and the West End

Covent Garden p86
National Gallery p78
Buckingham Palace p72
Westminster Abbey

River bus – a fun way to see many of the sights of Central London

The Lowdown

🚌 **Train** Charing Cross. **Tube** Westminster or St James's Park; Pimlico for Tate Britain. **Bus** Parliament Square: route numbers 3, 11, 12, 24, 53, 87, 88, 148, 159, 211 or 453; Tate Britain: 87, 88, C10, 185, 360, 436. **River bus** Westminster Pier to St Katherine's Dock daily, May–Sep; to Bankside on weekends and public holidays in winter. Seasonal services to Hampton Court, Kew Gardens to the west; Tower of London, Greenwich to the east

ℹ️ **Visitor information** Victoria Railway station, SW1E 5NE

🍴 **Supermarkets** Tesco Express, 8 Bridge St, SW1A 2JR (opposite Big Ben). Costcutter, 31 Horseferry Rd, SW1P 2AY **Markets** Strutton Ground (St James's Park tube), 8am–2:30pm Mon–Fri; and Tachbrook St (Pimlico tube) 8am–6pm Mon–Sat

🎪 **Festivals** New Year's Day Parade (1 Jan); Trooping the Colour, Horse Guards Parade (Jun); Mayor's Thames Festival (Sep); Festival of Remembrance, Whitehall (11 Nov); State Opening of Parliament (Nov); Christmas Carol Service, Westminster Abbey (23 & 24 Dec)

➕ **Pharmacies** Boots, 11 Bridge St, SW1A 2JR (across from Big Ben), open daily. Or search at www.nhs.uk/servicedirectories

🛝 **Nearest playgrounds** Victoria Tower Gardens (Lambeth Bridge end); Causton St playground; and playground in St James's Park

The Houses of Parliament, seen from across the River Thames

Trying on a uniform at the Household Cavalry Museum on Horse Guards Parade

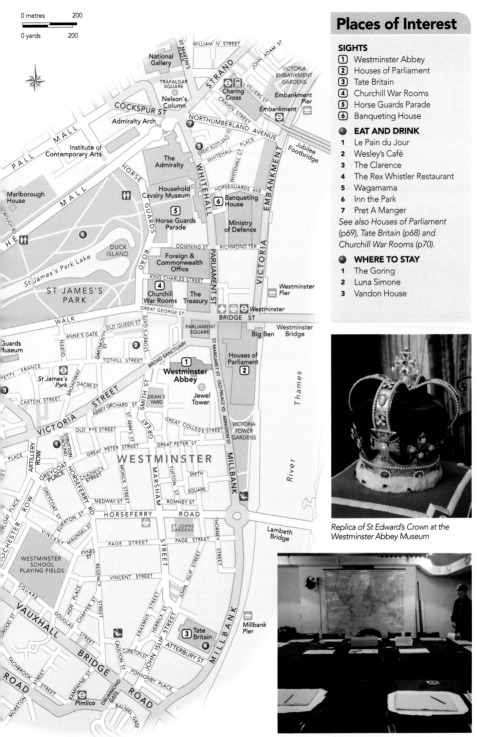

0 metres 200
0 yards 200

WILLIAM IV STREET
National Gallery
TRAFALGAR SQUARE
Nelson's Column
COCKSPUR ST
Admiralty Arch
STRAND
JOHN ADAM ST
VICTORIA EMBANKMENT GARDENS
Charing Cross
VILLIERS ST
CRAVEN STREET
Embankment Pier
Embankment
NORTHUMBERLAND AVENUE
MALL
Institute of Contemporary Arts
PALL MALL
The Admiralty
WHITEHALL
GREAT SCOTLAND YD
WHITEHALL CT PLACE
Jubilee Footbridge
Marlborough House
MALL
Household Cavalry Museum
HORSEGUARDS AVE
Banqueting House
EMBANKMENT
SPROUL RD
Horse Guards Parade
Ministry of Defence
St James's Park Lake
DUCK ISLAND
DOWNING ST
RICHMOND TER
Foreign & Commonwealth Office
VICTORIA
Westminster Pier
ST JAMES'S PARK
KING CHARLES STREET
Churchill War Rooms
The Treasury
PARLIAMENT ST
GREAT GEORGE ST
BRIDGE ST
Westminster
WALK
OLD QUEEN ST
PARLIAMENT SQUARE
Big Ben
Westminster Bridge
ANNE'S GATE
STOREY'S GATE
ST MARGARET ST
OLD PALACE YD
Guards Museum
QUEEN
DACRE ST
BROADWAY
OAKMOUTH ST
TOTHILL STREET
BROAD SANCTUARY
Westminster Abbey
Houses of Parliament
Thames
PETTY FRANCE
St James's Park
CAXTON STREET
STREET
ABBEY ORCHARD ST
DEAN'S YARD
Jewel Tower
ST ANN'S ST
SMITH ST
GREAT COLLEGE STREET
ABINGDON ST
VICTORIA TOWER GARDENS
River
VICTORIA
STRUTTON GROUND
OLD PYE STREET
GREAT PETER ST
GREAT PETER STREET
ARTILLERY ROW
GREYCOAT PLACE
HORSEFERRY
CHADWICK STREET
MONCK STREET
TUFTON ST
MILLBANK
WESTMINSTER
SMITH SQUARE
PLACE
GREYCOAT ST
ELVERTON ST
MEDWAY ST
ROMNEY ST
MARSHAM STREET
HORSEFERRY ROAD
ST JOHNS GARDENS
THORNEY ST
Lambeth Bridge
ROCHESTER ROW
VINCENT ST
MAUNSEL ST
PAGE STREET
PAGE STREET
FYNES ST
Millbank Pier
WESTMINSTER SCHOOL PLAYING FIELDS
REGENCY ST
VINCENT STREET
JOHN ISLIP STREET
SQUARE
HIDE PLACE
CHAPTER ST
MILLBANK
VAUXHALL
DOUGLAS ST
ERASMUS ST
HERRICK ST
Tate Britain
ATTERBURY ST
TACHBROOK
CUREBRIDGE
CAUSTON ST
CURETON ST
JOHN ISLIP ST
PONSONBY PLACE
ROAD
MORETON
Pimlico
RAMPAYNE ST
DRUMMOND GATE
BALNIEL GATE
ROAD

See also Houses of Parliament (p69), Tate Britain (p68) and Churchill War Rooms (p70).

Places of Interest

SIGHTS
1 Westminster Abbey
2 Houses of Parliament
3 Tate Britain
4 Churchill War Rooms
5 Horse Guards Parade
6 Banqueting House

● **EAT AND DRINK**
1 Le Pain du Jour
2 Wesley's Café
3 The Clarence
4 The Rex Whistler Restaurant
5 Wagamama
6 Inn the Park
7 Pret A Manger

● **WHERE TO STAY**
1 The Goring
2 Luna Simone
3 Vandon House

Replica of St Edward's Crown at the Westminster Abbey Museum

The shelter in the Churchill War Rooms, from where the prime minister conducted Britain's World War II campaign

① Westminster Abbey

Poets, princes and some rather smelly monks

Henry VIII ejected the Benedictine monks in 1540 when he dissolved the monasteries and founded the Church of England, but Westminster Abbey has retained its importance down the centuries. As well as witnessing the coronations of 40 kings and queens, the atmospheric building is also the final resting place of many world-famous writers, musicians and scientists. It is packed full of spooky tombs, sleeping knights and secret gardens, and there is even a creepy wax museum.

Gargoyle over the door of Westminster Abbey

Key Features

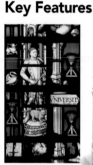

Dick Whittington Window This honours London's most famous lord mayor – his cat is hiding at his feet in the stained glass.

Dick Whittington Window

High Altar Queen Elizabeth II was crowned here in 1953, in front of 8,251 packed-in people. The gilded Coronation Chair is 700 years old – and has been carved with graffiti by naughty Westminster schoolboys.

Lady Chapel This 16th-century chapel has a plasterwork ceiling as delicate as a cobweb, and there are cheeky carvings under the choir stalls. Look for a wife thrashing her husband's bottom with some corn!

Poets' Corner The first great writer buried here was Geoffrey Chaucer, 600 years ago. The novelist Thomas Hardy's ashes are here, but not his heart, which is buried alongside his first wife in his beloved Dorset.

Cloisters These contain the earliest parts of the abbey, including the Pyx Chamber, a strong room where kings kept some of their treasure. The monks lived around the cloisters, and they even bathed here – though only four times a year.

Queen Elizabeth I's Tomb (above) is shared with Queen Mary Tudor.
Grave of the Unknown Warrior (left) This tribute to all who have lost their lives in war was created in 1920.

The Lowdown

🌐 **Map reference** 16 G1
Address 20 Dean's Yard, SW1P 3PA; 020 7222 5152; www.westminster-abbey.org

🚌 **Tube** Westminster. **Bus stop** Westminster Abbey or Victoria St. **River bus** Westminster Pier

🕐 **Open** 9:30am–4:30pm Mon–Fri (till 7pm Wed); 9:30am–2:30pm Sat. Last admission 1 hour before closing. On Sun and religious holidays, the abbey is open for worship only – all are welcome.

💲 **Price** £42–52; under-11s free

👫 **Skipping the queue** Tickets can't be pre-booked. Attending church services is free: the choir sings Evensong daily except Wed (5pm weekdays; 3pm weekends)

🚩 **Guided tours** Free audio tour; there are verger-led guided tours up to five times daily (£3)

👫 **Age range** 5 plus

👫 **Activities** Children's trail (ages 5–12) in English, French, German, Spanish, Italian; kids aged 5–12 can dress up as a monk in the museum (free). Art, dancing and drama workshops

on summer afternoons in College Garden (ages 5 plus, free).

⏱ **Allow** Up to 2 hours

♿ **Wheelchair access** Yes, via North Door; some areas inaccessible

☕ **Café** Open-air counter in the cloisters

🛍 **Shop** Outside the West Door

🚻 **Toilets** Near Poets' Corner

Good family value?
Plenty to dazzle here, though adult admission is expensive.

Prices given are for a family of four

College Garden, Westminster Abbey, once used by monks for growing herbs

Letting off steam

The tidy lawns and paths of **College Garden**, in the grounds of Westminster Abbey, are open Tuesday to Thursday only: concerts and children's events are held here in July and August. However, for a proper run-around, head for **St James's Park** with its lake and playground, at the Buckingham Palace end (see p74). If it rains, get even wetter at the **Queen Mother Sports Centre** (223 Vauxhall Bridge Road, SW1V 1EL; open daily), where the children's swimming pool has a great flume.

Eat and drink

Picnic: under £20; Snacks: £20–40; Real meal: £40–60; Family treat: £60 or more (based on a family of four)

PICNIC Le Pain du Jour (10 Strutton Ground, SW1P 2HP; 020 7222 3722; 7:30am–4pm Mon–Fri) is the pick of a parade of sandwich places along Strutton Ground, near St James's Park tube. Eat by the lake in St James's Park.
SNACKS Wesley's Café (Central Hall Westminster, Storey's Gate, SW1H 9NH; 020 7222 8010; 8am–4pm daily) is located downstairs at the Methodist Central Hall and serves hot and cold meals, as well as paninis, salads and sandwiches. It also offers a wide range of cakes, scones and biscuits in the afternoon.

Enjoying lunch at Wesley's Café, Methodist Central Hall

REAL MEAL There are limited options near Parliament Square so try **The Clarence** (53 Whitehall, SW1A 2HP; 020 7930 4808; 11am–10pm Mon–Sat; noon–9:30pm Sun), a scrubbed-up gastropub with half-price children's dishes (£5), including beef stew and gammon and eggs.
FAMILY TREAT The Rex Whistler Restaurant at Tate Britain (020 7887 8825; 11:30am–5pm daily) is a posh pillared dining room with food to match. One child under 13 can lunch for free with an adult eating a main and a dessert à la carte (£20–25). The murals, painted by Whistler in 1927, when he was still a student, make a jolly talking point.

Find out more

DIGITAL Create your own colourful coat of arms like those of the knights of Westminster Abbey at www.makeyourcoatofarms.com. Test your knowledge about Guy Fawkes and the Gunpowder Plot – and answer as quick as you can, to stop the fizzing fuse, at: www.bbc. co.uk/history/british/civil_war_ revolution/launch_gms_ gunpowder_plot.shtml.

The famous front door at No. 10 Downing Street

Next stop...

NO. 10 DOWNING STREET Stroll along Whitehall to peek through the railings into Downing Street, home of prime ministers since 1730. Until 1982 tourists could walk up and take photos of Number 10.
WESTMINSTER CATHEDRAL Near Victoria station is this impressive cathedral, which is the Catholic Church's headquarters in Britain (42 Francis Street, SW1P 1QW; www.westminstercathedral.org.uk; 8am–7pm Mon–Fri; 10am–1pm Sat & Sun). Zip up the 83-m (272-ft) tower for long views across London.

The Neo-Gothic Houses of Parliament, rebuilt in the 19th century after a massive fire

② Houses of Parliament

Home of UK democracy and those famous bongs

Officially called the Palace of Westminster, the Houses of Parliament began with Westminster Hall, built in 1097 by the son of William the Conqueror and little changed since. Guy Fawkes was tried here after trying to blow the building up in 1605, Sir Winston Churchill lay in state in 1965, and Henry VIII's tennis ball was found in the rafters, nearly 400 years after it got stuck there. Today, the hall is a pretty grand visitors' lobby – with its lofty timber roof, it feels like being inside an upturned Viking longship.

Free guided tours begin here and run all year for British residents, plus every Saturday and on weekdays in summer for paying visitors. When MPs are in session, or "sitting", it's also possible to attend a debate by queueing down the ramp on Cromwell Green. The tour passes through Westminster Hall and the shop, set inside St Stephen's Hall, where Spencer Perceval was shot dead in 1812 – Britain's only assassinated prime minister.

Where Guy Fawkes failed, a cleaner succeeded, accidentally burning down Parliament in 1834. Most of the building visible today was designed by Charles Barry in Victorian Gothic style and built in 1840–60 with sumptuous interiors by Augustus Pugin. The 75-minute tour is unstuffy and full of anecdotes

and follows the same route as the Queen when she attends the State Opening of Parliament each November. The tour reveals why Her Majesty arrives on a blue carpet, the location of her secret toilet, and why the statues of past prime ministers have shiny shoes. It doesn't visit Big Ben, though – that tour is only available to British residents (age 11 plus) who apply to their MP. The tower's iconic clock first ticked on 31 May 1859 and its famous "bongs" have heralded some BBC radio news bulletins since 1923.

The standard tour climaxes in the Commons Chamber, a surprisingly snug space just 20 m (66 ft) long – it can seat only 427 of Britain's 650 MPs. Visitors are able to stand where the prime minister does, but

sitting down on any of the seats is not allowed – only MPs can do that. Parliament Square, just outside, is home to several large statues of leaders and politicians.

Letting off steam
Victoria Tower Gardens (*Abingdon Street, SW1P 3*) has a grassy riverside, plus a small swing park.

③ Tate Britain

A masterpiece in every room

This site once stored prisoners, not paintings: in Victorian times the Millbank Penitentiary held convicts about to be shipped off to Australia as punishment. In 1897 Henry Tate, the sugar tycoon, paid for a national gallery, and it became the world's biggest collection of British art.

The Lowdown

🌐 **Map reference** 16 G1 **Address** St Margaret's Street, SW1A; 020 7219 3000; www.parliament.uk	🚶 **Age range** 7 plus; visitors attending debates must be silent.
🚌 **Tube** Westminster. **Bus stop** Bridge Street, Parliament St, Millbank. **River bus** Westminster Pier	🧑 **Activities** Good children's brochures are usually available at the Westminster Hall reception
🕐 **Open** 8am–11pm Mon–Thu; 8am–8pm Fri; 9am–6pm Sat	⏱ **Allow** 2 hours
💷 **Price** Attending debates is free.	♿ **Wheelchair access** Yes, all tours
🚻 **Skipping the queue** UK residents can arrange a free tour through their MP (six-month waiting list). Arrive early for tour.	🍴 **Eat and drink** *Snacks* Jubilee Café, off Westminster Hall (*10am–5:30pm Mon–Fri, till 6.15pm Sat*), is lovely, but open only to tour and debate goers. *Real Meal* Wagamama, (*76–98 Victoria Street, SW1E 5JD*) in Cardinal Place shopping centre, has a kids' menu.
📷 **Guided tours** Paid tours Mon–Fri Aug–Sep, plus Sat all year round: £37–60 (0844 847 1672; www.ticketmaster.co.uk/ housesofparliament)	🛍 **Shops** In St Stephen's Hall
	🚻 **Toilets** In Westminster Hall

Prices given are for a family of four

The Lowdown

🌐 **Map reference** 16 G3
Address Millbank, SW1P; 020 7887 8888; www.tate.org.uk/britain

🚇 **Tube** Pimlico, Vauxhall. **Bus stop** Millbank, Vauxhall Bridge Road. **River bus** Tate Boat (www.tate.org.uk/tatetotate) shuttles every 40 minutes to Tate Modern (see p148) during opening hours.

🕐 **Open** 10am–6pm (last admission 5:15pm); till 10pm first Fri of every month

💲 **Price** Free; special temporary exhibitions individually priced

👫 **Skipping the queue** Tickets for temporary exhibitions can be booked ahead online.

🚩 **Guided tours** Free tours daily; hand-held multimedia guide £3.50

👫 **Age range** 3 plus

👫 **Activities** Children's activity packs; Art Trolley on weekends and school holidays (free); occasional family workshops.

🕐 **Allow** 1–2 hours

♿ **Wheelchair access** Yes, Manton entrance, Atterbury Street

🍴 **Eat and drink** Snacks The Café has a kids' menu. *Family treat* The Rex Whistler Restaurant offers a free meal for one child under 13 when an adult orders two courses à la carte.

🛍 **Shops** Millbank and Manton entrances

👫 **Toilets** Manton entrance

The 30-room collection spans 500 years and includes everything from Hogarth to Hockney, Gainsborough to Gilbert and George. What's

actually on display varies, but there are always plenty of works to capture young imaginations: story pictures (perhaps *The Lady of Shalott* by John Waterhouse); scary pictures (try Bacon's *Figures at the Base of a Crucifixion*); pictures of animals (Stubbs's *Horse Devoured by a Lion*) and of children (Sargent's *Carnation, Lily, Lily, Rose*). The Pre-Raphaelites, with their fairytale lushness, go down especially well, and in the Modern and Contemporary galleries, children will be heartened to learn that bold stripes of colour (Bridget Riley) or splodges of paint (Gillian Ayres) can also qualify as genius. Beware, though: Damien Hirst's pickled sheep is lurking.

The gallery also encourages kids to scribble their way around. Begin at the Manton entrance and ask for an activity pack. "Secret Tate" is for ages 6–12 and very free-form, inviting children to design mosaics or copy a masterpiece. The "Post It!" pack for under-5s has an ingenious art box to build before setting off. Every weekend, a family Art Trolley is wheeled out from 11am–5pm, while the dedicated Tate Kids website (http://kids.tate.org.uk) is brimming with craft ideas and interactive games.

Letting off steam

Tucked away in a back street 5 minutes from the Tate, the terrific **Causton Street Playground** has a ball court, sandpit, paddling pool and play kit for ages 3–7.

The façade of Tate Britain

Picnic: under £20; **Snacks:** £20–40; **Real meal:** £40–60; **Family treat:** £60 or more (based on a family of four)

④ Churchill War Rooms

Hidden passages, secret messages

Everyone loves a secret labyrinth, and here's one right under the heart of London. The Churchill War Rooms are where Winston Churchill ran Britain's campaign against the Axis powers during World War II. This warren of chambers was designed to resist enemy bombs – just as well, as the House of Commons took a direct hit during the Blitz. The rooms became the nerve centre for picking up secret messages from the front, with some staff living like moles almost full time, even using sun-lamps to prevent Vitamin D deficiency.

What is enthralling is that along with a few shop-dummy typists and military men poised over maps, the rooms remain frozen in time, filled with original clutter and musty smells. Churchill's bedroom looks like he's just popped out for a quick cigar – which he liked to do, often climbing to the roof during Luftwaffe raids to watch.

The children's audio tour extends into the adjoining Churchill Museum,

Plotting the course of World War II in Churchill's Cabinet War Rooms

a 21st-century space that uses audio, film and touch-screen wizardry to canter through Churchill's career. Despite all the gizmos, this area will mainly interest older children.

Letting off steam

Cross the road into **St James's Park** (*see p74*), which has refreshment kiosks and plump ducks to feed.

The Lowdown

- 🌐 **Map reference** 10 F6
- **Address** Clive Steps, King Charles Street, SW1A; 020 7930 6961; http://cwr.iwm.org.uk
- 🚇 **Tube** Westminster, St James's Park. **Bus stop** Parliament Street, Parliament Square. **River bus** Westminster Pier
- ☉ **Open** 9:30am–6pm daily (last admission 5pm)
- 💲 **Price** £30–40, under-16s free
- 🏴 **Guided tours** No. Free audio guide
- 🕴 **Age range** 8 plus
- 🎨 **Activities** Children's audio guide (English only), plus War Rooms family trail. Kids' activity sheets for Churchill Museum downloadable from website. Occasional school holiday workshops for families.
- ⏱ **Allow** Up to 2 hours
- ♿ **Wheelchair access** Yes, use Great George Street entrance.
- 🍽 **Eat and drink** *Snacks* The Switch Room Café, halfway though the tour, sells main dishes and snacks.
- 🛍 **Shop** At the end of the tour
- 🚻 **Toilets** In ticket lobby

⑤ Horse Guards Parade

A polished performance

In Tudor times, the royal palace was at Whitehall, and Horse Guards Parade started life as Henry VIII's jousting yard. That's why Her Majesty's Life Guard stand sentry on the pavement here to this day. Every morning, the new guard trots in on horseback along The Mall from Hyde Park Barracks, silver helmets glinting, heading for the

changing ceremony – a 15-minute silent stand-off followed by lots of bellowing as the old guard departs. Beside the parade ground is the Household Cavalry Museum, displaying historic regimental memorabilia. The main attraction, though, is the cobbled stables – a glass wall in the museum looks right in on the troops as they groom their horses and prepare their kit. Most of the action happens at the guard-change time, and at 4pm, when the troops dismount. The smells are authentic, too! There is real armour

The Lowdown

- 🌐 **Map reference** 10 F6
- **Address** Horse Guards, Whitehall, SW1A; 020 7930 3070; www.householdcavalrymuseum.co.uk
- 🚇 **Tube** Westminster, Embankment, Charing Cross. **Bus stop** Whitehall. **River bus** Westminster Pier
- ☉ **Open** Changing the Guard, 11am daily (10am Sun); museum open 10am–6pm daily (Mar–Sep); till 5pm (Oct–Feb)
- 💲 **Price** £15–24
- 🏴 **Skipping the queue** To guarantee a good view of the guard change, arrive by 10:45am.
- 🏴 **Guided tour** No
- 🕴 **Age range** 4 plus
- 🎨 **Activities** Dressing-up uniforms and good age-specific museum quizzes. Pre-bookable school-holiday craft activities (free with an admission-paying adult)
- ⏱ **Allow** 1 hour
- ♿ **Wheelchair access** Yes
- 🍽 **Eat and drink** *Real meal* Inn the Park, nearby (*see p74*).
- 🛍 **Shop** Gifts and souvenirs
- 🚻 **Toilets** In the museum

Filling in a quiz-sheet kit inspection at the Household Cavalry Museum

Mounted sentries on Horse Guards Parade

for kids to try on, quiz sheets to complete and touch-screen TVs with footage of the guards talking about their work. Young recruits spend up to 12 hours a day buffing their uniforms and each morning the smartest one gets to be a mounted "boxman" or sentry, while the least polished is saddled with foot duty. So, is it acceptable for visitors to pull faces and make them smile? Permission denied!

Letting off steam

The spacious and well-tended lawns and lakes of **St James's Park** (see p74) are right opposite.

⑥ Banqueting House

Where a king lost his head

Four hundred years ago, English kings believed they were agents of God. James I threw dazzling courtly entertainments, or masques, in which actors cavorted as devils and beasts with the monarch restoring order at the end. Banqueting House was built in 1622 to stage them and designed by Inigo Jones, who excited London with the Neo-Classical architecture he had brought back from Italy.

Today, a visit begins with a film history in the Undercroft, moodily lit by candelabras. Then, head upstairs into the white-and-gold hall with its double-decker columns and painted ceiling. This was commissioned from Baroque master Peter Paul Rubens by Charles I and shows his father, King James I, rising gloriously into Heaven. Children are encouraged to lie on their backs and ogle the closest thing in the UK to the Sistine Chapel in Rome.

The lively audio guide tells the building's stories: such as the "touching the king's evil" ceremony, where sufferers of the hideous skin disease scrofula gathered to be "cured" by the monarch's touch.

Charles I inherited his father's belief in the superiority of kings over the common man. However, in 1649, just 11 years after his ceiling was finished, Charles was marched out of Banqueting House and had his head chopped off for treason.

Letting off steam

St James's Park (see p74) is across the road, via Horse Guards Parade, with activities for kids of all ages.

The Lowdown

🌐 **Map reference** 10 G6
Address Whitehall, SW1A; 0844 482 7777; www.hrp.org.uk/banquetinghouse

🚇 **Tube** Westminster, Charing Cross, Embankment **Bus stop** Whitehall. **River bus** Westminster Pier

🕐 **Open** 10am–5pm daily (last admission 4:30pm)

💷 **Price** £10–20, under-16s free. Free audio guide

🚶 **Skipping the queue** Rarely busy

🎧 **Guided tour** No

👫 **Age range** 9 plus

⏱ **Allow** Up to 1 hour

♿ **Wheelchair access** Limited. Call 020 3166 6155/6152 for details

🍽 **Eat and drink** Picnic Pret A Manger (1 Whitehall, SW1A 2DD; 020 7932 5216) offers eat in or out sandwiches and salads. Snacks The Portrait Café serves light meals (see p82).

🛍 **Shop** On the main stairwell, selling gifts and souvenirs

🚻 **Toilets** In the undercroft

Picnic under £20; **Snacks** £20–40; **Real meal** £40–60; **Family treat** £60 or more (based on a family of four)

Buckingham Palace and around

Each year, thousands press their noses to the gilded railings of Buckingham Palace, the headquarters of the royal family since 1837. The Palace has been open for pre-booked tours (August and September only) since 1993, but check the calendar to ensure your visit coincides with the Changing the Guard ceremony. Approach along Birdcage Walk from St James's Park Tube Station, and explore the children's playground en route. Then while away the afternoon around the lake in St James's Park, or wander across Green Park to window shop in the swish arcades along Piccadilly. It's all within walking distance.

Westminster and the West End

Covent Garden
p86

National
Gallery
Buckingham p78
Palace

Westminster
Abbey
p64

0 metres   200

0 yards   200

The small but compelling Guards Museum, filled with military kit from historic battles to modern-day wars

The Lowdown

🚆 **Train** Victoria (five-minute walk) or Charing Cross (10–15 minutes). **Tube** Victoria, St James's Park or Green Park. **Bus** Grosvenor Place: route numbers 2, 16, 36, 38, 52, 73, 82, 148, 436 or C2; or Buckingham Palace Rd: 11, 211, C1 or C10

ℹ️ **Visitor information** Victoria Railway Station (opposite platform 8) or Britain and London Visitor Centre, 1 Regent Street, SW1Y 4XT

🛒 **Supermarkets** Sainsbury's, 150 Victoria St, SW1E 5LB; Marks & Spencer, 78 Piccadilly, W1J 8AQ
Markets Arts & crafts market, St James's Churchyard, Piccadilly W1J 9LL; 11am–6pm Tue–Sat

🎊 **Festivals** St Patrick's Day Parade, Green Park (Sun nearest Mar 17); Trooping the Colour, Horse Guards Parade (any Sat in Jun); Virgin London Marathon, ends in The Mall (Apr); Royal Academy Summer Exhibition (Jun–Aug)

➕ **Pharmacies** Boots, 13 Cathedral Walk (7:30am–8pm Mon–Fri, 9am–6pm Sat). For 24-hour pharmacies search at www.nhs.uk/servicedirectories

🛝 **Nearest playground** St James's Park (Buckingham Palace end of Birdcage Walk)

One of the Queen's garden parties at Buckingham Palace

Places of Interest

SIGHTS
1. Buckingham Palace
2. The Royal Mews
3. Guards Museum
4. Royal Institution

● **EAT AND DRINK**
1. Inn the Park
2. The Parlour Restaurant at Fortnum & Mason
3. The Café at the Institute of Contemporary Arts
4. Benihana

5. Crumpets
6. Le Signore
7. Picnic Kiosk
8. Caffe Grana
9. Laduree
See also Royal Institution (p77) and Shopping (below)

● **SHOPPING**
1. Prestat
2. Burlington Arcade
3. Fortnum & Mason

● **PLACES TO STAY**
1. Brown's
2. Duke's
3. The Goring
4. Vandon House
5. Athenaeum Apartments
6. Flemings Apartments
7. 44 Curzon Street Apartments

Changing the Guard at Wellington Barracks, also home to the Guards Museum

Leafy trees around the lake in St James's Park, with the London Eye visible across the Thames

① Buckingham Palace
When the Queen's away, there are visits to pay

Full of priceless porcelain, jewelled cabinets and gold leaf, Buckingham Palace owes its splendour to George IV, who came to the throne in 1820 and lavished a fortune on it – but never lived here. Queen Elizabeth II first moved in as a 10-year-old princess, and now shares the palace with 350 staff, from cleaners to courtiers. Visitor tours operate in summer when Her Majesty is at her holiday home, Balmoral Castle in Scotland. Only 19 state rooms are open to the public – just as well, as there are 775 rooms in all.

Sentry guard

Key Features

Grand Staircase This was the centrepiece of George IV's extravagant conversion of the old "Buckingham House". The ornate bronze cast balustrade alone cost £200,000 in today's money.

Grand Staircase

State Ballroom The French-style ballroom is used for state banquets and conferring awards.

White Drawing Room This has a secret panel that swings back to allow the royals to appear as if by magic.

Throne room

State Dining Room

State Dining Room The dining table seats 46 guests, and the footmen carry special rulers to make sure cutlery and glassware are positioned correctly. The Queen always makes a final check!

Throne Room The two thrones here are embroidered with "ER" and "P" and were used by Elizabeth II and the Duke of Edinburgh at the coronation in 1953.

Letting off steam

St James's Park (020 7930 1793; www.royalparks.org.uk) is nearby, with a great playground for children aged up to 11 at the Palace end – it has a sandpit, kids-only toilets, a refreshment kiosk and picnic tables. Admire the geese and swans as they glide across the lake, but the kings of the park are the pelicans, fed at 2:30pm near Duck Island. The first pelicans were a gift from the Russian ambassador in 1664. There's a smart conservatory restaurant nearby (see right) and deck chairs for hire, band concerts on summer weekends, occasional guided walks… and no "keep off the grass" signs.

Prices given are for a family of four

Eat and drink

Picnic: under £20; Snacks: £20–40; Real meal: £40–60; Family treat: £60 or more (based on a family of four)

PICNIC Inn the Park (St James's Park; 020 7451 9999; www.innthepark.com; 8am–11am, noon–4:30pm, 6–11pm daily) is a lakeside eatery in the park, with wide windows and an eco-friendly turf roof. The children's menu is pricey but there are tasty "grab and go" sandwiches and luscious cakes that are perfect for eating on the surrounding lawns.

SNACKS The Parlour Restaurant at Fortnum & Mason (181 Piccadilly, W1A 1ER; 0845 300

Clambering over boulders in St James's Park sandpit

1707; www.fortnumandmason.com; 10am–7:30pm Mon–Sat, noon–5:30pm Sun) does superb ice-cream sundaes and hot chocolate, and has a handy toasted sandwich menu for under-8s.

The Lowdown

🌐 **Map reference** 15 D1
Address Buckingham Palace Road, SW1A; 020 7766 7300; www.royalcollection.org.uk

🚗 **Tube** Victoria, St James's Park.
Bus stop Buckingham Palace Rd

🕐 **Open** State Rooms Jul–Oct 9:30am–6:30pm (last admission 3:45pm). Changing the Guard May–Jul 11:30am daily; Aug–Apr alternate days; cancelled in heavy rain

💲 **Price** £47–72, under-5s free

👬 **Skipping the queue** Book tickets in advance online. The palace forecourt gets squeezed during the Changing the Guard – children will get a better view on nearby Friary Court, outside St James's Palace. Aim to be there before 11am

🚩 **Guided tours** Free audio guide in eight languages

👫 **Age range** 5 plus

🎨 **Activities** Children's audio guide (ages 7–11), plus garden nature trail on request (or downloadable online). Family room with free activities during summer holiday: design a hat for a garden party

🕐 **Allow** 2 hours

♿ **Wheelchair access** Yes, but must be booked in advance: 020 7766 7324

☕ **Café** On the garden terrace

🏷️ **Shop** Large shop at the end of the Palace gardens, at the end of the visit

🚻 **Toilets** In the garden at the end of visit

Good family value?
The palace tour is far from cheap, though the children's audio guide and sparky summer activities make it just about worth the money.

KIDS' CORNER

Wrap this
What gift would you give Her Majesty if she visited your home town? The strange presents she has received from foreign rulers include: two giant turtles, a jaguar, a canary, a canoe, an elephant called Jumbo, a pair of cowboy boots, the world's biggest pork pie, a pair of sunglasses, 12 tins of tuna and 15 tonnes of dried fruit. Actually, we made up one of those. Can you guess which one?

....

Answer at the bottom of the page.

TRICK A GROWN-UP
Ask an adult to tell you whether the Queen is at home. If the Union Jack is flying above the palace, they'll probably say yes. Wrong! It means the opposite. A red, blue and gold quartered flag called the Royal Standard is raised when Her Majesty is in residence.

Watch the birdie...
Look out for the birds on the lake in St James's Park. Score points for each one you spot:
1 **Coot** (small, black with a white forehead) 1 point
2 **Greylag goose** (big, grey with pink feet) 2 points
3 **Black swan** (black with a red beak) 3 points
4 **Pelican** (big, mainly white, with a big beak) 4 points
5 **Great crested grebe** (slim-necked with tufts on its reddish head) 5 points

....

Answer: The world's biggest pork pie

REAL MEAL The Café at the Institute of Contemporary Arts (020 7930 8619; www.ica.org.uk; noon–2:30pm, 5–10pm daily, till 8pm Sun), on The Mall, is a cool alternative to the chain restaurants on nearby Haymarket. No children's menu, but smaller portions of pasta and burgers on request. High chairs and baby-changing facilities, too.
FAMILY TREAT Benihana (37 Sackville Street, W1S 3DQ; 020 7494 2525; www.benihana.co.uk; noon–3pm daily, 5:30–10:30pm Mon–Sat; 5–10pm Sun) is cooking as theatre: the Japanese dishes sizzle up spectacularly on a teppan hot-plate at your table.

Shopping
After visiting the Queen, head for the aristocratic shops of St James's. **Prestat** (14 Princes Arcade, SW1Y 6DS) purveys deluxe chocolates and truffles, while in even more exclusive **Burlington Arcade** (Mayfair, W1; www.burlington-arcade.co.uk), which claims to be the world's first mall, the top-hatted security guards – Beadles – have been keeping the peace since 1819. **Fortnum & Mason** (181 Piccadilly, W1A 1ER) has elegant frock-coated assistants who look like escaped palace footmen. See if the kids will try the shop's chocolate-covered scorpions.

The confectionery counter inside Fortnum & Mason

Find out more
DIGITAL Take one of Buckingham Palace's most famous inhabitants, Queen Victoria, to the seaside, then help her to write a postcard, at www.museumnetworkuk.org/portraits/activities/activities.html.
FILM At the start of the 1996 film 101 Dalmatians, Anita and Roger fall into the lake (and in love) in St James's Park thanks to their dogs.

Next stop...
QUEEN'S GALLERY Just around the corner on Buckingham Gate, the Queen's Gallery (Apr–Nov; www.royalcollection.org.uk) shows off art, jewels and family heirlooms from the royal collections. There's also a good children's trail.

② The Royal Mews
A coach fit for Cinderella

This must be the most picturesque garage in London: a 200-year-old Georgian stable yard, complete with an ornate clock tower and surrounded by the cottage-like quarters of the Queen's coachmen and their families. It looks enchanting at Christmas, when Santa slides in on his regal sleigh to the Queen's annual children's party.

Up to 30 horses are stabled here – they go to school for two years before they are qualified to pull a coach. The trainers wave flags, blow trumpets and play the sound of cannon fire to prepare them for the London crowds. The horses even learn to stop at red traffic lights.

As well as Santa's sleigh, a visit takes in the Glass Coach that Lady Diana Spencer rode in to her wedding to Prince Charles in 1981, and the little donkey carriage (or barouche) once driven by Queen Victoria's children. Apparently, the latter came in handy to get to the bathrooms in the vast royal palaces. The biggest gasp of all is reserved for the Gold State Coach used for coronation parades, presented in full harness and looking every bit like it's been borrowed from Cinderella. It is so big they have to remove a wall to get it out of the building.

The magic of the Mews for most children, though, springs from being among the sounds and smells of a working stable in the heart of London – and, if they're lucky, there might be a horse or two to meet and greet at the exit.

Helping a guardsman with his job (and getting a photo) at Horse Guards Parade

Letting off steam

A few minutes along Buckingham Gate lies **St James's Park** *(see p74)*, with its excellent children's playground, just off Birdcage Walk.

③ Guards Museum
Royal sentries and toy soldiers

Part of Wellington Barracks, this modest museum fills a handful of basement rooms with the bloody exploits of the five British Guards regiments (and Household Cavalry). Learn the stories behind Charles II's musketeers, Wellington's overcoat and Florence Nightingale's medicine cup. Most compelling, perhaps, is the display of kit and mementos from the conflict in Afghanistan.

A quiz sheet for youngsters is usually available, and the kids can don a guard's tunic and bearskin for a photo, though there's an extra charge. If short of time, head for the toy soldier shop on the forecourt, which has shelf after shelf of brilliant thumb-sized battle scenes.

Outside, on the parade ground, troops line up at 11am ready to march to Buckingham Palace for the Changing the Guard ceremony *(see p75)*, and viewpoints here are usually less congested than the more famous observation points at the palace. There are often drills at other times too: listen out for the military drum beat booming out across St James's Park.

Letting off steam

The excellent **St James's Park** playground, complete with sandpit, is just across the road *(see p74)*.

The Lowdown

- 🌐 **Map reference** 16 E1
  Address Wellington Barracks, Birdcage Walk, SW1E; 020 7414 3271; *www.theguardsmuseum.com*
- 🚇 **Tube** St James's Park. **Bus stop** Victoria Street
- 🕐 **Open** 10am–4pm (last admission 3:30pm)
- 💷 **Price** £8–12
- 🚶 **Skipping the queue** Rarely busy
- 🚶 **Guided tours** No
- 👫 **Age range** Museum, 8 plus; shop, 5 plus
- 🤸 **Activities** Dressing-up, £6; ask about the children's quiz sheet
- ⏱ **Allow** Up to 1 hour
- ♿ **Wheelchair access** Yes, via lift
- 🍴 **Eat and drink** Picnic A kiosk by St James's Park lake *(Palace end)* sells snacks and ices. *Snacks* Caffé Grana *(St James's Park tube station)* sells snacks and hot food.
- 🛍 **Shop** On the right, just after the gates on Birdcage Walk, selling armies of toy soldiers
- 🚻 **Toilets** No

The Lowdown

- 🌐 **Map reference** 15 D1
  Address Buckingham Palace, SW1W; 020 7766 7302; *www.royalcollection.org.uk*
- 🚇 **Tube** Victoria, Green Park or Hyde Park corner. **Bus stop** Buckingham Palace Rd
- 🕐 **Open** end Mar–end Oct, 10am–5pm Sat–Thu. 1 Nov–22 Dec, 10am–4pm Mon– Sat (last admission 45 minutes before closing)
- 💷 **Price** £22–33, under-5s free
- 🚶 **Skipping the queue** Buy tickets online before visiting.
- 🚶 **Guided tours** Hourly; free
- 👫 **Age range** 5 plus

- 🤸 **Activities** Children's audio guide; unsupervised art room for ages 5–11 at weekends (free); occasional school holiday workshops.
- ⏱ **Allow** 1 hour
- ♿ **Wheelchair access** Yes, for more information, call 020 7766 7324
- 🍴 **Eat and drink** Picnic Crumpets (82 Buckingham Gate, SW1E 6PD) offers good sandwiches, toasted sandwiches... and, of course, crumpets. *Snacks* Le Signore (4 Palace Street, SW1E 5HY) is a reliable Italian café.
- 🛍 **Shop** On Buckingham Palace Rd
- 🚻 **Toilets** Near the entrance, with baby-changing facilities

Toy soldiers at the Guards Museum – perfect for children of all ages

Exploring the elements, Royal Institution

④ Royal Institution

A genius introduction to ground-breaking science

Smash glass, electrocute a frog and blow up a laboratory assistant. That's the irresistible promise of a visit to the "Science in the Making" exhibition at the Royal Institution. Luckily, the glass-smashing and frog-frazzling are achieved virtually, using the museum's ingenious eGuide – a hand-held console which plays interactive cartoons of historic experiments at regular points around the museum. Even so, it's a great way to get budding geniuses interested in the mysteries of science.

Fourteen Nobel Prize winners have worked at the Royal Institution,

so there are fascinating artifacts to see – Alessandro Volta's prototype battery, James Dewar's first vacuum flask and Michael Faraday's original transformer. The laboratory where Faraday first harnessed electricity survives just as it was in the 1850s. In a clever touch, the Institution has a laboratory right opposite, where scientists can sometimes be seen working on special projects, such as developing tiny nanomagnets that can find and zap cancer cells.

Most children will be more engaged by the eGuide and its amusing clips and games. The handy device also brings to life some of the most popular bits of the Royal Institution's celebrated Christmas lectures, which have been enthralling children since 1825. For example, learn how a toy kangaroo can unlock the secrets of gravity, and how to turn a bicycle wheel into a gyroscope.

Letting off steam

A 10-minute walk away along Piccadilly lie the grassy expanses of **Green Park** *(see p73)*, perfect for a run around, with deck-chair hire and refreshment kiosks.

The Lowdown

- 🌐 **Map reference** 9 D4
- 📍 **Address** 21 Albemarle St, W1S 4BS; 020 7409 2992; *www.rigb.org*
- 🚇 **Tube** Green Park or Piccadilly Circus. **Bus stop** Berkeley St or Piccadilly
- 🕐 **Open** 9am–9pm Mon–Fri
- 💲 **Price** Free
- 🎫 **Guided tours** No; free eGuide
- 👫 **Age range** 9 plus
- 🤸 **Activities** Hands-on science sessions six times a year (ages 5–12): £16–20
- ⏱ **Allow** Up to 2 hours
- ♿ **Wheelchair access** Yes
- 🍽 **Eat and drink** *Snacks* Laduree *(71 Burlington Arcade, W1J 0QX; www.laduree.fr/)* was established in Paris in 1862 and is a temple to French macaroons. *Family treat* Time & Space Restaurant, at the musuem has good-value set lunches. There is a less formal cafe too.
- 🚻 **Toilets** In the lobby

Michael Faraday glass egg, used to test theories about electricity

National Gallery and around

In one room, St George spears the dragon straight through the eye. In another, a teenaged queen is led blindfolded to the chopping block. Who said art galleries are boring? The National unlocks the stories behind every canvas, with kids' trails and workshops. Its Sainsbury Wing is the best way in for families – aim left when approaching across Trafalgar Square. The cinemas and street life of the West End are a short stroll up Charing Cross Road – and best explored by day. To see Piccadilly Circus and Hamleys toy shop, take the Bakerloo Line from Charing Cross.

Westminster and the West End

Covent Garden p86

National Gallery

Buckingham Palace p72

Westminster Abbey p64

Above *The grand porticoed entrance of the National Gallery, completed in 1838*
Below *Holbein's The Ambassadors (1533) shows two stately men with symbols of power*

The metal in the brass lions in Trafalgar Square reputedly came from French guns captured at the Battle of Trafalgar (1805)

Inside the National Portrait Gallery

The Lowdown

🚃 **Train** Charing Cross. **Tube** Charing Cross, Embankment or Leicester Square. **Bus** Trafalgar Square: routes 3, 6, 9, 11, 12, 13, 15, 24, 23, 29, 87, 88, 159, 176, 453; Piccadilly Circus: 3, 6, 9, 12, 13, 15, 22, 23, 88, 94, 139, 159, 453; Shaftesbury Avenue: 14, 19, 38. **River bus** Embankment Pier, services to Westminster and St Katharine's Dock (Crown River Cruises: 020 7936 2033; www.crownriver.com)

ℹ️ **Visitor information** Leicester Square; Britain & London Visitor Centre, 1 Regent St; or at Piccadilly Circus Tube Station

🍴 **Supermarkets** New Loon Moon Chinese supermarket, 9a Gerrard St, W1D 5PL; Tesco Metro, 17–25 Regent St, SW1Y 4LR **Markets** Berwick Street (food, fish, flowers) and Rupert Street (books, jewellery, hot food), both in Soho: 9am–6pm Mon–Sat

🎡 **Festivals** New Year's Day Parade, Trafalgar Square (1 Jan); Chinese New Year, Soho (Feb); St George's Day, Trafalgar Square (23 Apr); Kids' Week Theatre Festival, West End theatres (Aug); Regent Street Festival (Sep); Trafalgar Day Parade (Oct); London Film Festival, Leicester Sq cinemas (Oct); Christmas Lights, Regent Street (Nov–Dec)

➕ **Pharmacies** Boots, 5–7 Strand, WC2N 5HR (7:30am–8pm Mon–Fri, 9am–6pm Sat, 11am–5pm Sun). For 24-hour pharmacies search at www.nhs. uk/servicedirectories

🛝 **Nearest playgrounds** Phoenix Garden in St Giles-in-the-Fields churchyard, or in St James's Park (see p73)

0 metres 200
0 yards 200

Places of Interest

SIGHTS
1. National Gallery
2. Trafalgar Square
3. National Portrait Gallery
4. Benjamin Franklin House
5. Leicester Square
6. Piccadilly Circus
7. Hamleys

● EAT AND DRINK
1. Tesco Metro
2. The Café in the Crypt
3. Ed's Easy Diner
4. Portrait Restaurant
5. Leon
6. Patisserie Pompidou
7. Lupita
8. Häagen-Dazs Café
9. Little Lamb
10. Millies
11. The Rainforest Café
12. Fairgrounds Café
See also Trafalgar Square (p82), National Portrait Gallery (p82) and Hamleys (p85)

● SHOPPING
1. Marchpane
2. Mamas & Papas
3. TokyoToys

William Hamley's toy shop has been bewitching children since 1760 and is now a major tourist attraction

① National Gallery

Heroes and angels, monsters and murderers

Britain's richest art collection began life in 1824 with just 38 paintings. Now it has 2,300, from the vivid saints and serpents in the medieval galleries, to the iconic sunflowers and water lilies in the 19th-century rooms. With school groups sitting cross-legged in front of assorted canvases, there is plenty of happy hubbub throughout. Start at the audio guide desk, where family trails include Teach Your Grown-Ups About Art, a genius idea that turns children into instant experts.

National Gallery main entrance

Key Features

■ **Main Gallery Building** Paintings from 1500 to 1900 are displayed here.

■ **Sainsbury Wing** This houses the early Renaissance Collection of paintings from 1250 to1500.

Main entrance on ground floor

① **St George and the Dragon (1470)** Paolo Uccello illustrates two episodes from the story of St George in one picture: the knight's victory, and the rescued princess bringing the fearsome prey to heel. (Room 54)

② **Peepshow (1655–60)** A mind-boggling "perspective box" by Samuel Von Hoogstraten. Through the main window it all looks skewed, but have a look through the eyeholes for a surprise. (Room 25)

③ **Perseus Turning Phineas and his Followers to Stone (1680s)** An attacking army is petrified by the face of the snake-haired Medusa, a mythological event brilliantly captured by Luca Giordano. (Room 32)

④ **The Execution of Lady Jane Grey (1833)** Paul Delaroche's painting shows the doomed, blindfolded 17-year-old queen groping towards the chopping block. Gallery-goers wept when it was first exhibited in 1834. (Room 41)

⑥ **Sunflowers (1888)** Vincent van Gogh sold only one painting, for about £50, during his lifetime. His famous *Sunflowers* is now worth a million times that sum. The flowers symbolized happiness for him. (Room 45)

⑤ **Bathers at Asnières (1884)** Georges Seurat used his new technique – tiny dots of contrasting colour called pointillism – to make his paintings glow. (Room 44)

The Lowdown

⊕ **Map ref** 10 F4
Address Trafalgar Square, WC2N 5DN; 020 7747 2885; www.nationalgallery.org.uk

🚗 **Train** Charing Cross.
Tube Charing Cross or Leicester Square.
Bus stop Trafalgar Square. **River bus** Embankment Pier

🕐 **Open** 10am–6pm daily; until 9pm Fri. Closed 1 Jan, 24–26 Dec

💲 **Price** Permanent collection free; temporary exhibitions individually priced

👪 **Skipping the queue** The Sainsbury Wing entrance (corner of Trafalgar Square) is less busy. Arrive early for kids' workshops.

🚩 **Guided tours** "Taster tours" of the collection twice daily, plus Fridays at 7pm

👫 **Age range** 5 plus

👫 **Activities** Family audio tours (under-12s free), plus themed workbook trails: download these at www.nationalgallery.org.uk/families. Family Sunday sessions for under-5s and for 5–11s (2 hours; free). There are school holiday workshops, too.

⏱ **Allow** Up to 3 hours

♿ **Wheelchair access** Yes

☕ **Café** National Café (Level 0) for brunch, lunch and afternoon tea; National Dining Rooms (Level 1) for more formal dining

🛍 **Shop** Sainsbury Wing and main building, selling art-themed books, cards, prints, jewellery and gifts

🚻 **Toilets** All floors main building; Level 1, Sainsbury Wing

Good family value?
Excellent, thanks to the inventive kids' stuff. Visit the Art Start room (Sainsbury Wing) to find out what's happening on the day.

Letting off steam

Outside the gallery, in **Trafalgar Square** (see p82), there is fun to be had chasing pigeons, dodging spray from the fountains and scampering around Nelson's Column – though riding his famous lions is fraught with slippery danger. For softer landings, stroll 2 minutes through Admiralty Arch onto the well-kept lawns of **St James's Park** (see p74).

Chasing pigeons outside The National Gallery on Trafalgar Square

Eat and drink

Picnic: under £20; Snacks: £20–40; Real meal: £40–60; Family treat: £60 or more (based on a family of four)

PICNIC Buy supplies from the **Tesco Metro** supermarket behind St Martin's Lane (22–25 Bedford Street, WC2E 9EQ; 0845 677 9173; 8am–midnight Mon–Fri, 7:30am–11pm Sat, noon–6pm Sun) and walk down to Victoria Embankment Gardens for a picnic.
SNACKS The Café in the Crypt (Trafalgar Square, WC2N 4JJ; 020 7766 1158; www.smitf.org; 8am–8pm Mon–Tues; 8am–10.30pm Wed (jazz night ticket holders only after 7:30pm); 8am–9pm Thu–Sat; 11am–6pm Sun) serves super-fresh canteen-style dishes in the crypt of St Martin-in-the-Fields church.
REAL MEAL Ed's Easy Diner (London Trocadero, 19 Rupert Street, W1D 7PA; 020 7287 1951; www.edseasydiner.com; daily noon till late) is a temple to 1950s Americana, with hotdogs, shakes and retro jukeboxes at every table.
FAMILY TREAT Portrait Restaurant (National Portrait Gallery; 020 7312 2490; www.npg.org.uk; 10am–5pm

daily; 5:30–8:30pm Thu–Sat) offers half-size portions of its dishes for kids, with fantastic views of Admiral Nelson in Trafalgar Square, Big Ben, and the London Eye. Book well in advance for Saturday night dining.

Shopping

West End shopping heaven is close by, dominated by the seven storeys of hyperactive play at **Hamleys** (see p85). For vintage children's books, there is **Marchpane** (16 Cecil Court, WC2N 4HE), while designer toddlers enjoy **Mamas & Papas** (256–8 Regent Street, W1B 3AF), which also has a good café. Teenage anime fiends will love **TokyoToys**, in the Trocadero Centre (13 Coventry Street, W1D 7DH).

Find out more

DIGITAL Make a 3D perspective box like Samuel Van Hoogstraten's at http://kids.tate.org.uk/create/ sunsets_box.shtm.

Next stop…

ROYAL ACADEMY OF ARTS On nearby Piccadilly, the **Royal Academy** (www.royalacademy.org.uk) is another treasure house of British painting, with Art Detective family trails, downloadable guides and occasional free workshops for families. In summer, its café spills into the courtyard, and kids are even able to frolic in the fountains.
CLEOPATRA'S NEEDLE Stroll down to the Embankment and investigate this 3,500-year-old Egyptian obelisk, raised beside the river in 1878. Its guardian (19th-century) sphinxes are at child-friendly height for a photo.

The entrance courtyard of the Royal Academy of Arts, Piccadilly

The magnificent Cleopatra's Needle, situated on the Embankment

② Trafalgar Square

Lions and fountains

As monumental playgrounds go, Trafalgar Square, with its splashing mermaids and watchful lions, is as grand as it gets. This has been the official centre of London for 800 years – ever since Edward I erected the original "Charing Cross" here to remember his queen, Eleanor. The square was completed by Nelson's Column in 1840, and Britain's most famous naval commander gazes off towards Portsmouth, home of his flagship HMS *Victory*, from a 46-m (151-ft) plinth above the crowds.

At times of national celebration or mourning, people gather here: the square has seen anti-apartheid rallies, World Cup victory parades and a record-breaking performance by "the world's largest coconut orchestra". A big talking point has been the Fourth Plinth, vacant for decades because nobody could agree on what to erect there. It is now a yearly changing showcase for contemporary art, including (in 2009) Antony Gormley's *One and Other*, which invited 2,400 ordinary people to occupy the podium for 1 hour each – with eccentric results.

Visitors have always flocked here, but today more do so than ever before, thanks to a 2003 redevelopment, which pedestrianized the National Gallery side of the square, installed a café

Nelson's 5.5-m (18-ft) statue atop his column made of Dartmoor granite

and toilets, and drove out most of the 35,000 pigeons with falcons. Uniformed "heritage wardens" are now on 24-hour duty to help visitors.

Take cover
St Martin-in-the-Fields Church (020 7766 1100; www.smitf.org), beside the square, is home to the London Brass Rubbing Centre, where indoor fun can be had waxing William Shakespeare or King Arthur. Prices vary, instruction given. There's a good café and Saturday afternoon concerts most months (ages 5 plus). The church itself is worth a look, too.

③ National Portrait Gallery

Famous faces and much more

"The world's biggest collection of faces" numbers a jaw-dropping 160,000 portraits in all, and crams 1,000 of them onto the walls of its three gallery levels, from King Henry

VII (Room 1) to actor Ian McKellen, perhaps recognisable to youngsters as "Gandalf the Grey" (Room 37).

Begin with those schoolbook favourites, the Tudors, on Floor 2, where there are plenty of extravagantly dressed children to catch the eye: the future King Charles II, for example, painted by Anthony Van Dyck in full armour at the age of eight. It's an exaggeration of history, though: Charles didn't fight seriously until the Battle of Edgehill (1642)… when he was 12!

Floor 1 spans the Victorians to the 20th century, showcasing many names that kids may know: Beatrix Potter, LS Lowry, Paul McCartney, Princess Diana and Winston Churchill. A multimedia guide just for children reveals historical nuggets along the way: find out the grisly truth about Walter Raleigh's head, and meet the strange pet that Florence Nightingale kept in her pocket.

For celeb-spotting, though, the ground floor galleries win every time: the contemporary cast here might include JK Rowling, Lily Allen or

The Lowdown

🌐 **Map reference** 10 F4
Address St Martin's Place, WC2H; 020 7306 0055; www.npg.org.uk

🚗 **Train** Charing Cross. **Tube** Charing Cross, Leicester Square or Embankment. **Bus stop** Trafalgar Square

🕐 **Open** 10am–6pm Sat–Wed; 10am–9pm Thu–Fri

💲 **Price** Permanent collection free; temporary exhibitions individually priced

🎫 **Skipping the queue** Tickets for the free family art workshops are in high demand: they are put on sale one hour before the event

🚩 **Guided tours** No. Audio guide £3

👪 **Age range** 6 plus

👪 **Activities** Storytelling sessions (age 3 plus) and art workshops (age 5 plus) on 3rd Sat of every month; artist-led sessions in school holidays. Activity cards and audio tours for children from front desk.

🕐 **Allow** 2 hours

♿ **Wheelchair access** Yes

🍴 **Eat and drink** *Snacks* Portrait Café (*Floor -2*) offers light snacks and meals. *Real meal* Portrait Restaurant (*Floor 3*) is a great option for à la carte with a view.

🛍 **Shop** Ground floor

🚻 **Toilets** On Floor 0 and Floor 3

The Lowdown

🌐 **Map reference** 10 F5
Address WC2H; www.london.gov.uk/trafalgarsquare

🚗 **Train** Charing Cross. **Tube** Charing Cross, Embankment or Leicester Square. **Bus stop** Trafalgar Square

👪 **Activities** Annual events include St George's Day celebrations (Apr), the Diwali Festival (Oct or Nov) and Christmas carols in Dec; check website for listings.

🕐 **Allow** 1 hour

🍴 **Eat and drink** *Snacks* The Café on the Square (*10am–6pm daily*), under the central staircase, is a good lunch option. *Real meal* Leon (*73–6 Strand*), part of a chain of burgeoning "healthy fast food" restaurants, is in striking range.

🚻 **Toilets** Under the central staircase

Exterior of the National Portrait Gallery

A peaceful promenade with pretty flower displays in Victoria Embankment Gardens

David Beckham – though it pays to check online beforehand, because the faces change regularly. Kids can search for favourites using the computers in the mezzanine lounge.

Letting off steam
The fountains and lions – perfect for running around – are mere strides away in **Trafalgar Square**.

④ Benjamin Franklin House

Lightning flashes of inspiration and voices from the past

The tall-windowed townhouse at 36 Craven Street looks unremarkable at first, but its walls once contained a human whirlwind. Benjamin Franklin, American Founding Father, inventor, diplomat, and all-round Enlightenment hero, lived here for 16 years, working as deputy postmaster to the Colonies, inventing the lightning rod, measuring the Gulf Stream and calming unrest between England and America. The latter was unsuccessful – and by 1775, as the War of Independence loomed, Franklin had to flee or be arrested.

The house itself is an experiment in "museum as theatre" – visitors are whisked through its apartments by "Polly Hewson", Franklin's surrogate daughter, while being assailed by the smells of a Georgian kitchen, flashes of lightning from the laboratory, and the echoing voices of Franklin and his landlady. It's a

state-of-the-art effects show that older kids will find especially engaging. Franklin, ever the innovator, would have approved.

Letting off steam
It's a 2-minute walk to **Victoria Embankment Gardens**, which offers lunchtime concerts (May to August), and the Embankment Café (*www.embankmentcafe.co.uk*).

The Lowdown

- 🌐 **Map reference** 10 G5
- 📍 **Address** 36 Craven St, WC2N; 020 7839 2006; www. benjaminfranklinhouse.org
- 🚆 **Train** Charing Cross. **Tube** Charing Cross or Embankment. **Bus stop** Trafalgar Square or Strand
- 🕐 **Open** 12–5pm Wed–Mon. The Historical Experience runs at noon, 1pm, 2pm, 3:15pm, 4:15pm Wed–Sun
- 💲 **Price** £14–19
- 🚩 **Guided tours** Yes. Mon only (times as above): adults £3.50; under-16s free
- 👫 **Age range** 8 plus
- 🏃 **Activities** School holiday art and science workshops; period-dress Christmas party for kids
- ⏱ **Allow** 1 hour
- ♿ **Wheelchair access** No
- 🍴 **Eat and drink** Snacks Patisserie Pompidou (35 Villiers St, WC2N 6ND), sells sandwiches and salads. Real meal Lupita (13 Villiers Street, WC2N 6ND) dishes up Mexican fare in child-friendly tasting portions.
- 🚻 **Toilets** In the basement

Picnic under £20; **Snacks** £20–40; **Real meal** £40–60; **Family treat** £60 or more (based on a family of four)

⑤ Leicester Square

Blockbusters and buzz

Every autumn a gaudy funfair sets up in Leicester Square Gardens – which seems like overkill. This is already London's most garish entertainment zone, ringed by blockbuster cinemas (often host to starry premieres), fast-food palaces and souvenir stores manned by giant bears in guards' uniforms. There is also a squad of street artists scribbling caricatures of passers-by and usually a choice of buskers.

The square once had more illustrious residents, among them scientist Isaac Newton (1643–1727) and artists Joshua Reynolds (1723–92) and William Hogarth (1697–1764) – look for their statues here.

Although the atmosphere can be a bit grown-up at night, by day it's a buzzy place for all; traffic-free and with benches for lunch, it's a good spot to check out the evening's theatre bargains. The best ticket booth is TKTS on the south side of Leicester Square Gardens (Mon–Sat 10am–7pm, Sundays 11am–4pm).

A 2-minute walk away, around Gerrard Street, lies the lively and aromatic Chinatown (www. chinatownlondon.org), with its colourful pagoda gateways and authentic Chinese grocery stores, barbers and beauty parlours. Again, it's perhaps best explored by day.

The Lowdown

🌐 **Map reference** 10 F4

🚇 **Tube** Leicester Square or Piccadilly Circus. **Bus stop** Shaftesbury Avenue or Charing Cross Road

👫 **Activities** There are about 50 film premieres annually, mostly at the Odeon Leicester Square (0871 224 4007; www.odeon. co.uk). There's also a Christmas fair, occasional funfairs and music events. For Chinese New Year (late Jan or Feb), Chinatown comes alive with lion dances, acrobatics and music.

⏱ **Allow** 1 hour

🍴 **Eat and drink** Snacks Häagen-Dazs Café (14 Leicester Square WC2H 7NG; 020 7287 9577) has sumptuous ice cream. Real meal Little Lamb (72 Shaftesbury Ave, W1D 6NA) offers the chance to cook your own meal – dip titbits into communal hot and spicy broth (messy fun, best for older children).

🚻 **Toilets** Underground on the north side, with changing facilities.

Take cover

With 20 screens and more than 6,000 seats to choose from, it has to be the cinema if it rains. Check which of the latest films are showing at Odeon Leicester Square (0871 224 4007; www.odeon.co.uk), Vue (0871 224 0240; www.myvue.com) and the Empire (0871 471 4714; www.empirecinemas.co.uk).

Bustling with people and traffic, colourful Piccadilly Circus

⑥ Piccadilly Circus

Bright lights and amusement arcades

Piccadilly Circus is often used in books, film and television to signify London – children might know it as the scene of a horseback chase in Anthony Horowitz's Alex Rider novels, for example; it also starred as Dr Evil's lair in the first Austin Powers movie. Basically a traffic intersection, thanks to its power as a geographical signifier (and the Trocadero Centre), it's a focal point for visitors. Sit on the steps of the famous fountain (installed to honour philanthropist Lord Shaftesbury in 1893, and one of the first statues cast in aluminium) and take in the famous giant neon billboards, first erected in 1923.

The tube station is a good starting point for exploring London's Theatreland district – it has a Visitor Information desk and toilets. Right on the junction stands the **Ripley's Believe It Or Not** attraction (1 Piccadilly Circus, W1J 0DA;

The Lowdown

🌐 **Map reference** 10 E4

🚇 **Tube** Piccadilly Circus. **Bus stop** Piccadilly Circus

⏱ **Allow** 1 hour

🍴 **Eat and drink** Picnic Millies (Trocadero Centre, W1D 7DH) sells freshly baked cookies and ice cream. Real meal The Rainforest Café (20 Shaftesbury Ave, W1D 7EU) is an extraordinary themed restaurant, set in an animatronic jungle with monsoon soundtrack. Queues at weekends.

🚻 **Toilets** In the subway to Piccadilly Circus tube station.

The main thoroughfare in bustling Chinatown

Prices given are for a family of four

Enjoying a freaky exhibit at Ripley's Believe it or Not

www.ripleyslondon.com), part fun-park, part freak-show. It brings together bizarre curiosities from across the globe, from Maori cannibal forks to cars coated in crystals. Beware, though: it's implausibly expensive.

Take cover
Just along Coventry Street, **Funland** (10am–1am daily; www.funland.co.uk) is a juggernaut of an amusement arcade filling several noisy, neon-lit floors of the Trocadero Centre with wallet-emptying attractions: laser tag, dodgem cars, simulator rides, ten-pin bowling and 400 or so arcade games, paid for individually by coin or token. It's a youngster's paradise. Look out for an early-bird bargain deal on the bowling.

⑦ Hamleys
Toys, toys, toys

This emporium is considered by some to be "the world's finest toy shop". Kids certainly think so, and entering the seven-storey store on Regent Street feels like plunging headlong into a children's play heaven. Wandering jesters blow bubbles, conjurers make things magically disappear and tots gather, giggling, around the puppet theatre, while remote-control planes whizz overhead: it's undeniably fun. And that's just the ground floor. Other levels are themed: working up from the basement, they feature computer games and Lego; then board games and jigsaws; pre-school books and toys; dolls and dressing-up; hobbies, train sets and remote-control cars; and finally

The Lowdown

🌐 **Map reference** 9 D3
Address 188–196 Regent St, W1B; www.hamleys.com
🚇 **Tube** Piccadilly Circus or Oxford Circus. **Bus stop** Regent Street
🕐 **Open** 10am–8pm Mon–Fri; 9am–8pm Sat; noon–6pm Sun
🧍 **Activities** Lots of hands-on play tables in store, plus storytime sessions and costumed events, often linked to promotions. Real reindeer visit at Christmas.
⏱ **Allow** Up to 1 hour
🍲 **Eat and drink** *Picnic* Fairgrounds Café (74 Broadwick Street) has cakes and pastries. *Snacks* Regal Tea Café (top floor) invites kids to design their own dishes.
🚻 **Toilets** Top floor

action figures. If it all gets a little too manic, head to the princess-themed café on the top floor.
The equivalent of Hamleys for grown-ups is close by. **Carnaby Street** (www.carnaby.co.uk), somewhat changed since its 1960s heyday as the epicentre of Swinging London, is a pedestrianized precinct of mostly chain boutiques of casual wear, along with gift shops and cafés. Shop for children's gear at **David & Goliath** (15 Carnaby Street) and **Carry Me Home** (Kingly Court).

Letting off steam
It is only 5 minutes around the corner to grassy **Hanover Square** (Mayfair, W1): stop off along the way at **Sunflower Café** (3 Pollen Street, W1S 1NA) for picnic supplies.

Absorbed in a doll's house at Hamleys toy shop

Picnic under £20; **Snacks** £20–40; **Real meal** £40–60; **Family treat** £60 or more (based on a family of four)

Covent Garden and around

From the high art at the Royal Opera House to the low comedy of the street-corner clowns, children love the buzz of London's original public square. The pedestrianized piazza is safe for kids, and surrounded by the city's oldest theatre, its quirkiest church and the London Transport Museum. On summer weekends, the sheer volume of the crowds can overwhelm Covent Garden's charms: instead, consider visiting on a Monday, when the markets are quieter and the Opera House stages free lunchtime recitals.

Westminster and the West End

Covent Garden

National Gallery
p78

Buckingham Palace
p72

Westminster Abbey
p64

Places of Interest

0 metres 100
0 yards 100

SIGHTS

1. Covent Garden
2. St Paul's Church
3. Royal Opera House
4. Theatre Royal Drury Lane
5. London Transport Museum
6. Somerset House
7. Sir John Soane's Museum
8. Hunterian Museum
9. St Clement Danes

● EAT AND DRINK

1. Kastner and Ovens
2. Ella's Bakehouse
3. Masala Zone
4. Wahaca
5. Muffinski's
6. Gourmet Burger Kitchen
7. Zizzi
8. Hope and Greenwood
9. Boswell's
10. Rules
11. Paul
12. Strada
13. Caffè Nero (Kingsway)
14. Fleet River Bakery
15. Caffè Nero (Strand)

See also Royal Opera House (p90), London Transport Museum (p92) and Somerset House (p93)

● SHOPPING

1. Build-A-Bear Workshop
2. Games Workshop
3. Disney Store
4. Tintin Shop
5. Eric Snook's
6. Benjamin Pollock's Toyshop

● WHERE TO STAY

1. Renaissance London Chancery Court
2. Fleet River Bakery Rooms
3. Citadines Prestige Holborn-Covent Garden

A personal perfomance, given in the streets around Covent Garden

Street performers in front of the grand portico of St Paul's Church, in Covent Garden's West Piazza

Skeleton of a "giant" at the Hunterian Museum, one of the fascinating, varied and sometimes a little gory exhibits at the Royal College of Surgeons

Wonderful taxis, buses and trains from a bygone era at the London Transport Museum

The Lowdown

🚗 **Train** Charing Cross (5-minute walk away).
Tube Covent Garden, Leicester Square or Holborn.
Bus Nearest stops at Aldwych, route numbers RV1, 9, 13, 15, 23, 139 or 153; Strand: 6, 9, 11, 13, 15, 23, 87, 91, 139, 176. **River bus** Embankment Pier, beside Charing Cross – services to Westminster and St Katherine's Dock (*Crown River Cruises: 020 7936 2033; www.crownriver.com*)

🍴 **Supermarkets** Tesco Metro, 22–25 Bedford St, WC2 5RF; Marks & Spencer, 107–111 Long Acre, WC2 3RG.
Markets Antiques market, Mon; craft markets daily plus "Real Food" market on the East Piazza, Apr–Dec, 11am–7pm Thu (becomes Christmas market in Dec)

🎭 **Festivals** Punch & Judy, Covent Garden Piazza (1st Sun in Oct); May Fayre & Puppet, St Paul's Church Gardens (2nd Sun in May)

➕ **Pharmacies** Boots, 4 James St, WC2E 8BH; 8:30am–9pm Mon–Fri; 9am–9pm Sat; 11am–7pm Sun. For 24-hour pharmacies, visit *www.nhs.ukservicedirectories*.

🧸 **Nearest playground** Drury Lane Gardens, WC2N 5TH, 8am–dusk (*see p91*) and Phoenix Garden, WC2H 8DG

① Covent Garden
Fire-eaters, opera singers and lots and lots of cupcakes

From the Apple Market to the Apple Store, Covent Garden is London's best location for shopping as entertainment and an irresistible visitor attraction. It is scary to think it was almost bulldozed in the 1970s – locals fought to save it. The square was built by Inigo Jones in 1632, based on a Palladian piazza he had seen in Livorno, Italy. Today, it's full of child-pleasing fun, from the "living statues" along James Street to the street performers who dice with death daily outside St Paul's Church.

Key Sights

Apple Store
The world's largest Apple Store is a temple to technology, with classical columns, glass stairways and three storeys of hi-tech wizardry.

Jubilee Market
Squashed into the South Piazza, the souk-like passageways here are full of stalls selling trinkets and T-shirts – perfect pocket-money fodder. Monday is antiques day.

Street shows In 1662, Samuel Pepys saw England's first recorded Punch and Judy show outside St Paul's Church. Today, you can watch a mix of music, acrobatics and magic.

Apple Market
Once home to London's main produce market, this glass-roofed arcade now has craft stalls, fashion boutiques and West End divas singing arias al fresco in the South Courtyard.

Apple Store

Royal Opera House

JAMES STREET

COVENT GARDEN

RUSSELL STREET

KING STREET

HENRIETTA STREET

SOUTHAMPTON ST

St Paul's Church

London Transport Museum poster

The Young Dancer

London Transport Museum

The Young Dancer (1988) by Enzo Plazzotta, is said to portray Ninette de Valois, who founded the Royal Ballet in 1931.

Letting off steam
The piazza is cobbled and car-free, but for more room to race about, head for **Somerset House** (see p93). For a weatherproof option, walk north along Endell Street to the **Oasis Sports Centre** (020 7831 1804; www.gll.org/oasis), with indoor and outdoor swimming pools, a sun deck and towel hire.

Eat and drink
Picnic: under £20; Snacks: £20–40; Real meal: £40–60; Family treat: £60 or more (based on a family of four)

Prices given are for a family of four

PICNIC Kastner & Ovens *(52 Floral St, WC2E 9DA; 8am–4pm weekdays)* does fabulous quiches, pies, salads and mouth-watering cakes to take away. Pick up some treats for a picnic on the jaunty benches in **Neal's Yard** *(see opposite)*.

SNACKS Who does Covent Garden's best cupcakes? The classic choice is **Ella's Bakehouse** *(20a The Piazza, WC2E 8RB; 10am–7pm Mon–Sat; 10am–6pm Sun)*, a dapper 1950s-style place. There are plenty of other options nearby to satiate a sweet tooth. There's only one way to find out which one is best…

REAL MEAL Masala Zone *(48 Floral St, WC2E 9DA; 020 7379 0101; www.masalazone.com)* is a great option for Indian fare. The restaurant is super-friendly, its ceiling all a-dangle with Rajasthani puppets, and serves an authentic thali platter for kids.

FAMILY TREAT Wahaca *(66 Chandos Place, WC2N 4HG; 020 7240 1883; www.wahaca. co.uk)* offers a zingy take on Mexican cuisine, serving up authentic street food. There are child-size portions, high chairs and baby-changing facilities.

The Lowdown

KIDS' CORNER

⊕ **Map ref** 10 G3
Address Covent Garden Piazza,
WC2E 8HD; 0870 780 5001;
www.coventgardenlondonuk.com

🚗 **Tube** Covent Garden. **Bus stop**
Aldwych. **River bus**
Embankment Pier

🕐 **Open** Apple Market: 10:30am–
6pm daily (till 7:30pm Thu).
Jubilee Market: 9:30am–
6:30pm daily (till 5:30pm
weekends). Apple Store
(1 The Piazza, WC2E 8HA):
9am–9pm (noon–6pm Sun)

👫 **Skipping the queue** Covent
Garden tube can be a scrum
at rush hour and lunchtime;
consider walking from
Holborn, Temple, Leicester

Square or Charing Cross
(10–15 mins).

👫 **Age range** All

🎪 **Activities** Check website for
family street events – circus
workshops in summer holidays,
reindeer-petting at Christmas.

⏱ **Allow** 2 hours for shopping and
street entertainment

👫 **Toilets** West Piazza, beside St
Paul's Church; Tavistock Place
(with baby-changing facilities),
right of the Transport Museum.

Good family value?
Hours of free fun just window-
shopping and busker-watching –
but do put a pound in the hat
if the show is any good!

Benjamin Pollock's Toyshop, a jewel of a place selling creative and theatrical toys

Shopping

Plenty for all ages, from bear-making
at the **Build-A-Bear Workshop**
(9 The Piazza, WC2H 9HP) to table
warfare at the **Games Workshop**
(33 The Market, WC2E 8BE). There's
also a **Disney Store** (The Piazza,
WC2E 8HD) and the **Tintin Shop**
(34 Floral St, WC2E 9DJ). Best of all
are the area's historic toy emporia:
Eric Snook's (32 The Market, WC2E
8RE) – open since 1980 – and
Benjamin Pollock's Toyshop (44
The Market, WC2E 8RF), selling
paper theatres since 1880.

Find out more

DIGITAL Download a 19th-century
toy theatre to build and colour, at
the Victoria & Albert Museum site:
www.vam.ac.uk/collections/
theatre_performance/todoonline.
FILM The movie musical My Fair
Lady begins at the Royal Opera
House, where Henry Higgins sees
flower-seller Eliza Dolittle and vows
to turn her into "a proper lady".

Take cover

The **London Transport Museum**
(see p92) is a strong wet-weather
standby: its shop and café alone
should while away an hour.

Next stop...

NEAL'S YARD It's a short stroll
north to this cluster of healthfood
shops and New Age cafés painted
in bright colours. There is picnic
space, a magic mirror, and infinite
I-Spy potential.
ENGLISH NATIONAL OPERA
Kids who enjoyed their blast of
street opera can book a workshop
here (St Martin's Lane, WC2N 4ES;
020 7632 8484; www.eno.org).
Scheduled so that parents can take
in a matinée, Opera Tots is for ages
6 months to 4 years, Opera Stars
ages 7–12.

The shop and café in the fascinating London Transport Museum

That's the way to do it!
Three things you never knew
about Punch and Judy shows...
1 They arrived in Covent
Garden from Italy nearly
400 years ago. At first, the
performances were for adults.
2 Some early shows used a real
dog to play the part of Toby.
Good job they didn't use a real
baby – Mr Punch usually throws
him out of the window!
3 Punch and Judy men are
always called "Professor". They
make the squawky voice using
a mouthpiece called a swazzle.
Can you do a Mr Punch voice?
One way to do it is to pinch
your nostrils shut!

FESTIVE FACT
The craziest Covent Garden
event is the Great Christmas
Pudding Race held in December.
People dress up as Santas, elves
or reindeer and dash
over a series of
obstacles
carrying plum
puddings.
You can watch the
most recent race at www.
xmaspuddingrace.org.uk.

3-minute wonders
Covent Garden's amazing
entertainers have to audition
to win a chance to perform here,
and just like singers on a TV
talent show, they
only get 3
minutes to
impress! What
act would you
do to entertain
the judges?

The Lowdown

- **Map reference** 10 G4
- **Address** Bedford St, WC2E; 020 7836 5221; www.actorschurch.org
- **Tube** Covent Garden or Leicester Square. **Bus stop** Aldwych
- **Open** 8:30am–5pm Mon–Fri; times vary Sat; 9am–1pm Sun
- **Price** Donations
- **Activities** Services Tue–Thu & Sun; plus regular concerts
- **Allow** 30 minutes
- **Eat and drink** Snacks Muffinski's (5 King St, WC2E 8HN) offers fresh-from-the-oven muffins. Real meal Gourmet Burger Kitchen (13–14 Maiden Lane, WC2E 7NE) has fine tasty burgers.
- **Toilets** Next door, on the West Piazza

② St Paul's Church

The actors' Church

Where's the door? That's the mystery of St Paul's portico, with its soaring marble columns. The answer is: around the back. After Inigo Jones designed the church as the centrepiece of his new piazza in 1631, the Bishop of London insisted the altar must be at the eastern end, so that worshippers faced Jerusalem – which means this grand gateway was never used.

Today, it makes a perfect stage for Covent Garden's acrobats and clowns, which is fitting, since St Paul's has long been the "actors' church", and inside there are inscriptions remembering Charlie Chaplin,

Vivien Leigh and more. Children can hunt for the actor who first played Frankenstein's monster, Boris Karloff, and Percy Press, "King of Punch and Judy", whose memorial depicts the puppet pair.

Look out, too, for the church's vintage model theatre, which was once shown off in village halls to raise money for a London hostel where actors could lodge their children while they went on tour.

The first victim of the Great Plague of 1665–66, Margaret Porteous, is buried here. It went on to claim one in five Londoners.

Letting off steam

Escape the Covent Garden crowds in the church garden – but get there early to bag a bench for lunchtime.

③ Royal Opera House

Tenors, sopranos and pirouetting ballerinas

Home to both the Royal Opera and Royal Ballet companies, this showpiece theatre was begun in 1732 by John Rich, a famous harlequin who staged Britain's first pantomime. George Frederick Handel (1685–1759) was its musical director: he gave his *Messiah* its UK premiere here and also introduced the risqué dancing of Marie Sallé.

Following a makeover in the 1990s, the theatre has endeavoured to lessen opera's elitist image. Ticket prices have been reduced, there's a free recital most Mondays and

Drury Lane Gardens, a small playground for little ones in the backstreets

guided backstage tours daily. Tours start in the jaw-dropping auditorium, built in 1858, with its 15-m (50-ft) high stage and balconies dripping with gilt. Tours usually visit the Model Room, too, where doll's-house-size sets are delicately

The Lowdown

- **Map reference** 10 G3
- **Address** Covent Garden, WC2E; 020 7304 4000; www.roh.org.uk
- **Tube** Covent Garden. **Bus stop** Aldwych
- **Open** 10am–3pm Mon–Sat and for performances
- **Price** Show tickets start from £38
- **Skipping the queue** Tickets for free Monday recitals are released online nine days ahead, but most are held back till the day – 10am at the box office.
- **Guided tours** Mon–Sat (£34–40)
- **Activities** A free children's activity trail explores the public areas; creative workshops in May half-term; Christmas productions suit kids aged 6 and up
- **Age range** 8 plus (guided tours); 7 plus (workshops)
- **Allow** 75 minutes for the tour
- **Wheelchair access** Yes, lifts give access to most of the auditoria
- **Eat and drink** Snacks The rooftop terrace at the Amphitheatre Bar serves light lunches 10am–3pm. Real meal Zizzi (20 Bow St, WC2E 7AW) serves up scrumptious pizzas.
- **Shop** Covent Garden entrance and in Amphitheatre Bar before a show
- **Toilets** In the lobby

The green spaces of St Paul's Church garden, an oasis of calm in Covent Garden

Royal Ballet dancers performing Swan Lake at the Royal Opera House

constructed for every new show. But the highlight is peering into a Royal Ballet rehearsal studio, where the dancers might be pirouetting away.

Letting off steam
The tiny playground in **Drury Lane Gardens** (along Broad Court, then right on Drury Lane) used to be a graveyard! Today it has swings and slides for ages 3–7.

④ Theatre Royal Drury Lane
Theatrical magic and spooks

London's oldest working playhouse started life in 1663, when Charles II lifted the 11-year theatre ban imposed by Oliver Cromwell. The entire building would fit on the stage today: it was roofless and featured Britain's first ever female actors and the first proscenium arch or "picture box stage".

Today, the oak-lined lobby is worth a peek, or take a backstage tour run by actors in costume. Nell

An entertaining backstage tour at the historic Theatre Royal Drury Lane

Gwynne, actress and mistress of Charles II, reveals the royal retiring room where George V knighted the actor Frank Benson with his own prop sword, then it's down under the stage to see the trap doors.

Shows at "the Lane" have been famous for their spectacular special effects, including an earthquake and a horse race with 12 real horses running on a treadmill. *Miss Saigon*, which ran for 10 years and 4,263 performances, "landed" a real helicopter on the stage every time!

Letting off steam
To reach **Drury Lane Gardens** playground *(see left)*, head along Russell Street and turn left.

The Lowdown

- **Map reference** 10 H3
- **Address** Catherine St, WC2B; *www.reallyuseful.com/theatres*
- **Tube** Covent Garden or Holborn. **Bus stop** Aldwych
- **Open** Box office 10am–8pm
- **Price** Show tickets from £80
- **Guided tours** Twice daily, Mon–Sat (£32–6)
- **Age range** Tours suit ages 6 plus
- **Allow** 1 hour for the tour
- **Wheelchair access** Limited. Call 08444 124648 for information
- **Eat and drink** *Picnic* Hope and Greenwood *(1 Russell St, WC2B 5JD)* sells old-fashioned sweets. *Real meal* Boswell's *(8 Russell St, WC2B 5HZ)* offers sandwiches, salads, pastries and more.
- **Toilets** On request

Picnic under £20; **Snacks** £20–40; **Real meal** £40–60; **Family treat** £60 or more (based on a family of four)

⑤ London Transport Museum

This really is travelling back in time

Don't be put off by the subject matter – this is one of the most hooting, tooting museums in London. It crams 20 vintage buses, trams and trains into a steel-and-glass cavern once occupied by the Covent Garden flower market, and visitors get to climb aboard many of them to "take a drive". It's a hands-on experience, so hold tight!

Start on Level 2, up in the rafters, with its full-size sedan chair and London's earliest horse-drawn omnibus. Jump in and sit beside a top-hatted gent as he reels off the rules of the road, 1829-style. There are sound clips of crossing-sweepers (who cleared a path through the horse muck) and bus conductors, and cartoon quizzes to answer.

Level 1 has the first underground steam train from the 1860s, occupied by lifelike passengers, while vintage posters recall how the expansion of the tube sent London sprawling out into the suburbs. On a balcony is the Interchange, a push-button zone for children (age 7–11), where they can dress up as engine drivers and try their hand at driving the latest eco-friendly bus.

Younger kids will want to sprint straight to the open-plan and neon-lit ground floor (Level 0), with

Above One of the many vintage trains at the London Transport Museum
Below right Enjoying a hands-on experience – driving a bus

a dozen or so vehicles to explore, plus sit-in simulators where they can manoeuvre the "dead man's handle" that drives a modern-day tube train (once the adults get out of the way). There is a themed play corner for under-7s, with picnic tables alongside. Finally, it's out into the shop and café, with retro-cool posters for parents, die-cast models for kids, and Circle Line smoothies for all.

Letting off steam

The museum is comfortable about kids careering around. For outdoor frolics, head along Russell Street to **Drury Lane Gardens**, with slides and seesaws for ages 3–7; or across Strand into Somerset House *(see opposite)*.

On board a horse-drawn double-decker "London Omnibus", phased out in 1911

The Lowdown

🌐 **Map ref** 10 H3

📍 **Address** Covent Garden Piazza, WC2E 8RF; 020 7565 7299; *www.ltmuseum.co.uk*

🚇 **Tube** Covent Garden. **Bus stop** Aldwych

🕐 **Open** Sat–Thu 10am–6pm; Fri 11am–6pm

🎫 **Price** £27–37, under 12s free

👪 **Skipping the queue** Tickets give free entry for a whole year.

🚩 **Guided tours** No

👫 **Age range** 3 plus

🎨 **Activities** Collect cards from the ticket desk for kids to stamp as they go around the museum. Download trails from the website beforehand. There are free drop-in activities in school holidays.

⏱ **Allow** Up to 3 hours

♿ **Wheelchair access** Yes, but some vehicles are inaccessible

🍴 **Eat and drink** *Snacks* Upper Deck café-bar in lobby serves quick bites. *Family treat* Rules (35 Maiden Lane, WC2E 7LB; 020 7836 5314) serves classic British dishes.

🛍 **Shop** Gifts and memorabilia

🚻 **Toilets** Ground floor gallery

Splashing around in the Fountain Court, Somerset House

⑥ Somerset House

Enjoy a great day at the office

Somerset House looks like a palace, and originally there was one here, the scene of 17th-century royal masques (see p71). But the Palladian quadrangle we see today was actually the first ever purpose-built office block, for decades the home of tax inspectors and the register of births, deaths and marriages.

It is now open to the public, and the Embankment Galleries, by the riverside, house temporary shows on 20th-century fashion, design and photography, usually incorporating lots of interactive gizmos and family workshops. The Courtauld Gallery, by Strand, is a modest collection with several paintings that even little ones might know: Van Gogh with his ear bandaged, Manet's staring barmaid at the Folies-Bergère and Degas's graceful ballet dancers.

The big draw for families, though, is the spectacular Fountain Court in the centre, now a pleasure space where 55 water jets dance from Easter till October, just begging for youngsters to chase and splash. There are big-name pop concerts and family film matinées here in summer; while from November to January it becomes London's most glamorous ice rink, with cocktails, DJs and a giant Christmas tree.

Letting off steam

Fountain Court takes on a seaside feel in summer, with café tables at the edges and families spreading out towels and donning swimsuits.

The Lowdown

🌐 **Map ref** 10 H4
Address Strand, WC2R 1LA; 020 7845 4600; www.somersethouse. org.uk; 020 7848 2526; www. courtauld.ac.uk

🚇 **Tube** Temple. **Bus stop** Strand. **River bus** Embankment pier

🕐 **Open** Embankment Galleries and Courtauld Gallery 10am–6pm daily; Fountain Court 7:30am–11pm

💷 **Price** Embankment Galleries £22–32, under 12s free; Courtauld Gallery £12–18, under 18s free (free entry 10am–2pm Mon)

🎫 **Skipping the queue** Tickets for Saturday workshops are released at 1pm sharp. Book ahead for the popular ice rink (www.somerset house.org.uk/ice-rink)

🚩 **Guided tours** Thu and Sat (free)

👫 **Age range** All

👪 **Activities** Family fact-finding sheets for most temporary shows. Free art and fashion workshops on school-holiday weekends, plus every Sat for ages 6–12, and 1st Sun of the month for under-5s. There are studio days for teens in the school holidays.

🕐 **Allow** 1 hour

♿ **Wheelchair access** Yes

🍴 **Eat and drink** *Snacks* The Café at the Courtauld is cosy, with a patio garden, funky teapots and yummy cakes. *Real meal* Tom's Kitchen, in the Embankment wing, serves brasserie food in a refectory-style area, run by celebrity chef Tom Aikens.

🛍 **Shop** Rizzoli Bookshop sells art books; Courtauld Shop offers items inspired by the artworks.

🚻 **Toilets** Downstairs, on the Embankment side

Picnic: under £20; **Snacks:** £20–40; **Real meal:** £40–60; **Family treat:** £60 or more (based on a family of four)

⑦ Sir John Soane's Museum

3,000 years of history packed into one house

This townhouse museum comprises a warren of poky passages filled with wonders: a magic picture gallery, a monk's cell, even a real mummy's coffin from ancient Egypt.

Sir John Soane was a bricklayer's son who became a top architect: he designed the Bank of England in 1788. He brought his family to the house in 1792, and spent the next 45 years filling every nook and cranny with his bizarre collection of gargoyles, statues, busts and bric-à-brac from the ancient world. Luckily, before he died Soane insisted everything was left exactly as it was, for visitors to enjoy.

This means the house is one big time capsule. Audio guides lead the way, but watch out for Soane's tricks: mirrors where you can't see your feet; secret panels that reveal hidden paintings; even a writing desk hidden inside a statue. Best of all is the mummy's sarcophagus

Inside the fascinating Sir John Soane's Museum

down in "the Crypt", which belonged to Pharaoh Seti I. It is 3,300 years old and covered in hieroglyphics. Soane paid £2,000 for it, and threw a three-night candlelit party to celebrate.

Letting off steam

Lincoln's Inn Fields, opposite, was laid out in the 17th century by Inigo Jones. The lawns, once popular for duels, are green and wide. There are tennis courts (£7 per hour for a court, under-16s £2.60; 07525 278647).

The Lowdown

🌐 **Map reference** 10 H2
Address 13 Lincoln's Inn Fields, WC2A 3BP; 020 7405 2107; www.soane.org
🚇 **Tube** Holborn. **Bus stop** High Holborn, Aldwych or Kingsway
🕐 **Open** 10am–5pm Tue–Sat (last entry 4:30pm). Candlelit opening 6–9pm 1st Tue of each month
💲 **Price** Free
👫 **Skipping the queue** No pre-booking, so there are often large queues. Get there by 10am
🚩 **Guided tours** Sat 11am (£5); tickets on sale from 10:30am
👫 **Age range** 7 plus
🏃 **Activities** Children's audio tour must be downloaded before visiting. Imaginative holiday workshops for ages 7 plus (£18 full day, £10 half day).
⏱ **Allow** 1–2 hours
♿ **Wheelchair access** Limited, due to stairs. Contact 020 7405 2107
🍽 **Eat and drink** *Snacks* Paul (296–298 High Holborn, WC1V 7JH) offers filled baguettes and patisserie. *Real Meal* Strada (6 Great Queen Street, WC2B 5DH) does pizzas and classic Italian food.
👫 **Toilets** In the basement

The Lowdown

🌐 **Map reference** 10 H2
Address 35–43 Lincoln's Inn Fields, WC2A 3PE; 020 7869 6560; www.hunterianmuseum.org
🚇 **Tube** Holborn or Temple. **Bus stop** High Holborn, Aldwych or Kingsway
🕐 **Open** 10am–5pm Tue–Sat
💲 **Price** Free
👫 **Skipping the queue** Download the audio guide from the website for free before visiting; at the museum it costs £3.50
🚩 **Guided tours** Wed, 1pm (free)
👫 **Age range** 6 plus, though parental guidance advisable
🏃 **Activities** Half-term holiday sessions for families
⏱ **Allow** 1–2 hours
♿ **Wheelchair access** Yes, via Nuffield College entrance
🍽 **Eat and drink** *Picnic* Caffè Nero (77d Kingsway, WC2B 6ST) serves sandwiches and snacks. *Snacks* Fleet River Bakery (71 Lincoln's Inn Fields, WC2A 3JF) does sandwiches, salads and soup.
👫 **Toilets** In the basement

⑧ Hunterian Museum

Bones and body parts

The Hunterian might be the most stomach-turning museum in London – its website even has a "parental advisory" section – but most children are gripped by its sparkling cut-glass receptacles full of bits and pieces of bodies, weird wildlife and gruesome gadgets, all collected in the 18th century by John Hunter, the pioneer of modern surgery.

Hunter is not very well known these days, but he's the man who insisted surgery should be based on evidence – which meant cutting things up to show what they look like inside. He performed public dissections for his students at a time when only the bodies of hanged criminals could be used for medical science: don't miss the display about the notorious

Lincoln's Inn Fields, London's largest public square, a great place to stretch the legs

Items from the early days of anatomical discovery at the Hunterian Museum

KIDS' CORNER

Treasure Hunter
John Hunter collected an amazing 13,000 specimens from 400 kinds of plants and animals, as well as a few famous human items. See if you can track down…
1 An Irish giant's skeleton
2 A computer genius's brain
3 An extinct bird
4 A master criminal's bones
If you need help, the case numbers are below.

bodysnatchers who raided local graveyards to supply Hunter with corpses. These were bumped upstairs at his grand house in Leicester Square – a house big enough to hold his stuffed giraffe, the first ever seen in England.

The museum has an audio guide suitable for older children and adults, plus quiz sheets for ages 5–7 and 8–11. The upstairs gallery has gory TV clips of modern operations and there are art materials, moveable skeletons and tunics stuck with Velcro organs in a side room, which is usually open for kids (phone ahead to check).

Letting off steam
The well-tended lawns of **Lincoln's Inn Fields** are right opposite (see left), perfect for running around.

⑨ St Clement Danes

Home of a nursery rhyme?
The strange name of this church is said to come from the Vikings, who murdered and pillaged their way along what is now the River Thames in the 9th century. Finally defeated by King Alfred the Great, those with English wives were allowed to settle in this part of London.

St Clement's has been rebuilt twice: by Christopher Wren after the Great Fire of London (1666) and again after being blasted by German bombers in the Blitz (1941) – which is why it became the central church of the Royal Air Force. Aim to visit at 9am, noon, 3pm or 6pm, when

the church bells peal out the tune to the nursery rhyme *Oranges and Lemons*. First written down in 1744, some say it refers to local children who helped smugglers unload their cargo from the Thames, and were given fruit as a reward. Oranges and lemons are still handed out to children here today, as part of a service in March.

The church's creepiest treasure is in the crypt a chain that was used to clamp shut coffins to protect the recently deceased from the bodysnatchers who raided graveyards to steal corpses for medical research.

Letting off steam
Temple Gardens, at the bottom of Arundel Street, has slivers of grass, but for more space, head along the Strand to **Somerset House** (see p93).

The Lowdown

🌐 **Map reference** 11 A3
Address Strand, WC2 1DH; 020 7242 8282; www.raf.mod.uk/stclementdanes

🚇 **Tube** Temple. **Bus stop** Strand

🕐 **Open** 9am–4pm; services Wed, Fri and Sun

💲 **Price** Donations

⏱ **Allow** 30 minutes

🍴 **Eat and drink** *Snacks* Caffè Nero (181 Strand, WC2R 1EA), opposite, serves sandwiches and snacks. *Real Meal* The Courtauld Gallery Cafè (150 Somerset House, WC2R 0NR; daily 10am-5:40pm) is cooler, with quirky crockery and big cakes.

🚻 **Toilets** No

Just imagine…
The eccentric Sir John Soane invented an "imaginary friend", a monk named Brother John, and even created a room for him, complete with a skull! Do you have a favourite character from books, TV, films or games? Imagine if they lived with you. Get some paper and draw a bedroom for them. What would be inside it?

Find the goddess
Can you find an Egyptian goddess hiding in Sir John Soane's mummy case? She is Nut, goddess of the sky, who protected the dead and gave them food and wine in heaven.

Answers: 1 Charles Byrne's, Case 8
2 Charles Babbage's, Case 5 **3** Dodo,
Case 5 **4** Jonathan Wild's, Case 2

Bloomsbury
and Regent's Park

It's hard to beat this part of London for sheer spectacle: it has mummies and movie stars, lions and labyrinths. It's possible to go a full weekend without setting foot outside Regent's Park, thanks to its zoo, open-air theatre, canals and lakes, while the busy Madame Tussauds is nearby. If the vast treasures of the British Museum don't attract, then fascinating smaller museums cover canal boats, toys, medicine and more.

Bloomsbury and Regent's Park

The City and the East End

Westminster and the West End

Southwark and the South Bank

Kensington, Chelsea and Battersea

Highlights

British Museum
Among this museum's many marvels, the mummy galleries will always be the star attraction. Plan ahead and kids can even have a sleepover *(see p102)*.

Coram's Fields
London's top playground? This one is in the running, boasting zipwires, slides and sandpits, plus a farmyard *(see p106)*.

Wellcome Collection
Children get a cardboard moustache to wear during their visit here. Why? Who knows! It is part of the zaniest – and best – children's museum pack in London *(see p104)*.

ZSL London Zoo
Yes, there are lions and tigers, gorillas and giraffes, but George the scarlet macaw upstages them all in the daily Animals in Action live show *(see p110)*.

Puppet Theatre Barge
This red-and-yellow narrowboat at Little Venice is home to London's most delightful family theatre experience. Glide there along the canal from Camden *(see p111)*.

Camden Market
It's about as close as London gets to a souk. Older children especially love exploring the market's labyrinth of exotic stalls and shops *(see p112)*.

Left Clambering on one of the boats on display in the London Canal Museum
Above Getting up close to a tarantula at London Zoo

The Best of
Bloomsbury & Regent's Park

This well-to-do part of London divides neatly in two – one half cerebral, the other sensory. Both are walkable for even the littlest legs and filled with literary and artistic connections. To the east, stately Bloomsbury offers a day or two of family-friendly brainwork, its mix of unusual museums providing all manner of kids' activities. For more active fun or some relaxation, head west to the great green playground of Regent's Park.

A Year in Regent's Park

With or without a trip to London Zoo, little ones will adore **Regent's Park** (see p112). In spring, guided walks show off the blooms of the wildlife garden near York Bridge; or venture out on the boating pond. June is prime time for the roses in Queen Mary's Gardens, where the rock garden is perfect for hide-and-seek. The school summer holiday heralds playground sessions and sports coaching at The Hub, and there are matinée performances at the Open Air Theatre.

Come autumn, the tree-lined towpath along Regent's Canal is very colourful, and October's Frieze Art Fair dots eye-catching artworks around the park. By November, over-wintering wildfowl are swooping onto the lake from colder climes: Long Bridge is the best viewing spot. If it really freezes, warm up in the indoor rainforest pavilion at **ZSL London Zoo** (see pp110–11), or take in the Christmas show at the **Puppet Theatre Barge** (see p111). Whatever the season, the friendly Garden Café has a menu to match (see p111).

Storybook London

Pooh and Potter, Peter Pan and Paddington – many favourites from children's literature have links with this part of London. The original Winnie the Pooh lived at London Zoo (see pp110–11) in the 1920s: author AA Milne and his son Christopher Robin loved visiting the bear, and a statue now remembers Winnie in the zoo's Animal Adventure zone. Just across the fence in Regent's Park stood the home of Pongo and Missis, heroes of The Hundred and One Dalmatians; while over in Bloomsbury, a statue of Peter Pan and Tinkerbell stands outside Great Ormond Street children's hospital; Peter's creator JM Barrie donated the royalties from his play to hospital funds.

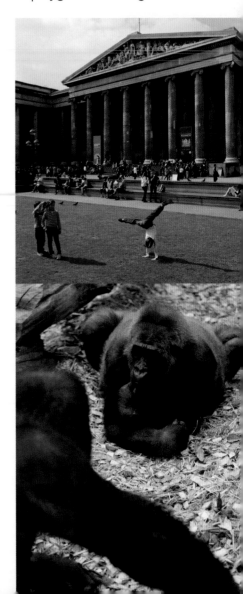

Above Playing on the forecourt of the British Museum
Below Gorillas lounging at ZSL London Zoo

Admiring the spring flowers in Regent's Park, one of London's most beautiful green spaces

It's a short walk from there to the **Charles Dickens Museum** (see p106), where the great Victorian novelist wrote *Oliver Twist* – see the window that Oliver scrambled through on his burgling mission with Bill Sikes. Wander up to the **British Library** (see p105) and flick through a digital version of Lewis Carroll's original manuscript for *Alice in Wonderland*, before heading home – preferably via platform 9¾ at King's Cross Station, Harry Potter's departure point for Hogwarts School of Witchcraft and Wizardry.

A Bloomsbury sketch

There's nowhere better in London for families to travel armed with sketchbook and pencils. An inspiring place to start is the **Cartoon Museum** (see p103), with its art room and monthly family workshops. Just up the road, **Pollock's Toy Museum** (see p104) devotes a gallery to the exquisite paper theatres stencilled and coloured by Benjamin Pollock and his family in Victorian times, and sells kits to construct at home. The **Wellcome Collection** (see p104) also encourages budding artists – its children's pack includes modelling clay and a mask-making kit – while the nearby **Foundling Museum** (see p106) invites young visitors to design a postcard inspired by its exhibition, and hosts family craft sessions each month.

Running out of paper? Never fear: the **British Museum** (see pp102–103) has the mother of all children's activity programmes – and hands out free art materials to every junior visitor.

A fun-filled weekend

There is always something afoot for families at the British Museum (see pp102–103), but especially on Saturdays. Arrive by 10am, check out the day's programme, then head for the Paul Hamlyn Library, which hands out children's packs and trails. Organized kids' activities get going at around 11am, usually in the magnificent Great Court. For lunch, escape to nearby Russell Square for a splash in the fountain, and pizza and ice cream from the terrace café. Just around the corner is **Coram's Fields** (see p106), one of London's very best playgrounds.

Sunday is all about **Camden Market** (see p114), a maze of stalls selling everything from musky smelling patchouli oil to vintage clothing. Younger children will especially like Camden Lock, with its jaunty narrowboat rides, and Yumchaa teashop is nice for elevenses. Escape before 1pm, when busy Camden Town tube station becomes exit-only, and hop two tube stops south to Euston, where the weird and wonderful Wellcome Collection (see p104) will amaze young and old alike with its array of curiosities. Don't miss the free tour at 2:30pm.

Left *Toys for sale at Stables Market, Camden Lock, a great place to browse, with 700 stalls and shops*

British Museum and around

With Sir Norman Foster's splendid Great Court, a cavernous igloo of white space, the British Museum has one of the grandest entrance lobbies in the world. All-action art workshops take place here every weekend, there is a dedicated children's shop and two cafés. The museum is free to visit and picnicking is permitted: throw in the marvellous playground at nearby Coram's Fields, and this must be London's best budget day out for families. Bloomsbury has a clutch of smaller museums too, devoted to toys, cartoons, canal boats and more.

Bloomsbury and Regent's Park

ZSL London Zoo p108

British Museum

The British Museum, packed with interesting and exotic exhibits from around the world

Exploring Pollock's Toy Museum, filled to bursting with toys, both past and present

Places of Interest

SIGHTS

1. British Museum
2. Pollock's Toy Museum
3. Wellcome Collection
4. British Library
5. Foundling Museum
6. Charles Dickens Museum
7. London Canal Museum

EAT AND DRINK

1. In Season
2. My Old Dutch
3. Meals
4. Hakkaan
5. Planet Organic
6. Patisserie Valerie
7. Giraffe
8. Kipferl
9. Simmons
10. Oz Café

See also British Museum (p102–103), Wellcome Collection (p104), British Library (p105), Foundling Museum (p106) and Charles Dickens Museum (p106)

PLACES TO STAY

1. Bedford
2. Alhambra
3. Arosfa
4. Arran House
5. Euro
6. Jesmond Dene

0 metres 200

0 yards 200

Bronze statue of Sir Isaac Newton outside the British Library

The Lowdown

🚐 **Tube** Tottenham Court Road or Holborn. **Bus** New Oxford Street: 8, 25, 55, 98; Great Russell Street: 8, 10, 14, 24, 25, 29, 55, 73, 98, 134, 390

ℹ️ **Visitor information** Holborn Information Kiosk, Kingsway, WC2B 6BG; Euston Travel Information Centre, Euston Rail Centre, NW1 2HS

🛒 **Supermarkets** Hannells Food & Wine, 52–56 New Oxford Street, WC1A 1ES; Sainsbury's Central, 129 Kingsway, WC2B 6NH; Waitrose, 23–39 The Brunswick Centre, WC1N 1AF **Markets** Chapel Market (food and household goods) Penton Street, N1 9PX, 9am–6pm Tue–Sat; 8:30am–4pm Sun (including farmers' market); Camden Passage antiques market, N1 8EA, 7am–2pm Wed, 8am–4pm Sat. Both are near Angel tube. Covent Garden's markets are also within (30-min) walking range *(see p86–7)*

🎪 **Festivals** Bloomsbury Festival, music and arts (Oct)

➕ **Pharmacies** Clockwork Pharmacy, 150 Southampton Row, WC1B 5AN (9am–7pm Mon–Fri; 9am–6pm Sat). For 24-hour pharmacies search at *www.nhs.uk/ servicedirectories*

🛝 **Nearest playgrounds** Alf Barrett Playground *(see p102)*, Coram's Fields *(see p106)* and Crabtree Fields *(see p104)*.

Exploring the fascinating Wellcome Collection

Enjoying one of the many attractions at the popular Coram's Fields playground and park

The Lowdown

🌐 **Map ref** 10 G1
Address British Museum, Great Russell Street, WC1B 3DG; 020 7323 8000; www.britishmuseum.org

🚇 **Tube** Tottenham Court Road or Holborn. **Bus stop** New Oxford Street, Great Russell Street

🕐 **Open** Galleries 10am–5:30pm daily; selected rooms till 8:30pm Fri. Great Court 9am–6pm Sun–Thu; till 8:30pm Fri

💲 **Price** Free. Special exhibitions charge entrance fees

🚩 **Guided tours** Free 30-min tours daily in selected galleries; multimedia guide £17

👫 **Age range** 3 plus

👫 **Activities** Children's audio tour with a choice of themes. Family workbook trails (ages 3–5 and 6–11) plus activity backpacks available until 3:30pm daily from Paul Hamlyn Library, as are free art materials. Object-handling in galleries 1, 2, 24, 33, 49 and 68 (11am–4pm). Free family activities and workshops on weekends and school holidays. Young Friends club (annual membership £20) arranges six sleepovers a year; www.britishmuseum.org/membership/young_friends.aspx

⏱ **Allow** At least 3 hours

♿ **Wheelchair access** Yes

☕ **Café** Court Cafés (Great Court, Ground Floor) serve snacks and sandwiches. Gallery Café (Ground Floor) has family-friendly hot dishes. Court Restaurant (Great Court, Upper Floor) serves an à la carte menu. Ford Centre for Young Visitors (Lower Floor) has a baby-feeding room and allows picnicking.

🛍 **Shops** Several – in the foyer and the Great Court

🚻 **Toilets** On all floors

Good family value?
Unbeatable, with lots of free stuff to hold children's interest, from activity backpacks to object-handling tables and weekend workshops. It's even permissable to bring your own sandwiches.

① British Museum
Heaps of human history under one roof

Pirate gold, a crystal skull, fanged demons – the British Museum is jammed full of wonders. Three floors of galleries chart two million years of human civilization across the globe, so it pays to be choosy. The Egyptian Collection (Rooms 61–66) and Living and Dying (Room 24) never fail to impress, with their mummies and skulls. Start in the Paul Hamlyn Library, for free kids' trails and backpacks.

Key Features

■ **Levels 4 & 5** Special exhibitions and Asia: Japan

■ **Level 3** Ancient Egypt, Greece and Rome; Middle East and Europe

■ **Levels 1 & 2** Asia: China, India, Korea, Southeast Asia

■ **Ground floor** America: North America and Mexico; Ancient Greece and Rome; Middle East and Egypt

■ **Level -1** Africa, Greek and Roman architecture

Entrance   Paul Hamlyn Library

Letting off steam
Alf Barrett Playground (Old Gloucester Street, WC1B 4DA), 10 minutes east of the museum on the corner of Old Gloucester Street and Gage Street, caters for kids up to age 13. Behind the museum, **Russell Square**, remodelled to its original 200-year-old Humphry Repton design, has the perfect fountain for splashing through, plus ice creams to enjoy from the terrace café.

Eat and drink
Picnic: under £20; Snacks: £20–40; Real meal: £40–60; Family treat: £60 or more (based on a family of four)

PICNIC In Season (37 New Oxford Street, WC1A 1BH; 020 7240 0768; www.inseasonsandwiches.co.uk) is a bright independent sandwich shop among a sea of chains. Eat your picnic in the pretty garden in nearby Bloomsbury Square.

SNACKS My Old Dutch (131 High Holborn, WC1V 6PS; 020 7242 5200; www.myolddutch.com) lets kids build their own crêpes –

Taking a break in the comfortable surroundings of Meals at Heals

anyone for a pineapple and red chilli pancake? It also does good smoothies and shakes.

REAL MEAL Meals (196 Tottenham Court Road, W1T 7LQ; 020 7636 1666; www.heals.co.uk), on the first floor of Heals, has child-friendly fare.

FAMILY TREAT Hakkasan (8 Hanway Place, W1T 1HD; 020 7927 7000; www.hakkasan.com) is at the forefront of contemporary Chinese cuisine and has a Michelin star. The "small eat" dishes are ideal for kids.

① Great Court Once an outside courtyard, this is now the largest covered public space in Europe.

② Rosetta Stone Carved with a pharaoh's decree from 196 BC, this is the museum's most visited treasure. It is written in three languages, which enabled experts to decode Egyptian hieroglyphs for the first time. (Room 4)

③ Abydos cat mummy The ancient Egyptians worshipped cats, mummifying thousands as offerings to the cat-goddess Bastet. (Room 62)

④ Pirate treasure Long John Silver's parrot squawked "pieces of eight" – and here they are. In Tudor times (c.1500–1600), these Spanish coins were worth about £50. (Room 68)

⑤ The Royal Game of Ur This Ludo-like dice game was played 4,500 years ago in Mesopotamia. Players raced across the board, trying to land on the lucky rosettes. (Room 56)

⑥ Ball game belt This toad-shaped belt featured in the world's oldest team sport, a type of volleyball played in ancient Mexico. Defeat could be dangerous – the losers were sacrificed to the gods! (Room 27)

⑦ Camera coffin The Ga people of Ghana have been fashioning these fantastical coffins since the 1950s to represent the dead person's interests – such as photography, eagles or planes. (Room 24)

⑧ Mold Cape Discovered in a Welsh burial mound, this Bronze Age cape was a pile of gold fragments, leaving curators with a giant jigsaw puzzle to tackle. (Room 51)

Find out more
DIGITAL The museum's website has a great zone just for children: skip through the centuries in the Time Explorer adventure game: www.britishmuseum.org/explore/young_explorers1.aspx.

Take out the lungs, liver and stomach, then pull the brain out via the nostrils...yeuch! Make your own mummy at www.bbc.co.uk/history/interactive/games/mummy_maker.

In the BBC Radio 4 series A History of the World in 100 Objects, British Museum director Neil MacGregor chose his world-changing artifacts. Download the series at www.bbc.co.uk/ahistoryoftheworld.

Next stop...
THE PETRIE MUSEUM Part of the University College of London, this museum (Malet Place, WC1E 6BT; Tue–Sat 1–5pm; www.ucl.ac.uk/museums/petrie) is stacked high with Egyptian items – and has an art table and Roman togas for children to model.

THE CARTOON MUSEUM This fun place (35 Little Russell St, WC1A 2HH; 10:30am–5:30pm Tue–Sat; noon–5:30pm Sun; www.cartoonmuseum.org) has an art room where kids can doodle their own masterpiece. British cartoons and comic art from the 18th century to the present day are on display. It also offers drop-in family cartooning on the second Saturday of the month and terrific school-holiday workshops for ages 8 plus.

Aspiring young cartoonists getting instruction at the Cartoon Museum

Pollock's Toy Museum

Playtimes from the past

Winding your way around the snaking stairways and attic rooms of this rickety old house feels like going back in time – which is appropriate, since they are filled with a treasure trove of toys spanning two centuries. Don't tell the children, but it's an irresistible nostalgia trip for parents, too.

The charming, idiosyncratic collection includes Schoenhut's Humpty Dumpty Circus from 1903, and a reconstructed early 20th-century boy's den, complete with dangerous-looking chemistry set and blow football. One room is devoted to the delicate but magical paper theatres of the Pollock family, whose renowned Victorian toy emporium spawned the museum in 1956. Other rooms concentrate on early teddy bears, toy soldiers and slightly spooky wax dolls.

The labels are yellowing and there's little to touch or play with, so give thanks for the toyshop at the end of the visit, stacked with superannuated treats – spinning tops, kaleidoscopes and classic card games such as Happy Families. Pollock's Toy Shop in Covent Garden (see p89) also sells great toys.

Letting off steam

One minute's walk south, **Crabtree Fields** (Whitfield Street, W1T 2BJ) has a fun-filled playground and an attractive pergola walkway.

Browsing among the exciting toys in the toyshop of Pollock's Toy Museum

Prices given are for a family of four

The Lowdown

- 🌐 **Map ref** 10 E1
  Address 1 Scala Street, W1T 2HL; 020 7636 3452; www.pollockstoytheatres.com
- 🚇 **Tube** Goodge Street. **Bus stop** Tottenham Court Road
- 🕐 **Open** 10am–5pm Mon–Sat (last admission 4:30pm)
- 💲 **Price** £14–20
- 🚩 **Guided tours** No
- 🎭 **Activities** Occasional toy theatre or puppet shows during school holidays (call to check)
- 🚻 **Age range** 5 plus
- ⏱ **Allow** 1 hour
- ♿ **Wheelchair access** Only to ground floor shop due to stairs.
- 🍴 **Eat and drink** Picnic Planet Organic (22 Torrington Place, WC1E 7HJ) is a healthy grocery-cum-café – picnic on Bedford Square; Snacks Patisserie Valerie (24 Torrington Place, WC1E 7HJ) sells less virtuous, delicious cakes.
- 🛍 **Shop** Toys and gifts
- 🚻 **Toilets** Ground floor

---

③ Wellcome Collection

Shrunken heads and massive moustaches

On a par with Ripley's Believe It Or Not (see p84) is the Wellcome Collection. This giant store of curiosities was collected by an eccentric adventurer called Henry Wellcome, who made his fortune as a medicine salesman, grew Victorian England's bushiest moustache, then travelled the world hunting for medical marvels. He returned with

Examining the curious medical exhibits in the Wellcome Collection

some very bizarre booty indeed: prepare to be amazed by a torturer's mask, a Peruvian mummy (minus bandages) and a peculiar device for blowing tobacco smoke up a drowning person's bottom.

The historical gallery is beautifully arranged: slide open drawers to hear sound clips about key objects or to reveal artifacts to touch. The curators are oddly ambivalent about younger visitors: they stress that some of the material has adult themes, yet the museum has produced one of the best children's explorer kits in London, with modelling clay, a false moustache and a guide to making a shrunken head. Parental discretion is needed – steer sensitive souls away from the birth and death cabinets, and focus instead on the exotic masks, votive amulets and celebrity ephemera (Napoleon's toothbrush, George III's hair).

The Wellcome's second gallery, Medicine Now, feels very different:

The Lowdown

- 🌐 **Map ref** 4 E6
  Address 183 Euston Road, NW1 2BE; 020 7611 2222; www.wellcomecollection.org
- 🚆 **Train** Euston, King's Cross or St Pancras. **Tube** Euston Square; Warren Street. **Bus stop** Euston Road, Euston Bus Station, Upper Woburn Place
- 🕐 **Open** 10am–6pm Tue–Sat, 11am–6pm Sun; till 10pm Thu
- 💲 **Price** Free
- 🚩 **Guided tours** Free 30-minute tours of the Medicine Now and Medicine Man galleries at 2:30pm on Sat and Sun respectively

- 🚻 **Age range** 6 plus, though parental guidance advisable
- 🎭 **Activities** Young Explorers Pack for under-14s. Events programme tends to be adult-focused
- ⏱ **Allow** 2 hours
- ♿ **Wheelchair access** Yes
- 🍴 **Eat and drink** Snacks The Museum café offers light lunches, muffins and pies; Real meal The British Library restaurant offers a more substantial feed (see right)
- 🛍 **Shop** Books, gifts and collection-based souvenirs
- 🚻 **Toilets** On all floors

The spacious courtyard of the British Library

starkly lit and stylish, and devoted to modern wonders such as Dolly the cloned sheep and the human genome. Downstairs in the lobby there are temporary exhibitions on health and well-being, plus a cool café with free Wi-Fi and screens for browsing the museum's collection.

Letting off steam
Nearby **Gordon Square Garden** *(Gordon Square, WC1H 0AR)* has a full 100-m (330-ft) lawn, and there's a toddler play-park in adjacent **Woburn Square** *(WC1H 0AB)*.

④ British Library
Sshhh! – a temple for books and the printed word

Fourteen million books, three million sound recordings, almost a million journals and newspapers… and just one permanent public gallery. For such a vast institution, the British Library offers thin pickings for the general visitor, especially for families – guided tours are pitched at adults and under-18s are barred from accessing the sound archives.

However, the Treasures Gallery offers a changing collection of important tomes, from England's first printed book, the *Gutenberg Bible* (c.1455), to Leonardo's Da Vinci's notebooks, a draft score of Handel's *Messiah*, and Captain Scott's South Pole diaries. For children, the displays are saved from dryness by sound stations where they can listen to bursts of Brahms or the Beatles, and especially by the Turning the Pages interactive displays with touch-screen browsing. Flick through Lewis Carroll's original *Alice's Adventures Under Ground*,

with the author's own pictures; or novelist Jane Austen's History of England, written when she was 15 – she had very neat handwriting, too.

Letting off steam
There is a small swing park along Judd Street, across the Euston Road, or walk south for about 15 mintues to **Coram's Fields** *(see p106)*.

The Lowdown

🌐 **Map ref** 4 F4

📍 **Address** 96 Euston Road, NW1 2DB; 0843 208 1144; *www.bl.uk*

🚆 **Train** King's Cross or St Pancras. **Tube** King's Cross St Pancras. **Bus stop** Euston Road

🕐 **Open** 9:30–6pm Mon, Wed–Fri; 9:30am–8pm Tue; 9:30am–5pm Sat; 11am–5pm Sun

💲 **Price** Free

🎫 **Guided Tours** Free Viewing Gallery tours at 11am Mon, Wed, Fri; Library Tour (£29.50) same days at 3pm, plus 10:30am and 3pm Sat. Free conservation tour 2pm Thu; audio tours are downloadable online beforehand.

👫 **Age range** 7 plus

👫 **Activities** Occasional free family workshops during school holidays, linked to temporary exhibitions.

⏱ **Allow** 1 hour

♿ **Wheelchair access** Yes, via lifts and ramps

🍴 **Eat and drink** *Snacks* Peyton & Byrne Café (open daily), upper ground floor, has quality snacks and free Wi-Fi; *Real meal* The first-floor restaurant (9:30am–5pm Mon–Fri; 9:30am–4pm Sat) offers stir-fries and salads.

🛍 **Shop** Ground floor near the entrance

🚻 **Toilets** On all levels

⑤ Foundling Museum

A poignant tale of children lost and found

No single room in any London museum tells a more moving story than the main gallery here. In the early 18th century, before orphanages were established, a thousand babies were abandoned in London's back streets each year – most of them reluctantly – by their destitute mothers. Pioneering shipwright Thomas Coram (1668–1751) led a heroic 20-year campaign to launch a Foundling Hospital to take them in.

The story has all the ingredients of a blockbuster, from the hospital's celebrity patrons (George Frideric Handel performed his *Messiah* to raise funds; William Hogarth donated paintings, which still hang upstairs) to anguished mothers drawing lots to discover whether their tiny bundles would be saved by the orphanage. Today, visitors get to experience the lottery too – if

Dressing up in a rich child's costume at the Foundling Museum

they draw out a black ball, their "baby" is rejected. There are recordings of interviews with former foundlings (the hospital finally closed in 1953), and most heartrending of all, a collection of tokens left behind by mothers who hoped one day to reclaim their child.

Themed activity packs help to focus young minds on the story, while in the immaculate Georgian picture gallery, kids can dress up, or browse in the reading corner – which includes *Hetty Feather*, a tale about a Victorian inmate by Jacqueline Wilson. Better still, the book is a perfect way to whet the appetite before a visit.

Letting off steam

Just across the square, **Coram's Fields** *(93 Guildford St, WC1N 1CN; www.coramsfields.org)* is not so much a playground as a kids' kingdom, with its Olympic-sized paddling pool, mini-farmyard, toddler play sessions, zip-wire and sports pitches.

The Lowdown

- 🌐 **Map ref** 4 G6
  Address 40 Brunswick Square, WC1N 1AZ; 020 7841 3600; www.foundlingmuseum.org.uk
- 🚃 **Train** King's Cross, St Pancras. **Tube** Russell Square. **Bus stop** Russell Square, Gray's Inn Road
- 🕐 **Open** 10am–5pm Tue–Sat, 11am–5pm Sun
- 💲 **Price** £15–25, under 16s free
- 🏷️ **Guided tours** No. Downloadable audio tours from website only
- 👫 **Age range** 3 plus
- 🏃 **Activities** Free treasure-hunt trails (ages 3–12) and activity backpacks (ages 3–5 and 5–8). Drop-in family workshops 1st Sat of each month, plus Thu–Fri in school holidays.
- ⏱️ **Allow** Up to two hours
- ♿ **Wheelchair access** Yes
- 🍽️ **Eat and drink** *Snacks* The museum's Coram Café does light lunches and cream teas and has a children's menu. *Real meal* Giraffe *(19–21 Brunswick Centre, WC1N 1AF; 020 7812 133)* serves burgers, sausages and pizzas and has a kids' menu.
- 🛍️ **Shop** In reception, selling toys and collection-inspired gifts
- 🚻 **Toilets** Lower ground, ground and first floor

⑥ Charles Dickens Museum

Oliver Twist's birthplace

The creator of Oliver, Tiny Tim and Little Nell loved children – he had 10 of his own after all. A leading proponent of child welfare in poverty-stricken Victorian London, Dickens lived at this smart Holborn townhouse from 1837–9, and wrote *Oliver Twist* and *Nicholas Nickleby* here.

The building has been preserved as Dickens knew it, and original furniture, manuscripts and interesting memorabilia such as the

The Lowdown

- 🌐 **Map ref** 4 H6
  Address 48 Doughty Street, WC1N 2LX; 020 7405 2127; www.dickensmuseum.com
- 🚃 **Tube** Russell Square or Chancery Lane. **Bus stop** Gray's Inn Place; Theobald's Road
- 🕐 **Open** Daily 10am–5pm (last admission 4:30pm)
- 💲 **Price** £20–28, under 10s free
- 🏷️ **Guided tours** Group bookings
- 👫 **Age range** 8 plus
- 🏃 **Activities** Free children's trail; occasional family activities
- ⏱️ **Allow** 1 hour
- ♿ **Wheelchair access** Yes, via ramp but some limitations due to age of building
- 🍽️ **Eat and drink** *Picnic* Buy sandwiches at the small onsite café. Eat in the courtyard garden. *Snacks* Kipferl (www.kipferl.co.uk), at Coram's Fields playground, is a kiosk café with an Austrian flavour.
- 🛍️ **Shop** Sells memorabilia
- 🚻 **Toilets** Basement floor

Having fun in the exciting Coram's Fields playground and park

quills he used are on display. There are Victorian cookery demonstrations and the house is animated by sound clips of Dickens' words. After a major refurbishment, the museum is more child-friendly, with regular family activities and a kids' trail.

Letting off steam

Coram's Fields *(see left)*, with its playground, pool and other exciting attractions is just around the corner.

⑦ London Canal Museum

Horse dung and ice cream

Britain's canal age endured for longer than one might imagine – barges carrying cargo were still moving through Battlebridge Basin on the Regent's Canal in the 1960s. That's good news for the museum that now sits here, because lots of fascinating oral history survives – pick up the antique-style telephones and listen to William Tarbit describe what it was like to live and work on the canals: how he had to crawl into his narrowboat's coal box to clean it – aged three! – and how he snared rabbits and pheasants for his mother's poacher's pie.

The museum has a traditional feel, with an authentic 1850s warehouse setting. It is half filled by the vintage barge *Coronis*, on which younger children can play. The cramped cabin might once have accommodated a family of six. Step out onto the wharf for a look at some modern narrowboats, and

visit the re-created blacksmith's workshop and stable upstairs.

The museum's other theme is guaranteed to get kids' tastebuds tingling: the Victorian ice cream trade. The underground chasm in the downstairs gallery once stored vast blocks of ice, imported on barges from Norway by the pioneering pudding-maker Carlo Gatti in the days before refrigeration. And never fear – there is ice cream for sale at the museum shop.

Letting off steam

A 10-minute walk via York Way and Goods Way leads to **Camley Street Natural Park** *(12 Camley Street, NW1 0PW; www.wildlondon.org. uk)*, a canalside wildlife oasis set in a former coal yard amid the bustle of King's Cross. The visitor centre offers activities from 10am–5pm daily, and at weekends there is pond-dipping and insect hunts.

Interactive display showing how a lock's mitre gate works

KIDS' CORNER

Tiny tokens

At the Foundling Museum, find the tokens left behind by mums so they could identify their children if they returned. Which of these objects is NOT in the case: thimble, hairpin, fish, nut, pencil sharpener, coin. What would you leave behind? Why not draw a picture of it?

Answer at the bottom of the page.

Yum yum!

How would you like to eat these dishes from the Foundling Hospital's Victorian menu?
• Gruel: thin porridge made with barley and water
• Pease pottage: mashed-up peas mixed with spices
• Flummery: bland blancmange made with stewed fruit

THE FAMOUS FOUNDLING

Imagine living at the Foundling Hospital for your whole life. John Brownlow was abandoned there as a baby and later took charge of the hospital, running it until he was 72. John was so kind to children that Charles Dickens borrowed his name for Mr Brownlow, the caring gentleman in his story *Oliver Twist*.

Treat time

At the Canal Museum, see if you can find the names of these two ice-cream treats enjoyed by Victorian children...
1. A soft scoop served in a little glass
2. A slice of ice cream wrapped in paper
Get them right and you might be able to have an ice cream!

Answers Pencil sharpener – they were invented nearly 100 years later! **Treats 1** Penny lick **2** Hokey-pokey

The Lowdown

🌐 **Map ref** 4 H3
Address 12–13 New Wharf Road, N1 9RT; 020 7713 0836; *www. canalmuseum.org.uk*

🚆 **Train** King's Cross, St Pancras. **Tube** King's Cross. **Bus stop** Caledonian Road, Pentonville

🕐 **Open** 10am–4:30pm Tue–Sun (last admission 4pm); till 7:30pm on 1st Thu of the month

🎫 **Price** £10, under 4s free

🚩 **Guided tours** There is an audio tour, which must be downloaded beforehand from the website to an MP3 player.

👫 **Age range** 5 plus

👪 **Activities** Small play corner with books and building blocks; family trails, guided boat trips on some

summer Sundays, plus children's activity days every Tuesday in Aug. Website has kids' pages and a downloadable walk from Camden.

🕐 **Allow** 1–2 hours

♿ **Wheelchair access** Yes

🍴 **Eat and drink** *Snacks* Simmons (32 Caledonian Road, N1 9DT) is a tiny, trendy teahouse. Drop in for a pot of tea and a cupcake in the afternoon, or a fruit beer in the evening. *Real meal* Oz Café (53 Caledonian Road, N1 9BU) is a cheery lunchtime diner serving pasta and paninis.

🛍 **Shop** Sells books, pottery and model barges

🚻 **Toilets** Ground floor

ZSL London Zoo and around

There are gorillas and tigers to see of course, but these days London Zoo gives centre stage to its smaller creatures, devoting walk-through enclosures to monkeys and meerkats, penguins and sloths. Wait for some sunshine, and dedicate a full day to get the best value for the entrance fee. The nearest Tube station is Camden Town, but it gets congested on Sundays, when the area's manic markets are in full swing. Consider travelling to Baker Street or Regent's Park station, and walking across Regent's Park, with a game of hide-and-seek along the way. Another great option is a canal tour from Camden Lock.

An "Animals in Action" demonstration at ZSL London Zoo

Far left Youngsters enjoying a costumed talk at the Wallace Collection
Left Elegant bandstand in Regent's Park

Places of Interest

SIGHTS
1. ZSL London Zoo
2. Regent's Park
3. Camden Market
4. Jewish Museum
5. Madame Tussauds
6. Sherlock Holmes Museum
7. The Wallace Collection

EAT AND DRINK
1. Whole Foods Market
2. Gelato Mio
3. Strada
4. The Garden Café
5. The Cow and Coffee Bean
6. The Honest Sausage
7. Yumchaa
8. The Ice Wharf
9. Toasted
10. Caffè Nero
11. The Boathouse
12. Caffè Saporito
13. Nando's
14. Fratelli Deli Café

See also Jewish Museum (p113) and Wallace Collection (p115)

PLACES TO STAY
1. The Landmark
2. Blandford
3. Hart House
4. Lincoln House
5. New Inn
6. 23 Greengarden House

Below Browsing at Camden Lock Crafts Market

CHALK FARM RD

Stables Market

Camden Lock Village

Camden Lock Market

Camden Market

The Pirate Castle

KENTISH TOWN RD

CAMDEN

Camden Town

BAYHAM ST

CAMDEN HIGH ST

Jewish Museum

DELANCEY ST

PRINCE ALBERT ROAD

Canal

(Regent's

ZSL London Zoo

Regent's Park

REGENT'S PARK

QUEEN MARY'S GARDENS

Boating Lake

Sherlock Holmes Museum

Madame Tussauds

Baker Street

The Stardome

St Marylebone Parish Church

MARYLEBONE

The Wallace Collection

WIGMORE STREET

0 metres 500

0 yards 500

The Lowdown

🚆 **Train** Camden Road or Marylebone. **Tube** Camden Town, St John's Wood. **Bus** Prince Albert Road: route number 274; Parkway: C2. **Canal** Services from Camden Lock to Little Venice, daily in summer, weekends in winter (www.londonwaterbus.com; www.jasons.co.uk)

ℹ️ **Visitor information** See pp100–101

🛒 **Supermarkets** Somerfield, 131–133 Camden High Street, NW1 7JR; Morrisons, Chalk Farm Road, NW1 8AA; Waitrose, 98–101 Marylebone High Street, W1U 4SD **Markets** Camden Markets (fashion, crafts, antiques, gifts) 10am–6pm daily. Marylebone Farmers' Market (mainly produce, Cramer Street Car Park, W1U 4EW) 10am–2pm Sun. Cabbages & Frocks Market (food, fashion, crafts), St Marylebone Parish Church, NW1 5LT, 11am–5pm Sat. Church Street Market (food, clothes, bric-a-brac), Church Street, NW8 8DT, 8am–6pm Mon–Sat. Alfies Antique Market, 13–25 Church St NW8 8DT, 10am–6pm Tue–Sat.

🎪 **Festivals** Taste of London (food/restaurant festival), Regent's Park (Jun); Pride London (diversity and equality festival) – parade begins Baker Street (Jun–Jul); Frieze Art Fair, Regent's Park (Oct)

➕ **Pharmacies** JP Pharmacy, 139 Camden High Street, NW1 7JR (9am–6pm Mon–Sat; 10am–4pm Sun). Boots, 173–175 Camden High Street, NW1 7JY (8am–6pm Mon; 8am–7pm Tue, Wed & Fri; 9am–7pm Thu; 8:30am–6pm Sat; 11am–5pm Sun). For 24-hour pharmacies, visit www.nhs.uk/servicedirectories

🛝 **Nearest playgrounds** Regent's Park, NW1 4NR: Marylebone Green, Gloucester Gate, Hanover Gate; Primrose Hill, Prince Albert Road, NW1 4NR; Paddington Street Gardens W1U

The Lowdown

🌐 **Map reference** 3 B3
Address Regent's Park, NW1 4RY; 020 7722 3333 and 0844 225 1826; www.zsl.org

🚗 **Train** Camden Road Station. **Tube** Camden Town, St John's Wood. **Bus stop** Prince Albert Road; Parkway. **Canal** Scheduled service along Regent's Canal between Camden Lock and Little Venice, daily April–September, plus winter weekends (www.londonwaterbus.com).

🕙 **Open** 10am–5:30pm daily (till 4pm in winter); animal houses close 30 minutes earlier.

💲 **Price** £60–70, under 3s free (optional 10% surcharge supports conservation work); online saver offers 10% reduction for families (2+2 or 1+3).

👫 **Skipping the queue** Online tickets allow fast-track admission. Head straight for Gorilla Kingdom, before the queues build.

🚩 **Guided tours** No

👫 **Age range** All

👫 **Activities** Daily programme might include otter feeding, tarantula handling, goat grooming and the Animals in Action show. Plus storytelling in the Animal Adventure teepee and badge-making or brass-rubbing in the Activity Den

⏱ **Allow** At least half a day

♿ **Wheelchair access** Yes – however, there are two steep ramps that need caution

🍽 **Eat and drink** Oasis Restaurant offers hot lunches, including children's portions, baby food and a pick-and-mix picnic counter. Also Animal Adventure Café, seasonal pancake and hot dog stands, and picnic lawns.

🛍 **Shops** Near entrance and in Barclay Court

🚻 **Toilets** Near entrance, in Oasis Restaurant and around zoo

Good family value?

It's wildly expensive, though cut-price deals can sometimes be found online. To get value for money, arrive early, pick up the "Dayplanner" events leaflet, and plot the day carefully.

Prices given are for a family of four

① ZSL London Zoo
Face to fang with the world's wildlife

An architectural oddity, ZSL London Zoo is full of strange 1930s buildings, but it also has a new gorilla compound, an interactive children's zoo and a "penguin beach". Kids will be kept busy tiptoeing along the balancing bars in the monkey enclosure, crawling into an aardvark's burrow, or smiling at sloths in the walk-through rainforest. The zoo's watchword is "immersive", and it brings visitors closer to the animals than ever before.

Key Features

① **Butterfly Paradise** A walk through butterfly house set in a giant inflatable caterpillar. The fluttering insects sometimes mistake brightly dressed visitors for flowers, so watch out for hitchhikers!

② **Blackburn Pavilion** Home to jewel-coloured hummingbirds and splendid sunbirds, this steamy tropical bird-house is themed on Victorian explorers. Get ready to take flight!

③ **Rainforest Life** This hothouse takes visitors right in among snoozing sloths and scurrying tamarin monkeys, which chase along the creepers overhead.

Reptile House

Exit

Aquarium

Animal Adventure **Entrance** **Snowdon Aviary**

④ **Gorilla Kingdom** A splendid moated enclosure brings visitors eye to eye with a troop of western lowland gorillas. The star attraction is the cute youngster, born here in 2010.

⑤ **BUGS!** There are handling sessions here and views of bird-eating spiders, naked mole rats and the zoo's bug experts in their laboratory.

⑥ **Animals in Action** The zoo's captivating live show runs daily in the amphitheatre. Kids watch wide-eyed as George the Macaw and Archie the Owl swoop on the stage.

Letting off steam

If crawling among porcupines and knuckle-walking with gorillas doesn't tire out your flock, there is formal play equipment at the zoo, next to Butterfly Paradise and in the Animal Adventure zone. Beyond the zoo, head for the Gloucester Gate entrance to **Regent's Park**, which has a spacious playground and (just south of its enclosure) an exciting tangle of tree trunks arranged for scrambling, where children really can make like monkeys.

Climbing in the Animal Adventure zone playground

Eat and drink

Picnic: under £20; Snacks: £20–40; Real meal: £40–60; Family treat: £60 or more (based on a family of four)

PICNIC Whole Foods Market *(49 Parkway, NW1 7PN; 020 7428 7575; www.wholefoods market. com; 8am–9pm Mon–Sat, 10am–8pm Sun)* is on the way from Camden Town Tube station to the zoo, with healthy, high-class picnic food. Throw a rug down in Regent's Park to eat it.

SNACKS Gelato Mio *(138 St John's Wood High Street, NW8 7SE; 020 0011 3889; www. gelatomio.co.uk; 7.30am–10:30pm Mon–Fri, 9am–10:30pm Sat–Sun)* serves possibly the tastiest authentic Italian ice creams and sorbets in London. Choose from a wide range of classic flavours.

REAL MEAL Part of a chain, the Italian restaurant **Strada** *(40–42 Parkway, NW1 7AH; 020 7428 9653,*

www.strada.co.uk) is a welcoming spot for lunch, with a kids' menu and activity pack.

FAMILY TREAT The Garden Café *(Inner Circle, Regent's Park, NW1 4NU; 020 7935 5729, www. thegardencafe.co.uk)*, is set in an idyllic location in Regent's Park and specializes in seasonal English cooking – including a set two-course menu for children.

Find out more

DIGITAL ZSL London Zoo's interactive website has kids' pages that mix animal fact-finding with games. Learn how to weigh a meerkat, make your own colourful animal mask or catch up with the babies born recently at the zoo: *www.zsl.org/kids*

Dramatic performance for children on the Puppet Theatre Barge

Next stop...

TOWPATH TRAIL Regent's Canal runs right through the zoo. Escape the excitement with a tranquil walk along the towpath to Camden, with its chaotic, exotic markets *(see pp112–13)*. Head west, perhaps by waterbus, and you'll reach Little Venice, a genteel canal quarter with flower-festooned narrowboats and the delightful **Puppet Theatre Barge**, which puts on seasonal shows for children (nearest tube station Warwick Avenue; 020 7249 6876, www.puppetbarge.com).

Choosing between the many mouthwatering flavours of ice cream at Gelato Mio

② Regent's Park

Playgrounds and playhouses

On a sunny day, few stretches of ground in London lift the spirits quite like Regent's Park. There is just so much to do here: hide-and-seek and ducks to feed for toddlers; football coaching and adventure playgrounds for older children; an open-air theatre and smart dining for mum and dad; even rose gardens and band concerts for granny and grandad.

The park looks wonderful, too: first laid out in 1811 by John Nash, the Buckingham Palace architect, for his great patron the Prince Regent, it was opened to the public 30 years later. There are four excellent playgrounds here (each with attendants and toilets), which often stage activities during school holidays. The elegant Inner Circle has a labyrinthine tangle of snaking pathways, Chinese bridges and cascades, plus the celebrated open-air theatre, which usually includes a family-friendly Shakespeare play in its summer season.

To the west, the pretty boating lake attracts grey herons and has rowing boats and pedalos for hire. Nearby, the Holme Green bandstand stages sedate jazz on Sunday evenings from June to August, when deckchairs can be

Messing about on the water, always a fun option for children in Regent's Park

rented too. There are a number of wildlife walks and allotment workshops in season, including Get Growing family sessions; while to the north of the park, what looks like a crashed flying saucer among the football pitches is actually The Hub (*0207 935 2458*), offering a wide range of sports for all ages and holiday sports camps for kids.

Take cover

If it rains, it's a short stroll to the Odeon Camden (*14 Parkway, NW1 7AA; 0871 224 4007; www.odeon. co.uk*), which offers several film screenings every afternoon.

③ Camden Market

London's most bizarre bazaar

For a first-time visitor, plunging into Camden's maelstrom of markets can feel a little like tumbling down Alice in Wonderland's rabbit hole. It is a passport to an incense-scented alternative universe where the tattooed and pierced buy and sell jewellery, clothes, music, novelties, furniture and food from right across London's vivid cultural spectrum. Take a deep breath, hold on tight to little hands, and go with the flow.

The gentlest introduction is Camden Lock, a cute courtyard right beside Regent's Canal, where prettily painted narrowboats chug out to Little Venice past ZSL London Zoo. The market hall next door majors in sparkly crafts and accessories, from earrings and scarves to candles and carvings, and there's a tasty parade of multi-ethnic food stands. Behind here, things get more chaotic: the labyrinthine Stables Market occupies the site of the stables, horse hospital, warehouses and vaults connected with the canal trade in Victorian times – hence the bronze carthorses that spring out from assorted corners. Teenagers love the groovy goth-punk vibe, while the characterful Horse Tunnel area has more grown-up bric-à-brac.

Just across Chalk Farm Road is Camden Lock Village, another zone of mostly street-fashion stalls set in wooden cabins – look out for the food stands with mopeds as seating.

The Lowdown

- 🌐 **Map ref** 3 B4
  Address London NW1 4NR; *020 7486 7905; www.royalparks. org.uk/regents*
- 🚆 **Train** Marylebone, Euston. **Tube** Regent's Park, Baker Street, Great Portland Street, Camden Town, St John's Wood. **Bus stop** Prince Albert Road, Parkway, Marylebone Road, Baker Street
- 🕐 **Open** 5am till dusk daily (park office 8:30am–4pm)
- 💲 **Price** Free
- 🚩 **Guided tours** Free wildlife walks from spring to autumn (check website)
- 👫 **Age range** All
- 🧍 **Activities** Four playgrounds, with summer holiday activity programme (check website); bandstand and open-air theatre (May–Sept, 0844 826 4242; www.openairtheatre.org;

  backstage tours £3); boating lakes (boat hire £20, Apr–Sep, daily from 10:30am; 020 7724 4069); holiday sports camps (020 7935 2458); pay-and-play tennis (020 7486 4216).
- ⏱️ **Allow** Up to a full day
- ♿ **Wheelchair access** Yes, the park has level access and there are specially adapted toilets
- ☕ **Eat and drink** *Picnic* The Cow and Coffee Bean (*St Mary's Gate, Chester Road; 0207 224 3872; 9am–8pm in summer, 10am–3pm in winter*) serves a selection of sandwiches, alongside milkshakes, ice cream and delicious cakes. *Snacks* The Honest Sausage (*The Broadwalk; 020 7224 3872; 8am–7pm in summer, 9am–4pm in winter*) offers breakfast and light lunches, which can be enjoyed on its spacious terrace.
- 🚻 **Toilets** Throughout the park, including all playgrounds

The Lowdown

🌐 **Map ref** 3 C1

Address Camden High Street, NW1; 020 7284 2084; *www.camdenlock.net*

🚇 **Tube** Camden Town, Chalk Farm. **Bus stop** Chalk Farm Road, Camden Town Station. **Canal** London Waterbus (*www.londonwaterbus.com*) and Jason's Trip (*www.jasons.co.uk*) run daily in spring and summer; London Waterbus runs winter weekends

🕙 **Open** 9:30am–6pm daily

💲 **Price** Free

👪 **Skipping the queue** The market heaves at weekends: 1–5:30pm Sun, Camden Town tube station is exit only. Weekdays are quieter.

🧍 **Age range** 7 plus

🏃 **Activities** Canal trips *(see above)*

⏱ **Allow** Up to 2 hours

♿ **Wheelchair access** Yes, via lifts (disabled toilet in Unit 23 on the Stables market level).

🍴 **Eat and drink** *Snacks* Yumchaa (*91–92 Camden Lock Place, NW1 8AF; www.yumchaa.com*) offers a huge variety of teas and cakes. *Real meal* The Ice Wharf (*28 Jamestown Road, NW1 7BY; www.jdwetherspoon.co.uk/home/pubs/the-ice-wharf*) overlooks the lock and has a good kids' menu.

🚻 **Toilets** Various; basement of Stable Market, bridge of Middle Yard.

Letting off steam

Primrose Hill, a 10-minute walk via the canal towpath, is a lofty northern satellite of Regent's Park popular with kite fliers. The Pirate Castle (*020 7267 6605; www.thepiratecastle.org*), a canalside youth club offering kayaking sessions for ages 8–17 on Tue, Thu and Sat, plus most weekdays in summer holidays, is on the way.

Exploring the bustling Camden Lock crafts market

---

④ Jewish Museum
A poignant 1,000-year immigrant odyssey

From the life of the Victorian prime minister Benjamin Disraeli to that of Auschwitz survivor Leon Greenman, the Jewish Museum puts an emphasis on personal stories. You can get a free taste of the museum from the ground-floor gallery, but the history hall is the highlight, tracing the 1,000-year story of Britain's Jewish community, from their arrival with William the Conqueror in 1066. The senses are engaged: smell the chicken soup in a re-created East End street, play a board game based on the Jewish diaspora or try Yiddish karaoke. Especially poignant for kids are the keepsakes from the Kindertransport, carried by the 10,000 Jewish children who fled Nazi Germany in 1939.

Letting off steam

It's a 5-minute walk along Parkway to Gloucester Gate playground, in **Regent's Park**.

The Lowdown

🌐 **Map ref** 3 D2

Address 129–131 Albert Street, NW1 7NB; 020 7284 7384; *www.jewishmuseum.org.uk*

🚇 **Tube** Camden Town, Mornington Crescent. **Bus stop** Delancey Street, Camden High Street. **Canal** Camden Lock (*www.londonwaterbus.com; www.jasons.co.uk*)

🕙 **Open** 10am–5pm Sun–Thu; 10am–2pm Fri (last admission 30 minutes earlier)

💲 **Price** £18

🏴 **Guided tours** No

🧍 **Age range** 7 plus

🏃 **Activities** Family workshops on occasional Sundays and in school holidays, include glass-painting, candle-making and drumming

⏱ **Allow** 1–2 hours

♿ **Wheelchair access** Yes

🍴 **Eat and drink** *Snack* Toasted (*96 Parkway, NW1 7AN; 020 7482 4866; www.toastedcafe.co.uk*) is a cool little café with comic-strip décor and board games. *Real meal* The museum's Kosher Café has bagels, salt beef and a special kids' menu.

🛍 **Shop** Ground floor

🚻 **Toilets** All floors

KIDS' CORNER

Animal hunt

Regent's Park is home to all kinds of wildlife, including herons, owls, kestrels and hedgehogs. They are often shy and keep away from humans, though some creatures can be found whenever you visit. Look out for a giant newt, a bronze vulture and a sleek wooden jaguar. The park also has a "talking bench". Can you find it?

DOTTY!

Have you read *The Hundred and One Dalmatians*? Dodie Smith's book is set in Regent's Park, where Pongo and Missis live with their owners, the Dearlys, at 1 St Andrew's Place, near Chester Walk Gate. You can follow their nightly walk to the top of Primrose Hill, where they yelped for help to all dogdom during the "Twilight Barking".

Crazy Camden

The road from Camden Town tube to Camden Market must have the best shop-fronts in London. See if you can tick off these strange sights:
• A fierce dragon
• A Union Jack boot
• A giant scorpion
• A climbing cat
• A nose-diving plane.

Giddy-up!

In Victorian times, hundreds of horses were stabled in the Camden Market area. They pulled cargo between the canal, the railway and the roads, and Camden goods yard was the biggest in the world. How many horses can you spot? Score a point for every one you see and five points if you find a farrier – he's a man who fits horseshoes.

Picnic under £20; **Snacks** £20–40; **Real meal** £40–60; **Family treat** £60 or more (based on a family of four)

Iconic red telephone boxes outside the world-famous Madame Tussauds

⑤ Madame Tussauds
Schmooze with the stars

No attraction in the capital divides opinion quite like Marie Tussaud's 175-year-old waxwork show. Despite the pricey admission, visitors queue around the block – and that's really the problem. The galleries can get crowded, defeating the main purpose of a visit – to have your photograph taken with Lady Gaga, Zac Efron or Johnny Depp. Small children may even struggle to see

The Lowdown

🌐 **Map ref** 3 B6
📍 **Address** Marylebone Road, NW1 5LR; 0871 894 3000; www.madametussauds.com/london
🚇 **Train** Marylebone. **Tube** Baker Street. **Bus stop** Marylebone Road, Baker Street
🕐 **Open** 9:30am–5:30pm Mon–Fri; 9am–6pm Sat–Sun
💲 **Price** £99–109. Half-price tickets after 5pm, online only
🏃 **Skipping the queue** Book online for fast-track entry; online tickets are about 10 per cent cheaper.
👪 **Age range** 5 plus
👪 **Activities** Free family activity pack, available online only: www.madametussauds.com/London/BuyTickets/Families.aspx
⏱ **Allow** 2 hours
♿ **Wheelchair access** Yes, apart from the Spirit of London moving ride. No prams allowed in attractions.
☕ **Eat and drink** *Snacks* Caffè Nero (*Marylebone Road, NW1 5LR; 8am–6:30pm Mon–Fri; 9am–7:30pm Sat–Sun*) serves small eats. *Real meal* The Boathouse (*Boating Lake, Hanover Gate, Regent's Park, NW1 4NR; 0207 724 4069*) sells pizzas, pastas and salads.
🛍 **Shop** In the exit lobby
🚻 **Toilet** A-list Party and Sports zones

Rubbing shoulders with a waxwork of actress and singer Miley Cyrus

their heroes in the melee. But go when it's quieter, ideally on a weekday morning, and there's no denying the glamour of walking into the first hall – a celebrity party where the likes of Daniel Radcliffe, Robert Pattinson and Miley Cyrus are waiting for their close-up. Most of the models are spookily lifelike, and there are no ropes to segregate visitors from "VIPs", so you really can rub shoulders with the stars. Younger children may prefer the Hollywood hall, with its rampaging dinosaur and giant Shrek, while downstairs they can play simulated tennis and football (queues permitting), as Becker and Beckham look on.

In the basement, the Scream horror gallery has live serial killers jumping out of shadowy corners – not for the under-13s. Younger kids can head straight for the two attractions at the end; a ride through London's history in a black cab and a 4D animated experience in which Spider Man, the Hulk and Wolverine battle baddies in modern London.

Letting off steam
Regent's Park is very close – from York Gate, turn right to find the Marylebone Green playground.

⑥ Sherlock Holmes Museum
Home of the world's most famous detective

It's hard to think of many museums devoted to fictional characters – and indeed, some fans refuse to believe that Sir Arthur Conan Doyle's great detective didn't exist. There is a file of genuine letters

The Lowdown

🌐 **Map ref** 3 A6
📍 **Address** 221b Baker Street, NW1 6XE; 020 7224 3688; www.sherlock-holmes.co.uk
🚇 **Train** Marylebone. **Tube** Baker Street. **Bus stop** Baker Street, Marylebone Road
🕐 **Open** 9:30am–6pm daily
💲 **Price** £20–30
🏃 **Guided tours** None
👪 **Age range** 8 plus
⏱ **Allow** Up to 1 hour
♿ **Wheelchair access** No, due to stairs
☕ **Eat and drink** *Snacks* Caffè Saporito (*14 Melcombe Street, NW1 6AH*) sells lovely cupcakes. *Real meal* Nando's (*113 Baker Street, W1U 6RS*) serves tasty Portuguese-style food.
🛍 **Shop** Next door
🚻 **Toilet** In basement

here, from people around the world, asking for Sherlock Holmes's help with solving their own personal mysteries.

Holmes the sleuth, repeatedly revived by Hollywood, lives on in this moody Victorian townhouse, though kids unfamiliar with the tales will feel a little clueless. The first mystery is the address: why is 221b Baker Street between numbers 237 and 241? Inside, staircases creak, gas-lamps splutter and Dr Watson lurks on the landing, ushering visitors into Holmes's study to sit in his chair, or even puff on his pipe.

Youngsters in period hats, outside the front door of 221b Baker Street

The other five rooms are filled with clues and murder weapons from his famous cases. It is atmospheric, if rather kitschy, and there's not much on more recent screen adaptations. One puzzle remains: why isn't the cleaner dressed up as Mrs Hudson?

Letting off steam

Regent's Park is 2 minutes away, with pedaloes and a playground at nearby Hanover Gate.

⑦ The Wallace Collection

No Gromit, but lots of armour and The Laughing Cavalier

First impressions can be deceptive. The Wallace Collection looks like a typical hushed and highbrow museum of old, a marbled mansion dripping with weighty chandeliers and gilt-framed Old Masters. Even its splendid restaurant has bibbed waiters and pricey food.

However, the Wallace is very keen to woo families: it has teamed up with pupils from a nearby school to create a children's "acoustiguide" and I-Spy trails, and has published a kids' art book based on key exhibits, for sale in the shop.

The collection was mostly put together by the Francophile Fourth Marquess of Hertford in the 1800s and is especially strong on French furniture and Sèvres porcelain – look out for Catherine the Great's tea set. Children will be most excited by the rooms full of gleaming armour displays, which include Rajput warrior regalia and medieval knights on horseback. Upstairs, a series of stuccoed salons are lined with fine art, including Titians, Rembrandts, 22 Canalettos and a certain very famous jovial horseman.

Letting off steam

There is an excellent playground at **Paddington Street Gardens** *(Paddington Street, W1U 4EF; ages 3–11)*, just north of the museum.

The Lowdown

- 🌐 **Map ref** 9 B2
- **Address** Hertford House, Manchester Square, W1U 3BN; 020 7563 9500; *www. wallacecollection.org*
- 🚗 **Train** Marylebone. **Tube** Bond Street, Baker Street. **Bus stop** Baker Street, Oxford Street
- 🕐 **Open** 10am–5pm daily
- 🏷 **Price** Free
- 🚩 **Guided tours** General tours Wed, Sat, Sun 11:30am and 3pm; themed tour daily 1pm
- 👫 **Age range** 5 plus
- 👫 **Activities** Two free children's trails plus multimedia guide with touch-screen games (£4). There is armour to try on in the Conservation Gallery. Little Draw art workshops 1st Sun of the month (1:30–4:30pm), plus family events in school holidays
- ⏱ **Allow** 2 hours
- ♿ **Wheelchair access** Yes
- 🍴 **Eat and drink** *Snacks* Fratelli Deli Café *(108 Wigmore Street, W1U 3RW; 020 7487 3100)* sells solid Italian staples and tasty light bites. *Real meal* The French-style Wallace Restaurant offers great brasserie lunches, afternoon teas and dinner on Fri and Sat.
- 🛍 **Shop** Ground floor
- 🚻 **Toilets** Lower ground floor

A "Meet Marie Antoinette" costumed talk at the Wallace Collection

Picnic under £20; **Snacks** £20–40; **Real meal** £40–60; **Family treat** £60 or more (based on a family of four)

The City
and the East End

Now synonymous with global money markets and the Bank of England, the City of London (or Square Mile) is also where London began – the Romans built a wall around it in AD 200, parts of which still survive. The area is brimful of brilliant buildings and history. The vibrant East End has undergone a radical transformation since Jack the Ripper's time and is now filled with a host of stylish galleries and fun Sunday markets.

Bloomsbury and
Regent's Park

**The City and
the East End**

Westminster
and the
West End

Southwark and
the South Bank

Kensington,
Chelsea and
Battersea

Highlights

The Monument
Climbing this memorial comes with a deep sense of occasion – 311 steps to the top, then out onto a blustery balcony 50 m (164 ft) above the City (see p124).

Tower of London
The Tower's famous Beefeaters deliver the most entertaining tour in London. Ask them what happened to the luckless Duke of Monmouth (see pp122–3).

St Paul's Cathedral
It is polite to whisper in church – but high inside the dome here, a whisper travels further than most. The curious acoustics are captivating for kids (see pp130–1).

Postman's Park
This picnic-friendly spot houses a most touching memorial – hand-painted tiles recall people who gave their lives to save others. Bring a hankie (see p136).

Bank of England Museum
This museum is surprisingly welcoming to families – no sign of a pinstripe suit – and where else can you lift up a gold ingot worth more than a house (see p132)?

Here be dragons
Dragons are the City's legendary guardians, and there's great fun to be had tracking them down on statues and street signs. Start hunting at the Guildhall (see p133).

Left Stately and magnificent, St Paul's Cathedral is one of London's most famous landmarks **Above** The fascinating engine room at Tower Bridge

The Best of
The City and the East End

With 300,000 workers and only 10,000 residents, the City is best tackled at the weekend. The focus of the area is a triangle of top attractions: the Tower of London, St Paul's Cathedral and the Museum of London, one of the capital's most exciting museums for families. Meanwhile, beyond the shiny towers of the financial quarter, a lively young arts community has blossomed around Old Spitalfields Market and the Whitechapel Gallery.

A City weekend

For families, the ideal City weekend begins on Saturday morning with Family Film Club at the **Barbican** (see p138), where curators wheel out activities on trolleys before the movie. There's a great foodhall for lunch and also a deli, so if the weather's kind, walk to **Postman's Park** (see p136) for a picnic. Next, head for **St Paul's Cathedral** (see pp128–9) (it's closed to visitors on Sundays). It offers a family multimedia guide with hidden facts especially for younger visitors.

On Sunday, begin with brunch and a browse at **Old Spitalfields Market** (see p138). Don't linger too long, though, because the **Tower of London** (see pp122–3) is waiting. A tour with a Beefeater is a great introduction, while children get to meet medieval damsels and fire crossbows in the armoury display. Round off the weekend with a bite to eat at nearby **St Katharine's Dock** (see p126).

Roaming with Romans

The City of London was first established by the Romans in the 1st century and many traces of them can still be seen. Start at the **Museum of London** (see pp136–7), which has a mock 2,000-year-old street and offers young visitors an activity pack full of Roman fun and games.

Around the corner on Noble Street stands the best surviving part of Roman London's defensive wall, which once stretched all the way from modern-day Tower Bridge to Blackfriars. Next,

Below Looking down at the intricate floor of St Paul's Cathedral from the Whispering Gallery stroll east along Gresham Street to the **Guildhall Art Gallery** (see p133) to see the remains of a Roman amphitheatre. A sound and light show brings gladiatorial combat back to life.

Head south to Queen Victoria Street to see the remains of the 3rd-century Temple of Mithras, then hit **Leadenhall Market** (see p124), once the site of London's original Roman forum, to eat.

Nursery-rhyme London

It's amazing how many children's nursery rhymes have their roots in London's history. Begin tracing them at **St Olave's church** (see p125), where a plaque recalls the burial of Old Mother Goose in 1586. St Olave was an 11th-century Norwegian king who saved London from invading Vikings by towing away London Bridge with his ships – which probably inspired *London Bridge is Falling Down*. The spooky skulls on the church's gateway remember the plague victims buried here, so why not play a game of *Ring-a-Ring-o-Roses* in nearby Seething Lane Gardens? "We all fall down" is thought to refer to people dying of the plague.

Next, head for **The Monument** (see p124), built after the Great Fire of 1666, for a rousing chorus of *London's Burning*.

Finish at **St Mary-le-Bow Church** (see p131) whose great bell is mentioned in *Oranges and Lemons*, and also tolled to call back Dick Whittington to become Lord Mayor of London: Dick's statue presides over nearby Guildhall Yard (see p133).

Money, money, money

From pirate treasure to gold bars, there's no escaping money in the world's second-biggest banking centre. Goldsmiths first gathered here

*Above View of the Tower of London from the River Thames
Below Guildhall Art Gallery bringing the gladiator combat of London's Roman amphitheatre to life*

in the 15th century and a walk along Lombard Street takes in London's earliest finance houses, with their curious banking signs. After gazing at some modern temples of Mammon (the Lloyd's Building, the "Gherkin"), visit the **Bank of England Museum** (see p132), where children can see a £1,000,000 note.

Nearby, 100 years ago, workmen dug up the world's finest cache of Tudor gems: the Cheapside Hoard. These may originally have been plundered by pirates, and some now glitter at the **Museum of London** (see pp136–7). Even they are outshone, of course, by the Crown Jewels at the **Tower of London** (see pp122–3).

Tower of London and around

Begun in 1078 by William the Conqueror to subdue his new Anglo-Saxon citizens, the Tower of London has extended its special brand of hospitality to the likes of Anne Boleyn, Guy Fawkes and Captain Blood. There's a full day of family fun here, so book online to skip the queues, and try to avoid weekends. The Tower, the Monument and St Katharine's Dock all have an outdoor dimension, so this area is good to visit on a sunny day.

The City and the East End

Museum of London p134

St Paul's Cathedral p128

Tower of London

Places of Interest

SIGHTS

1. Tower of London
2. The Monument
3. Leadenhall Market
4. All Hallows by the Tower
5. Tower Bridge
6. St Katharine's Dock
7. Whitechapel Gallery

● **EAT AND DRINK**

1. Paul
2. Ebb
3. Bodean's
4. Chez Gerard
5. Jonathan's Sandwiches
6. Pod
7. Pret A Manger
8. Pizza Express
9. Bubble Café
10. Café Rouge
11. Capstans
12. Ping Pong

See also Tower of London (p122), Leadenhall Market (p124) and Whitechapel Gallery (p127)

● **PLACES TO STAY**

1. Apex City of London
2. Grange City
3. Hamlet (UK)

The iconic Tower Bridge, with its pinnacled towers

The enormous Monument, which commemorates the Great Fire of London

Far left The magnificent Tower of London, seen from across the River Thames **Left** The attractive and vibrant marina at St Katharine's Dock

Enjoying an arts and crafts workshop at the cutting-edge Whitechapel Gallery

The Lowdown

🚗 **Train** Fenchurch Street, Cannon Street or Tower Gateway (Docklands Light Railway). **Tube** Tower Hill, Monument, Aldgate or Aldgate East. **Bus** Tower Bridge Approach: route numbers 42, 78, RV1; Tower Hill: 15, 25, 100; Gracechurch Street (for the Monument): 35, 40, 47, 48, 149, 344. **River bus** Tower Pier, to Embankment and Woolwich Arsenal via London Eye, Greenwich (0870 781 5049, www.thamesclippers.com); to Greenwich and Westminster via London Eye (020 7740 0400; www.citycruises.com). St Katharine's Pier, circular to Westminster via Embankment, Festival Pier, Bankside Pier (020 7936 2033; www.crownriver.com); to Westminster and Thames Barrier via Greenwich (020 7930 4097; www. thamesriverservices.co.uk)

ℹ️ **Visitor information** See pp128–29

🛒 **Supermarkets** Tesco Metro, 6 Eastcheap, EC3M 1AE; or (much larger) Waitrose at 41 Thomas More Street, St Katharine's Dock, E1W 1YY **Markets** St Katharine's Dock (food), 10am–4pm Fri. Leadenhall Market (general), 11am–4pm Mon–Fri. Petticoat Lane Market (clothing), Middlesex Street, E1 10am–2:30pm Mon–Fri; 9am–2pm Sun

🎏 **Festivals** City of London Festival, music and arts (Jun–Jul); The Mayor's Thames Festival, Tower Bridge (Sep); Leadenhall Market Winter Festival and Christmas lights (from mid-Nov)

➕ **Pharmacies** Boots, 54 King William St, EC4R 9AA (7:30am–7pm Mon–Fri). For 24-hour pharmacies, visit www. nhs.uk/servicedirectories

🧒 **Nearest playground** Tower Hill Gardens, corner of Tower Hill and Minories Hill

① Tower of London
A pop-up-book castle in modern London

With its stories of beheadings, child-slayings and torture, the tower has a gory appeal for kids. There are ramparts to patrol, spiralling staircases, dank dungeons and chambers full of treasure. The interiors are interactive, too: meet a minstrel in Henry III's medieval palace, try on a helmet in the Peasants' Revolt exhibit and fire a crossbow in the White Tower. Touching the Crown Jewels is still banned, however – the last time the guards allowed that in 1671, Colonel Blood tried to stuff them down his breeches.

A Beefeater standing guard

Key Features

Jewel House The Crown Jewels, including the royal sceptre, which holds one of the largest diamonds in the world, are stored here.

White Tower This houses Henry VIII's armoury – visitors can handle the replica weapons.

Wakefield Tower This has a rack for stretching, manacles for dangling and the "scavenger's daughter", for crushing people to a pulp.

Traitors' Gate Prisoners, many on their way to die, entered the Tower by boat through these gates.

Entrance

Traitor's Gate

Bloody Tower Known as such after the strange disappearance here of 12-year-old Edward V and his 9-year-old brother in 1483. Their uncle, Richard III, was next in line to the throne and is the prime suspect.

The ravens Caged at night, the six ravens are now the only prisoners here. Legend says that if they ever leave, the tower and the kingdom will fall.

Beauchamp Tower The walls are etched with prisoners' graffiti. The inscription "Jane" recalls Lady Jane Grey, who was executed at the age of 17.

Tower Green Queen Anne Boleyn, one of Henry VIII's wives, was beheaded here. She expected a late pardon, so no coffin was made. They buried her in an arrow box.

The Lowdown

🌐 **Map ref** 12 G4
Address Tower of London, EC3N 4AB; 0844 482 7777; www.hrp.org.uk/toweroflondon

🚗 **Train** London Bridge, Fenchurch Street, Tower Gateway (Docklands Light Railway – DLR). **Tube** Tower Hill. **Bus stop** Tower Bridge Approach, Tower Hill. **River bus** Tower Pier and St Katharine's Pier

🕐 **Open** Mar–Oct, Tue–Sat 9am–5:30pm; Sun–Mon 10am–5:30pm; Nov–Feb till 4:30pm (last admission 30 minutes earlier)

💷 **Price** £55

👫 **Skipping the queue** Book online beforehand (prices are lower,

too); or the day before your visit from ticket office on Tower Hill

👉 **Guided tours** Free 45-minute tours every 30 minutes; themed audio tours (extra charge)

👫 **Age range** 5 plus, although torture exhibition and Yeoman Warder tour can be scary.

👫 **Activities** Activity books available free from the Welcome Centre. Downloadable family trails, and an Explore Kit that also covers HMS *Belfast* and Tower Bridge. Costumed interpreters daily in St Thomas's Tower, plus free family fun days on 1st Sat of the month and regular school-holiday children's events.

Tower Moat ice rink, Nov–Jan (extra charge; www.toweroflondonicerink.com).

⏱ **Allow** At least half a day

♿ **Wheelchair access** Limited – there's a downloadable map of accessible areas on the website.

☕ **Café** The Armouries Café offers children's meal deals, high-chairs and a microwave for baby food.

🛍 **Shops** Five shops selling play armour, books and sweets

👫 **Toilets** Behind Waterloo Block

Good family value?
London's most popular visitor attraction – and it deserves to be.

Enjoying a picnic in the sunshine in the Tower of London's grounds

Letting off steam

There's plenty of running-about room inside the Tower, along the ramparts and on the grass, while riverside **Tower Wharf** is traffic-free, and boasts picnic benches and cannons for youngsters to clamber over. Alternatively, cross Tower Hill to the corner of **Minories Hill**, where you'll find a new playground with swings and slides.

Eat and drink

Picnic: under £20; Snacks: £20–40; Real meal: £40–60; Family treat: £60 or more (based on a family of four)

PICNIC Picnicking is encouraged at the Tower. Try the moat (during the summer months), the benches around the White Tower, or the riverside at Tower Wharf, where popular patisserie **Paul** (daily 8am–6pm) sells super sandwiches.

SNACKS Head for St Katharine's Dock, and **Ebb** *(Ivory House, E1W 1AT; 020 7702 9792)*, a cute coffee house by the water that sells good milkshakes and boasts comfortable seats and a vibrant atmosphere.
REAL MEAL Bodean's *(16 Byward Street, EC3R 5BA; 020 7488 3883; www.bodeansbbq.com; noon–11pm, till 10:30pm Sun)* offers sizzling barbecue dishes, as well as delicious salads and vegetarian options. One child eats free with an adult between noon and 5pm daily.
FAMILY TREAT Chez Gerard *(14 Trinity Square, EC3N 4AA; 020 7480 5500; www.chezgerard. co.uk; weekdays only noon–11pm)* offers upmarket French brasserie fare that appeals to children and adults alike, and has a friendly attitude to families.

Find out more

DIGITAL See if you have what it takes to don some armour, grab a weapon and challenge King Henry VIII, at *henryviiidressedtokill. viral-game.co.uk/*. Dress a medieval knight in armour, then sort out his greaves from his gauntlets at *www. ictgames.com/knightinarmour.html*.

Next stop...

TRINITY SQUARE GARDENS Across Tower Hill in this park *(Tower Hill, EC3N)*, a plaque marks the site of the Scaffold, where 125 churchmen and nobles were publicly beheaded while jugglers and acrobats entertained the crowd. Their heads were placed on spikes along London Bridge.

Youngsters sword-fighting against the impressive backdrop of the Tower

② The Monument
Climb up among the rooftops for views over London

Three centuries before the London Eye, it was possible to admire the city's skyline from 50 m (164 ft) aloft. The view is hard earned: there are 311 corkscrewing steps to reach the caged platform atop The Monument, erected by Sir Christopher Wren in the 1670s to remember the Great Fire of London.

The fire broke out in September 1666, in a bakery in nearby Pudding Lane, and within three days it had reduced 13,000 homes, 87 churches and St Paul's Cathedral to ashes. The good news: it also saw off the Great Plague, which had wiped out 100,000 people the year before.

The Monument is still the world's tallest free-standing column and must have been a marvel in its day. Wren built a laboratory in the basement for conducting his experiments, but soon it was open for visitors. The climb is a challenge for little legs, but well worth it to emerge among the spires and skyscrapers of modern London. The telescope commentaries are hardly worth bothering with; instead, just savour the fabulous views. There is a certificate for everyone who makes it down again intact.

Letting off steam

Still got some puff left after the big climb? A few minutes east, via Lower Thames Street, is the bombed-out shell of the church of St Dunstan in the East (Dunstan's Hill, EC3R), now a garden and perfect for a picnic.

The viewing deck at the top of Wren's grand Monument

Prices given are for a family of four

The Lowdown

- 🌐 **Map ref** 12 F4
  Address Monument Street, EC3R 8AH; 020 7626 2717; *www.themonument.info*
- �︎ **Train** Cannon Street. **Tube** Monument. **Bus stop** Gracechurch Street
- 🕙 **Open** 9:30am–5:30pm daily (last admission 5pm)
- 💲 **Price** £8–12; combined ticket with Tower Bridge Exhibition £26–36
- 🚶 **Skipping the queue** At weekends, arrive before 11am to avoid waiting
- 🚶‍♀️ **Age range** 5 plus
- ⏱ **Allow** 30 minutes
- ♿ **Wheelchair access** No
- ☕ **Eat and drink** *Picnic* Jonathan's Sandwiches *(17 Cullum St, EC3M 7JJ)*, sells excellent salt beef sandwiches. *Snacks* Pod *(75 King William St, EC4N 7BE)* serves good salads, noodles and wraps.
- 🚻 **Toilets** In nearby Monument Street

③ Leadenhall Market
From Dick Whittington to Harry Potter

This area has a fascinating 600-year history – and it really looks the part. The warren of cobbled arcades is encased in fancy ironwork and lit by quaint lanterns, while pillars gleam in bold carousel colours – cream, claret and green. Snarling dragons guard every corner and there are topsy-turvy taverns and streetwise shoeshine stands. It's like looking into a Victorian kaleidoscope.

The centre of Roman London was here – the ruins of its 1st-century basilica, the same length as St Paul's Cathedral, lie buried beneath the Lamb Tavern. In 1411, the merchant Richard (Dick) Whittington, of pantomime fame, donated Leadenhall to the City of London, and by 1800 it was Europe's best-supplied market, specialising in beef and game.

The arcades were designed in 1881, and now host gourmet butchers and cheesemongers, slick brasseries and bars, plus Pandora's Box and Ben's Cookies for sweet treats. As a family lunch spot, Leadenhall has genuine wow factor – especially when you reveal the Harry

The interior of historic Leadenhall Market, with its bustling cafés

Potter connection. Bull's Head Passage was transformed into Diagon Alley, where our hero buys his wand in *Harry Potter and the Philosopher's Stone*.

Letting off steam

Head towards the Tower of London, to the excellent new playground on the corner of Minories (see p123).

The Lowdown

- 🌐 **Map ref** 12 F3
  Address Gracechurch Street, EC3V 1LR; 020 7929 1073; *www.leadenhallmarket.co.uk*
- 🚗 **Train** Fenchurch Street, Bank (DLR). **Tube** Bank or Monument. **Bus stop** Gracechurch Street
- 🕙 **Open** Mon–Fri 7am–6:30pm; market stalls 11am–4pm
- 💲 **Price** Free
- 🚶 **Skipping the queue** Aim to be there before 1pm, when the eateries fill up with City workers
- 🚶‍♀️ **Activities** Winter Festival with lunchtime concerts (mid-Nov); City Lights Family Festival, September
- ♿ **Wheelchair access** Yes
- ☕ **Eat and drink** *Snacks* Chop'd *(1 Leadenhall Mkt, EC3V 1LR)*, serves hearty but healthy stews, broths and sandwiches. *Real meal* Ortega *(26–27 Leadenhall Mkt, EC3R 5AS)* gets busy at lunchtime but the tapas are good.
- 🚻 **Toilets** In Monument Street

Grim skull and bone reliefs above the entrance to St Olave's church

④ All Hallows by the Tower

Boudicca, beheadings… and brass-rubbing

London's oldest church is packed to the tower-top with quirky history, from the battles of Boudicca to beheaded bodies and the glowing embers of the Great Fire of 1666.

Begin in the crypt, where a pristine chunk of 2nd-century pavement was uncovered in 1926, along with a layer of ash dating from Queen Boudicca's burning of the city in AD 60. There's also an intricate model of Roman London to look at and scraps of salvaged pottery from imperial days.

Fast forward to Saxon times – an archway survives from the original 7th-century church, revealed suddenly when a bomb blasted the building during World War II. In the 16th century, All Hallows took in the headless corpses from Henry VIII's execution scaffold *(see p123)*, including that of Sir Thomas More. The church survived the Great Fire of London thanks to the quick wits of Admiral William Penn (father of Penn of Pennsylvania fame), who blew up nearby buildings to create a fire-break. Meanwhile, Penn's next-door neighbour, Samuel Pepys, climbed the steeple to watch the blaze – having first buried his prized truckle of Parmesan in his garden.

If that doesn't impress the kids, they can take home their very own medieval knight – the church's visitor centre offers brass-rubbing sessions most weekday afternoons.

Letting off steam

Cross Byward Street into Seething Lane Gardens to St Olave's Church – worth a peek for its spooky skulls and crowded plague graves. The woman thought to be responsible for bringing the plague to London is buried here, along with nursery-rhyme character Mother Goose.

Above *The Saxon archway from the original 7th-century All Hallows*
Below *Exposed Roman pavement inside All Hallows*

The Lowdown

- 🌐 **Map ref** 12 G4
  Address Byward Street, EC3R 5BJ; 020 7481 2928; www.ahbtt.org.uk
- 🚆 **Train** Fenchurch Street, Tower Gateway (DLR). **Tube** Tower Hill, Monument. **Bus stop** Tower Hill
- 🕐 **Open** 8am–6pm Mon–Fri; 10am–5pm Sat–Sun; Sung Eucharist service, 11am Sunday
- 💷 **Price** Free
- 🏃 **Activities** Brass-rubbing most weekdays 2–4pm, £5 (call to check). Occasional themed walking tours in the City, £6 (www.londoncitywalks.co.uk). Free tours of the church most afternoons (Apr–Sept)
- ♿ **Wheelchair access** Yes
- 🍴 **Eat and drink** *Picnic* Pret A Manger (12 Byward Street, EC36R 5AS; 7am–6pm Mon–Fri, 9am–5pm Sat–Sun; www.pret.com) offers a wide variety of reliable sandwiches and salads. *Real meal* Pizza Express (1 Byward Street, EC3R 7QN; 11:30am–11pm Mon–Sat, 11:30am–5pm Sun; 020 7626 5025; www.pizzaexpress.com) is a perennial favourite with families.
- 🚻 **Toilets** In Tower Place, next door

Tower Bridge opening to allow a high-masted boat through

⑤ Tower Bridge
The legend of the flying bus driver

"Tawdry … pretentious … absurd". When Tower Bridge opened in 1894, the architecture critics didn't think much of Horace Jones's flamboyant Gothic design. Today, it is London's number-one icon, and its drawbridge-style bascules (the "see-saw" parts) are still raised 1,000 times a year to allow ships to pass. The patriotic paint scheme, first added in 1977 to mark the 25th anniversary of the accession of Queen Elizabeth II, used 22,000 litres (4,840 gallons) of red, white and blue paint.

The bridge's high walkways were designed for pedestrians – but nobody wanted to climb the 300 stairs to use them. Today, an elevator whisks visitors 42 m (138 ft) up onto the twin gantries, for breathtaking views along the river. Little ones may need lifting up to get the full impact, though there's an Explore Kit to keep them occupied, and stickers to collect en route.

Displays focus on bridge trivia, including stories about straying whales, cheeky fighter pilots and Albert Gunter, the "flying bus-driver", who found himself airborne in 1952 when the bascules opened while his number 78 bus was still crossing the bridge.

The exhibition continues in the Victorian engine rooms, showing off the shiny steam turbines that powered the bridge until 1976, when oil, electricity and hydraulics took over. Here, kids can get to grips with interactive models: for example, sit an unsuspecting sibling in a chair, turn a handle, and watch them suddenly lurch skywards.

Letting off steam
At the southern end of the bridge, on the right as you cross north to south, lies **Potters Fields** (*www.pottersfields.co.uk*). It is possibly the most panoramic picnic spot in London.

⑥ St Katharine's Dock
London's floating treasure trove

Hidden behind a phalanx of high buildings, St Katharine's Dock is one of London's loveliest backwaters, where a powerhouse of the Industrial Revolution has been transformed into a jaunty marina lined with yachts and waterside cafés. It's a great place to kick back after tramping around the Tower of London.

The dock's roots as a shipping hub date back to the 10th century, when King Edgar granted 5 ha (13 acres) to 13 knights, with permission to trade. It grew into a prosperous and important mercantile area over the centuries. In the 1820s, the great civil engineer Thomas Telford built the basins we see today, and their warehouses were stacked high with treasure from across the British Empire – marble, ivory, wine, spices and perfume. As late as the 1930s, St Katharine's was reckoned to hold the world's largest concentration of portable wealth.

These days, the warehouses have been turned into office blocks and the money is not in the cargoes, it's in the boats themselves. For children, a wander among the yachts and pleasure cruisers is a glorious glimpse into life afloat.

Boats in the pretty marina at St Katharine's Dock

The Lowdown

🌐 **Map ref** 12 H5
Address Tower Bridge Road, SE1; 020 7403 3761; *www.towerbridge.org.uk*

🚃 **Train** Fenchurch Street, London Bridge, Tower Gateway (DLR). **Tube** Tower Hill. **Bus stop** Tower Bridge Approach. **River bus** Tower Pier, St Katharine's Pier

🕑 **Open** Apr–Sep 10am–6:30pm; Oct–Mar 9:30am–6pm (last admission one hour earlier)

💷 **Price** £18–24, under 5s free; combined ticket with The Monument £26–36

👪 **Skipping the queue** Buy tickets online to avoid queuing

🚩 **Guided tours** Available for groups of 10 or more only (extra charge)

👫 **Age range** 5 plus

👫 **Activities** A kids' passport, from the ticket desk, has stickers to collect. Separate Explore Kit must be downloaded beforehand (also covers Tower of London, HMS *Belfast* and All Hallows by the Tower). School-holiday activities might include Victorian games and storytelling.

🕐 **Allow** 1 hour

♿ **Wheelchair access** Yes, via lifts and an alternative ramped route

🍽 **Eat and drink** *Picnic* Bubble Café (Blossom Square Kiosk, SE1 2JP) is right under the southern supports of the bridge, with terrace tables adjoining Potters Fields and the Thames. *Real meal* Café Rouge (50 St Katharine's Way, St Katharine's Dock, E1W 1AA; 020 7702 0195; *www.caferouge.co.uk*) is a chain French bistro set in a pretty spot beside St Katharine's Dock.

🛍 **Shop** At end of visit

🚻 **Toilets** In South Tower and Engine Rooms

The Lowdown

🌐 **Map ref** 12 H5
Address St Katharine's Way, E1W 1LA; 020 7488 0555; www. skdocks.co.uk

🚇 **Train** Fenchurch Street, Tower Gateway (DLR). **Tube** Tower Hill. **Bus stop** Tower Hill Approach, East Smithfield. **River bus** St Katharine's Pier, Tower Pier

🤾 **Activities** Fine food market on Fri outside Dickens Inn (10am–4pm). Check website for lock opening times – a good time to see boats enter and exit the dock.

👫 **Age range** All

⏱ **Allow** Up to 1 hour

♿ **Wheelchair access** Yes

☕ **Eat and drink** *Picnic* Capstans (*St Katharine's Way, E1W 1LD*) serves doorstep sandwiches, hot bites and more substantial dishes. *Real meal* Ping Pong (*Tower Bridge House, E1W 1BA*) sells tasty, reliable Chinese food.

🚻 **Toilets** Near Starbucks coffee shop (*Cloister Walk, E1W 1LA*)

Letting off steam
The Tower Hill/Minories playground (*see p123*) is reached via the underpass to Tower Hill tube station.

⑦ Whitechapel Gallery

Art on the edge
Little Miss Muffet is menaced by a malevolent tarantula. A cute teddy bear suffers an extremely grisly disembowelling. When commissioning artists to mastermind a new exhibition for children, Jake and Dinos Chapman may not seem like an obvious

Creating a masterpiece in one of the Whitechapel Gallery's workshops

choice. But the Whitechapel Gallery likes to push boundaries.

The gallery has been at the cutting edge of contemporary art since 1901, introducing the likes of Frida Kahlo, Jackson Pollock and Gilbert & George to British audiences. In 2009 a £13 million revamp doubled the exhibition space and added a dedicated children's studio on the top floor. The Chapman Brothers' 2010 summer show typified the Whitechapel's thought-provoking approach to art for kids.

The gallery offers free workshops and family days most weekends, and 1–2 day courses (cost varies), inspired and often led by artists. Available all the time is the Make It Yours art detective kit, loaded with scrapbook, stickers and drawing materials.

Letting off steam
Head past Aldgate tube station to find the playground overlooking the Tower of London (*see p123*).

The Lowdown

🌐 **Map ref** 12 H2
Address 77–82 Whitechapel High Street, E1 7QX; 020 7522 7888; www.whitechapelgallery.org

🚇 **Train** Liverpool Street, Tower Gateway (DLR). **Tube** Aldgate East. **Bus stop** Whitechapel High Street, route numbers 15, 25, 115, 135.

🕐 **Open** Tue–Sun 11am–6pm; Thu till 9pm

💲 **Price** Free; charge for special temporary exhibitions

👫 **Age range** 4 plus

🤾 **Activities** Free children's trail suits ages 4–12; regular weekend and school-holiday children's workshops (check website)

⏱ **Allow** 1 hour

♿ **Wheelchair access** Yes

☕ **Eat and drink** *Snacks* The gallery's café-bar claims to make London's best brownies. *Family treat* For something more upscale, try the Gallery Dining Room

🛍 **Shop** Selling art books and cards

🚻 **Toilets** Ground, basement and 2nd floor

St Paul's Cathedral and around

Left smouldering by the Great Fire of London in 1666, London's grandest church owes its modern-day magnificence to the great Renaissance architect Christopher Wren, who spent almost 40 years on his masterpiece. Best visited at the weekend, its most dramatic approach with children is on foot via the pedestrianized promenade from Millennium Bridge. Join a guided walk (free for under-12s) from the nearby City of London Information Centre, then climb the cathedral's famous dome and enjoy the fantastic views of the city's skyline.

The City and the East End

Museum of London
p134

Tower of London
p120

St Paul's Cathedral

The Millennium Bridge, linking the Tate Modern on Bankside with St Paul's Cathedral and the City

Places of Interest

SIGHTS

1. St Paul's Cathedral
2. Bank of England Museum
3. Dr Johnson's House
4. Guildhall Art Gallery

● **EAT AND DRINK**

1. Tea
2. The Café at St Paul's
3. Byron
4. Barbecoa
5. Chop'd
6. Tortilla
7. The Natural Kitchen
8. Ye Olde Cheshire Cheese
9. Hummus Bros
10. The Café Below

● **WHERE TO STAY**

1. Cheval Calico House

Mosaic of a crocodile at Nelson's tomb in St Paul's Cathedral, made by women prisoners at Woking Gaol in the 19th century

The Whispering Gallery in St Paul's Cathedral – a whisper against its walls is audible on the opposite side

The Lowdown

Train Blackfriars, Cannon Street, City Thameslink. **Tube** St Paul's, Mansion House. **Bus** Fleet Street/Cannon Street: route numbers 4, 11, 15, 23, 26, 76, 172; Threadneedle Street (for Bank of England): 8, 11, 23, 26, 242, 388; Cheapside (for Guildhall): 8 and 25. **River bus** Blackfriars Pier, weekday-only services between London Eye and Woolwich (0870 781 5049; www.thamesclippers.com); and Blackfriars Pier to Putney via Chelsea (01342 820605; www. thamesrivertaxi.com)

i **Visitor information** City of London Information Centre, St Paul's Churchyard, EC4M 8BX

Supermarkets M&S Simply Food, 3a One New Change, EC4M 9AF; Sainsbury's Local, 10 Paternoster Square, EC4M 7DX; Tesco Metro, 80b Cheapside, EC2V 6EE **Markets** Leadenhall Market (mostly fine food), 11am–4pm Mon–Fri; Leather Lane Market (North of Holborn Circus; mixed stalls), 9am–2:30pm Mon–Fri

Festivals London Maze history festival, Guildhall (Apr); City of London Festival, music and arts (Jun–Jul); Pearly Kings and Queens Harvest Festival, St Mary-le-Bow (Sep); The Lord Mayor's Show, procession from Mansion House and fireworks (2nd Sat in Nov); Christmas at St Paul's, carols and services (Dec)

Pharmacies Boots, 107 Cheapside, EC2V 6DN (7am–7pm weekdays; 9am–6pm Sat; 10am–4pm Sun). For 24-hour pharmacies, visit www. nhs.uk/servicedirectories

Nearest playground Fortune Street Park, Fortune Street, EC1 0RY (north of the Barbican)

A hands-on experience with a real gold ingot at the Bank of England Museum

① St Paul's Cathedral
Possibly the most spectacular church in Christendom

Boasting Britain's biggest bell, Europe's largest crypt and a dome weighing 64,000 tonnes, St Paul's is a superlative building. Its shadowy crypt is full of famous tombs, including those of the Duke of Wellington, Florence Nightingale and Admiral Nelson, but what children will adore is counting the steps to the Whispering Gallery, and the magical sound effects they can create there. The family audio guide keeps things fun, with cartoons, quizzes and nuggets of trivia designed to dazzle even grown-ups.

Wellington Monument

The Lowdown

- **Map ref** 11 D3
  Address The Chapterhouse, St Paul's Churchyard, EC4M 8AD; 020 7246 8350 or 020 7246 8357; www.stpauls.co.uk

- **Train** Cannon Street, Blackfriars. **Tube** St Paul's, Mansion House. **Bus stop** St Paul's Churchyard. **River bus** Blackfriars Pier

- **Open** 8:30am–4:30pm Mon–Sat (last admission 4pm); cathedral galleries 9:30am–4:15pm. Attending services is free, including Evensong, 5pm Tue–Sat and 3:15pm Sun

- **Price** £34–50, under 6s free

- **Skipping the queue** Buy tickets online beforehand – it's cheaper and allows use of the new fast-track entrance.

- **Guided tours** Free 90-minute tours four times daily, plus multimedia guide

- **Age range** 6 plus

- **Activities** Family multimedia guide (English only); or download self-guided children's tours before visiting.

- **Allow** Up to 2 hours

- **Wheelchair access** Yes, except for the Whispering, Stone and Golden galleries and the south entrance, which are reached via many steps.

- **Café** The café in the crypt (see opposite), plus the more formal restaurant alongside.

- **Shop** In the crypt, selling books and souvenirs

- **Toilets** Beside the café

Good family value?
Cheaper than Westminster Abbey – and a visit includes a free workout to reach one of the most spectacular views in London.

Key Features

The Dome It's as heavy as 50,000 elephants, so Wren cleverly designed a dome within a dome, to bear the weight. As it was built, he was hauled up in a basket twice a week to inspect it.

Old St Paul's The old cathedral, at 149 m (489 ft), was taller than the new one (111 m / 364 ft), as a model in the crypt shows.

① Golden Gallery Lying at the highest point of the dome, it's a pull up all those steps. It's worth the effort – visitors are rewarded with a spellbinding view across London at the top.

② Whispering Gallery The quirky acoustics inside the spectacular dome throw a whisper all the way around the walkway, making this an atmospheric echo chamber kids will love.

Oculus This exciting multimedia show, in the former Treasury in the crypt, brings the cathedral's 1,400 years of history to life.

Florence Nightingale's Tomb

Oculus

Florence Nightingale's Tomb The hospital reformer first came to prominence as a nurse during the Crimean War (1853–6). She was the first woman to receive the Order of Merit.

Wellington Monument This tribute to one of Britain's most famous soldiers is in the North Aisle. He died in 1852 – his tomb is in the crypt.

Nelson's Tomb Buried in a coffin hollowed out of the mast of a defeated French flagship, Horatio Nelson gets star billing in the centre of the crypt. Look for seafaring symbols in the mosaic floor.

A quiet spot under the shade of the trees in the gardens at St Paul's Cathedral

Letting off steam

The cathedral's churchyard has small lawns to loll on, or there are the **Festival Gardens** right next door, with a sunken lawn, cooling wall fountain and a great view back to the Dome. Alternatively, how about a romp on the panoramic rooftop of **One New Change** (www.onenewchange.com), the sleek new shopping centre just east of the cathedral? Six floors high, it claims to be London's loftiest public terrace, and there's a café, too.

Eat and drink

Picnic: under £20; Snacks: £20–40; Real meal: £40–60; Family treat: £60 or more (based on a family of four)

PICNIC Tea (1 Paternoster Square, EC4M 7DX; 020 7248 6606) has designer decor and designer brews, along with organic savouries to take away – perhaps into neighbouring Paternoster Square, whose stone benches are broad enough for a full family picnic.
SNACKS Located in the crypt of the cathedral, **The Café at St Paul's** (9am–5pm, Sun noon–4pm), is open to all and specializes in classic British food. Pick a ploughman's lunch from the "Barrow in the Crypt", with ingredients sourced from Borough Market (see p150).
REAL MEAL Lots of options in the One New Change centre, including **Byron** (17 Upper Cheapside Passage, EC2V 6AG; 020 7246 2580; www.byronhamburgers.com). Serving classy burgers (and knickerbocker glories!), Byron has a dedicated children's menu that includes all the usual favourites.
FAMILY TREAT Barbecoa (20 New Change Passage, EC4M 9AG; 020 3005 8555; www.barbecoa.com; noon–11pm daily) is the hot ticket here, co-owned by celebrity chef Jamie Oliver and majoring in chargrilled meats. There are seafood starters and fish of the day. There is no children's menu but the chef will happily adapt dishes to suit children's tastes.

Find out more

DIGITAL Fight alongside Lord Nelson in the Trafalgar Origins game: www.channel4.com/play-win/trafalgar-origins. Family trails are available to download from the St Paul's website; www.stpauls.co.uk
FILM The children's classic *Mary Poppins* has lovely dreamlike sequences featuring St Paul's, including the "Feed the Birds" scene on the cathedral's steps.

Next stop. . .

ST MARY-LE-BOW CHURCH
Walk along to St Mary-le-Bow church (Cheapside, EC2V 6AU), another Christopher Wren gem, with an extravagant tower and a golden dragon atop its steeple. It's said you must be born within the sound of Bow Bells to be a true Cockney. There's a very cosy café in the crypt (see p133).
GUIDED WALKS AND TOURS
Opposite St Paul's, the City Information Centre (Cannon St, EC4M 8BX) is the starting point for daily walks exploring the oldest part of London: discover more Wren churches or learn about Samuel Pepys (adults £6, under-12s free).

The "feed the birds" scene from the 1964 film Mary Poppins, set outside St Paul's

② Bank of England Museum

Crack a safe, grab some gold

Walking into the grand hall of this museum is one of the more surprising experiences in London. There are kids everywhere: piloting hot-air balloons, designing bank notes, cracking safes. This playroom approach strives to make simple economics palatable to young minds – never an easy task.

The hot-air balloon works as an effective metaphor for the nation's finances and kids can get their hands on the controls. Nearby, there's a safe to unlock with the help of quiz answers gathered from around the room.

The rest of the museum is more sober and includes a £1 million note and a gold ingot worth more than £300,000, which children can try their hand at lifting. Look out for the showcase featuring Ratty and

The Sir John Soane-designed building housing the Bank of England Museum

Mole, creations of *Wind in the Willows* author Kenneth Grahame (1859–1932), who was secretary to the bank from 1879 to 1908.

Letting off steam

The skyscrapers of the **Broadgate Centre** (*Eldon Street, EC2M 2QT*) enclose traffic-free squares, including grassy **Exchange Square**, with its train-set view down into Liverpool Street Station, and **Broadgate Circle**, whose ice rink is open daily Oct–Jan (*www.broadgateinfo.net*).

③ Dr Johnson's House

The home of an English eccentric

He collected orange peel, wore the same clothes for weeks, and liked to start every journey with the same foot. But the eccentric Samuel Johnson was a London legend, and

Dressing up in period costume in Dr Johnson's House

The Lowdown

- 🌐 **Map ref** 12 E3
  Address Threadneedle Street, EC2R 8AH; 020 7601 5545; *www.bankofengland.co.uk/museum*
- 🚃 **Train** Cannon Street or Bank (DLR). **Tube** Bank. **Bus stop** Threadneedle Street
- 🕐 **Open** Weekdays only 10am–5pm (last admission 4:45pm)
- 💲 **Price** Free
- 👤 **Skipping the queue** Queues rare
- 🚩 **Guided tours** None, but free audio tour
- 👫 **Age range** 5 plus
- 🏃 **Activities** Five different children's trails, graded from pre-school to ages 15–17. School holiday events.
- ⏱ **Allow** 1 hour
- ♿ **Wheelchair access** Yes, via ramps, please call in advance
- 🍴 **Eat and drink** *Snacks* Chop'd (*1–3 Leadenhall Market, EC3V 1LR; 0207 626 3706; www.chopd.co.uk; 7am–3pm Mon–Fri*) offers all-natural healthy food. *Real meal* Tortilla (*28 Leadenhall Market, EC3V 1LR; 0207 929 7837; www.tortilla.co.uk; 11:45am–7pm Mon–Fri*) does finger-licking Mexican fast food.
- 🛍 **Shop** Souvenirs and gifts
- 🚻 **Toilets** At the rear of museum

The Lowdown

- 🌐 **Map ref** 11 B3
  Address 17 Gough Square, EC4A 3DE; 020 7353 3745; *www.drjohnsonshouse.org*
- 🚇 **Tube** Chancery Lane.
  Bus stop Fleet Street
- 🕐 **Open** Mon–Sat 11am–5:30pm; Oct–Apr till 5pm
- 💲 **Price** £10–18
- 👤 **Skipping the queue** Queues rare
- 🚩 **Guided tours** None; Johnson's London walks, 1st Wed of the month (*see website*)
- 👫 **Age range** 9 plus
- 🏃 **Activities** Free kids' guide. Occasional concerts and jazz evenings. Activities and trails are organised during school holidays
- ⏱ **Allow** Up to 1 hour
- ♿ **Wheelchair access** No, there are some unavoidable steps.
- 🍴 **Eat and drink** *Picnic* The Natural Kitchen (*15–17 New Street Square, EC4A 3AP; 0203 012 2123; www.thenaturalkitchen.com; 8am–10pm Mon–Fri*) has a fresh feel to its take-away food. *Real meal* Ye Olde Cheshire Cheese (*145 Fleet Street, EC4A 2BU; 020 7353 6170*) is a 17th-century pub full of character.
- 🛍 **Shop** Selling books, booklets, posters and souvenirs
- 🚻 **Toilets** Basement

the great and the good gathered at his house off Fleet Street to enjoy his witty conversation. Today, Dr Johnson is remembered mainly for his English dictionary, compiled here in the 1750s, with a team of scribes who copied literary snippets to illustrate 42,000 definitions. It took nine years to write, during which the debt-ridden Johnson once had to barricade the door with his bed to fend off bailiffs.

Johnson's jokes will fly over the heads of most children, but there is a film telling his story and a dressing-up rack of Georgian frockcoats to try on. Point out the spiked window above the door, to deter burglars from smuggling boy accomplices inside; and challenge kids to track down Hodge, Johnson's spoilt cat. Clue: he's out on the tiles.

Letting off steam

Head west across Fetter Lane to **Lincoln's Inn Fields** (WC2A) with its picnic-perfect lawns and public tennis courts (see p94).

④ Guildhall Art Gallery

Where gladiators fought

Dragons, Dick Whittington, Britain's biggest painting and a ruined Roman amphitheatre – these are just some of the unlikely attractions at the Guildhall Gallery. It stands beside the 15th-century Guildhall, seat of City government since medieval times, whose courtyard has a statue of Dick Whittington, every child's favourite Lord Mayor. The yard is menaced on all sides by dragons, the City's armorial emblem – ideal for a game of I-Spy.

The gallery itself is dominated by John Singleton Copley's eye-popping painting *The Siege of Gibraltar* (1791) – so big that it occupies two floors. Youngsters may prefer the Undercroft Galleries downstairs, lined with sentimental Victorian pictures of children, including John Everett Millais' funny portraits of his daughter dozing off in church.

The main reason to come here, though, lurks in a dark cavern in the basement – the ruins of London's 2,000-year-old Roman amphitheatre, stumbled upon by archaeologists in 1988. In Roman times, up to 6,000 people sat here to watch bloody animal fights, public executions and gladiatorial combat – to the death. Scant foundations survive, but children won't notice that, because spotlights and sound effects do a brilliant job of bringing the arena to life. Stride in through the eastern entrance, as gladiators once did long ago, past the pens used to hold wild beasts, and listen to the deafening roar of the crowd.

The Lowdown

🌐 **Map ref** 12 E2
Address Guildhall Yard, Gresham Street, EC2V 5AE; 020 7332 3700; www.guildhall-art-gallery.org.uk

🚇 **Tube** St Paul's, Bank, Moorgate. **Bus stop** Cheapside

🕐 **Open** 10am–5pm Mon–Sat; noon–4pm Sun (last admission 30 minutes earlier)

💷 **Price** £5–10, under 16s free

🚶 **Skipping the queue** Queues rare; go after 3:30pm (or any time Fri) for free admission

👫 **Guided tours** Fri pm only (free)

👫 **Age range** 5 plus

👫 **Activities** Sketching tables in the Undercroft Galleries

⏱ **Allow** Up to 1 hour

♿ **Wheelchair access** Yes

🍽 **Eat and drink** *Snacks* Hummus Bros (128 Cheapside, EC2V 6BT; 020 7726 8011; www.hbros.co.uk; 11am–4pm Mon–Fri) offers hummus and pitta breads with tasty toppings. *Real meal* The Café Below (Cheapside, EC2V 6AU; 020 7329 0789; www.cafebelow.co.uk; 7:30am–9pm Mon–Fri) serves imaginative, rustic European dishes in the snug 1,000-year-old crypt of St Mary-le-Bow Church.

🛍 **Shop** Near reception

🚻 **Toilets** Floor C by cloakroom

Letting off steam

St Mary Aldermanbury Garden (EC2 2EJ), behind the Guildhall, has picnic benches and a majestic bust of William Shakespeare. The master playwright's contemporaries, John Hemynge and Henry Condell, are commemorated in the gardens; it is to them that we owe the printing of Shakespeare's *First Folio* of work.

The Siege of Gibraltar, *one of the UK's biggest paintings, at the Guildhall Art Gallery*

Picnic under £20; Snacks £20–40; Real meal £40–60; Family treat £60 or more (based on a family of four)

Museum of London and around

A £20 million revamp has made the Museum of London a supremely welcoming place for families, from the pink-shirted "hosts" to the hands-on exhibits that animate London's story. Arrive on foot along Aldersgate Street from St Paul's tube station, and take the escalator on the right-hand pavement. Weekends are the prime time to visit, when there are fewer school parties, free family events on Sundays and children's films every Saturday at the nearby Barbican. To combine the museum with Old Spitalfields Market, take the Hammersmith & City line from Barbican to Aldgate East.

The City and the East End

Prisoners' elegant graffiti in an 18th-century cell at the Museum of London

Built in 1757, the Lord Mayor's state coach in the Museum of London is beautifully crafted and still used for the Lord Mayor's Parade

Places of Interest

SIGHTS
①	Museum of London
②	The Barbican
③	Old Spitalfields Market
④	Museum of the Order of
	St John

🔴 EAT AND DRINK
1	Carluccio's
2	Farm
3	Barbican Foodhall

4	Malmaison Brasserie
5	Patisserie Valerie
6	The Luxe
7	Benugo
8	Dose
*See also The Museum of London
(pp137) and the Barbican (p138)*

🔴 PLACES TO STAY
1	Market View by Bridge Street
2	MiNC Eagle Court

The Lowdown

🚗 **Train** Moorgate (5-minute walk), Liverpool Street, Farringdon (10-minute walk); Shoreditch High Street (for Spitalfields Market). **Tube** Barbican, Moorgate, St Paul's. **Bus** Moorgate; route numbers 4, 56; London Wall: 100; Barbican tube station: 153; King Edward Street: 8, 25, 242, 521

ℹ️ **Visitor information** *See pp128–29*

🛒 **Supermarkets** Waitrose, 6L Cherry Tree Walk, EC1Y 8NX. Marks & Spencer, 70 Finsbury Pavement, EC2A 1SA
Markets Leather Lane Market (mixed stalls), 9am–2:30pm Mon–Fri. Broadgate Farmers' Market, 2nd and 4th Thu of the month. Petticoat Lane Market (clothing), Middlesex Street, E1, 10am–2:30pm Mon–Fri; 9am–2pm Sun. Spitalfields Market (antiques, fashion and art), 10am–4pm Thu–Fri; 9am–5pm Sun

🎪 **Festivals** East Festival, arts (Mar). Blaze Festival, music and dance, Barbican Centre (Jun–Jul). City of London Festival, music and arts (Jun–Jul). Story of London Festival, history (Oct). London Children's Film Festival, Barbican Centre (Nov); Spitalfields Music Festivals (Jun–Jul; Dec–Jan)

➕ **Pharmacies** Portman's Pharmacy, Cherry Tree Walk, EC1Y 8NX (9am–6:30pm Mon–Fri; 9am–5pm Sat). For 24-hour pharmacies, visit *www.nhs.uk/servicedirectories*.

🏞️ **Nearest playgrounds** Christ Church play area (Commercial Street, E1 6LY); Fortune Street Park (Fortune Street, EC1Y 8)

Face to face with a goat at the popular Spitalfields City Farm

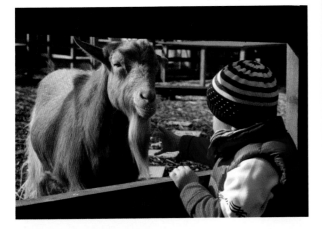

① Museum of London
Don't touch? Don't be so old-fashioned!

It's not easy to bring 450,000 years of history to life for children, but the Museum of London does just that, using a mix of interactive gadgetry and eye-catching presentation. The upstairs rooms are arranged chronologically and are packed with prehistoric skulls and Roman treasures, while the Galleries of Modern London resemble a series of spectacular stage-sets – including a shadowy Georgian prison cell and a Victorian high street. The excellent activity trails and backpacks encourage kids to explore.

Bronze age shield and helmet c.350–50 BC

Key Features

① **Victorian Walk** Window-shop along a lively Victorian high street, complete with toy shop, pub, bank and barber's shop. The fixtures and fittings are all original.

② **Wellclose Prison Cell** Enter the dark, claustrophobic cell from a 1750 debtors' prison, its walls scratched with the names of desperate inmates and echoing with their pleas for mercy.

③ **Archaeology in Action** Get to grips with ancient pottery and other precious booty found in London at the artifact-handling sessions held here most days.

Entrance

Entrance level History of London from 450,000 BC to the 1660s: Roman London; Medieval London; War, Plague and Fire

Lower Galleries History of London from 1670s to Today: Expanding City; Victorian Walk; People's City; Modern London

④ **Evacuees' Trunks** Lift the lids to read real-life letters from schoolchildren on the eve of World War II – and discover what they packed for their flight from London.

⑤ **Georgian Pleasure Gardens** Explore this re-creation of an 18th-century park, with its harlequins, acrobats and elegant ladies in fancy hats. Children were expected to behave like miniature adults.

⑥ **Bill and Ben** Find out what children's TV was like in the 1950s, by exploring the wall of toys and TV screens in the museum's new Playtime Zone.

The Lowdown

🌐 **Map ref** 11 D2
Address 150 London Wall, EC2Y 5HN; 020 7001 9844; www.museumoflondon.org.uk

🚇 **Tube** Barbican, Moorgate, St Paul's. **Bus stop** Moorgate Street, Barbican Station, London Wall

🕐 **Open** 10am–6pm daily

💲 **Price** Free

👫 **Skipping the queue** Grab a ticket on arrival for the guided tours – they are free, but numbers are limited

🚩 **Guided tours** Free tours of specific galleries four times a day; plus guided walks around the City monthly

👫 **Age range** 4 plus

🎨 **Activities** Free activity sheets from welcome desk for ages 4–7 and 7–11, plus backpacks themed on Roman and Medieval London. Computer quizzes and costumes to try on are distributed throughout the galleries. There are also object-handling sessions most days, plus free family events every Sun and in school holidays.

⏱ **Allow** At least 2 hours

♿ **Wheelchair access** Yes

🍴 **Cafés** The museum's Benugo café sells good sandwiches and salads, and has a kids' lunch deal

and high-chairs. The Sackler Hall café does lighter bites. Plus, there's an indoor picnic area in the Clore Learning Centre, across the forecourt.

🛍 **Shop** In the entrance lobby, selling books, cards and posters related to the exhibitions

🚻 **Toilets** Behind lobby area

Good family value?
Absolutely crawling with children, and with all the hands-on activities and trails, it's easy to see why.

Nursery Garden at the Museum of London – one of two small gardens

Letting off steam

The nearest playground is 10 to 15 minutes away, at Forts are at Rotunda Gardens (5-minute walk) and Fortune Street (10–15 minute walk). **Postman's Park** is much closer, just across Aldersgate Street beside St Botolph's church. It doesn't have climbing apparatus, but there is a small spread of lawns and benches, plus the moving George Frederic Watts Memorial, which honours ordinary folk who sacrificed their lives saving others. Each is remembered on a painted tile, and there are several poignant tales of childhood bravery to discover.

Eat and drink

Picnic: under £20; Snacks: £20–40; Real meal: £40–60; Family treat: £60 or more (based on a family of four)

PICNIC Carluccio's *(12 West Smithfield, EC1A 9JR; 020 7329 5904; www.carluccios.com/caffes/smithfield)*, just up the road, beside the splendid Victorian halls of Smithfield meat market, offers a generous spread of deli-style delights. Opposite, the shady benches of West Smithfield Park make ideal picnic territory. Postman's Park (see left) is also a good picnic spot.

The Sackler Hall coffee shop in the Museum of London.

SNACKS Head towards Smithfield Market, where **Farm** *(91 Cowcross Street, EC1M 6BH; 0207 253 2142; www.farmcollective.com; weekdays only 7am–3:30pm)* offers delicious, carefully sourced pies and fishcakes at reasonable prices, served by friendly and efficient staff.

REAL MEAL The **Barbican Foodhall** *(Barbican Centre, Silk Street, EC2Y 8DS; www.barbican. org.uk/restaurants-bars; 9am–8:30pm, from 11am–8pm Sun)* serves up a variety of no-nonsense main courses and salads in its buffet overlooking the arts centre's courtyard. There are even a few board games available to keep the kids entertained.

FAMILY TREAT The plush burgundy-and-black **Malmaison Brasserie** *(18–21 Charterhouse Square, EC1M 6AH; 020 7012 3700; www.malmaison.com; noon–2:30pm, 6pm–10:15pm)* has a serious commitment to sourcing seasonal and local ingredients. It is also a very family-friendly place, offering smaller portions for children on request.

Find out more

DIGITAL The museum's website has history-themed games and challenges for kids: survive life as a medieval apprentice, or help aliens dig up household objects from the past. Lots more at *www. museumoflondon.org.uk/Explore-online/Games/*. Play "Roman snakes and ladders", and discover more about real historic artifacts on the way, at *http://romans.tulliehouse. co.uk/flash/snakes/index.htm*.

Next stop...

DENNIS SEVERS' HOUSE After breezing through London's entire history in half a day, try a different kind of museum: Dennis Severs' House *(Sun noon–4pm, Mon 6–9pm: bookings required for eve session; 18 Folgate Street, E1 6BX; www.dennissevershouse.co.uk)* is a unique time capsule created by a Canadian designer. He furnished his home as a series of still-life tableaus spanning two centuries, as though the occupants have just stepped outside. It's not for younger children, though.

② The Barbican

Cartoons and crazy art

If you're looking for somewhere to lose the children, the Barbican might just be it. With its innumerable entrances and tangles of stairways and courtyards, Europe's biggest multi-arts complex is a little difficult to navigate. Never fear – head for the main entrance round the back on Silk Street, which curves down into the heart of things.

Inside is a vast black-and-orange bunker packing in two theatres, two art galleries, a music and dance space, a library, three restaurants and three cinemas.

Bustling Old Spitalfields Market filled with a variety of stalls

Ensconced in the Saturday Film Club at the Barbican

There is always something happening and it's often for kids, from the Family Film Club every Saturday morning to a fistful of annual festivals, including the London Children's Film Festival in November and Animate the World in May. The Curve Gallery on Level 0 showcases the kind of conceptual art that's guaranteed to excite the imagination of children, and the library on Level 2 also has a great children's section.

Check the website to find out what's on, or just drop in and enjoy the food hall, overlooking an urban lake with lily-pads and a waterfall.

Letting off steam

Walk north along Whitecross Street to **Fortune Street Park** (see p136), where swings and scrambling nets will keep the kids happy.

③ Old Spitalfields Market

London's liveliest and coolest market place

The first market at "Spittle Fields" was licensed to sell flesh, fowl and roots by King Charles I in 1638, but the area's wholesale green-grocers outgrew the site in 1991, paving the way for an inventive community of craftspeople and designers to move in.

Today, Spitalfields Market is cutting-edge cool and on a busy Sunday up to 1,000 traders specializing in vintage fashion, bespoke jewellery and gifts set up stalls. The vibe is youthful and positive – a winner with fashion-conscious kids. Stalls operate every day except Monday and Saturday, but Sunday is when things really get going.

Don't miss a browse among the offbeat boutiques that have popped up in adjoining streets, too – they include Queen's (111b Commercial Street, E1 6BG), for girly accessories wrapped in pink tissue and fairydust; and Wood 'n' Things (57 Brushfield Street, E1 6AA), for high-quality toys and dolls. The market's "food village" serves aromatic dishes from the world over, while a fine foods market runs on Thursday, Friday and Sunday in nearby Crispin Place.

Just south of Old Spitalfields, along Middlesex Street, lies historic Petticoat Lane Market, a more down-to-earth affair where traders have been shouting their wares since the 1750s – mostly street clothing, leather goods and shoes.

The Lowdown

- 🌐 **Map ref** 11 D1
  Address Silk Street, EC2Y 8DS; 020 7638 4141, Box Office 020 7638 8891; www.barbican.org.uk

- 🚃 **Train** Liverpool Street, Farringdon, Blackfriars. **Tube** Barbican. **Bus stop** Barbican tube station, London Wall

- 🕐 **Open** 9am–11pm Mon–Sat; noon–11pm Sun

- 💲 **Price** Shows and exhibitions individually priced. Access to Curve Gallery, library, restaurants and courtyard is free

- 🎟 **Skipping the queue** Online booking available for most events

- 🚩 **Guided tours** Architecture tours Wed, Sat and Sun; £28

- 👫 **Age range** All

- 🧍 **Activities** Family Film Club (Sat 10:30am) lays on art activities

before the film: £5 (£3 members, sign up for free online). Special teenager tickets for London Symphony Orchestra concerts and talks. Do Something Different weekends (Mar & Jul) offer activities for all. Check website for full programme

- ♿ **Wheelchair access** Yes, via Silk Street entrance

- 🍴 **Eat and drink** *Snacks* Barbican Foodhall (see p137) offers deli fare, which can be eaten on its courtyard tables. *Family treat* The Barbican Lounge (Level 1) and Searcy's (Level 2) are more formal.

- 🛍 **Shops** Foyer Shop (Level G) selling CDs and books; Art Gallery Shop (Level 3) selling souvenir books and posters

- 🚻 **Toilets** On most levels

The Lowdown

🌐 **Map ref** 12 G1

Address 105a Commercial Street, E1 6BG; 020 7375 2963; www.visitspitalfields.com

🚃 **Train** Liverpool Street. **Tube** Liverpool Street, Aldgate East. **Bus stop** Commercial Street, Bishopsgate

🕐 **Open** Spitalfields: 10am–4pm Tue–Fri; 9am–5pm Sun; shops: 11am–7pm daily. Petticoat Lane: 10am–2:30pm Mon–Fri; 9am–2pm Sun

🅿 **Price** Free

🧍 **Age range** All

🧍 **Activities** Spitalfields Music Festival, biannually in Jun–Jul and Dec–Jan (www.spitalfieldsmusic.org.uk)

♿ **Wheelchair access** Yes, the market is accessible but may be difficult to navigate if busy.

☕ **Eat and drink** Snacks Patisserie Valerie (37 Brushfield Street, E1 6AA) offers salads, wraps and gorgeous homemade Italian ice cream. Real meal The Luxe (109 Commercial Street, E1 6BG) serves brilliant brunches.

🚻 **Toilets** In the market and surrounding restaurants and cafés

Letting off steam

There is a small play area beside Christ Church, opposite the market on Commercial Street. Alternatively, head east to Buxton Street, where kids can commune with Bayleaf the donkey, Bentley the goat and friends at **Spitalfields City Farm** (closed Mon; admission free; Buxton Street, E1 5AR; www.spitalfieldscityfarm.org).

Costumed guide at the Museum of the Order of St John

④ Museum of the Order of St John

From nurses to knights

There's something distinctly magical about visiting the historic home of real knights in the heart of London. The building certainly looks the part – built in 1504, it is a remnant of the priory of the Knights Hospitaller, the medieval crusaders who went from helping sick pilgrims in Jerusalem to fighting Saladin.

The museum uses TV screens, armour and artifacts to relay its stirring story of chivalric sacrifice. A separate gallery is devoted to the St John's Ambulance movement, the 20th-century reincarnation of the order, still based here. It may be fairly conventional, but the museum succeeds in bringing history to life.

Letting off steam

The peaceful lawns at **Rotunda Gardens** (West Smithfield, EC1A 9BD) belie its grisly past as an execution site. Those executed include the Scottish knight William Wallace (1305); today there is a jolly new playground.

The Lowdown

🌐 **Map ref** 11 C1

Address St John's Gate, St John's Lane, EC1M 4DA; 0207 324 4005; www.museumstjohn.org.uk

🚃 **Train** Farringdon. **Tube** Farringdon. **Bus stop** Farringdon Road, Clerkenwell Road

🕐 **Open** 10am–5pm Mon–Fri; 10am–5pm Sat

🅿 **Price** Free (optional donation £5)

🎫 **Guided tours** 11am and 2:30pm (free) Tue, Fri and Sat

🧍 **Age range** 8 plus

🧍 **Activities** Challenge Trail (ages 6–11) plus sticker trail for younger kids (free); actor-led interpretation sessions; drop-in craft activities, 3rd Sat of the month, plus school-holiday workshops.

♿ **Wheelchair access** Main galleries are accessible, but crypt and upper floor are reached via stairs.

☕ **Eat and drink** Picnic Benugo (116 St John Street, EC1V 4JS; 020 7253 3499; www.benugo.com) does made-to-order sandwiches and salads for eating in or out. Snacks Dose (70 Long Acre, EC1A 9EJ; 020 7600 0382; www.dose-espresso.com) serves up great salads, homemade bread and cakes.

🛍 **Shop** A small gift shop

🚻 **Toilets** Ground floor

Southwark
and the South Bank

The South Bank first blossomed as an arts district in 1951, when it was chosen as the focal point for the Festival of Britain. However, it took another 50 years, and the opening of the London Eye, for the area to finally become a prime visitor destination. Today, it offers an irresistible array of family-friendly attractions, from Shakespeare's Globe and Tate Modern to the National Theatre and IMAX Cinema.

Bloomsbury and
Regent's Park

The City and
the East End

Westminster
and the
West End **Southwark and
the South Bank**

Kensington,
Chelsea and
Battersea

Highlights

The *Golden Hinde*
Every child loves a pirate fancy-dress party – and there's no more authentic place to enjoy one than aboard Sir Francis Drake's gorgeous treasure galleon. Ahoy, matey *(see p150)*!

Borough Market
The stalls of this bustling market allow brave gastronomes to explore many of the world's cuisines. Pick up a picnic, then head for the tables outside Southwark Cathedral *(see p150)*.

Imperial War Museum
Despite the planes, tanks and guns, what kids will remember

most about this museum are the personal stories, and the mud and madness of its World War I Trench Experience *(see p166)*.

River Thames RIB-boat tour
When sightseeing starts to feel a little sedate, jump aboard this speedboat for a spray-drenched blast past the London Eye and other riverside sights *(see p161)*.

The Old Operating Theatre
On Saturday afternoons, limbs are swiftly lopped off in a bloodcurdling demonstration of Victorian surgery at this museum. Needless to say, most children love it *(see p151)*.

Left *Fun and frolics on the Golden Hinde – youngsters come face to face with a buccaneer during a "Pirate Days" activity session* **Above** *Marine life at the Sea Life London Aquarium*

The Best of
Southwark & the South Bank

For all its imposing parks and squares, London never really had one long, traffic-free promenade – until the 21st-century transformation of the South Bank. A walkway now stretches virtually unbroken along the Thames from Tower Bridge to the London Eye, offering a terrific pleasure trail for families. Runners rush, seagulls soar, speedboats skim… and when the tide goes out, there's even a beach.

A South Bank stroll

Start at Tower Hill Tube station, and cross Tower Bridge to pick up The Queen's Walk past the imposing bulk of **HMS Belfast** (see pp154–5). From here, the City's skyline is visible across the water. At London Bridge, turn left and take the stairs down beside **Southwark Cathedral** (see p150), where Borough Market (see p150) may be in full swing (Thu–Sat) – a great place to gather a picnic for later.

Return to the river, where you'll soon pass a brace of brilliant attractions, **Shakespeare's Globe** (see pp146–7) and **Tate Modern** (see p148), both very welcoming for families. Beyond Blackfriars Bridge, break out your lunch among the craft studios and cafés of **Gabriel's**

Wharf (see p163), then press on past the **Southbank Centre** (see p164) to the **London Eye** (see pp160–61), its glass capsules guaranteed to elicit gasps from all. Cross Westminster Bridge to the Tube station and Big Ben – a fitting finale to a River Thames walk.

Dressing-up time

Who do you want to be today? A sea captain or a pirate? Perhaps a fighter pilot or a star of the Elizabethan stage? A clutch of museums along the South Bank offer children the chance to act the part. **Shakespeare's Globe** (see pp146–7) has sound booths where kids can play Juliet or King Lear, and there are occasional drama workshops during matinee performances.

Below The naval gunship HMS Belfast on the Thames

Younger kids may prefer the **Golden Hinde** (see p150), a replica of Sir Francis Drake's globetrotting Tudor galleon, which holds regular pirate sleepovers for families.

Nearby, the **Britain at War Experience** (see p156) recalls life on the home front during World War II, with a well-stocked dressing-up corner and a mattress under a table in case of an air-raid. **HMS Belfast** (see pp154–5) is perhaps the most atmospheric of all, evoking life on a battleship with the help of a lively children's audioguide and the chance to be a pint-sized admiral.

The world's a stage

At the southern end of Waterloo Bridge is a true village for the arts, from classical music to comedy, cinema to circus. There is always plenty going on, and families are well catered for, especially during the summer festival season. The highlight is the three-month Watch This Space Festival at the **National Theatre** (see p162), which transforms the riverside into an all-singing, all-dancing performance space, complete with a dedicated children's programme.

Virtually next door, the **Southbank Centre's** (see p164) summer celebration focuses on the Udderbelly pop-up theatre, housed in an upside-down purple cow. The British Film Festival follows in October, at the nearby **BFI** (see pp162–3) – and at any time of year, it offers free film and TV in its Mediatheque suite, plus monthly film-making workshops for kids at the BFI IMAX, Britain's largest cinema screen.

In a weekend

The essential Southwark weekend begins on Saturday morning, gathering cosmopolitan edibles from Borough Market (see p150). Kids love soaking up the sounds, smells and free samples, and Monmouth coffee shop (2 Park Street, SE1 9AB) does all-you-can-eat bread and jam for £3, perfect for elevenses. Afterwards, sign up for a story-filled tour at **Shakespeare's Globe** (see pp146–7) – family fundays are on the second weekend of every month. Picnic by the river, then head off to **Tate Modern** (see p148) for the art trails.

On Sunday, head for the dark side, getting up early to beat the queue at the **London Dungeon** (see p156). Afterwards, if you can stomach it, the nearby George Inn (see p147), an atmospheric old coaching tavern, serves Sunday roast. Then it's off to view the spooky potions and pickled parts at the **Old Operating Theatre** (see p151), which has a herb-handling session at 2pm.

Shakespeare's Globe and around

The Globe is a genuine time-travel experience for children, set in a thatched theatre straight from a picture book. River bus services dock at Bankside Pier, opposite the gates. The theatre is just one of several attractions on the South Bank, so book ahead for the auditorium tour, then build the day around it. Families can happily spend a full day on museum-going, pavement-dining and people-watching – while barely encountering a single car.

Southwark and the South Bank

Shakespeare's Globe

London Eye p158

HMS *Belfast* p152

Southwark Cathedral, the oldest cathedral in London, dating from the 7th century

The open-roofed Shakespeare's Globe theatre – a lively experience for all

The Lowdown

🚗 **Train** Blackfriars and London Bridge stations are about a 10-minute walk away; Cannon Street, about 15 minutes away.
Tube London Bridge, Mansion House, Cannon Street.
Bus Southwark Bridge Road: route number 344; Southwark Street: RV1, 381; London Bridge: 17, 21, 35, 40, 43, 47, 133, 141, 149, 343, 521.
River bus Bankside Pier, en route from Westminster to St Katherine's Dock (020 7936 2033; www.crownriver.com); and from London Eye to Greenwich (020 7001 2222; www.thamesclippers.com). The Tate to Tate Boat (020 7887 8888; www.tate.org.uk/tatetotate) shuttles between Tate Britain and Tate Modern during gallery opening hours.

ℹ️ **Visitor information** City of London Information Centre (see pp128–9)

🍴 **Supermarket** Marks & Spencer Simply Food, Bankside, 90 Southwark St, SE1 0HX; open daily
Market Borough Market, 8 Southwark St, SE1 1TL, www.boroughmarket.org.uk (fine foods), 11am–5pm Thu, noon–6pm Fri, 8am–5pm Sat

🎊 **Festivals** Shakespeare's Birthday festivities, the Globe (Apr); Sam's Day, the Globe (Jun); Coin Street Festival, Bernie Spain Gardens (Jun–Jul); The Mayor's Thames Festival (Sep); Bankside Winter Festival (Dec)

➕ **Pharmacies** Boots, 8–11 Hays Galleria, SE1 2HD; 020 7407 4276 (7:45am–6:15pm Mon–Fri). For 24-hour pharmacies, visit www.nhs.uk/servicedirectories

🛝 **Nearest playground** Little Dorrit Park (SE1); Mint Street Adventure Playground (see p146; www.mintstreet.org.uk)

Rive

Blackfriars Bridge

Oxo Tower

THE   QUEEN'S   WALK   THE   QU

BERNIE SPAIN GARDENS

Banksid Galler

Gabriel's Wharf

BARGEHOUSE STREET   UPPER GROUND

BLACKFRIARS

HOPTON STREET

UPPER GROUND

BROADWALL

DUCHY ST

RENNIE STREET

STAMFORD STREET

ROAD

PARIS GARDEN

BURRELL

HATFIELDS

CHANCEL ST

BEAR LANE

MEYMOTT ST

DOLBEN ST

GAMBIA

JOAN

STREET

Southwark

UNION   ST

THE CUT

BLACKFRIARS ROAD

NELSON SQUARE GARDENS

NELSON SQUARE

UFFORD ST

SURREY ROW

POCOCK STREET

0 metres   100
0 yards   100

Testing the torture equipment at the Clink Prison Museum

Tasting delicious Spanish food at Brindisa, Borough Market

Places of Interest

SIGHTS

1. Shakespeare's Globe
2. Tate Modern
3. Clink Prison Museum
4. The *Golden Hinde*
5. Southwark Cathedral
6. The Old Operating Theatre

● EAT AND DRINK

1. Borough Market
2. Café 2
3. Swan at the Globe
4. OXO Tower Brasserie
5. Amano
6. Gourmet Burger Kitchen
7. Caffè Nero
8. Fish!
9. De Gustibus
10. The George Inn

See also Shakespeare's Globe (p147), Tate Modern (p148) and Southwark Cathedral (p151)

● WHERE TO STAY

1. All Seasons Southwark Rose
2. London Bridge

Examining primitive surgical equipment at the Old Operating Theatre

① Shakespeare's Globe

The roar of the greasepaint, the smell of the crowd

In Shakespeare's time, going to the theatre was not the genteel experience it is today. Rival acting troupes competed to attract an audience – who would drink, fight and shout at the actors during plays packed with murder, magic and comedy. The original Globe was built nearby in 1597, after Shakespeare and his company, the Chamberlain's Men, transported a playhouse, timber by timber, across the Thames from Shoreditch. Today's open-air theatre, a near replica, opened in 1997 – and the crowd is still encouraged to heckle.

Detail from the Globe's gates

Key Features

THE GLOBE IN 1600

The actors Until 1661, boys as young as 13 performed the female roles. Many died early, poisoned by the lead in their heavy face make-up.

The plays *Hamlet, Macbeth* and *Romeo and Juliet* all had their premieres at the original Globe Theatre. Shakespeare often performed minor roles in his own plays.

The audience 3,000 people would cram inside for a play. It cost a penny to watch from the pit – in summer, it got so smelly, these spectators were called "penny stinkards".

THE GLOBE TODAY

The building It uses 16th-century materials, such as hand-made bricks and wooden pins, not nails. The thatched roof was the first in the city since the Great Fire of London.

The theatre season runs from April to October. After the monthly Child's Play workshops, kids get to sneak in to watch the end of the Saturday matinee.

The stage Look out for trapdoors (above and below), which allow surprise entrances by devils or ghosts in puffs of smoke, or angels and fairies flying down on ropes.

Letting off steam

When the tide is out, get down to the riverside in front of **Gabriel's Wharf** for a bit of beach time (check the tides at *www.pla.co.uk*). There is a stretch of grass in front of nearby Tate Modern, but for swings and slides, head south to **Mint Street**

At Gabriel's Wharf, kids can play on the beach in the centre of the city

Prices given are for a family of four

Adventure Playground *(Lant St, SE1 1QP)*, or to **Nelson Square Garden** *(Nelson Square, SE1)*, near Southwark Tube station.

Eat and drink

Picnic: under £20; Snacks: £20–40; Real meal: £40–60; Family treat: £60 or more (based on a family of four)

PICNIC Borough Market
(8 Southwark St, Borough, SE1 1TL; www.boroughmarket.org.uk; 11am–5pm Thu, noon–6pm Fri, 8am–5pm Sat) makes foraging for food a gastronomic, globetrotting adventure, though it's not cheap: its classy picnic offerings include Spanish hams and cheeses at

Brindisa (*www.brindisa.com*) and German bread from The Backhaus Bakery (*www.backhaus.co.uk*).
SNACKS Café 2 *(Tate Moden, Bankside, SE1 9TG; 0207 887 8888; www.tate.org.uk/modern; open daily)* allows one child to eat for free at lunchtime when an adult chooses a main course. The café serves soup, many other savoury dishes, cakes and homemade smoothies.
REAL MEAL Swan at the Globe *(21 New Globe Walk, SE1 9DT; 020 7928 9444; www.swanattheglobe. co.uk; open daily)* is located right next to the theatre with a great view of the river Thames, and specializes in upmarket pub food, including a set menu for kids.

The Lowdown

🌐 **Map ref** 11 D4
Address 21 New Globe Walk, Bankside, SE1 9DT; 020 7902 1400; www.shakespeares-globe.org

🚗 **Train** Blackfriars, Cannon Street, London Bridge. **Tube** London Bridge, Cannon Street. **Bus stop** Southwark Bridge Road, Southwark Street. **River bus** Bankside Pier

🕐 **Open** Apr–Oct: 9am–5pm daily; Nov–Mar: 10am–5pm; plus performances (see website)

💲 **Price** Museum: visit £35–45, under 5s free. Theatre tickets from £5

🏃 **Skipping the queue** During the theatre season (late Apr–Oct), auditorium tours are mornings only; afternoon tours focus on the remains of the Rose Theatre, contemporary with the Globe.

👉 **Guided tours** 40-minute tour included in the museum visit

👫 **Age range** 6 plus

🤺 **Activities** Live demonstrations of stage combat, Elizabethan stage costumes or printing most days in the museum (phone to check). Family activity weekends (2nd weekend of month) and school holiday workshops, free with museum admission. During theatre season, Child's Play drama workshops (ages 8–11, £12.50) coincide with occasional Saturday matinees.

🕐 **Allow** Up to 2 hours

♿ **Wheelchair access** Yes, via lifts and ramps

☕ **Café** In the theatre lobby; plus the Swan at the Globe (see below left)

🏷️ **Shop** Selling theatre merchandise and souvenirs

🚻 **Toilets** Inside exhibition space

Good family value?
The exhibition is pricey, but there's plenty happening for children, and show tickets cost as little as £5.

Fresh artisan bread sold at The Flour Station, Borough Market

FAMILY TREAT OXO Tower **Brasserie** (Bargehouse St, SE1 9PH; 020 7803 3888; www.harveynichols.com/oxo-tower-london; open daily), eight storeys above the river, feels like dining in the sky: European cooking for grown-ups, spaghetti bolognese or sausages for kids.

Find out more
DIGITAL Watch the BBC's *Shakespeare: the Animated Tales*, collected together at www.squidoo.com/shakespeareforchildren. For more William Shakespeare activities, including themed word searches, jigsaws and mazes, visit www.folger.edu/shakespeare

Next stop. . .
THE GEORGE INN Head across Southwark to the George Inn (77 Borough High St, SE1 1NH) to see London's last surviving galleried coaching tavern. In the days before formal playhouses, actors performed in the cobbled courtyards of inns like this one (note: children are admitted only when accompanied by an adult).
UNICORN THEATRE The Unicorn Theatre (147 Tooley St, SE1 2HZ; 020 7645 0560; www.unicorntheatre.com) is London's dedicated children's playhouse, with a full programme of family shows plus kids' workshops before its Sunday performances.

The purpose-built Unicorn Theatre, close to Tower Bridge

2 Tate Modern

Shattering, splattering, exploding... art

There's no need to worry whether children will enjoy Tate Modern. Whether it's a Jackson Pollock splatter painting, Henri Matisse's colourful collages, or Claes Oldenburg's make-believe hamburgers, chances are they have already created something along the same lines at school or in their bedroom. If not, they soon will, after a wander around London's most mind-expanding art gallery. Copying Niki de Saint Phalle, who created her paintings by shooting at them, should probably be discouraged, however.

Housed in the tall-chimneyed former Bankside Power Station, Tate Modern was a smash hit from the moment it opened in 2000, and a £215 million redevelopment has doubled the exhibition space to help soak up its five million annual visitors. The gallery offers masses for children. A dedicated team occupies the family concourse on Level 3 every weekend afternoon, suggesting art trails and challenges for kids aged five and above. The "Interactive Zone" on Level 5 is available full time, with touch-screen consoles and video clips that illuminate and explain the collection. The children's audio tour is strong on quizzes and puzzles, and there's even a "Tate Trumps" game to download as an app for iPhone – collect seven favourite works

then pit them against art chosen by friends. Exploring the gallery is less daunting than it first appears: while there are seven storeys in all, the permanent collection is only on levels 3 and 5, and is grouped by theme into four wings. A great approach is to let kids lead the way, wandering the 20 or so rooms on each floor in search of appealing pieces. Rewarding stops include Room 2 of the "Poetry and Dream" wing, for Dali and Magritte; Room 7 of "Material Gestures", for Pollock and Monet; and "States of Flux" Room 1, for Roy Lichtenstein's

Whaam! Inevitably, a few works should have a "parental guidance" warning, notably Ana Mendieta's visceral self-portraits ("Energy and Process", Room 4). Don't miss the Turbine Hall, right at the bottom, housing a single, huge installation.

Letting off steam

Tate Modern's new extension (opening 2012) opens up into a piazza and lawns to the south and west of the gallery, with space for kids to play. The **Millennium Bridge** is a great spot for watching the Thames water traffic.

The Lowdown

- **Map ref** 11 C5
  Address Bankside, SE1 9TG; 020 7887 8888; www.tate.org.uk
- **Train** Blackfriars, Cannon Street, London Bridge. **Tube** Southwark, London Bridge, Cannon Street. **Bus stop** Southwark Bridge Road, Southwark Street. **River bus** Bankside Pier.
- **Open** 10am–6pm Sun–Thu; 10am–10pm Fri–Sat (last admission to exhibitions: 45 mins before closing)
- **Price** Turbine Hall and permanent collection free; temporary shows charge
- **Skipping the queue** The extension should ease weekend congestion
- **Guided tours** Free 45-minute tours daily at 11am, noon, 2pm and 3pm, each covering one of the four wings of the permanent collection. There are one-hour tours of temporary shows – times and prices vary.

- **Age range** All
- **Activities** Free guided kids' activities (age 5 plus) every Sat & Sun noon–4pm, also Thu & Fri in school holidays. Family zone with art books and materials on Level 3; an under-5s' zone on level 5 and free art trails (age 5 plus) from information desks on Levels 1 and 2. Kids' multimedia guide from Levels 2 and 3 (£3.50).
- **Allow** At least 2 hours
- **Wheelchair access** Yes
- **Eat and drink** Snacks Café 2 (Level 2) has good-value lunch deals for under-12s, also sandwiches and pastries. Real meal Tate Modern Restaurant (Level 7) has river views and a more ambitious menu; also open for dinner Fri–Sat.
- **Shops** Levels 1, 2 and 4 selling art books, jewellery, prints and exhibition souvenirs
- **Toilets** All levels; baby-changing facilities on Level 1

Above The Millennium Bridge over the Thames links St Paul's and Tate Modern
Left The heart of Tate Modern is the towering Turbine Hall

Waxwork inmate undergoing punishment at the grisly Clink Prison Museum

③ Clink Prison Museum

The original London dungeon

Medieval Southwark was outside the jurisdiction of London's civic authorities, and was a lawless place notorious for bear fights, drinking dens and brothels – all licensed by the bishops of Winchester, whose palace stood here on the south bank of the Thames. A gaol was needed to control the area, and in 1144 the Clink was opened – a place so infamous that its name became a byword for prisons across the land.

Inside the small, dingy cells of this subterranean attraction, waxwork inmates, recorded shrieks and replica torture equipment are used to tell the gory story of crime and punishment up to 1780, when the Clink locked up for the last time. Information boards describe a 12th-century trial by ordeal (walk across red-hot irons without injury and you're innocent)

Clambering over a steam-train climbing frame in Little Dorrit Park, SE1

and the priestly persecutions of Bloody Mary. It is more histrionic than historical, and maybe a bit too spooky for the under-8s. Ghoulish children will enjoy trying on the scold's bridle or placing their head on the executioner's chopping block. Visitors are able to download a picture of their visit afterwards.

Letting off steam

Head south along Bank End Park and Redcross Way to **Little Dorrit Park** (off Little Dorrit Court, SE1), which has play equipment.

The Lowdown

- 🌐 **Map ref** 12 E5
  Address 1 Clink Street, SE1 9DG; 020 7403 0900; www.clink.co.uk
- 🚉 **Train** London Bridge. **Tube** London Bridge. **Bus stop** Southwark Bridge, Southwark Street, Borough High Street. **River bus** Bankside Pier
- 🕐 **Open** Jul–Sep: 10am–9pm daily; Oct–Jun: 10am–6pm Mon–Fri, 10am–7:30pm Sat & Sun
- 💷 **Price** £15–25
- 🚩 **Guided tours** Groups only
- 🚻 **Age range** 8 plus
- 🕐 **Allow** Up to 1 hour
- ♿ **Wheelchair access** There are nine steps to get down to the musem.
- ☕ **Eat and drink** Snacks Amano (Clink Street, SE1 9DG; 7am–11pm Mon–Fri, 9am–10pm Sat & Sun) serves flatbreads and wraps. *Real meal* Gourmet Burger Kitchen (Soho Wharf, Clink Street, SE1 9DG; www.gbk.co.uk; 11:30am–10pm daily) does mini versions of its burgers for kids.
- 🛍️ **Shop** Gift shop selling souvenirs
- 🚻 **Toilets** No

④ The *Golden Hinde*

Ahoy there me hearties!

This beautiful replica of a Tudor galleon sits majestically on the river alongside the cafés and office blocks of Bankside, as if moored there just a minute ago by pirates. Indeed, miniature mutineers swarm aboard regularly, during the pirate days and sleepovers staged for families.

The *Hinde* is a full-size reproduction of Sir Francis Drake's flagship, which circumnavigated the world in the 1570s, discovering California and plundering much Spanish loot along the way. Rewards could be high – after one profitable trip, even a lowly cabin boy became the equivalent of a millionaire.

A rudimentary handout describes the decks, rigging and artillery – but aim to visit at the weekend if possible, when excellent tour

Dressed up and pretending to fire a cannon on the Golden Hinde

guides are on board to help. Sit in Drake's chair in the captain's cabin and marvel at how the cramped quarters once accommodated up to 80 crew – even little ones will need to duck down to explore the gloomy gun deck. Most Saturdays there are costumed family fun days: grab a cutlass and eye-patch and learn how to weigh anchor and fire a cannon.

Letting off steam

Head south along Borough High Street to **Little Dorrit Park** (*off Little Dorrit Court, SE1*).

⑤ Southwark Cathedral

Pilgrims, poets and posh provisions

The "archaeology chamber" in Southwark Cathedral's millennium wing is a window on nearly 2,000 years of worship beside London Bridge. A 4th-century Roman religious icon was unearthed here, and there is a stone coffin from the medieval Priory of St Mary Overie.

The church we see today is mostly 14th century. Geoffrey Chaucer's pilgrims in *The Canterbury Tales* began their journey from a nearby tavern, and the fabulous tomb of Chaucer's contemporary John Gower lights up the cathedral's nave with its carousel colours – red, green and gold. Look out for a 500-year-old stone "corpse", emaciated in its shroud – perfect for spooking the children. However, the best known

memorial remembers William Shakespeare, who spent 12 years working at the nearby Globe Theatre – characters from some of his plays cavort in a stained-glass window above.

From Thursday to Saturday, the stalls of Borough Market (*see p146*) lap around the cathedral railings, adding greatly to the atmosphere of the neighbourhood. London's oldest food market was chartered by Edward III in 1406, although it is unlikely to have sold ostrich burgers or Burmese curry powder back then. The market now specializes in delectable ingredients from across Europe and beyond, and sampling the food is encouraged – but steer clear on Saturday mornings after 10am, when the area gets super-busy.

Letting off steam

The Cathedral has an outside area with tables, and beyond that there is a small square beside the river.

Gilded Mary and Jesus, a detail of the Great Screen, Southwark Cathedral

The Lowdown

🌐 **Map ref** 12 E5
Address Pickfords Wharf, Clink Street, SE1 9DG; 020 7403 0123; www.goldenhinde.com

🚆 **Train** London Bridge. **Tube** London Bridge, Monument. **Bus stop** Borough High Street. **River bus** Bankside Pier

🕙 **Open** 10am–5:30pm daily

💲 **Price** £18–28

👪 **Skipping the queue** Best to book ahead for a family workshop

🚩 **Guided tours** Costumed tours or pirate dress-up days every Sat (family £20, including admission)

👫 **Age range** 5 plus

👫 **Activities** 2-hour pirate workshops for families most Saturdays (plus some weekdays in school holidays) – come in costume. Also regular sleepovers for ages 5–10, accompanied by an adult (£40pp). Call or check website

⏱ **Allow** 1 hour for self-guided visit

♿ **Wheelchair access** No, due to the steep stairs and low ceilings

🍴 **Eat and drink** *Picnic* Caffè Nero (*3 Cathedral Street, SE1 9DE; 7am–9:30pm Mon–Fri, 8am–9:30pm Sat & Sun*) overlooks the ship, or try the stalls at Borough Market (*see p146*).

🛍 **Shop** At the ticket shop selling souvenirs

🚻 **Toilets** At the ticket shop

The Lowdown

🌐 **Map ref** 12 E5

Address London Bridge, SE1 9DA; 020 7367 6700; www. southwarkcathedral.org.uk

🚆 **Train** London Bridge. **Tube** London Bridge, Monument. **Bus stop** Borough High Street. **River bus** Bankside Pier

🕐 **Open** 8am–6pm Mon–Fri, 8:30am–6pm Sat & Sun; services include choral evensong daily. Borough Market: 11am–5pm Thu, noon–6pm Fri, 8am–5pm Sat

💲 **Price** Donations

🚩 **Guided tours** Groups only (adults £5; under-12s £2.50); walking tours also available

🧍 **Activities** Regular concerts

⏱ **Allow** Up to 1 hour

♿ **Wheelchair access** Yes, via lifts or fixed and portable ramps

🍴 **Eat and drink** *Snacks* The Refectory café serves lunch and cakes. *Real meal* Fish! *(Cathedral Street, SE1 9AL; 020 7407 3803; 11:30am–11pm Mon–Thu, noon–11pm Fri–Sun) offers seafood.*

🛍 **Shop** Selling cathedral souvenirs, cards, books and gifts

🚻 **Toilets** At the west end of Lancelot's Link, near the entrance

⑥ The Old Operating Theatre

The church that dripped blood

This macabre museum makes an interesting counterpoint to the London Dungeon *(see p156)*, just around the corner. Whereas the Dungeon is a schlocky horror show, this is an authentic slice of Victorian

The small surgeon's table at the heart of The Old Operating Theatre

gore, inside the attic of 300-year-old St Thomas's Church. It shows off Europe's oldest surviving operating theatre, established in 1822 to serve nearby St Thomas's Hospital, where student surgeons once gathered to watch limbs being chopped off poor patients – without anaesthetics.

Howls of real torment once rang through the rafters here, and the museum's entrance could hardly be spookier – it is reached via a spiral staircase in the church's tower. The first chamber to visit is the Herb Garret, storehouse of the hospital apothecary in centuries past, and stacked with musty animal skins and bizarre potions, much like a witch's pantry. Harry Potter fans will adore the vibe here. The operating room is a creepy space too – literally a theatre, with the surgery table as the stage, steeply banked viewing stands, a box of sawdust to soak up the blood of amputees and a corridor of murderous-looking surgical instruments.

Letting off steam

Little Dorrit Park *(see left)* has a small playground for children.

The Lowdown

🌐 **Map ref** 12 E5

Address 9a Saint Thomas Street, SE1 9RY; 020 7188 2679; www. thegarret.org.uk

🚆 **Train** London Bridge. **Tube** London Bridge. **Bus stop** London Bridge

🕐 **Open** 10:30am–5pm daily

💲 **Price** £14–24

🧍 **Skipping the queue** Capacity is tight, so book ahead for events

🧍 **Age range** 7 plus

🧍 **Activities** Free demonstrations, at 2pm Sat and Sun (age 7 plus), might feature herbal medicine or 19th-century speed surgery. There's an imaginative programme of family

activities in the school holidays: call ahead or check website.

⏱ **Allow** 1 hour

♿ **Wheelchair access** limited

🍴 **Eat and drink** *Snacks* De Gustibus *(4 Southwark Street, SE1 1TQ)* is an artisan bakery on the edge of Borough Market *(see above)*. *Real meal* The George Inn *(77 Borough High Street, SE1 1NH; 020 7407 2056; noon–9pm Mon–Sat, noon–5pm Sun) serves traditional pub fare.*

🛍 **Shop** Selling quirky and original gifts and presents with a medical theme

🚻 **Toilets** On entrance level before entering (requires a key)

HMS *Belfast* and around

HMS *Belfast*, the most powerful battle cruiser in Britain's World War II fleet, is now a floating museum. Visiting with kids is an immersive experience, but avoid inclement days, and check the website for kid's activities. Back on shore, this pedestrianized strip of riverside is perfect for families. Older kids will enjoy the ghoulish attractions of the London Dungeon, while young history buffs will love trying on the uniforms in Winston Churchill's Britain at War Experience.

The Modernist building housing the Design Museum, founded in 1989 and one of the first design museums in the world

Inside the interactive Operations Room on board HMS Belfast

The Lowdown

Train London Bridge, a five-minute walk away; Tower Gateway (DLR). **Tube** London Bridge, Monument, Tower Hill. **Bus** Tooley Street: route numbers 47, 343, 381, RV1; London Bridge: 17, 21, 35, 40, 43, 47, 133, 141, 149, 521. **River bus** London Bridge City Pier, on riverbus route between Woolwich Arsenal and London Eye (0207 001 2222; *www. thamesclippers.com*)

Visitor information City of London Information Centre (*see pp128–9*)

Supermarkets Marks & Spencer Simply Food, 6 More London Place, SE1 2DA; Costcutter, 134 Tooley Street, SE1 2TU **Markets** Borough Market, *see pp144–5*; Bermondsey Farmers' Market, Bermondsey Square, SE1 3UN (mostly food, plus flowers and garden plants), 10am–2pm Sat

Festivals City of London Festival, music and arts (Jun–Jul); the Mayor's Thames Festival, music, arts and markets (Sep)

Pharmacies Boots, 8–11 Hays Galleria, SE1 2HD; 020 7407 4276; 7:30am–6:30pm Mon–Fri, 10am–6pm Sat. For 24-hour pharmacies, visit *www.nhs.uk/ servicedirectories*

Nearest playground Tanner Street Park (*SE1*); Little Dorrit Park (*SE1*); St John's Churchyard (*SE1*); Leathermarket Street Gardens (*SE1*)

0 metres 100

0 yards 100

The London Dungeon is inhabited by all manner of creepy characters

Tower Pier

HMS *Belfast*

London Bridge City Pier

THE LANE

QUEEN'S

River

Thames

Tower Bridge

Hay's Galleria

WALK

The Scoop

City Hall

TOOLEY

POTTERS FIELDS

THE

SHAD

QUEEN'S

THAMES

Butler's Wharf

Winston Churchill's Britain at War Experience

HOLYROOD STREET

STREET

GAINSFORD STREET

LAFONE STREET

CURLEW STREET

SHAD THAMES

WALK

QUEEN ELIZABETH STREET

Design Museum

CRUCIFIX LA

BARNHAM ST

DRUID STREET

FAIR

ST JOHN'S CHURCHYARD

ROAD

TOOLEY STREET

BRIDGE

DRUID STREET

KNOWSFIELDS

KIRBY GROVE

HARDWICKE ST

BERMONDSEY

GROUNDS

BRUNSWICK CT

Fashion & Textile Museum

WHITE'S

TOWER

STREET

LEATHERMARKET STREET GARDENS

LEATHERMARKET STREET

TANNER STREET

TANNER STREET PARK

MOROCCO STREET

LAMB WALK

LONG

LANE

BERMONDSEY

Getting a thorough soaking in the fountains in the sculptural gardens next to City Hall

Places of Interest

SIGHTS

1. HMS *Belfast*
2. London Dungeon
3. Winston Churchill's Britain at War Experience
4. Design Museum

● **EAT AND DRINK**

1. Le Pont de la Tour
2. Caffè Paradiso
3. Dim T
4. Browns Bar & Brasserie
5. Absolutely Starving
6. Café Rouge
7. Pod
8. Ask

See also HMS Belfast (pp154–5) and the Design Museum (p157)

● **WHERE TO STAY**

1. London Bridge
2. London Tower Bridge

① HMS *Belfast*

Action stations – on one of Britain's great battleships

She was built in 1937, in the same Northern Irish shipyard as the *Titanic*, but on a quiet day, HMS *Belfast* feels more like the *Marie Celeste*. What could be more atmospheric than exploring a great warship in battle trim, populated only by visitors and the ghosts of the 800 seamen who once manned her? Generators buzz, orders crackle through the speakers and nowhere is off-limits to children, who can swarm down ladders and along gangways, into gun turrets and mess decks accompanied by the lively audio guide.

Signalling with semaphore flags

The Lowdown

🌐 **Map reference** 12 G5
Address Morgan's Lane, Tooley Street, SE1 2JH; 020 7940 6300; http://hmsbelfast.iwm.org.uk

🚃 **Train** London Bridge (a five-minute walk); Tower Gateway (DLR). **Tube** London Bridge, Monument, Tower Hill. **Bus stop** Tooley Street, London Bridge. **River bus** London Bridge City Pier, en route between Woolwich Arsenal and London Eye (020 7001 2222; www.thamesclippers.com).

🕐 **Open** Mar–Oct: 10am–6pm daily; Nov–Feb: till 5pm (last admission one hour earlier).

💷 **Price** £27–37, under 16s free; including a voluntary donation

🔫 **Guided tours** Free audio guide (also in French, German and Spanish); children's audio guide

🚶 **Age range** 7 plus

🤸 **Activities** Family drop-in activities on last weekend of month, 11am–1pm and 2–4pm; object-handling sessions for all ages on some weekends and in school holidays.

⏱ **Allow** 2 hours

♿ **Wheelchair access** Limited due to the nature of a warship. See website for details.

☕ **Café** The Walrus Café, Zone 3

🛍 **Shop** In ticket hall

🚻 **Toilets** On the quarterdeck, ask staff for the key

Good family value?
For maximum value, make time for the hands-on Life at Sea exhibition on Deck 3, with knots to tie and kitbags to lift.

Key Features

① **Admiral's Cabin** HMS *Belfast* became the flagship of Britain's Far East Fleet, and in the admiral's command room, children can don uniforms and scan for enemy craft.

② **Quarterdeck** The ship's parade ground and exercise yard, this was mainly reserved for officers. It is where visitors board – don't forget to salute!

■ **Bridge** The compass platform at the front was where the captain controlled the ship.

■ **Superstructure** This part of the ship held the gun turrets, funnels, life boats, fore mast and main mast.

■ **Deck Two** This housed a forward mess deck, where the crew would sleep and eat, as well as the officers' mess.

■ **Deck Three** As well as the Admiral's cabin, this held the boiler, whose steam powered the turbines and the propeller.

■ **Deck Four** This held the shell room and gun guidance system, as well as the ship's wheel and steering gear.

■ **Deck Five** Home to the forward and aft engine rooms, as well as smaller shells and the submarine detection device.

③ **Anchor** If the electric winch failed, it took 144 men to turn the capstan and raise the ship's main anchor. It is as heavy as an elephant (5.5 tonnes).

④ **Shell Room** The shells line up like giant bowling pins here. They were loaded into a carousel and then hoisted up to the four main gun turrets.

⑤ **Operations Room** In the ship's nerve centre, *Belfast's* finest hour is re-created – when she helped sink the German battleship *Scharnhorst* at the Battle of the North Cape in 1943.

⑥ **Gun Turret** Swivel in the turret captain's chair and imagine unleashing *Belfast's* guns on a target 23 km (14 miles) away.

Taking a break in Potters Field Park, right next to Tower Bridge.

Letting off steam

Potters Fields Park is a spread of lawn beside Tower Bridge. Behind it, across Tooley Street, **St John's Churchyard**, on Fair Street, has a small play area; or there's a larger playground at **Tanner Street Park**, further along Tower Bridge Road. Older children might enjoy junior sessions at **White's Grounds Skate Park** (*Crucifix Lane, SE1 3JW*), which caters for ages 11–16: call 020 7525 1102 for details.

Eat and drink

Picnic: under £20; Snacks: £20–40; Real meal: £40–60; Family treat: £60 or more (based on a family of four)

PICNIC Le Pont de la Tour (*36d Shad Thames, SE1 2YE; 020 7403 8403; www.lepontdelatour.co.uk; 7:30am–8pm weekdays, 9am–6pm weekends*) has a great deli with good bread, an impressive cheese counter and gourmet goodies galore. Grab a picnic and head to nearby Potters Fields Park where there is plentiful rug-spreading space.

SNACKS The designer Docklands haunt of Shad Thames has an array of good eateries, including **Caffè Paradiso** (*45 Shad Thames, SE1 2NJ; 020 7378 6606; www. pizzaparadiso.co.uk; 8am–7pm daily*), a Sicilian-style hangout offering piled-high patisserie and proper ice cream.

REAL MEAL Dim T (*2 More London Place, SE1 2DP; 020 7403 7000; dimt.co.uk; noon–11pm daily*), just ashore from HMS *Belfast*, creates a wide range of Asian-fusion dishes, including Thai curries and crispy duck, while children can choose between a bento box or dim-sum selection basket.

FAMILY TREAT There are posher places along Butler's Wharf, but **Browns Bar & Brasserie** (*Shad Thames, SE1 2YG; 020 7378 1700; www.browns-restaurants.co.uk; 10am–11pm Mon–Sat, till 10:30pm Sun*) does dependable British classics, such as shoulder of lamb or calves' liver and bacon. It also makes kids welcome with its two-course children's menu.

Find out more

DIGITAL HMS *Belfast's* online games zone features an interactive archive about life on board, and kids can try commanding a mission based on the ship's real-life exploits in the Arctic at: *hmsbelfast.iwm.org. uk/server/show/nav.475*

Next stop. . .

LONDON FIRE BRIGADE MUSEUM For more heavy-duty hardware, head for the nearby London Fire Brigade Museum (*94a Southwark Bridge Rd, SE1 0EG; 020 8555 1200; www.london-fire. gov.uk/ourmuseum.asp*), which has shiny red engines to admire and uniforms to try on: tours run 10:30am & 2pm Mon–Fri, booking essential (adults £5, children £3).

Examining fire engines from the past at the Fire Brigade Museum.

② London Dungeon

Gruesome tales of London's grisly past

This is the closest Central London gets to a theme park (with prices to match) – a glossy visitor experience featuring haunted-house sets, zombie actors and a couple of short, sharp, thrill-rides. Visitors are ushered through a gloomy labyrinth of torchlit rooms showcasing dark chapters from the city's history – from the Black Death and Bedlam to Sweeney Todd and Jack the Ripper – via dismembered corpses and heads on spikes. There's a generous helping of audience participation: children should stand at the back or expect to be locked in a torture chamber, burnt at the stake or operated on by the butcher surgeon.

The Lowdown

- 🌐 **Map ref** 12 F5
  Address 28–34 Tooley Street, SE1 2SZ; 020 7403 7221; www. the-dungeons.co.uk

- 🚗 **Train** London Bridge. **Tube** London Bridge. **Bus stop** Tooley Street, London Bridge. **River bus** London Bridge City Pier

- 🕐 **Open** 10am–5pm daily (from 9:30am during peak times), plus occasional late-night opening

- 💲 **Price** £83–93; book online for reductions. Also look for discount vouchers online

- 🚶 **Skipping the queue** Fast-track entry can be booked in advance (extra charge). On weekends and holidays, arrive 30 minutes before opening to avoid long queues.

- 🚩 **Guided tours** Guided performances throughout

- 👫 **Age range** 8 plus (parental discretion advised)

- 🕐 **Allow** 90 minutes, plus queuing

- ♿ **Wheelchair access** Limited due to uneven floors and a few steps; some rides are restricted

- 🍴 **Eat and drink** Snacks Absolutely Starving (51 Tooley St, SE1 2QN; 020 7407 7417; 7am–9:45pm Mon–Fri, from 9:30am Sat & Sun) has a hot buffet. Real meal Café Rouge (Hay's Galleria, Tooley St, SE1 2HD; 020 7378 0097; 8:30am–11pm Mon–Fri, 9am–10:30pm Sat & Sun) has a kids' menu.

- 🛍️ **Shop** At end of tour

- 🚻 **Toilets** After ticket office

The entrance to the London Dungeon – enter if you dare

It's all played for laughs (watch out for chamber pots being emptied from medieval windows) – the young cast act with gusto, and the Ripper rooms are especially atmospheric – though younger children might find themselves howling more in terror than delight.

Just across Tooley Street, the London Bridge Experience (10am–5pm Mon–Fri, 10am–6pm Sat & Sun; 0800 043 4666; www. thelondonbridgeexperience.com) offers a similar schtick with less convincing historic tableaus, but the "London Tombs" horror maze, which caps the visit, is genuinely nerve-shredding, as visitors are stalked by chainsaw-wielding serial killers. Definitely not for pre-teens.

Letting off steam

Walk east along Tooley Street to **St John's Churchyard** (Fair Street, SE1), which has a small playground and grassy areas for picnics.

③ Winston Churchill's Britain at War Experience

A recreation of London life – and death – during the Blitz

Among London's many museums of soldiery and warmongering, this is perhaps the most poignant, exploring life on the home front during World War II. It begins strongly: air raid sirens blare and an elevator whisks visitors down into a recreated Tube shelter; Londoners would rush to stations to shelter from Nazi bombs. Mannequins huddle on makeshift bunks, posters warn that "Careless talk costs lives", and an excellent newsreel uses real-life testimonies to tell the dreadful story of the war.

The main galleries feature mostly low-tech displays of costumes, cuttings and memorabilia: children can listen to recordings of factory girls and young evacuees talking about life in wartime; and can try on tin hats, gas masks and uniforms. Many exhibits have been donated by visitors, giving the museum a make-do-and-mend feel that is appropriate for the period. The big finish is a noisy, smoking evocation of houses being bombed during the Blitz – a bit scary for very young children, and slightly tasteless for everyone with its scattering of severed limbs.

Letting off steam

Walk east along the riverside to grassy **Potters Fields Park** (The Queens Walk, SE1 2AA).

Trying on gas masks at Winston Churchill's Britain at War Experience

The Lowdown

- 🌐 **Map ref** 12 F5
  Address 64–6 Tooley Street, SE1 2TF; 020 7403 3171; www.britainatwar.co.uk
- � **Train** London Bridge. **Tube** London Bridge. **Bus stop** Tooley Street, London Bridge. **River bus** London Bridge City Pier
- 🕐 **Open** Apr–Oct: 10am–5pm daily; Nov–Mar till 4:30pm
- 💲 **Price** £29–39; book online for reductions.
- 🚶 **Age range** 7 plus
- ⏱ **Allow** 90 minutes
- ♿ **Wheelchair access** Yes
- ☕ **Eat and drink** *Picnic* Absolutely Starving (*see London Dungeon Lowdown for details*) has a deli counter. *Snacks* Pod (*7 More London Place, SE1 2RT; 020 7174 0374; www.podfood.com; 7:30am–5pm Mon–Fri*) offers healthy food such as superfood salads.
- 🛍 **Shop** At the end of the tour
- 🚻 **Toilets** At back of main gallery

④ Design Museum
A modern temple to design

A big part of the appeal of this museum is its setting on Butler's Wharf, a chunk of London's revitalized Docklands. The approach is along Shad Thames, whose overhead walkways were used in Victorian times to wheel tea and spices from the quayside, but now link luxury loft apartments, their courtyards parked with convertibles instead of carthorses. A stroll around here will certainly appeal to kids' imaginations.

One of the ever-changing exhibitions at the Design Museum

The Design Museum itself is arranged over three floors of an appropriately cool white building. There is no permanent collection, instead temporary shows focus on avant-garde architecture, furniture or fashion. It can be a bit esoteric for children, but there's a family workshop or tour most months, linked to current exhibitions, while the free under-12s' activity sheet encourages kids to doodle their own designs.

If the kids enjoy this sort of thing, consider combining a visit with the nearby Fashion & Textile Museum (83 Bermondsey Street, SE1 3XF; 020 7407 8664; www.ftmlondon.org; 11am–6pm Tue–Sat), which lays on school holiday workshops.

Letting off steam
The **Butler's Wharf** waterfront is a good place to dash around – it is littered with old anchors to clamber over. For softer surroundings, head towards Tower Bridge to **Potters Fields Park**.

The Lowdown

- 🌐 **Map ref** 12 H6
  Address 28 Shad Thames, SE1 2YD; 020 7403 6933; www.designmuseum.org
- 🚗 **Train** London Bridge, Tower Gateway (DLR station). **Tube** London Bridge, Tower Hill. **Bus stop** Tooley Street, Tower Gateway, Jamaica Road, Tower Bridge. **River bus** Tower Pier, St Katherine's Pier
- 🕐 **Open** 10am–5:45pm daily (last admission: 5:15pm)
- 💲 **Price** £22–32, including £1 voluntary donation (under 12s free)
- 🚩 **Guided tours** Occasional tours of specific exhibitions, some geared towards families
- 🚶 **Age range** 5 plus
- 🏃 **Activities** Free activity sheet for under 12s. Sun pm workshops for ages 5–11 most months (book in advance, £4). School holiday courses for age 12-plus focus on specific design disciplines.
- ⏱ **Allow** 1 hour
- ♿ **Wheelchair access** Yes
- ☕ **Eat and drink** *Snacks* The Blueprint Café in the museum serves gourmet pies and pastries. *Real meal* Ask (*34 Shad Thames, SE1 2YG; 020 7403 4545; www.askrestaurants.com; noon–11pm Mon–Thu, noon–11:30pm Sat, noon–10:30pm Sun*) serves pasta and pizza and has a kids' menu.
- 🛍 **Shop** On the ground floor, selling excellent designer goods
- 🚻 **Toilets** On the ground floor

London Eye and around

Erected in 2000, the London Eye is a genuine wow for kids, especially if approached on foot from Waterloo station. Book ahead to ride – but not before checking the weather forecast, because rain blots the views. That's good advice for the eclectic South Bank, which can be bleak on a wet day, although it embraces the National Theatre, the London Aquarium and Britain's biggest cinema screen as well as a motley crew of street entertainers.

Southwark and the South Bank

Shakespeare's Globe p144

London Eye

HMS Belfast p152

The London Eye in front of the Sea Life London Aquarium, on the South Bank

Places of interest

SIGHTS

1. London Eye
2. National Theatre
3. BFI Southbank
4. Gabriel's Wharf
5. Southbank Centre
6. Sea Life London Aquarium
7. London Film Museum
8. Imperial War Museum
9. Florence Nightingale Museum

● EAT AND DRINK

1. Zen Café
2. Zen China
3. Riverside Terrace Café
4. Le Pain Quotidien
5. Canteen
6. Mezzanine
7. The Riverfront
8. Benugo Bar & Kitchen
9. House of Crepes
10. Gourmet Pizza Company
11. Concrete at the Hayward
12. Skylon Restaurant
13. Ned's Noodle Bar
14. Aji Zen Canteen
15. Café Roma
16. The Garden Café
17. Yo! Sushi
18. Troia
See also National Theatre (p162), BFI Southbank (pp162–3) and London Film Museum (p165)

● WHERE TO STAY

1. Park Plaza
2. Premier Inn

Dinosaur skeleton from Night at the Museum 2 at the London Film Museum

0 metres 200
0 yards 200

The Lowdown

🚗 **Train** Waterloo, a 5-minute walk away. **Tube** Waterloo, Westminster, Lambeth North. **Bus** Belvedere Road: route number RV1; York Road: 76, 77, 211, 341, 381, 507; Westminster Bridge: 12, 53, 148, 159, 211, 453. **River bus** London Eye Millennium Pier: riverbus services to Woolwich Arsenal (0870 781 5049; *www. thamesclippers.com*); and to Greenwich via the Tower (020 7740 0400; *www.citycruises. com*). Also services from Westminster Pier *(see p64)*

ℹ️ **Visitor information** Britain and London Visitor Centre, Waterloo station, SE1 7LY

🛒 **Supermarkets** Costcutter, 17–19 York Road, SE1 7NJ; Sainsbury's, 101 Waterloo Road, SE1 8UL; Iceland, 112–113 Lower Marsh, SE1 7AE **Markets** South Bank Book Market, BFI Southbank, daily; Real Food Market, Royal Festival Hall, Southbank Centre, 11am–8pm Fri–Sat; noon–6pm Sun; Lower Marsh street market, SE1 (mixed stalls), 8am–6pm Mon–Sat (Wed 10am–3pm)

🎪 **Festivals** Coin Street Festival, mixed arts, Bernie Spain Gardens (Jun–Jul); Meltdown Festival, music, Southbank Centre (Jun); Watch This Space, family arts, National Theatre (Jun–Sep); The Mayor's Thames Festival (Sep); BFI London Film Festival (Oct)

➕ **Pharmacies** Boots, Waterloo Station, SE1 7LY (7am–10pm Mon–Fri; 8am–10pm Sat; 9am–9pm Sun (closed 2–3pm daily). For 24-hour pharmacies, visit *www.nhs.uk/ servicedirectories*

🍃 **Nearest playgrounds** Archbishop's Park, *(Lambeth Palace Road, SE1 7LQ)*; Jubilee Gardens *(Belvedere Road, SE1 7XZ)*; Geraldine Mary Harmsworth Park *(Kennington Road, SE11)* Bernie Spain Gardens *(Duchy Street, SE1 9NL)*

Rockets, planes and armoured cars at the Imperial War Museum

Enthralled by an inquisitive ray at the Sea Life London Aquarium

The Lowdown

🌐 **Map ref** 10 H6
Address County Hall, Westminster Bridge Road, SE1 7PB; 0871 781 3000, www.londoneye.com

🚗 **Train** Waterloo, a 5-minute walk away. **Tube** Waterloo, Westminster. **Bus stop** Belvedere Road, York Road, Westminster Bridge. **River bus** London Eye Millennium Pier, Westminster Pier

🕐 **Open** Sep–Mar: 10am–8:30pm daily; Apr–Jun: till 9pm; Jul & Aug: till 9:30pm; closed 2 weeks in mid-Jan for maintenance

💲 **Price** £56–66 (book online for 10 per cent discount). Time-flexible and fast-track tickets cost extra

👫 **Skipping the queue** Jul and Aug are busiest; avoid the 11am–3pm peak and arrive 30 minutes before flight time. Fast-track tickets are the same price for adults and children.

🚩 **Guided tours** None. Audio guide costs £5 extra (£4.50 if booked online)

👫 **Age range** 5 plus

🤸 **Activities** Free "4D" film experience included in ticket. Kids' puzzle sheet downloadable from website only. In winter, the ice-rink in Jubilee Gardens carries a separate charge.

⏱ **Allow** 1 hour

♿ **Wheelchair access** Yes (carer can travel for free)

☕ **Café** *Snacks* Zen Café, with outlets beside Jubilee Gardens and inside County Hall, sells snacks and drinks. *Real meal* Zen China inside County Hall is a more grown-up alternative, specializing in traditional Chinese cuisine.

🎗 **Shop** Opposite ticket office, selling souvenirs

🚻 **Toilets** Downstairs at County Hall

Good family value?
It's expensive for 30 minutes, but there's a saving for combined admission to sister attractions Madame Tussauds and London Dungeon. On a budget? Consider the OXO Tower (see p147) instead.

① London Eye
Take a spin over London

How does it feel to be a seagull soaring above London? Find out during a ride on "the world's tallest cantilevered observation wheel". Rising 135 m (443 ft) above the Thames, the London Eye opened as part of the city's millennium celebrations. A serene 30-minute "flight" in one of its glass eggs offers views stretching 40 km (25 miles) – on a clear day you might even be able to see Windsor Castle!

Key Features

The capsules Each of the 32 capsules weighs 10 tonnes, can hold 25 passengers and rotates at 26 cm (10 in) per second. Celebrity fliers have included Prince Harry, Kate Moss, the Jonas Brothers…and Kermit the Frog!

The spec The wheel cost £70 million, weighs 2,100 tonnes and is supported by two 60-m (197-ft) cables. It was floated up the Thames in sections, assembled and then slowly raised using the cables.

The structure Although no longer the world's tallest observation wheel (the 165-m (541-ft) Singapore Flyer takes that prize for now) it is the largest cantilevered wheel, as it is supported by an A-frame on one side only.

The ride The slow-moving capsules mean the wheel can be boarded without it stopping, and the gentle ascent is entirely unscary.

Extras A 4-minute "4D" cinema show in the ticket hall is free for London Eye travellers. It uses dry ice, bubbles and "real rain" to simulate an aerial journey over London.

The view On a clear day, Windsor Castle, 40 km (25 miles) west of London, is visible – although Wembley Stadium's arch, 12 km (7 miles) away to the northwest, is a better bet.

Imaginative playground at Archbishop's Park, next to Lambeth Palace

Letting off steam

Jubilee Gardens (Belvedere Road, Southbank SE1 7XZ), beside the Eye, has lawns and a playground, and is best for younger children. The colourful **Archbishop's Park** (Carlisle Lane, SE1 7LE), a 10-minute walk away, was designed by children and is probably a better bet. If it's wet, there are hours of mindless pleasure to be had at **Namco Station** inside County Hall (10am–midnight daily; www.namcofunscape.com), which has three beeping, flashing floors of arcade games, dodgem cars and bowling alleys.

Eat and drink

Picnic: under £20; Snacks: £20–40; Real meal: £40–60; Family treat: £60 or more (based on a family of four)

PICNIC For provisions, check out the weekend **Real Food Market** held behind Royal Festival Hall. The hall's **Riverside Terrace Café** (Royal Festival Hall, SE1 8XX; 020 7921 0758; www.southbankcentre.co.uk; 10am–11pm) becomes an outdoor eating space in summer.
SNACKS Le Pain Quotidien (12–13 Festival Walk, Belvedere Rd, SE1 8XX; www.lepainquotidien.com; 7:30am–11pm Mon–Fri, 8am–11pm Sat, 9am–10pm Sun) offers superior tartines, salads and snacks.

The stylish Canteen restaurant behind the Royal Festival Hall, South Bank

REAL MEAL Canteen (Royal Festival Hall, Belvedere Road, SE1 8XX; 0845 686 1122; www.canteen.co.uk; 8am–11pm Mon–Fri, 9am–11pm Sat, 9am–10pm Sun) serves up a stylish take on English classics (roasts, steak and chips), and its kid's menu offers half portions of most dishes. The restaurant also gives out activity books and there are badges to collect.
FAMILY TREAT Mezzanine (National Theatre, South Bank, SE1 9PX; 020 7452 3600; www.nationaltheatre.org.uk; 5:15pm–11pm Mon–Sat, plus weekend lunchtimes) is a grown-up Modern European restaurant with a seasonal menu, but it also does half portions for kids and themed food to link with family shows. Green eggs and ham, anyone?

Find out more

FILM The Eye has starred in more than one Hollywood blockbuster. It almost comes crashing down in the 2007 comic-book caper *Fantastic Four: Rise of the Silver Surfer*, while in the 2004 movie *Thunderbirds*, Thunderbird 2 lands right beside it in Jubilee Gardens.

A London Duck Tour amphibious vehicle splashing into the Thames

Next stop. . .

SIGHTSEEING TOURS The Eye is high, but there are several unusual ways to see the city at a faster pace. Spin your own wheels by hiring bikes from the **London Bicycle Tour Company** (from £3.50 per hour; 020 7928 6838; www.londonbicycle.com), at Gabriel's Wharf; get soaked on a spray-drenched 40 mph (65 kph) speedboat ride from the London Eye Pier (020 7928 8933; www.londonribvoyages.com); or see the sights by both land and water on an ingenious, amphibious **London Duck Tour** (020 7928 3132; www.londonducktours.co.uk), starting from Chicheley Street, SE1.

② National Theatre

London's top family arts destination

Britain's largest theatre complex was built on the South Bank in 1976. It was designed by Sir Denys Lasdun in the Brutalist architectural style, with lots of concrete and sharp edges, which people seem to either love or hate. Luckily it's the interior that counts, and that has three auditoria showing a terrific mix of classic drama and new writing, providing something for everyone. It's worth just dropping in, too, as the lobby areas embrace four restaurants, two exhibition spaces (photography figures strongly) and a small stage for free live music before curtain-up most evenings.

Enjoying an auditorium tour at the Olivier Theatre, part of the National Theatre

Guided tours include a visit to the fan-shaped Olivier Theatre, modelled on ancient Greek theatres, and a glimpse of the scenery workshops backstage, where children can get up close to props from recent plays, such as Alice the mare, a puppet from the smash-hit show *War Horse*, based on Michael Morpurgo's novel for children. The liveliest time to come is June to September, when the theatre hosts a madcap family performance festival, mostly outdoors and largely free. It might include trampolining Belgian clowns in Theatre Square or interactive puppetry in the Playspace, an inflatable auditorium just for kids.

Letting off steam

Bernie Spain Gardens (*Upper Ground, SE1 9PP*), just east along the river, offers grassy spaces. **Jubilee Gardens** (*Belvedere Road, SE1 7XZ*), in the opposite direction, has a decent playground.

③ BFI Southbank

Britain's largest big-screen experience

Crouching right under Waterloo Bridge, London's art-house cinema hub opened as the National Film Theatre in 1953, and now has four screens, a gallery for celluloid-based art and a very slick cocktail lounge. The programme generally has something for families: the 2011 Disney 50 season showed every cartoon feature the studio has made.

For children who need a screen fix even when sightseeing, there is also the free Mediatheque room: simply choose a booth and access a menu of 2,000 movies and TV shows from the world's biggest screen archive. The children's list spans *Robin Hood* and *The Railway Children* to *Watership Down*.

The Lowdown

- 🌐 **Map ref** 11 A5
  Address South Bank, SE1 9PX; 020 7452 3000; www.nationaltheatre.org.uk

- 🚆 **Train** Waterloo or Waterloo East (both a 5-minute walk), Charing Cross (10 minutes). **Tube** Waterloo, Embankment. **Bus stop** Waterloo Bridge, Upper Ground, Waterloo Road, Stamford Street. **River bus** Festival Pier (Westminster to St Katherine's route; 020 7936 2033; www.crownriver.com); London Eye Millennium Pier; Embankment Pier (across Golden Jubilee Bridges).

- 🕐 **Open** 9:30am–11pm Mon–Sat, noon–6pm Sun

- 💲 **Price** Show tickets vary, from £10–40+; standing tickets are sold on the day only, £5

- 🎟 **Guided tours** Usually 10:15am, 10:30am, 12:15pm, 12:30pm, 5:15pm, 5:30pm Mon–Fri; 10:30am, 12:15pm Sat; 12:30pm Sun. Adults £7.50, under-18s £6.50; call 020 7452 3400.

- 👪 **Age range** All

- 🏃 **Activities** Foyer concerts 5:45pm Mon–Sat and lunchtimes Sat & Sun (free). The Big Wall in the main foyer has touch-screen clips and information about current shows. Talks and workshops programme, mostly for adults. Watch This Space festival (Jun–Sep) has events Tue–Sun; Playspace programme runs in school summer holiday

- ⏱ **Allow** Up to 1 hour

- ♿ **Wheelchair access** Yes

- 🍽 **Eat and drink** *Snacks* Lyttelton Café (Ground floor) and Olivier Café (Levels 2–3) serve hot and cold dishes pre-theatre. *Real meal* Terrace Bar & Food (Level 2) offers meze-style bites, with a focus on fresh seasonal ingredients.

- 🛍 **Shop** On the ground floor selling books, texts, programmes, posters, recordings and gifts

- 🚻 **Toilets** In theatres and foyers

BFI Southbank, a big attraction for film buffs of all ages

Nearby, the more commercial **BFI IMAX** is contained in a giant glass drum outside Waterloo Station, where the likes of Harry Potter and Shrek loom 20-m (66-ft) tall on Britain's largest screen. Look out for the monthly Film Funday workshops, where kids get to animate their own movie before the main screening, or dress up as their heroes.

Letting off steam
Jubilee Gardens (see left).

The Lowdown

- **Map ref** 11 A5
  Address Belvedere Road, SE1 8XT; 020 7928 3232 (IMAX enquiries 020 7199 6000); www.bfi.org.uk
- **Transport** See National Theatre (left)
- **Open** 9:45am–11:30pm daily (till 11pm Sun); Mediatheque noon–8pm Tue–Sun
- **Price** Seat prices vary – all tickets cost £5 on Tue. Mediatheque free
- **Skipping the queue** Book ahead for Film Fundays (020 7928 3232)
- **Activities** Film Fundays, usually on last Sun of each month, free with cinema tickets
- **Wheelchair access** Yes
- **Eat and drink** Real meal The Riverfront (020 7401 3332; www.riverfrontbarandkitchen.com) does burgers, salads and grills. Family treat Benugo Bar & Kitchen (020 7401 9000; www.benugobarandkitchen.com) is more formal, but offers children's dishes on Film Fundays.
- **Shop** Selling postcards, DVDs, BFI merchandise and books, including those for the more serious film connoisseur
- **Toilets** In the foyer

④ Gabriel's Wharf
Boutiques and bicycles

It's heartening that this little oasis of "alternative culture" can thrive in such a go-getting strip of Central London, and that's thanks to Coin Street Community Builders – a gang of residents who banded together in 1984 to save the site from property developers. They've created a perky area of pastel-painted craft studios and cafés right

by the Thames, with lots of appeal for families: it has a giant mural, bicycle hire (see p161), and a bevy of carved wooden beasts, some of them made for tots to ride on. Just beyond looms the Art Deco **OXO Tower**, with a small art gallery on the ground floor, bijou design shops along its balconies and a viewing platform at the summit.

Letting off steam
Bernie Spain Gardens (Upper Ground, SE1 9PP), just east along the river has running-about room.

Some of the pretty, pastel-painted buildings at Gabriel's Wharf

The Lowdown

- **Map ref** 11 A5
  Address 56 Upper Ground, SE1 9PP; 020 7021 1686; www.coinstreet.org
- **Train** Blackfriars, Waterloo. **Tube** Southwark, Waterloo. **Bus stop** Stamford Street, Blackfriars Bridge, Waterloo Bridge, Upper Ground, Waterloo Road. **River bus** Blackfriars Millennium Pier, Bankside Pier
- **Open** Shops, studios and Oxo Gallery 11am–6pm Tue–Sun. Restaurants and cafés till late
- **Price** Free, including Oxo Gallery and Oxo Tower Walkway
- **Age range** All
- **Activities** Sport and dance drop-in classes are available at the nearby Colombo Centre (34–68 Colombo St, SE1 8DP; 020 7261 1658; http://jubileehalltrust.org/colombo/).
- **Eat and drink** Snacks House of Crepes (56 Upper Ground, SE1 9PP; 020 7401 9816; 8am–4pm) is one of several options at Gabriel's Wharf. Real meal Gourmet Pizza Company (59–65 Upper Ground, SE1 9PP; 020 7928 3188; 11:30am–11pm daily) serves traditional Italian dishes and tasty pizzas with inventive toppings.
- **Toilets** Next to the Studio 6 bar/restaurant

⑤ Southbank Centre

Music, dance, art, poetry, comedy... and purple cows

The Southbank Centre comprises three main venues, the Hayward Gallery, the Queen Elizabeth Hall and the Royal Festival Hall, which together showcase all manner of music, art, dance and performance.

The Hayward Gallery is a cavernous contemporary art space that often puts on innovative and interactive shows. For example, its 2011 "Move" exhibition let visitors swing on monkey rings, don gorilla suits and pummel punchbags. The Royal Festival Hall, built for the 1951 Festival of Britain, is filled with exhibition, performance and eating areas. Its eclectic line-up includes Friday Lunch, a free gig in the Foyer Bar (Level 2); and family workshops most weekends in the Clore Ballroom, reflecting current shows. The gingerbread bake-off to complement *Hansel and Gretel* was especially memorable.

Since 2009, the Centre has staged a summer arts festival in the Udderbelly, a pop-up theatre in Jubilee Gardens set inside a giant upside-down purple cow. Its theme for 2012 is the Olympics.

Letting off steam

Jubilee Gardens (*Belvedere Road, SE1 7XZ*) has a playground, and from May–Oct, kids will love playing in Jeppe Hein's "walk-in fountain" on the Festival Hall terrace.

Free concert in the Foyer Bar of the Royal Festival Hall

Prices given are for a family of four

Mesmerising creatures of the deep in the Sea Life London Aquarium

The Lowdown

- 🌐 **Map ref** 10 H5
  Address Belvedere Road, SE1 8XX; 020 7960 4200; www.southbankcentre.co.uk. Hayward Gallery: 0844 875 0073
- 🚃 **Train** Waterloo, Waterloo East, Charing Cross. **Tube** Waterloo, Embankment. **Bus stop** Waterloo Bridge, Upper Ground, Waterloo Road, Stamford Street. **River bus** Festival Pier; London Eye Millennium Pier; Embankment Pier.
- 🕐 **Open** Royal Festival Hall 10am–11pm daily; Hayward Gallery 10am–6pm daily. Queen Elizabeth Hall opens 90 minutes before show time
- 💲 **Price** Performances individually priced, likewise Hayward Gallery exhibitions (reductions for ages 12–16; under-12s free)
- 👫 **Activities** For the full programme, visit www.southbankcentre.co.uk/find/family. The Waterloo Sunset Pavilion (Hayward Gallery 10am–6pm daily) has six monitors showing cartoons suitable for all.
- ♿ **Wheelchair access** All venues
- ☕ **Eat and drink** *Snacks* Concrete at the Hayward (*Hayward Gallery; 020 7921 0758; 10am–11pm Tue–Thu, 10am–10pm Fri & Sat, 10am–6pm Sun & Mon*) serves toasties. *Family treat* Skylon Restaurant (*Royal Festival Hall; 020 7654 7800; noon–2:30pm, 5:30pm–10:30pm Mon–Sat, noon–4pm Sun*) offers upmarket food.
- 🛍️ **Shops** Festival Terrace sells design-led gifts. Royal Festival Hall shop celebrates the artistic programme. Hayward Gallery offers gifts, books and cards.
- 🚻 **Toilets** All venues

⑥ Sea Life London Aquarium

Find Nemo and outstare a shark

It is said that we know more about deep space than we do about the deep oceans. After visiting the London Aquarium, that claim seems entirely plausible. Its three floors of tanks showcase more than 500 marine species, including amazing fish that change colour, fish that change sex, fish that glow in the dark, and fish that look like snowflakes, butterflies or boulders.

The aquarium tunnels under County Hall, its galleries snaking through vaults that echo with ambient music, which can feel a bit claustrophobic at busy times. The main tanks rise through two storeys and are so large that the fish-tank furniture includes a whale skeleton and several Easter Island-style sculpted heads. A walk-through glass tunnel brings children eye to beady eye with turtles, rays and murderous-looking sand tiger sharks. In other zones, kids may get to stroke a starfish or help out with the daily fish feeds, though interactivity is fairly limited. The big climax is the Shark Walk, which dares visitors to tiptoe over a glass platform right above the killers.

Letting off steam

Try **Jubilee Gardens** (*see left*), or spacious **Archbishop's Park** (*Carlisle Lane, SE1 7LE*), just to the south on Lambeth Palace Road.

The Lowdown

🌐 **Map ref** 10 H6

Address County Hall, Westminster Bridge Road, SE1 7PB; 0871 663 1678; www.visitsealife.com/London

🚆 **Train** Waterloo. **Tube** Waterloo, Westminster. **Bus stop** Belvedere Road, York Road. **River bus** London Eye Millennium Pier.

🕐 **Open** 10am–6pm Mon–Thu, 10am–7pm Fri–Sun (last admission: 1 hour earlier)

💲 **Price** £60–70 (10 per cent saving by booking online). 25 per cent discount after 3pm

🚶 **Skipping the queue** Priority Entrance (more expensive) ticket-holders skip most of the queue.

👫 **Age range** 3 plus

👫 **Activities** Feeding sessions at 11:30am, 1:30pm, 3:30pm and 4:30pm daily; plus shark feeds 2:30pm Tue, Thu and Sat.

⏱ **Allow** Up to 1½ hours

🍴 **Eat and Drink** *Picnic* Ned's Noodle Bar *(3E Belvedere Road, SE1 7GQ; 020 7593 0077; noon–11:15pm Mon–Sat, till 10:15pm Sun)* does kids' noodle boxes. *Snacks* Aji Zen Canteen *(County Hall; 020 7928 7766; noon–10:30pm Mon–Sat, till 10pm Sun)* is another tasty option.

🛍 **Shop** Selling gifts and souvenirs

👫 **Toilets** All floors

⑦ London Film Museum

From Batman to the Borrowers

This museum is an oddity: an eclectic collection of movie memorabilia arranged along the panelled corridors of London's former council building. It's not the most professional production, but there's enough to grab the attention of most children, especially if they like superheroes and sci-fi.

Superman flying over the Statue of Liberty in the British Film Museum

For younger visitors, the best bit comes right at the beginning, as an animatronic *T. rex* from *Night at the Museum 2* jerks menacingly to life just fingertips from the crowd. For maximum shriek value, don't tell them about it beforehand. Across the hall stands the Headless Knight from *Harry Potter* – or perhaps it's just his outfit, donated by ace movie armourer Terry English!

There are detailed exhibitions on the Lambeth-born legend Charlie Chaplin, and the pioneering *Jason and the Argonauts* monster-maker, Ray Harryhausen; while the centrepiece of the museum is a circular chamber housing assorted props and costumes, including Christian Bale's *Batman* suit, the Thunderbird 4 submarine and outsize pepperpots from *The Borrowers*. The walk-in *Star Wars* set, complete with C3PO and R2D2, may excite dads more than their offspring; it costs £7 extra to have a photo taken here.

Letting off steam

Jubilee Gardens *(see left)* and Archbishop's Park *(see left)* have space for kids to run around.

The Lowdown

🌐 **Map ref** 10 H6

Address County Hall, Westminster Bridge Road, SE1 7PB; 020 7202 7040; www.londonfilmmuseum.com

🚆 **Transport** See Sea Life London Aquarium *(above)*

🕐 **Open** 10am–5pm Mon–Fri (11am Thu); 10am–6pm Sat; 11am–6pm Sun (last adm: 1 hour earlier)

💲 **Price** £33–43; under 5s free

🎫 **Guided tours** £25; groups of 15 or over get a free tour

👫 **Age range** 6 plus

⏱ **Allow** Up to 2 hours

♿ **Wheelchair access** The museum is on the 1st floor, but there is a lift – please call ahead

🍴 **Eat and drink** Coffee lounge with vending machine; County Hall and the Southbank Centre have several dining options

🛍 **Shop** Selling film souvenirs

👫 **Toilets** On the first floor

German Focke Wulf 190, North American P-51 Mustang and British Spitfire at the IWM

⑧ Imperial War Museum (IWM)

War stories and weaponry

Housed in what used to be the Bethlem Royal Hospital, this enormous museum tries hard not to be too gung-ho about its subject. But some kids (and adults) are bound to coo over the vast main hall, literally filled to the rafters with warplanes, tanks, missiles and other deadly hardware. Highlights include British Field Marshall Bernard Montgomery's tank, a Nazi V2 rocket and a one-man submarine.

The IWM makes a real effort to appeal to families through a changing series of well-thought-out galleries and exhibitions. The fabulous Children's War, charting the story of World War II through the eyes of its younger victims, has now closed, to be replaced by a brand-new family at war exhibit,

Memorial to the Soviet dead of World War II, Geraldine Mary Harmsworth Park

Prices given are for a family of four

also focusing on the 1939–45 war. The displays can be unflinching, but are always accessible, with stories to listen to and games to play such as spot the enemy bomber.

On the Lower Ground Floor, twin galleries explore the two world wars in serious detail, leavened by occasional touch-screen puzzles and quizzes. Children may choose to fast-forward to the Trench Experience, a dark bunker that plunges visitors into the sights, sounds and stink of a Somme battlefield; and the Blitz Experience, intricately re-creating a bombed-out London street.

The second and third floors contain an exhibition on the

Up periscope! Children getting hands-on at the Imperial War Museum

Holocaust, some parts of which might be too graphic for pre-teens (under 11s are not allowed to enter).

Letting off steam

The IWM is set in **Geraldine Mary Harmsworth Park** (*Kennington Road, SE11*), which has a café, a fine playground, and an indoor play centre for under 5s – or under 12s during school holidays – which is open 1pm–4pm weekdays.

The Lowdown

🌐 **Map ref** 17 B2
Address Lambeth Rd, SE1 6HZ; 020 7416 5000; www.iwm.org.uk

🚆 **Train** Waterloo, Elephant and Castle. **Tube** Lambeth North, Elephant and Castle, Waterloo. **Bus stop** Lambeth Road, Kennington Road, St George's Road

🕐 **Open** 10am–6pm daily (last admission: 5:45pm)

💷 **Price** Free; temporary exhibitions individually priced

🚩 **Guided tours** Free tours at weekends only (11:30am and 1:30pm), plus audio guides for adults and children

👫 **Age range** 6 plus, but some exhibitions may be unsuitable for pre-teens

👫 **Activities** Cinema screenings most days (times vary). Frequent weekend storytelling, crafts and drama workshops for ages 6 and above, usually tied to temporary exhibitions, plus school holiday family activities: check website

⏱ **Allow** Up to 3 hours

♿ **Wheelchair access** Yes, via Park entrance – sometimes parts of exhibitions are not accessible

🍴 **Eat and drink** *Picnic* Café Roma (*Geraldine Mary Harmsworth Park, SE11*) offers ices, shakes and good-value kids' lunch bags. *Snacks* The Garden Café (*Lambeth Palace Rd, SE1 7LB; 020 7401 8865; www. gardenmuseum.org.uk; 10:30am–5pm daily*) is part of the Garden Museum, set in the former St Mary-at-Lambeth church. The museum has garden history displays and an art cart for children, and the menu at the homely vegetarian café changes daily according to what's in season.

🛍 **Shop** Lower ground floor, selling books, CDs, posters and gifts

🚻 **Toilets** Lower ground floor

⑨ Florence Nightingale Museum

Throwing light on the Lady With The Lamp

This one-room museum, beside the ambulance bay at St Thomas's Hospital, deserves top marks for making this woman's extraordinary life story so engaging. Florence Nightingale worked as a nurse during the Crimean War (1853–6), and founded Britain's first school of nursing in 1860. The museum is partitioned into three eye-catching "pavilions": the first hemmed by hedgerows to represent Nightingale's gilded youth; the next clad in Turkish tiles, to evoke the Crimean War; the third a mock-up of the bedroom where she spent most of her later life. She was often ill, but became the most popular woman in Victorian England thanks to her tireless campaigning for health reform. Kids can see the figurines that sold by the thousand to Florence's fans, along with her pet owl (stuffed, of course) and that famous lamp.

Florence Nightingale is a genuinely interesting character, but there are also several gadgets to help keep kids' attention, not least the ingenious "stethoscope" audio guide. Touch-screen challenges invite children to pack a medicine chest with useful kit for the battle-field, or wash their hands then scan them for germs. Elsewhere, short films bring the history of nursing up to date – including a look at the MRSA menace raging through modern hospitals. The Lady With The Lamp would not approve.

Letting off steam

Just 3 minutes' walk along Lambeth Palace Road is **Archbishop's Park** (Carlisle Lane, SE1 7LE), with a playground, a nature garden and tennis courts (0845 130 8998) for hire.

The Lowdown

- 🌐 **Map ref** 16 H1
- **Address** 2 Lambeth Palace Road, SE1 7EW; 020 7620 0374; www.florence-nightingale.co.uk
- 🚗 **Train** Waterloo. **Tube** Waterloo, Westminster. **Bus stop** Westminster Bridge, York Road, Lambeth Palace Road. **River bus** London Eye Millennium Pier, Westminster Pier
- 🕐 **Open** 10am–5pm daily
- 💷 **Price** £16–26
- 🚩 **Guided tours** None. Free audio guides for adults and children aged 7–11, plus I-Spy trail for younger ones
- 🧍 **Age range** 5 plus
- 🧑‍🎨 **Activities** Themed art-and-craft activities in school holidays: check website for details. Museum website's dedicated Kids' Zone has fact sheets
- ⏱ **Allow** Up to 2 hours
- ♿ **Wheelchair access** Yes
- 🍴 **Eat and drink** Snacks Yo! Sushi (County Hall, Belvedere Rd; 020 7928 8871; noon–11pm Mon–Sat, till 7pm Sun). Real meal Troia (3F Belvedere Road, SE1 7GQ; 020 7633 9309; noon–midnight daily) is a Turkish diner.
- 🛍 **Shop** Selling a range of quirky souvenirs
- 🚻 **Toilets** On the ground floor

Using a stethoscope to listen to the audio tour at the Florence Nightingale Museum

Picnic under £20; **Snacks** £20–40; **Real meal** £40–60; **Family treat** £60 or more (based on a family of four)

Kensington,
Chelsea & Battersea

With its world-class museums and fine parks, this wedge of West London feels like a purpose-built family entertainment zone. And in the 1850s, that is more or less what it was. A new cultural quarter in Kensington rose from the proceeds of the 1851 Great Exhibition, while across the river, plant-hunter John Gibson created Battersea Park for the masses. Tying the two together is the King's Road, lined with designer shops and restaurants.

Bloomsbury and
Regent's Park

The City and
the East End

Westminster
and the
West End

Southwark and
the South Bank

**Kensington,
Chelsea and
Battersea**

Highlights

Science Museum
If you think science is boring, think again. The galleries here are filled with interactive hi-tech wizardry, and the live science shows are a blast (see p180–81).

Natural History Museum
This great museum's collection runs to 70 million specimens – animals, insects, fossils, plants and skeletons. But beware: the T rex comes alive (see p182–3)!

Victoria and Albert Museum
There's a maze of galleries here so it can be hard on the feet. If that's the case, take a break in the palatial paddling pool (see p184).

Battersea Park
Meet the monkeys at Battersea Park Children's Zoo, then ape them at London's wildest adventure playground (see p188–9).

Kensington Palace
There's nowhere more regal to take high tea than Queen Anne's Orangery at Kensington Palace – they even serve a special child's version (see p176).

Harrods
For everything your child never knew they needed – how about a diamond-encrusted Monopoly set, bespoke rocking-horse or a doll in their own image (see p181)?

Left *Wooden pirate galleon, the impressive centrepiece of the Diana Princess of Wales Memorial Playground, Kensington Gardens* **Above** *Meerkat at Battersea Park Children's Zoo*

The Best of
Kensington, Chelsea and Battersea

South Kensington's three famous museums – the Science Museum, the Natural History Museum and the Victoria and Albert Museum (V&A) – represent one of the greatest gatherings of wonders in the world. And they're all free. If the children tire of all this learning, the open spaces of Kensington Gardens and Battersea Park are perfect places to let off steam.

Free for all

This affluent area is one of London's best places for a weekend of free family activities. Start at the **Science Museum** (see pp180–81) on Saturday: arrive at 10am to get first go on the Launchpad gallery's hands-on experiments, then see the auditorium's lively shows; after that, hit the basement picnic zone (cheaper than the cafés). Round off with the 3:30pm tour in the Exploring Space gallery.

On Sunday, take in some pageantry as Her Majesty's horse guards trot under Wellington Arch (see p177) at 10:30am. Afterwards, feed the ducks on the Serpentine lake (see p174) in **Hyde**

Left The Peter Pan-themed Diana Princess of Wales Memorial Playground *Below* Traditional pedalo fun on the Serpentine

Life-size model of a blue whale, the largest-ever creature on the planet, at the Natural History Museum

Park, then leave the park via the playground at Edinburgh Gate and head to the **V&A** *(see p184)*, which runs free drop-in family workshops till 5pm.

Wet, wet, wet ...

Who doesn't love making a splash – whether it's running a hand through the water from a pedalo in **Battersea Park** *(see p188)*, or total immersion at the Serpentine Lido *(see p174)*, which is open from Jun–Sep and has a paddling pool for little ones. Or you could try the Peter Pan paddling pool at the Diana Princess of Wales Memorial Playground *(see p172)* in Kensington Gardens.

The museums get in on the act too: the V&A *(see p184)* allows summer paddling in its courtyard, while in the basement playroom at the **Science Museum** *(see pp180–81)*, kids can splash around with water. In winter, when the weather's wet, head for the Chelsea Sports Centre pool *(see p190)* and jump right in.

Encounters with nature

With three great parks and the world's biggest collection of birds, beasts and botany, this area is a great place to introduce children to nature. The main draw is the **Natural History Museum** *(see p182–3)* – so vast that it warrants a day's exploration. First off, book a place on a behind-the-scenes Spirit Collection Tour and consult the film schedule at the Attenborough Studio. Pick up a free children's backpack from the welcome desk and head off to see prehistoric monsters or cheeky monkeys. From 2:30pm, the Investigate Centre invites families to study real specimens.

There is a meerkat enclosure at **Battersea Park Children's Zoo** *(see p190)*, while just across the Thames, the **Chelsea Physic Garden** *(p191)*

is another hive of animal activity – its holiday workshops include pond-dipping, creepy-crawly handling and herbalism for beginners.

Season by season

In Hyde Park *(see p174)*, spring begins with a bang, with a 41-gun salute on 21 April for the Queen's birthday. From Easter, pedalos and rowing boats glide over the Serpentine, while at the **Natural History Museum** *(see p182–3)*, they open their wildlife garden and pop-up butterfly house. The Chelsea Flower Show *(see p187)* bursts into bloom in May.

July sees the **Serpentine Galleries** *(see p176)* launch their summer season and entertainers perform at the Diana Princess of Wales Memorial Playground *(see p174)*. The Proms, an eight-week summer season of orchestral concerts, begin at the **Royal Albert Hall** *(see p185)*.

Winter is festival time. November brings fireworks in **Battersea Park** *(see p188)* and the city's Christmas bash, Winter Wonderland, in **Hyde Park** *(see p174)*, with Santa, skating and *glühwein*.

A ring-tailed lemur, one of the popular small primates at Battersea Park Children's Zoo

Kensington Gardens, Hyde Park and around

Inspired by the story of Peter Pan, with its pirate galleon and tree full of pixies, the Diana Princess of Wales Memorial Playground in Kensington Gardens is the perfect place to let imaginations run wild. The playground is situated next to the late Princess's Kensington Palace home, with Hyde Park next door for more outdoor fun. Most kids' stuff is concentrated south of the Serpentine swimming lido, making Knightsbridge, on the Piccadilly Tube line, the best route in.

Kensington, Chelsea and Battersea

Kensington Gardens and Hyde Park

Science Museum p178

Battersea Park p186

0 metres 200
0 yards 200

The ornate Albert Memorial, Kensington Gardens, commissioned by Queen Victoria after the death of her husband, Albert

Victoria Gate pet cemetery

Places of interest

SIGHTS
1. Hyde Park and Kensington Gardens
2. Kensington Palace
3. Serpentine Galleries
4. Apsley House

EAT AND DRINK
1. Mount Street Deli
2. Broadwalk Café
3. Serpentine Bar & Kitchen
4. The Cookbook Café
5. Hyde Park Tennis Centre Café
6. Lido Café Bar
7. Hard Rock Café
See also Kensington Palace (p176)

SHOPPING
1. Selfridges

WHERE TO STAY
1. Mandarin Oriental
2. Royal Garden
3. The Parkwood at Marble Arch

Cooling off on a hot day at the Diana Princess of Wales Memorial Fountain

Right The Serpentine Galleries, built in 1934 as a Tea Pavilion, and now home to modern art
Far right Speakers' Corner in Hyde Park, a bastion of public speaking for 150 years

The Lowdown

🚗 **Rail** Paddington (a five-minute walk). **Tube** Marble Arch, Lancaster Gate, Queensway (all Central Line); Knightsbridge, Hyde Park Corner (both Piccadilly Line). **Bus** Park Lane: route numbers 2, 10, 16, 36, 73, 74, 82, 137, 148, 414, 436; Marble Arch: 6, 7, 23, 98, 113, 159; Bayswater Road: 94, 274, 390; Knightsbridge: 9, 10, 52, 452

ℹ **Visitor information** Old Police House, Hyde Park, W2 2UH (www.royalparks.org.uk); Victoria Railway Station (see pp64–5)

🛒 **Supermarkets** Sainsburys Local, Marble Arch Tower, 55 Bryanston Street, W1H 7AA; West One Food Fayre, 85 Duke Street, W1K 5PG
Markets Bayswater Road Market (art, jewellery), 10am–6pm Sun; Notting Hill Farmers' Market (food), Kensington Church Street, 9am–1pm Sat; Portobello Market 8am–7pm Mon–Sat, 8am–1pm Thu; Fri Easter–Oct, Sat all year (fashion, antiques)

🎪 **Festivals** Royal Gun Salutes, near Speakers' Corner (6 Feb, 21 Apr, 2 Jun and 10 Jun); Hard Rock Calling, rock music, (Jun); Wireless Festival, pop music, (Jul); Notting Hill Carnival, Aug Bank Holiday weekend; Winter Wonderland, Christmas festival (Nov–Jan)

➕ **Pharmacies** Bliss Chemists, 5–6 Marble Arch, W1H 7EL (9am–11:30pm daily). For 24-hour pharmacies visit www.nhs.uk/ServiceDirectories

🛝 **Nearest playgrounds** There are three in the parks, at Edinburgh Gate (Hyde Park); Diana Princess of Wales Memorial Playground and Westbourne Gate (both Kensington Gardens)

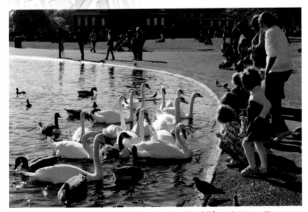

The Round Pond in Kensington Gardens, popular with wildlife and visitors alike

① Kensington Gardens and Hyde Park

Visit one park and get another one free!

The ever-youthful Peter Pan first sprang to life in Kensington Gardens – his creator JM Barrie lived nearby – and it remains a great place for those who've never really grown up. Along with neighbouring Hyde Park, it offers picnic and play opportunities galore – on both land and water. Children's entertainers perform here daily throughout the summer, and the Diana Princess of Wales Memorial Walk cleverly links together all the highlights.

Peter Pan statue by the Serpentine

Key Features

Diana Memorial Walk

Kensington Palace (see p176)

Peter Pan statue

Albert Memorial

① **The Serpentine** Eat beside it, swim in it, row across it, or seek out herons and cormorants in its wilder reaches or swans and geese around its edge.

② **Diana Princess of Wales Memorial Fountain** Created in 2004, in memory of Princess Diana, this is less a fountain than a spot for dipping toes.

③ **Speakers' Corner** A place for budding orators and eccentrics to address people on any subject they choose. Sunday is the busiest day.

④ **Diana Princess of Wales Memorial Playground** As well as a galleon, there is a music trail and a teepee encampment. Nearby, the ancient Elfin Oak is alive with fairy folk carvings made by Ivor Innes in the 1920s.

The Lowdown

🌐 **Map ref** 8 G4
Address Park Office, Rangers Lodge, W2 2UH; 020 7298 2000; www.royalparks.org.uk.

🚗 **Tube** Marble Arch, Queensway, Lancaster Gate. **Bus stop** Black Lion Gate; Marlborough Gate; Marble Arch; Hyde Park Corner; Edinburgh Gate; Royal Albert Hall; Palace Gate.

🕐 **Open** Hyde Park: 5am–midnight daily; Kensington Gardens: 6am–dusk daily

💲 **Price** Free

🚩 **Guided tours** Free 90-minute guided walks monthly in both parks (020 7298 2083); 45-minute Albert Memorial tours 1st Sun of month (2pm & 3pm), Mar–Dec (020 7936 2568)

👪 **Age range** All

Activities Daily children's entertainment from Jul–Aug at the Diana Princess of Wales Memorial Playground (020 7298 2141) and the Serpentine Lido (020 7706 3422). Lido and paddling pool open May: 10am–6pm Sat & Sun; Jun–mid-Sep: 10am–6pm daily (adults £4, ages 3–15 £1). Hyde Park Tennis & Sports Centre has pay-and-play tennis all year (020 7262 3474). The Boathouse offers boat and pedalo hire, Easter–Oct: 10am–dusk (£25/hour; 020 7262 1330). Solarshuttle boat rides, Mar–Sep: weekends and public hols; Jun–Aug: daily (020 7262 1330; www.solarshuttle.co.uk)

⏱ **Allow** Up to a full day

♿ **Wheelchair access** There are free electric buggies which give half-hour rides around the park.

🍴 **Cafés** Serpentine Bar & Kitchen (see right) or Lido Café Bar (020 7706 7098; www.lidohydepark.co.uk). Plus snacks at Hyde Park Tennis Centre Café (summer 9am–9pm, winter 10am-4pm; 020 7262 3474) and Broadwalk Café (see right), as well as at kiosks.

🚻 **Toilets** At Serpentine Road, the Lookout, Marble Arch (Hyde Park); Palace Gate, Lancaster Gate, Black Lion Gate, Marlborough Gate (Kensington Gardens)

Good family value?
The park and its three playgrounds are free; swimming and tennis are affordable; only boat hire is pricey.

Take cover

If it rains, **Queens Ice and Bowl** (17 Queensway, W2 4QP; 020 7229 0172; www.queensiceandbowl. co.uk; Mon–Sun 10am–11pm) is a 2-minute walk north of Black Lion Gate, and offers ice-skating (£41–51; skate hire from £2) and tenpin bowling (£7 per person). Alternatively, Kensington's trio of mighty museums (see pp180–84) are just a short walk away via Exhibition Road and entirely free.

Youngsters ice-skating at Queens Ice and Bowl

Eat and drink

Picnic: under £20; Snacks: £20–40; Real meal: £40–60; Family treat: £60 or more (based on a family of four)

PICNIC Delicatessens are more decadent than usual around here. Try Mayfair's **Mount Street Deli** (100 Mount Street, W1K 2TG; 020 7499 6843, www.themountstreetdeli.co.uk; 8am–8pm Mon–Fri, 9am–6pm Sat). **SNACKS Broadwalk Café** (020 7034 0722; www.companyofcooks. com; summer: 8am–8pm; winter: 10am–4pm), by the Diana Princess of Wales Memorial Playground, has a "playcafé" menu for kids.

The Lido Café Bar, on the banks of the Serpentine

REAL MEAL Serpentine Bar & Kitchen (020 7706 8114; www. serpentinebarandkitchen.com; 8am–9pm daily) overlooks the lake and has a pre-teen menu with fishfingers and toasted sandwiches for under £5.

FAMILY TREAT The Cookbook Café (1 Hamilton Place, Park Lane, W1J 3QY; 020 7318 8563, www. cookbookcafe.co.uk; 6:30am–11am; noon–3pm; 6pm–10pm daily; weekend brunch 12.30pm–4pm) is cool, casual and costly, with hefty Market Table lunches plus a monthly children's cookery class.

Shopping

The mammouth **Selfridges** department store is nearby (400 Oxford Street, W1A 1AB; 0800 123400, www.selfridges.com).

Find out more

DIGITAL A self-guided walk around Hyde Park can be downloaded at www.royalparks.gov.uk/Hyde-Park. aspx: click "main attractions" on the interactive map, then click on a point of interest to get a download. **FILM** The biopic *Finding Neverland* (2004), starring Johnny Depp, used the real Kensington Gardens for the scenes where author JM Barrie first enchanted children with tales of Peter Pan, Wendy and Captain Hook.

Next stop. . .

PORTOBELLO ROAD MARKET If it's Saturday, walk west from Black Lion Gate to explore Portobello Road Market (8am–7pm; www. portobelloroad.co.uk), reputedly the world's biggest antiques jamboree. Children should seek out Mr Punch's Old Toys (Unit 18, Admiral Vernon Arcade, W11 2DY) and Victoriana Dolls (101 Portobello Rd, W11 2QB). **HYDE PARK STABLES** For a canter beside the Serpentine, contact Hyde Park Stables (020 7723 2813, www. hydeparkstables.com), which offers riding lessons on Rotten Row, the 300-year-old royal carriageway. From £64 per hour, beginners welcome.

Putting a pony and young rider through their paces at Hyde Park Stables

② Kensington Palace

A palace full of princesses

It was in 1689 that Kensington Palace first became a royal home, when William of Orange asked architect Christopher Wren to turn a Jacobean manor into a place fit for a king. On 20 June 1837, 18-year-old Princess Victoria woke in her bed here to discover she was queen, and by the 1930s, so many minor royals were quartered in "Princesses' Court" that Edward VIII called it "an aunt heap". But the palace is best known as the long-time home of Diana, Princess of Wales – and as a showcase for her gorgeous array of gowns. William and Kate, the Duke and Duchess of Cambridge, now have an apartment here, too.

Major refurbishment in 2011–12 has opened up much of the palace, allowing visitors better access to the elegant courtyards, which they can enjoy before touring the highlights of the Royal Ceremonial Dress Collection, with its 12,000 historic garments. Other exhibitions reveal the public and private lives of queens – Mary II, Anne and especially Victoria – and detail the trials and tribulations that come with being a princess, by exploring the lives of Princess Margaret and, of course, Diana.

Letting off steam

Head to the nearby **Diana Princess of Wales Memorial Playground** for a run around (see p174).

The Lowdown

- **Map ref** 7 D5
- **Address** Kensington Gardens, W8 4PX; 0844 482 7777; www.hrp.org.uk/KensingtonPalace
- **Tube** High Street Kensington, Queensway. **Bus stop** Bayswater Road, Knightsbridge
- **Open** Mar–Sep: 10am–6pm daily; Oct–Feb: 10am–5pm daily (last admission: 1 hour earlier)
- **Price** £34–52 (including voluntary donation), under-5s free
- **Skipping the queue** Book online to dodge the ticket queue – it's slightly cheaper, too
- **Age range** 5 plus
- **Activities** Free family craft activities in school holidays. Online "fun and games" zone has children's trails and Tudor sewing patterns
- **Allow** Up to 2 hours
- **Wheelchair access** Yes, to all floors
- **Eat and drink** *Snacks* The Broadwalk Café (see p175) is lovely when the sun shines. *Real meal* The palace's 300-year-old Orangery is an elegant place for breakfast, a light lunch or afternoon tea (winter: noon–5pm; summer till 6pm). The restaurant has a super kids' menu, and even does a special children's version of afternoon tea.
- **Shop** Selling gifts and souvenirs
- **Toilets** On the ground floor

③ Serpentine Galleries

Art in the gardens

These two outstanding – and often underrated – galleries showcase modern and contemporary art. The original gallery looks, from the outside, like a twee 1930s tea pavilion – but step indoors, and surprises lurk. The four stark whitespaces have held exhibitions by Andy Warhol, Damien Hirst and Jeff Koons. Typically, there are five shows a year, and from July to October the gallery spills onto the surrounding lawns, when it invites big names such as Frank Gehry to design a pavilion to host "Park Nights" – a theatre, music and film performance programme. Meanwhile, an artist-led Family Sunday workshop takes place most months, and includes hands-on craft activities.

The second gallery is housed in the Grade II-listed Palladian-style Magazine building across the lake. This satellite gallery, opened in 2012 in time for the Olympics, focuses on young artists, and there is an outdoor Playscape to encourage all ages to play around with art.

The Lowdown

- **Map ref** 8 F6
- **Address** Kensington Gardens, W2 3XA; 020 7402 6075; www.serpentinegallery.org
- **Tube** Knightsbridge, South Kensington, Lancaster Gate. **Bus stop** Knightsbridge
- **Open** 10am–6pm
- **Price** Free
- **Age range** Call ahead to check suitability of current show
- **Activities** Free Family Sunday workshop most months (noon–5pm). Check website for full programme
- **Allow** 1 hour
- **Wheelchair access** Yes
- **Eat and drink** *Snacks* Hyde Park Tennis Centre Café (020 7262 3474) offers simple snack fare. *Real meal* Lido Café Bar serves lunches and home-made ice cream (020 7706 7098; www.lidohydepark.co.uk).
- **Shop** In reception, selling art books and cards
- **Toilets** On the ground floor

The grand entrance gates at Kensington Palace

Prices given are for a family of four

Letting off steam

The galleries are surrounded by open, grassy areas, and there's a playground at the nearby **Serpentine Lido** (see p174).

Children's art workshop at the Serpentine Galleries, a major modern art venue

④ Apsley House

At home with Old Nosey

A door-plate outside Apsley House, known as "Number One, London", says: "To the private apartments of the Duke of Wellington." This mansion on Hyde Park Corner is still part-occupied by descendents of Arthur Wellesley, the first Duke of Wellington, Britain's greatest general and the hero of the Battle of Waterloo (1815). The duke bought the house in 1817, two years after his triumph over Napoleon, and it has been restored to the dazzle of its Regency heyday, filled with the paintings, porcelain and silver given to him by kings and emperors.

Riding along the pleasant bridleways through Hyde Park

In his day, Wellington was said to be "the most famous man in Europe", though his troops nicknamed him "Old Nosey" – and Apsley's jolly children's trail encourages kids to hunt for his aquiline profile all over the house. A giant statue of Napoleon stands in the stairwell, but the highlight is the Waterloo Gallery – with works by Goya, Rubens and Velazquez – where children can lie supine and scan the painted ceiling.

Apsley's front window looks out to Wellington Arch, commissioned by George IV as a grand gateway to Buckingham Palace. An admission fee buys you access to exhibits and a balcony view of the Household Cavalry en route to the Changing the Guard ceremony (see p70).

Letting off steam

Hyde Park is Apsley's back garden and the nearest playground is at the park's Edinburgh Gate.

The Lowdown

- 🌐 **Map ref** 9 B6
  Address 149 Piccadilly, Hyde Park Corner, W1J 7NT; 020 7499 5676; www.english-heritage.org. uk/apsleyhouse
- 🚆 **Train** Victoria. **Tube** Hyde Park Corner. **Bus stop** Hyde Park Corner
- 🕐 **Open** Apr–Oct: 11am–5pm Wed–Sun; Nov–Mar till 4pm (last admission: 30 minutes before closing). Wellington Arch opens at 10am
- 💷 **Price** £18–28. Wellington Arch: £12–18. Joint ticket £20–33
- 🚹 **Skipping the queue** The Horse Guards ride through Wellington Arch most days at 10:30am and 11:30am – come early for a view
- 🚩 **Guided tours** Free 15-minute gallery talks daily (times vary)
- 🚻 **Age range** 7 plus
- 🧗 **Activities** Free audio guide. Free children's trail from visitor desk or downloadable online
- ⏱ **Allow** 1–2 hours
- ♿ **Wheelchair access** No, due to unavoidable steps
- ☕ **Eat and drink** *Snacks* Serpentine Bar & Kitchen (see p175) is great for lunches. *Real meal* Hard Rock Café (150 Old Park Lane, W1K 1QR; 020 7629 0382; www. hardrock.com) is a themed burger joint with an under-11s' menu.
- 🛍 **Shop** On the ground floor, selling specialist books and memorabilia
- 🚻 **Toilets** In the basement

Picnic: under £20; **Snacks:** £20–40; **Real meal:** £40–60; **Family treat:** £60 or more (based on a family of four)

Science Museum and around

Prince Albert's dream of a new cultural quarter funded by profits from his 1851 Great Exhibition, ballooned into a trio of colossal free museums south of Hyde Park. From South Kensington Tube station, pedestrian tunnels lead directly to the Science Museum and Natural History Museum, while the Victoria & Albert is just across Exhibition Road. The Science Museum is an especially powerful magnet for kids, using every trick of 21st-century technology to bring its subject to life. This area is a great destination in winter, with almost everything under cover (including indoor playrooms and an IMAX cinema).

Kensington, Chelsea and Battersea

Kensington Gardens and Hyde Park *p172*

Science Museum

Battersea Park *p186*

Captivated by a statue in the Victoria & Albert Museum

Taking part in a demonstration at the Science Museum

| 0 metres | 200 |
| 0 yards | 200 |

Diplodocus skeleton in the Natural History Museum

The Lowdown

🚌 **Tube** South Kensington. **Bus** Exhibition Road, South Kensington Tube station: route numbers 14, 49, 70, 74, 345, 414, 430, C1; Kensington Road: 9, 10, 52, 452

ℹ️ **Visitor information** Victoria Railway Station (*see pp64–5*)

🛒 **Supermarkets** Waitrose, Gloucester Arcade, 128 Gloucester Rd, SW7 4SF **Markets** South Kensington Farmers' Market, Bute Street, SW7, 9am–2pm Sat

🎪 **Festivals** Ideal Home Show, Earls Court (Mar); Real Food Festival, Earls Court (May); Earls Court Festival, mixed arts (Jun–Jul); BBC Proms, Royal Albert Hall (Jul–Sep); London Design Festival, Victoria & Albert Museum (Sep); Festival of Remembrance, Royal Albert Hall (Nov)

➕ **Pharmacies** Boots, 203–205 Brompton Road, SW3 1LA (9am–7pm Mon–Sat; 11am–6pm Sun). Harrods Pharmacy, 87–135 Brompton Road, SW1X 7XL (10am–8pm Mon–Sat; noon–6pm Sun). For 24-hour pharmacies, visit *www.nhs.uk/ServiceDirectories*

🛝 **Nearest playground** Climbing frame at Hyde Park Tennis Centre, near Alexandra Gate; larger playground near Edinburgh Gate

Harrods' Toy Kingdom – guaranteed to excite children young and old

Places of Interest

SIGHTS
1. Science Museum
2. Natural History Museum
3. Victoria & Albert Museum
4. Royal Albert Hall

● EAT AND DRINK
1. Partridges
2. Morelli's Gelato
3. The Treehouse
4. Café Consort
5. L'Opera

See also Science Museum (p181), Natural History Museum (p183), Victoria & Albert Museum (p184) and Royal Albert Hall (p185).

● SHOPPING
1. Harrods

● PLACES TO STAY
1. Crowne Plaza
2. Mandarin Oriental
3. The Beaufort
4. Number Sixteen
5. Beaufort House
6. Fraser Place Queens Gate

① Science Museum
Putting the fizz into physics

Fly with the Red Arrows, fire up a pedal-powered TV set or launch a space probe: the Science Museum offers an explosively entertaining day out. With seven storeys filled with wonders, there's plenty to occupy young and old here. At every turn it's playtime – whether in the Launchpad zone, with its child-friendly experiments, or Antenna, where kids can study scientific breakthroughs. Best of all is the look of the museum – a sci-fi universe of neon-lit galleries that makes just being there an adventure.

Replica of Sir Isaac Newton's telescope

Key features

① **Who Am I?** An intriguing interactive gallery using face-morphing, sex-switching gadgets and personality tests to explore human identity.

② **Atmosphere** Play games on the tabletops, walk across oceans and see how the environment adjusts in this climate-change hall controlled by its visitors.

③ **Fly Zone** Soar with the Red Arrows in a "3-D aerobatic experience" (ages 4 plus), or take the controls in a "Fly 360°" simulator (9 plus).

④ **Launchpad** This kids' gallery has lots of hands-on experiments and science shows with audience participation.

■ **Fifth Floor** Veterinary History, History of Medicine.

■ **Fourth Floor** Glimpses of Medical History.

■ **Third Floor** Launchpad, Flight and the Fly Zone, plus Health and 18th-century medicine.

■ **Second Floor** Energy, Computers, Mathematics, Ships, Docks and Diving, and Atmosphere.

■ **First Floor** Materials, Communication, the Cosmos, Time, Agriculture and Who Am I?

■ **Ground floor** Energy and the power of steam, Exploring Space, Making the Modern World and Pattern Pod for families.

■ **Basement** The Garden gallery and a display on labour-saving gadgets for the home.

⑤ **The Garden** This basement playroom invites pre-schoolers to get to grips with the material world, via water troughs, junk instruments and a "building site" climbing frame. It's mayhem!

⑥ **Eagle capsule** This full-size replica of the Apollo 11 craft that put Armstrong and Aldrin on the moon in 1969 is in the Exploring Space gallery.

Letting off steam

The museum's own The Garden playroom (ages 3–6, basement) and Pattern Pod (ages 5–8, ground floor) are both rule-free romping spaces. For alfresco action, head 5 minutes along Exhibition Road into **Hyde Park** for tennis, playgrounds and pedaloes. The area between

The very open and child-friendly spaces of Hyde Park – perfect for picnics

Prices given are for a family of four

Rotten Row and the South Carriage Drive is set aside for Frisbee and ball games.

Eat and drink

Picnic: under £20; Snacks: £20–40; Real meal: £40–60; Family treat: £60 or more (based on a family of four)

PICNIC Partridges (21 Gloucester Rd, SW7 4PL; 020 7581 0535; www. partridges.co.uk; 8am–11pm daily) offers superior cold cuts and nibbles.
SNACKS Morelli's Gelato (87–135 Brompton Road, SW1X 7XL; 020 7730 1234; www.harrods.com; 9am–9pm Mon–Sat, 11:30am–6pm Sun), in Harrods' ground-floor food hall, is a theatrical ice-cream parlour.

REAL MEAL The Treehouse (87–135 Brompton Road, SW1X 7XL; 020 7730 1234; www.harrods. com; 11am–7pm Mon–Sat, 11:30am–6pm Sun), on the fourth floor of Harrods, next to the toy department, is the store's family diner, with burgers and milkshakes to eat and giant jigsaws to play with.
FAMILY TREAT The Royal Albert Hall's **Café Consort** (0845 401 5045; www.royalalberthall.com; 8:30am–10pm daily) is a sleek and grown-up place to dine before (or during) a show. It has free jazz or world music most Friday lunchtimes (12 noon to 1:30pm) and over Sunday brunch, and an enticing menu for under-12s.

The Lowdown

🌐 **Map reference** 14 F2
Address Exhibition Road, SW7 2DD; 0870 870 4868; *www.sciencemuseum.org.uk*

🚗 **Tube** South Kensington. **Bus stop** Exhibition Road, South Kensington Tube station: route numbers 14, 49, 70, 74, 345, 414, 430, C1; Kensington Road: 9, 10, 52, 452

🕐 **Open** 10am–6pm daily (until 7pm during school holidays); last admission 5:15pm; plus 6:45–10pm on last Wed of month (adults only)

💷 **Price** Free. Charges apply for IMAX 3-D cinema (£27–80), simulator rides and some temporary exhibitions

👫 **Skipping the queue** Launchpad is the big draw for kids, so arrive at 10am and head there first. The gallery is quieter when the live science shows are on.

🚩 **Guided tours** Free 30-minute tours (ages 13 plus) at 1pm, 2pm and 3pm most days, focusing on specific galleries. Spaced Out family tours and Cockroach tours (with costumes) start at 11:30am and 3:30pm at weekends

👫 **Age range** All

🏃 **Activities** Free 20-minute science shows, seven times daily (ages 7 plus); storytelling (under-7s) weekends at 1:30pm – both in Launchpad. School

holiday shows feature Albert Einstein, aviator Amy Johnson and more. Live science experiments sometimes invite museum-goers to take part in research. World Wonders and Contemporary Art trails for older children are downloadable online. Monthly Science Night sleepovers, usually on Fridays, for ages 8–11 (minimum group size six, including parent/guardian, £45pp)

⏱ **Allow** Up to a day

♿ **Wheelchair access** Yes, all floors

☕ **Cafés** Revolution Café serves buffet-style lunches; Deep Blue Café is a waiter-service family diner – both on ground floor. Eat Drink Shop (Basement) and Fly Café (Floor 3) do snacks and drinks. Picnic area in Basement

🛍 **Shop** On the ground floor, filled with brain-testing games, toys and clever souvenirs

🚻 **Toilets** All floors except 5

Good family value?

The IMAX cinema and flight simulators charge, but with science shows, family tours and hands-on galleries galore, there is more than enough free stuff to fill a day. To avoid being pestered for pennies for the kids' rides, steer clear of the café next to the Fly Zone.

Find out more

There are entertaining and fact-packed digital mini-sites devoted to the museum's galleries online at *www.sciencemuseum.org.uk/onlinestuff*, which also has more than a dozen brain-expanding computer games: work out how to help the Energy Ninjas beat climate change, or build cuddly "Things" using chromosomes and genes.

Next stop. . .

ALBERTOPOLIS Explore the museums of Exhibition Road on foot with an architectural scavenger hunt from the Royal Institute of British Architects, downloadable at *http://www.architecture.com/Library DrawingsAndPhotographs/Albertopolis/ExploringSouth Kensington/ScavengerHunt.aspx*

HARRODS When little (and big) brains start to ache, there's always Harrods (*87–135 Brompton Road, SW1X 7XL*), cascading with fairylights. London's most over-the-top department store caters for kids on the fourth floor, with its Toy Kingdom and "children's fashion rooms". The pet department is fun, too, with doggie four-poster beds and cookbooks for cats.

Harrods' Toy Kingdom – where future Formula One stars start out

② Natural History Museum

Life on Earth – in 70 million specimens

Imagine a dinosaur rampaging around a cathedral. That's the scene that confronts children entering the hallowed Central Hall of the Natural History Museum – and it's sure to grip them from the start. A full-size diplodocus dominates the lobby, and a sharp left turn from here leads into the dinosaur gallery, stalked by scores of skeletal monsters from prehistoric times.

This is just the beginning of the museum's extraordinary expedition through life on Earth. In other halls, a blue whale dangles from the ceiling, leaf ants scurry and an earthquake simulator shakes. On the lower ground floor, the Investigate Centre has shelf after shelf stacked with exhibits for kids to hold and examine. And don't miss the Darwin Centre, housed in a great white cocoon, which uses wall-to-wall digital wizardry to reveal how the museum collects and conserves its 70 million specimens.

Families should begin their visit at the welcome desk in the Central Hall. The free Explorer backpacks guide under-8s on exciting investigations into the natural world, well-equipped with binoculars, magnifying glass and clue book. There are also six Discovery booklets themed on mammals, dinosaurs or rocks for

Key Features

① **Investigate Centre** This invites children aged 7–14 to grab trays loaded with skins, skulls, rocks and bones, and view them under a microscope. Open 2:30–5pm daily, weekends and holidays 11am–5pm.

② **Dinosaur Hall** See a giant animatronic Tyrannosaurus rex lunge to life here. The beast was eight times more powerful than a lion, and could have swallowed a human whole.

③ **The Vault** This treasure room shows off the museum's most precious stones, including the cursed Purple Sapphire and the Nakhla meteorite, which proves there was once water on Mars.

■ Second Floor	■ Ground Floor
■ First Floor	■ Lower Ground

④ **Quake simulator** Walk into a Japanese supermarket and hold on tight as a re-creation of the 1995 Kobe earthquake shudders the floor. Meanwhile, CCTV screens show scenes from the real thing.

Entrance

⑤ **Central Hall** Under the vaulted arches here, the museum's most astonishing exhibits line up, including Dippy the diplodocus, Britain's only woolly mammoth skull, and the enormous egg of the extinct, so-called elephant bird.

⑥ **The Human Biology Zone** Head here for an entertaining skip through the body and brain. Scan microscopic liver cells, wander inside a womb, and have a go at fun memory tests and optical illusions.

⑦ **Darwin Centre** Inside this giant eight-storey white cocoon, jab the walls to examine beetles and butterflies, plan a field expedition, or question real-life researchers as they study in their lab.

children aged 5–7 and 8–11 (£1 each). For pre-schoolers, there's the Bookasaurus dinosaur trail (free). In the Darwin Centre, pick up a NaturePlus smartcard, which allows digital specimens to be scanned during a visit, for online investigation at home.

Science Focus specimen-handling sessions take place in the Darwin Centre and selected other galleries: weekdays 10:45am–2pm, weekends 11:15am–3pm, whilst the Family Earth Lab explores the fascinating world of rocks and fossils (weekends 11am–1pm). And there are art and crafts sessions for ages 5–12 on the first and third Saturday of the month (11am–1pm, 2–4pm); and puppet storytelling for under-7s on the last Sunday (noon and 1:30pm).

Free 30-minute Nature Live shows and talks (ages 8 plus) run in the Attenborough Studio, weekdays at 2:30pm, weekends and school holidays 12:30pm and 2:30pm; the studio also screens nature documentaries daily. Monthly Dino Snores museum sleepovers are open to ages 8–11 – minimum five children and one adult per party; £46 per person.

Check the museum website for the school holiday events programme, which typically includes live actors performing in character as famous figures from science. In

Beehive in the Natural History Museum's Wildlife Garden

recent summers, a temporary butterfly house has been erected on the East Lawn (typically Apr–Sep). Finally, there is lots to explore and investigate on the Kids Only web pages, including nature-cams, games and picture galleries.

Letting off steam

The museum's East and West lawns, on Cromwell Road, welcome picnickers, and the neighbouring Wildlife Garden, with its working beehives, pond and wide variety of other natural habitats is a great place to explore and is open from April to October (10am–5pm).

The Lowdown

🌐 **Map reference** 14 F2
Address Cromwell Road, SW7 5BD; 020 7942 5011; *www.nhm.ac.uk*

🚇 **Tube** South Kensington or Gloucester Road (both on Circle, District and Piccadilly lines).
Bus stop South Kensington; Exhibition Road

🕐 **Open** 10am–5:50pm daily; last admission 5:30pm. After Hours opening (till 10:30pm, last Fri of month) offers live music, debates, films and food

💲 **Price** Free. Some temporary exhibitions charge

🧍 **Skipping the queue** Spirit Collection tour has limited places: book on arrival at museum, or by phone after 10:15am on the day.

🚩 **Guided tours** Free 30-minute Spirit Collection tour (ages 8 plus) goes backstage at the Darwin Centre up to four times daily. Extended 50-minute tour at 3.15pm weekdays

👫 **Age range** All

👫 **Activities** Monthly Nature Live Nights open up the museum after hours, mainly for adults (see website)

⏱ **Allow** Up to a day

♿ **Wheelchair access** Yes

☕ **Cafés** The museum's striking galleried restaurant in the Green Zone (11am–5pm) serves ploughman's lunches and hot dishes, and offers a hearty children's menu and a family roast lunch deal at weekends (four for £30). The Central Hall Café does lighter bites and kids' lunch bags, plus there's a basement snack bar and picnic area

🛍 **Shops** There are three. The main shop near the entrance has imaginative nature-themed gifts; Dino Store and Earth Shop sell dinosaur- and planet-themed items

👫 **Toilets** On all floors

Picnic: under £20; **Snacks:** £20–40; **Real meal:** £40–60; **Family treat:** £60 or more (based on a family of four)

③ Victoria & Albert Museum

A labyrinth of artistic delights

For a first-time visitor, wandering the 145 galleries of the Victoria & Albert Museum (V&A) can feel like being in a very odd dream: turn a corner, and there's a hall hung with the enormous Raphael Cartoons; climb a staircase, and there's a chamber encrusted with Fabergé gems. Room after room is crammed with the world's most dazzling array of decorative arts – glass, ceramics, sculpture, furniture, textiles, silver and more, spanning five continents and 5,000 years. Perhaps it's best to forget the museum map and just roam, so the most dramatic galleries come as a breathtaking surprise. The Cast Courts, for example, are dominated by a towering 30-m (98-ft) replica of Rome's Trajan's Column, chopped in half to fit under the ceiling.

For children, the V&A can be a little overwhelming, especially since most exhibits are presented very conventionally – don't expect the interactive thrills of the Science and Natural History museums. However, the British galleries on Levels 2 and

The entrance of the Victoria & Albert Museum, designed by Aston Webb

4 include a series of ante-rooms with hands-on activities, one for each historical period. These follow a repeating format, with a dressing-up corner (Victorian crinolines, Tudor gauntlets); a design table (weave a tapestry, make a bookplate); and a construction puzzle (piece together a chair, build a model of the Crystal Palace). They best suit well-behaved over-7s, though younger visitors are catered for by the museum's kids' backpacks, stuffed with stories, toys and jigsaws to unload while walking around – themes include Chinese

art, medieval life and Georgian furniture. There are family events laid on every weekend, too.

The V&A's toy collection is now held at its sister museum in Bethnal Green *(see pp206–7)*, but by way of compensation, objects from the defunct Theatre Museum at Covent Garden are displayed in a suite of rooms on Level 3. These are unmissable with kids; they feature backstage film clips from West End shows, a mock-up of pop diva Kylie Minogue's dressing-room, doll-size models of theatrical sets, and flamboyant costumes from *The Lion King*. There are outfits to try on, too.

Letting off steam

The V&A's majestic courtyard garden has lawns and a summer café – plus what must be London's grandest paddling pool, which welcomes waders during warm weather.

The Lowdown

🌐 **Map ref** 14 G2
Address Cromwell Rd, SW7 2RL; 020 7942 2000, www.vam.ac.uk

🚇 **Tube** South Kensington.
Bus stop Exhibition Road, South Kensington tube station

🕐 **Open** 10am–5:45pm Sat–Thu; 10am–10pm Fri (selected galleries open late)

💷 **Price** Free; some temporary exhibitions charge (all free for under-12s)

🎟️ **Skipping the queue** Advance booking advised for temporary shows or events, available up to 48 hours ahead (020 7907 7073)

🚩 **Guided tours** Free 1-hour tours at 10:30am, 12:30pm, 1:30pm and 3:30pm daily, plus 7pm Fri. Tours of Medieval & Renaissance (11:30am) and British (2:30pm) galleries daily; Theatre & Performance, 2pm Mon–Fri.

👫 **Age range** 5 plus

🎒 **Activities** Eight different backpacks for ages 5–12, available till 4pm from Sackler Centre (Level 0) and (at weekends) from front desk; plus activity trails devoted to

Tudor and Silver galleries; and Picnic Parties (ages 7–12). Free family Drop-in Design sessions every Sun (10:30am–5pm); free 25-minute Gallery Plays every Sat (11am, 1pm, 3pm). Regular Sat workshops for ages 11–19 on photography, fashion and theatre *(www.vam.ac.uk/create)*, plus school holiday events (www.vam.ac.uk/families).

⏱️ **Allow** At least 2 hours

♿ **Wheelchair access** Yes; building is Grade I-listed – occasional chair lifts are used to visit all areas

🍽️ **Eat and drink** *Snacks* L'Opera *(241 Brompton Rd, SW3 2EP; 020 7052 9000; www.lopera.co.uk; 8:30am–11pm)*, across the road from the museum, is an opulent patisserie-deli. *Real meal* The V&A's Café *(10am–5:15pm, Fri till 9:30pm)*, the world's oldest museum restaurant, offers half-price main courses for under-10s.

🛍️ **Shop** Gift and bookshop

🚻 **Toilets** On all levels

The Cast Courts in the V&A, housed in two vast galleries, make a real impression.

The North Porch of the Royal Albert Hall, viewed from the Albert Memorial

④ Royal Albert Hall

Crown prince of concert venues – home of the Proms

Wagner and Verdi; Einstein and Shackleton; Frank Sinatra and Jay Z; Nelson Mandela and the Dalai Lama; the Beatles and the Rolling Stones – they've all appeared here. Does any concert hall in the world have a roster of greats to rival this one? Squatting like a big pink blancmange on the edge of Kensington Gardens, the Royal Albert Hall is the most instantly recognizable performance space in London – and is every bit as iconic on the inside, as its daily front-of-house tours reveal.

The hall opened in 1871, fulfilling Prince Albert's vision of a venue "for the advancement of the arts and sciences", and improbably, it is still part-supported by profits from his Great Exhibition of 1851, staged across the road in the Crystal Palace. Best known today for the pomp and circumstance of the annual BBC Proms classical music season, it also hosts rock, jazz, comedy and circus performances, film launches and Masters tennis.

Children can't help but feel the glamour of the elliptical red auditorium, with its dome full of flying saucers (part of the complex acoustics) – especially since the upbeat guided tours approach it via the Queen's retiring rooms behind the royal box. Tours also peek into the balustraded "smoking gallery" up in the eaves, where £5 standing tickets can be had for most shows.

Letting off steam

The green lawns of **Kensington Gardens** are across the road – head north past the Round Pond for the Diana Princess of Wales Memorial Playground (*see p174*).

The Lowdown

- 🌐 **Map ref** 14 F1
  Address Kensington Gore, SW7 2AP; 0845 401 5045; *www.royalalberthall.com*
- 🚇 **Tube** South Kensington, High Street Kensington. **Bus stop** Kensington Rd, Queen's Gate, Exhibition Rd
- 🕐 **Open** Box office 9am–9pm daily. Performance times vary
- 💷 **Price** Show tickets vary; from £20
- 👫 **Skipping the queue** For tours, advance booking recommended
- 🚩 **Guided tours** 1-hour tours about six times daily (10:30am–4:30pm), except during matinees, £17. Occasional back-stage tours, too (check website)
- 👫 **Age range** 6 plus on guided tours
- 👫 **Activities** Occasional free family concerts during school holidays; regular jazz and comedy shows in the Elgar Room, plus Classical Coffee Mornings most Sundays at 11am (charges apply).
- ♿ **Wheelchair access** Yes, via ramps and lifts
- 🍴 **Eat and drink** *Real meal* the Elgar Room is an informal restaurant. *Family treat* Coda offers more formal modern British cooking and a cocktail bar. (both on Level 3, and open two hours before shows).
- 🛍 **Shop** Near box office
- 🚻 **Toilets** In lobby

Battersea Park and around

Battersea Park boasts a Thames-side promenade, a bucolic boating lake, a miniature zoo and the city's most action-packed adventure playground (in the southwest corner). Approach on foot from Sloane Square Tube station (a 10-minute walk), perhaps diverting along Royal Hospital Road to the National Army Museum, which offers an indoor play zone for younger children – handy when it's wet.

Kensington, Chelsea
and Battersea

Kensington Gardens
and Hyde Park
p172

Science Museum
p178

Battersea
Park

The Chelsea Physic Garden, created in 1673 to help with
the identification of medicinal plants

The beautiful surroundings at Battersea Park Lake

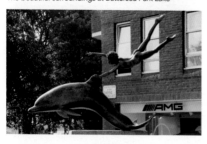

Boy with a Dolphin,
Cheyne Walk,
created by David
Wynne in 1975

Places of Interest

SIGHTS
1. Battersea Park
2. Battersea Park
   Children's Zoo
3. National Army
   Museum
4. Chelsea Physic
   Garden

● **EAT AND DRINK**
1. Le Pain Quotidien
2. The Stockpot
3. San Gennaro
4. The Gallery Mess
5. Made in Italy
6. My Old Dutch
See also Battersea Park

(p188), Battersea Park
Children's Zoo (p190),
National Army Museum
(p190) and Chelsea
Physic Garden (p191)

● **PLACES TO STAY**
1. Sydney House

Above *Getting a taste of life in the trenches at the National Army Museum*
Above right *Brown capuchin monkey at Battersea Park Children's Zoo*

The Lowdown

🚗 **Rail** Battersea Park or Queenstown Road (5-minute walk). **Tube** Sloane Square (10 minutes), Pimlico (15 minutes). **Bus** Chelsea Bridge: route numbers 44, 137, 452; Battersea Park Station: 156, 344; Chelsea Embankment: 170, 360; Battersea Bridge: 19, 49, 319, 345; King's Road: 11, 22, 211. **River bus** Cadogan Pier, on River Taxi route between Blackfriars and Putney, peak hours only Mon–Fri (01342 820600; *www.thamesexecutivecharters.com*)

ℹ️ **Visitor information** Victoria Railway station, (see pp64–5)

🛒 **Supermarkets** Waitrose, 196–198 King's Road, SW3 5XP; Tesco Metro, 275–277 Battersea Park Road, SW11 4LU; Here, 125 Sydney Street, SW3 6NR
Markets Battersea High Street Market (mixed), 9am–4pm Sat; Chelsea Antiques Market, King's Road, 10am–6pm Mon–Sat; Pimlico Road Farmers' Market, Orange Square, 9am–1pm Sat

🎪 **Festivals** BADA Antiques & Fine Art Fair, Duke of York Square (Mar); RHS Chelsea Flower Show, Royal Hospital Chelsea (May); Masterpiece Art Fair, Royal Hospital Chelsea (Jun–Jul); Bastille Day, Battersea Park (Jul); Battersea Park fireworks (Nov)

➕ **Pharmacies** Healthchem, 166–168 Battersea Bridge Rd, SW11 3AW; 9:30am–7:30pm Mon–Fri, 9am–6pm Sat. For 24-hour pharmacies, visit *www.nhs.uk/ServiceDirectories*

🚼 **Nearest playground** Adventure playground and toddler area inside Sun Gate (southwest corner) in the park; St Luke's Park (see p191).

① Battersea Park

London's best adventure playground

It may lack the royal pedigree of Regent's Park or Kensington Gardens, but Battersea Park has its fair share of exotica. Meet monkeys and meerkats at the children's zoo, take tea beside fantastical fountains, hide behind palms in Britain's original sub-tropical gardens and meditate beside a Japanese peace pagoda. What's more, Battersea is the only major city-centre park with a Thames-side promenade, thronging at weekends with baby buggies, roller-skaters and some of the best-dressed joggers in the world.

Pagoda statue

Key Features

① **Peace Pagoda** Built by Japanese monks in 1984 as a shrine to universal peace, the four gilded sculptures here recount Buddha's path to enlightenment.

Recumbent Cycling Half-bike, half-go-kart, these curious "lie-down" contraptions are rentable for all ages. If that sounds too intrepid, there's a toddlers' train.

② **Pleasure Gardens** During the 1951 Festival of Britain, Londoners flocked to the Battersea Pleasure Gardens for the funfair and flowers. Today, there is a fairytale tea terrace to enjoy.

③ **Millennium Arena** The park's main sports hub has an eight-lane running track, 19 floodlit tennis courts, all-weather pitches and a gym. It's open to all.

④ **Pump House Gallery** The Victorian engine house now hosts changing exhibitions of contemporary art.

Children's Zoo (see p190)

⑥ **Boating Lake** A wooded idyll sprinkled with tree-branch bridges, the lake has sculptures by Henry Moore and Barbara Hepworth, a waterside café and boats for hire.

⑤ **Sub-Tropical Gardens** Created by John Gibson, with finds from his orchid-hunting expeditions in India, this caused a sensation in 1860s London.

The Lowdown

🌐 **Map reference** 15 A6
Address Park Offices, Battersea Park, SW11 4NJ; 020 8871 7530, *www.wandsworth.gov.uk/parks*

🚗 **Rail** Battersea Park or Queenstown Road. **Tube** Sloane Square (Circle and District lines) or Pimlico (Victoria line). **Bus stop** Chelsea Bridge, Battersea Park Station, Chelsea Embankment, Battersea Bridge. **River** Cadogan Pier

🕐 **Open** Daily 8:30am–dusk

💲 **Price** Park admission free; charges apply for zoo, boating, cycle hire and sports pitches

🚩 **Guided tours** None; self-guided walk leaflets from Park Office (open weekdays only, 9am–5pm)

👫 **Age range** All

🧒 **Activities** Adventure Playground weekdays 3:30pm–7pm; weekends and school holidays 11am–6pm; toddler park open all hours. Land train runs July–August. Cycle hire weekends and holidays from 10am (from £7 per hour; 020 7498 6543, *www.londonrecumbents.co.uk*). Boat hire Easter to September, weekends and school holidays only (£11 per half-hour; 020 7262 1330, *www.solarshuttle.co.uk*). Frequent school holiday art workshops at Pump House Gallery (020 8871 7572, *www.pumphousegallery.org.uk*). Millennium Arena open weekdays 7am–10pm, weekends 7:30am–7:30pm (020 8871 7537); tennis bookings (020 8871 7542). Occasional funfairs in school and bank holidays.

⏱ **Allow** Half a day

☕ **Cafés** Family-run La Gondola al Parco (*near Rosery Gate, open 8.30am–8pm in summer, winter till 4pm; 020 7978 1655*) does home-style Italian staples and a kids' menu, by the lakeside. The Tea Terrace Kiosk (*9am–dusk*) has snacks; plus weekend sandwich van with picnic tables, outside the adventure playground.

🚻 **Toilets** Near fountains, zoo entrance and adventure playground.

Good family value?
The brilliant playground is free; the zoo, cycling and boating are affordable. What's not to like?

Take cover

The Adventure Playground is kid heaven and has a staffed indoor clubhouse with ping-pong, table football and craft activities (for opening times, see Lowdown). Just across the river is **Chelsea Sports Centre** (*Chelsea Manor Street, SW3 5PL; 020 7352 6985, www.nuffieldhealth.com*), with good-value swimming, including junior lessons (pool open weekdays 6:30am–10pm; Sat 8am–7:30pm; Sun 8pm–10pm).

Eat and drink

Picnic: under £20; Snacks: £20–40; Real meal: £40–60; Family treat: £60 or more (based on a family of four)

PICNIC Le Pain Quotidien (*201 King's Road, SW3 5ED; 020 7486 6154, www.lepainquotidien.co.uk; 8am–10pm Mon–Sat, till 7pm Sun*) serves a wide selection of breads, cakes, pastries and tarts. The light lunches offered include delicious salads and soups.

SNACKS The endless menu at **The Stockpot** (*273 King's Road, SW3 5EN; 020 7823 3175; 8am–11:30pm Mon–Sat, 11:30am–11pm Sun*) should please even the fussiest young palate – there are traditional English dishes as well as a huge range of continental favourites. Takeaways are also available – and it's very cheap for Chelsea.

REAL MEAL South of the park, **San Gennaro** (*22 Battersea Park Road, SW11 4HY, 020 7622 0475, www.sangennaro.co.uk; 5pm–10:30pm daily*) is a super-authentic, super-friendly pizzeria – evenings only, but half-price before 6:30pm.

Enjoying lunch at the Lemon Tree Café in the Battersea Park Children's Zoo

FAMILY TREAT The Gallery Mess (*Saatchi Gallery, Duke of York's HQ, King's Road, SW3 4RX; 020 7730 8135, www.saatchi-gallery.co.uk; 10am–11:30pm Mon–Sat, till 7pm Sun*) does deceptively sophisticated comfort food and a £10 two-course menu for under-12s. Daily specials using fresh seasonal ingredients and a constantly changing menu means there is something for everyone. Champion of Damien Hirst and Tracy Emin, the Saatchi is a bastion for provocative new art: while the kids are eating, sneak around the gallery to check if the current show is too shocking for them.

Find out more

DIGITAL Print off a copy of this orchid, or draw it yourself, and then colour it in to recreate the exotic and beautiful flowers from the Sub-Tropical Gardens in Battersea Park: *www.coloring-pictures.net/drawings/flowers/orchid-flower.php*

Families enjoying a tour of Stamford Bridge football ground

Next stop. . .

CHELSEA FOOTBALL GROUND
A 20-minute walk via Albert Bridge (or a ride on the number 11 bus from the King's Road) brings the story of association football up to date: from Battersea-based Wanderers FC, who won the first FA Cup back in 1872, to modern-day maestros Chelsea FC. For football lovers, there is the opportunity to have a 1-hour tour of the club's stadium, Stamford Bridge, which run daily from 11am–3pm, except on match-days (£42; 0871 984 1955, *www.chelseafc.com/tours*). Nearby Brompton Cemetery (*open 8am to 8pm during the summer, 8am to 4pm in winter*) is worth a look too, for its Beatrix Potter connections.

② Battersea Park Children's Zoo

Mingle with meerkats and ogle an otter

Chinchillas have the softest fur of any creature on Earth; brown capuchin monkeys smear garlic on their bodies to smell nice; and meerkats can sneak up on scorpions and bite off their stings. This modest menagerie can't compete with London Zoo, with its gorillas and lions, but compensates with intriguing titbits about the behaviour of its cute inhabitants.

The zoo is all about catering for kids – every resident seems to have a name, from Piggle and Wiggle the pigs to Morris and Murray the talking mynah birds – and at weekends children can help feed some of the animals. As well as several small primates, the zoo features child-friendly farm animals, interesting birds from emus to zebra finches, and a Mouse House filled

The ever-popular meerkat enclosure at Battersea Park Children's Zoo

with pet–size animals; there's also a butterfly garden. Stars of the show are the meerkats, and kids get to crawl through a tunnel into their compound, popping their heads up for a closer view.

Two hours is ample time here, even allowing for a long frolic in the excellent playground, which includes a full-size fire engine to "drive", hay bales to clamber on and an enormous sandpit.

Take cover
The zoo is mostly outdoors, so on a really rainy day, flee across the river for a swim, trampoline or jungle gym at **Chelsea Sports Centre** *(Chelsea Manor Street, SW3 5PL).*

The Lowdown

- 🌐 **Map ref** 15 B6
  Address North Carriage Drive, Battersea Park, SW11 4NJ; 020 7924 5826; www.
  batterseaparkzoo.co.uk
- 🚃 **Rail** Battersea Park, Queenstown Road. **Tube** Sloane Square, Pimlico. **Bus stop** Chelsea Bridge, Battersea Park Station, Chelsea Embankment, Battersea Bridge. **River bus** Cadogan Pier
- 🕐 **Open** Apr–Sep:10am–5:30pm daily; Nov–Mar till 4:30pm (last admission: 30 minutes earlier)
- 💲 **Price** £26–32
- 👫 **Age range** 3 plus
- 🤸 **Activities** Feeding times at weekends and school holidays: otters and meerkats 11am, 2:30pm; monkeys 11:30am, 3pm; farm animals noon and 3:30pm. Storytime Wednesdays in Feb and Mar; drop-in activities during school holidays (check website).
- ⏱ **Allow** Up to 2 hours
- ♿ **Wheelchair access** Yes, via ramped entrance
- ☕ **Eat and drink** *Snacks* Lemon Tree Café in the zoo serves sandwiches, soup and cakes. *Real meal* La Gondola al Parco *(see p188)*, beside the boating lake, offers hot dishes.
- 🛍 **Shop** Near the ticket office
- 🚻 **Toilets** Near the gift shop

③ National Army Museum

Tiny troops most welcome

Climbing chronologically through five levels of halls, this museum fills every inch with displays telling the story of the British Army from 1066 to the present. See the skeleton of Napoleon's horse, clamber through a World War I dugout, and light up a toy-soldier war zone to see how Wellington won the Battle of Waterloo. The liveliest areas for children are two Action Zones lined with hands-on kit and quizzes. In Victorian Soldier, a game of chance determines their army rank and whether they'll survive their service. In The World's Army, an interactive map plays out various battles and troop movements from the two world wars. Kids can borrow two prop-packed backpacks themed on World War II spies and military art.

On the face of it, a soft-play area for tots themed on war and conflict is a tricky idea to pull off. Thankfully, the museum's Kids' Zone eschews guns and grenades and sticks to climbing nets, rocking horses and khaki-based dressing-up. It can get a bit manic at weekends, but the room offers a useful safety valve after a tour of the galleries.

Next door to the museum is The Royal Hospital Chelsea, famed as the home of the scarlet-coated Chelsea Pensioners since 1682. Christopher Wren's chapel and the Great Hall are free to visit (10am–noon and 2–4pm; 020 7881 5200; www.chelsea-pensioners.co.uk).

Young recruits learning how to fire a rifle at the National Army Museum

The Lowdown

🌐 **Map ref** 15 A5
Address Royal Hospital Road, Chelsea, SW3 4HT; 020 7730 0717; www.national-army-museum.ac.uk

🚇 **Tube** Sloane Square. **Bus stop** Royal Hospital Road, Chelsea Bridge Road, King's Road. **River bus** Cadogan Pier

🕐 **Open** 10am–5:30pm daily

💷 **Price** Free; some temporary exhibitions charge

👫 **Skipping the queue** Free Kids' Zone operates on timed ticket system; it is sometimes reserved for private parties – check online

👫 **Age range** Kids' Zone ages 3–10; galleries and Action Zone 6 plus

👫 **Activities** Kids' Zone; children's backpacks suits ages 6–10. Family activities during school holidays and occasional weekends, led by costumed cavalry officers or sergeant-majors (check website).

🕐 **Allow** Up to 2 hours

♿ **Wheelchair access** Yes

☕ **Eat and drink** *Snacks* Base Café, in the museum, offers a short menu of hot dishes and snacks. *Real meal* Made in Italy (249 King's Road, SW3 5EL; 020 7352 1880; www.madeinitalygroup.co.uk; noon–11:30pm Mon–Sat, noon–10:30pm Sun) serves pizza by the metre.

🛍️ **Shop** Selling gifts, toys and books on military topics

👫 **Toilets** On the Ground and Lower Ground levels

Letting off steam
The Hospital grounds are open 10am – dusk (from 2pm Sun), or cross King's Road to the playground at **St Luke's** (*Cale Street, SW3 3QU*), where kids can act out their own play battle.

Pomegranates growing in the Chelsea Physic Garden

④ Chelsea Physic Garden
Calling all plant detectives

"Warning!" says the sign at Chelsea Physic Garden. "Many plants here are poisonous and can kill!" London's oldest botanical garden was opened in 1673 by the Worshipful Society of Apothecaries to study medicinal plants, and includes a Poison Bed, a Tropical Corridor and Perfumery, as well as an 18th-century rockery made from Icelandic lava, in its rambling walled plot beside the Thames. It feels like a charming secret garden.

The ingenious Shelf Life display cultivates nearly 100 plants inside the packaging of food and medicines that are made from them, while the main focus for kids is the inventive family sessions sprinkled through the school holidays. These include garden photography, herbal medicine workshops, paper-making, creepy-crawly handling and (best of all) CSI Chelsea, a crime-solving day looking into forensic pathology.

Letting off steam
Head across the river to **Battersea Park** for plenty of room to play.

The Lowdown

🌐 **Map ref** 15 A5
Address 66 Royal Hospital Road, SW3 4HS; 020 7352 5646; www.chelseaphysicgarden.co.uk.

🚇 **Tube** Sloane Square. **Bus stop** Royal Hospital Road, Chelsea Bridge Road, King's Road. **River bus** Cadogan Pier

🕐 **Open** Apr–Oct: noon–5pm Tue–Fri, noon–6pm Sun and Bank Holidays (last admission: 30 minutes earlier)

💷 **Price** £26–32

👫 **Guided tours** Free most days, times vary

👫 **Age range** Most family activity sessions target ages 7 plus

👫 **Activities** School holiday family programme, themes vary, booking essential (£5.50 per person, including accompanying adult)

🕐 **Allow** 1 hour

☕ **Eat and drink** *Snacks* Tangerine Dream Café (open from 12:30pm), in the garden, serves homemade hot lunches and afternoon teas. *Real meal* My Old Dutch (221 King's Road, SW3 5EJ; 020 7376 5650; www.myolddutch.com; 10:30am –10:45pm Mon–Sat, 10:30am–10pm Sun) is a cosy creperie.

🛍️ **Shop** Selling garden-related products

👫 **Toilets** Beside shop

KIDS' CORNER

Name that beast!
Bet you've never seen these animals before! Track them down at Battersea Park Zoo, identify them, and draw them in your sketchbook.

Answers at the bottom of the page.

OINK!
Did you hear about the pig that fell in love with a donkey? Poor old Wiggle the pig fell head over heels for Smokey, and liked to follow him around, nuzzling his legs with her snout. Battersea's zookeepers had to put them in separate paddocks, to stop Wiggle pestering Smokey!

Word wars
Soldiers brought back many new words from their travels across the British Empire, which became part of the English language. Can you guess which countries these words came from: toboggan, safari, pyjamas, ketchup, khaki? Find the answers in the Army Museum's Victorian Soldier zone.

Bug heaven
Can you spot some ways in which the Chelsea Physic Garden makes wildlife feel at home? Here are three tips for creating a nature reserve in your own garden:
1 Leave a messy wild corner, piled with twigs and leaves, for animals to hibernate under.
2 Plant lavender, aubretia, catmint and marjoram. Butterflies love them!
3 Sink a plastic bowl into the ground as a tiny pond, adding gravel and pond weed.
For more ideas, visit www.bbc.co.uk/nature/animals/wildbritain/gardenwildlife

Answers: 1 Coati **2** Degu **3** Cavy

Beyond
the City Centre

Spread out beyond the city centre are scores of terrifically appealing attractions, including some of London's most-fun museums and its widest, wildest open spaces. For families, several are too good to miss, including toy heaven at the Museum of Childhood, a glimpse into outer space at the Royal Observatory, and the world in one garden at Kew. The Tube, train and bus network makes them all accessible within about an hour.

Highlights

Kew Gardens
Kew invites kids to burrow into a badger's sett, get inside a giant flower, or perch bird-like on the treetop walkway *(see p228)*.

RAF Museum
The Air Force museum has a whole squadron of simulated flying machines to pilot – a hang-glider, a Spitfire and even a Eurofighter jet *(see p218)*.

Horniman Museum
Among the voodoo shrines and stuffed walruses at this quirky museum, the Music Gallery stands out – touch the table-tops and instruments strike up *(see p222)*.

Wembley Stadium
Touring the stadium is a trip to dreamland for football-crazy kids (and adults), climaxing when they climb those famous steps to view the FA Cup *(see p219)*.

V&A Museum of Childhood
London's noisiest museum? The Museum of Childhood, with its rocking-horse races, Punch & Judy shows and toys *(see p208–9)*.

Royal Observatory
At the Royal Observatory in Greenwich, kids can mastermind a mission to Venus, dodge a meteorite shower or even watch a big-screen Big Bang *(see p201)*.

Left *Mudchute Park and Farm, a pastoral corner of London in the shadow of the gleaming skyscrapers of Canary Wharf* **Above** *One of a huge number of exciting exhibits on show at the O2's British Music Experience.*

The Best of
Beyond the City Centre

When it comes to visitor attractions, London's riches extend far beyond the Tower of London, Buckingham Palace and Regent's Park. Families who venture out from the centre will be richly rewarded, whether they go east to hip Hoxton, west into well-to-do Richmond and Kew, north to the pleasure grounds of Hampstead Heath or south to the splendours of Greenwich. Here are some itineraries that will help you pick out the plums.

A Greenwich weekend

If Greenwich were outside London, it would vie with Windsor, Oxford and Bath. There is so much to see here by the Thames. An exciting way to arrive is on the Docklands Light Railway (DLR), gliding through the skyscrapers of Canary Wharf. Hop off for the **Museum of London Docklands** (see p202), where there's a programme of events every Saturday. Carry on to Greenwich for lunch at Discover Greenwich (see p200), then ramble through the **Old Royal Naval College** (see p200) and visit the **Cutty Sark** (see p198).

On Sunday, pick up a picnic at Greenwich Market (see see p199) and head for Greenwich Park. When its playground and pedal boats pall, dip into the free Discover Sundays kids' programme at the **National Maritime Museum** (see p200). For a star-studded finish, book family tickets for a blast into the Sky Tonight at the **Royal Observatory** planetarium (see p201).

Life out east

Beyond the pie-and-mash cliché, East London offers a rich mix of multicultural influences and terrific places to see. The starting point for families is the **V&A Museum of Childhood** (see pp208–9) at Bethnal Green – parents can browse the vintage toys while their kids go nuts in play zones scattered about the building.

Just one Tube stop further east, in Mile End, is the **Ragged School Museum** (see p213), offering an eye-opening Victorian classroom experience; while to the west, the **Geffrye Museum** (see p210) is all historical interiors and family action. Get to the Geffrye by bus (26, 48 or 55), or on foot via **Weavers Fields Adventure Playground** (see p209) and **Hackney City Farm** (see p210). On a sunny day, however, most kids would opt for a bus ride north to London Fields (see p211), with its sparkling outdoor lido. Spooky **Sutton House** (see p212) is also within easy reach.

Below Narrowboats moored on the Hertford Union Canal, in Hackney's Victoria Park

Above The Old Royal Naval College, Greenwich, designed by Sir Christopher Wren Middle The Climbers and Creepers indoor playground at Kew Gardens Bottom Horse and pony riding for little ones at Richmond Park

Gods and monsters

The **Horniman Museum** *(see pp222–3)*, a mish-mash of macabre masks and mad musical instruments – is the kind of place that turns kids on to museum-going. It's easy to fill a whole day here: activities include watching the honey bees and harvest mice in the Nature Base and the lively object-handling sessions every weekend afternoon. The museum is free, and nearby **Dulwich Park** *(see p224)*, with its boats, bicycles and café, is great for a lunchtime breather.

The Horniman also combines well with **Crystal Palace Park** *(see pp224–5)*, a 30-minute bus ride south (176 or 197). It is full of Victorian character, with Punch & Judy shows in summer, spooky statues left over from Joseph Paxton's Crystal Palace, and the unmissable Dinosaur Court, 30 life-size monsters beside a lake.

Wilderness diary

Yes, metropolitan London does have wilderness, albeit in child-size chunks. To find some, head southwest, where a trio of natural oases offer year-round treats for wildlife-watchers.

Spring is a great time to visit the **London Wetland Centre** in Barnes *(see p230)*. Sand martins swoop in from sub-Saharan Africa, Easter is full of fluffy ducklings, and there are walks to hear the dawn chorus. In summer, head to **Richmond Park** *(see p232)*, hiring bikes to see Isabella Plantation as the azaleas burst into flaming blooms. In October, the park's red deer spar in their autumn rut. It's never winter inside the steamy glasshouses at **Kew Gardens** *(see p228–9)*, and its Tropical Extravaganza fills February with spectacular orchid flowers.

Greenwich and around

They don't quite match Manhattan, but the shiny towers of Canary Wharf make a dramatic splash on London's eastern horizon. Once the world's largest port, this docklands quarter was reborn as a hive of business, entertainment and the high life. Arrive on the Docklands Light Railway (DLR) from Bank or Tower Gateway for a futuristic trip through the skyscrapers. Alight at West India Quay for the Museum of London Docklands; or at Mudchute for its city farm. Royal Greenwich, birthplace of Henry VIII, can be reached by DLR or river bus. Packed with museums and markets – all walkable – it's an irresistible summer's day out.

Places of Interest

SIGHTS

1. Greenwich
2. Old Royal Naval College
3. National Maritime Museum
4. Royal Observatory Greenwich
5. Museum of London Docklands
6. Mudchute Park and Farm
7. British Music Experience
8. Eltham Palace
9. Firepower Museum
10. Thames Barrier

⬤ EAT AND DRINK

1. Nevada Street Deli
2. Paul Rhodes
3. Trafalgar Tavern
4. Rivington Grill Greenwich
5. Wasabi
6. Las Iguanas

See also Greenwich Park (p198), Old Royal Naval College (p200), Royal Observatory (p201), Museum of London Docklands (p202), Mudchute Park and Farm (p202), Eltham Palace (p204), Firepower Museum (p204) and Thames Barrier (p205)

⬤ WHERE TO STAY

1. Hilton London Docklands
2. Novotel Greenwich
3. Ramada London Docklands
4. Fox Apartments

0 kilometres 1

0 miles 1

An array of colourful puppets on sale at Greenwich Market

Above *Vanbrugh Castle – a private residence on the borders of Greenwich Park*
Left *Making friends with the goats at Mudchute Park and Farm, Isle of Dogs*

Thames river bus in front of the Old Royal Naval College, Greenwich

The Lowdown

🚗 **Train** Docklands Light Railway (DLR) runs from Bank and Tower Gateway to Cutty Sark and Greenwich stations, via Canary Wharf/Docklands. Mainline trains run to Greenwich and Maze Hill from Charing Cross. **Tube** Canary Wharf and North Greenwich (for the O2) are both on the Jubilee Line. **River bus** Services run to Greenwich Pier from Westminster and Embankment and stops en route

ℹ️ **Visitor information** Pepys House, 2 Cutty Sark Gardens, SE10 9LW; 0870 608 2000; *www.visitgreenwich.org.uk*

🍴 **Supermarkets** Marks & Spencer Simply Food, 1–2 Cutty Sark Station, SE10 9EJ. **Markets** Greenwich Market (food, crafts, antiques) 10am–5:30pm Wed–Sun; Clocktower Market,

Greenwich High Road (vintage, jewellery, books) 10am–5pm Sat–Sun; Blackheath Farmers' Market 10am–2pm Sun

🎪 **Festivals** The London Marathon begins in Greenwich Park (Apr); Greenwich and Docklands International Festival, performance arts (Jun); Blackheath Bike and Kite Festival (Jun); Great River Race, starting point (Sep)

➕ **Pharmacies** Pharmacy Meridian, 16 Greenwich Church Street, SE10 9BJ (9am–5:30pm Mon–Fri; till 1pm Thu); Duncans, 193–195 Greenwich High Road, SE10 8JA (9am–7pm Mon–Fri; 9:30am–4pm Sat). For 24-hour pharmacies, search at *www.nhs.uk/servicedirectories*

🎯 **Nearest playgrounds** Greenwich Park Playground; Millwall Park playground

① Greenwich
Where east meets west

As well as periscopes and telescopes, pedaloes and playgrounds, roaming deer, jewelled lizards, exploding stars, a singed sailing ship, and Nelson's bloody breeches, Greenwich is also the official home of Greenwich Mean Time in 1847. So there's not a second to waste: climb to the top of the hill and see the glossy lawns of Greenwich Park spread out below, with space for squirrel-chasing, pedal-boating, and plenty of hands-on history.

A ship's figurehead

Key Features

Pavilion Tea House
Playground
⑦
②
③ ⑥
④
Bandstand
①
⑤

① Wildlife Centre Hides and viewpoints overlook the park's herd of deer, while the Secret Garden Wildlife Centre hosts monthly family open days.

② Boating lake Boats and pedaloes are available from Easter to October; the playground hosts concerts in summer.

③ Greenwich Market From Wednesday to Sunday, the market jumps with stalls selling food, vintage clothing and a variety of crafts.

④ Royal Observatory Home of Greenwich Mean Time and the Prime Meridian of the World, The Royal Observatory is the official starting point for each new day and year.

⑤ Wernher Collection Enamelled skulls and an opal-encrusted lizard pendant shine among the paintings and porcelain collected by diamond magnate Julius Wernher (Sunday–Wednesday, www.english-heritage.org.uk).

⑥ Cutty Sark Built in 1869, this Victorian tea clipper was the fastest of its day. Damaged by fire in 2007, it was restored in time for the 2012 Olympics.

⑦ Trafalgar Tavern This atmospheric old pub teetering on a prow of land above the Thames is Greenwich's unofficial figurehead.

The Lowdown

🌐 **Map ref** 18 H3
Address Greenwich Tourist Information, Pepys House, 2 Cutty Sark Gardens, SE10 9LW; 0870 608 2000; www.visitgreenwich.org.uk

🚗 **Train** Greenwich Maze Hill, or Blackheath (mainline); Cutty Sark or Greenwich (DLR). **Tube** North Greenwich, then bus number 188. **Bus stop** Cutty Sark. **River bus** Greenwich Pier: on Embankment to Woolwich Arsenal route (0870 781 5049; www.thamesclippers.com); plus from Westminster (www.thamesriverservices.co.uk; www.citycruises.com)

🕐 **Open** 6am daily (closing times seasonal, 6–9:30pm); park closed to traffic 10am–4pm and all day at weekends. Visitor information centre open 10am–5pm

💲 **Price** Free

🚩 **Guided tours** From visitor information centre near Greenwich Pier, 12:15pm, 2:15pm daily (£6–16; under-16s free)

👫 **Age range** All

👫 **Activities** Boat hire (Easter–Oct); playground; pay-and-play tennis and golf putting (020 8293 0276); bandstand concerts on summer weekends (www.royalparks.gov.uk/greenwich-park). Family open days at Secret Garden Wildlife

Centre, last Sat of month (www.friendsofgreenwichpark.org.uk). Full events calendar at www.visitgreenwich.org.uk

⏱ **Allow** At least a day

☕ **Cafés** Pavilion Tea House (see p201) and Cow and Coffee Bean (020 8293 07035; www.companyofcooks.com), both in Greenwich Park

👫 **Toilets** At Discover Greenwich, Royal Observatory, children's playground and Blackheath Gate

Good family value?
Excellent. Vast amounts to do, much of it blissfully free.

Letting off steam

Greenwich Park Playground has a Wendy house, scrambling tubes and a sandpit, and the boating lake is right next door. If it rains, Arches Leisure Centre *(Trafalgar Road, SE10 9UK; 020 8317 5020)* is close by, with family swimming – phone ahead to check the times of family sessions. Both Greenwich Theatre *(Crooms Hill, SE10 8ES; 020 8858 7755; www.greenwichtheatre.org. uk)* and the pleasingly retro Greenwich Picture House *(180 Greenwich High Road, SE10 8NN; 0871 902 5732; www.picturehouses. co.uk)* have regular family shows and screenings.

Greenwich Park Playground, traditional fun for younger children

Eat and drink

Picnic: under £20; Snacks: £20–40; Real meal: £40–60; Family treat: £60 or more (based on a family of four)

PICNIC Nevada Street Deli *(8 Nevada Street, SE10 9JL; 020 8293 9199; www.nevadastreetdeli. co.uk)* offers fresh and sophisticated sandwiches and other picnic fare.
SNACKS Paul Rhodes *(37 King William Walk, SE10 9HU; 020 8858 8995; www.rhodesbakery.co.uk)*, the artisan baker, does unbeatable sandwiches, pastries and cupcakes.
REAL MEAL Trafalgar Tavern *(Park Row, SE10 9NW; 020 8858 2909; www.trafalgartavern.co.uk; food served noon–10pm Mon–Sat, till 4pm Sun)* has been serving

One of the many enticing artisan food stalls in Greenwich Market

The light, airy and octagonal Pavilion Tea House, Greenwich Park

whitebait platters since the 1830s. They're still on the menu, alongside many other fresh fish dishes, but no longer caught in the Thames.
FAMILY TREAT Rivington Grill Greenwich *(178 Greenwich High Road, SE10 8NN; 020 8293 9270; www.rivingtongreenwich.co.uk; 10am–11pm Tue–Sun)* serves smart seafood and home-made British classics (shepherd's pie, bangers and mash, fish fingers); from 11am–2pm on Sat, one child (aged 2–12) eats free with an adult – advance booking is essential.

Shopping

Greenwich Market *(Durnford St, SE10 9HZ; www.shopgreenwich. co.uk)* has a mind-boggling spread of hot and cold food, especially at weekends. Alongside all the food stalls are antique shops, vintage clothing stores, an array of gift and craft stores and lots of lovely toy shops.

Find out more

DIGITAL In 1515, King Henry VIII had a tiltyard built at Greenwich Palace for jousting tournaments. Find out more about the Tudor joust, and have a go online, at: *www.tudorbritain.org/joust*

Next stop...

MERIDIAN DUCK TOURS *(020 7096 2053; www. meridianducks.com)* These tours offer a great view of Greenwich from both land and water in half-boat, half-bus yellow amphibious vehicles, launched daily from Cutty Sark DLR station. For a gentler adventure, saddle up for a children's donkey ride on nearby Blackheath: they start from Duke Humphrey Way *(10am–5pm weekends and school holidays).*

The symmetrical Thameside façade of the Old Royal Naval College

② Old Royal Naval College

Home for old sea dogs

Set on riverside lawns, with the silver towers of Canary Wharf rising across the water, Sir Christopher Wren's double-domed palace is the best collection of Baroque buildings in Britain. Except this wasn't a palace, it was a residential home for injured soldiers. Queen Mary II commissioned the complex in the 1690s, and until 1869, seamen spent their days here drinking, gambling and dragging their wooden legs to the river and back.

Today, the college's slick Discover Greenwich visitor centre introduces the place's maritime history – it was the Royal Naval College from 1873–1998 – using lots of tactile gadgetry. There's a dressing-up box, self-guided family trails and crafty children's workshops in the school holidays. Daily guided tours specialize in the kind of horrible history that kids love, including the grisly story of how Horatio Nelson returned from the Battle of Trafalgar

in 1805 – preserved inside a barrel of brandy. Nelson's body lay in state in the Painted Hall, London's answer to Rome's Sistine Chapel, which must be the finest dining hall in Europe – the old sailors once ate their mutton and beans here. Tours also visit the College's underground skittle alley, with its musket ball missiles – and don't miss a peep into the quadrangle now occupied by Trinity College of Music, where tubas parp and pianos tinkle from every window.

Letting off steam

Greenwich Park's well-equipped children's playground is nearby, just across Romney Road.

③ National Maritime Museum

Dive into the depths of Britain's nautical past

Bigger than the average cruise liner, the National Maritime Museum's central hall – a shiny glass cube full of whirring propellers and winking lighthouses – makes an instant impact on children. Prize exhibits

The Lowdown

🌐 **Map ref** 18 G2

Address 2 Cutty Sark Gardens, SE10 9LW; 020 8269 4747; www.oldroyalnavalcollege.org

🚃 **Train** Cutty Sark (DLR) or Maze Hill (5-minute walk). **Bus** Cutty Sark. **River bus** Greenwich Pier

🕐 **Open** Grounds 8am–6pm; Discover Greenwich visitor centre, Painted Hall and Chapel, 10am–5pm

💲 **Price** Free

🏴 **Guided tours** 90-minute tours given by yeoman guides daily, 2pm (£10–20, under-16s free)

👫 **Age range** All

🧍 **Activities** Family trails (£1 each, or download them from the website). Drop-in craft workshops every Fri in

school holidays (small charge); plus occasional archaeology workshops and shows (check website)

🕐 **Allow** 2 hours

♿ **Wheelchair access** Yes

🍴 **Eat and drink** *Snacks* The King William Undercroft (020 8269 2131; noon–2:30pm Tue–Sun) serves classic lunch fare, including Sunday roasts. *Real meal* The Old Brewery café-bar (020 3327 1280; www.oldbrewerygreenwich.com; café 10am–5pm; restaurant 6–11pm) has a riverside courtyard and children's sandwiches.

🛍️ **Shop** Discover Greenwich centre sells innovative gifts and souvenirs

🚻 **Toilets** Discover Greenwich centre

The Lowdown

🌐 **Map ref** 18 G3

Address Romney Road, Greenwich, SE10 9 NF; 020 8858 4422; www.nmm.ac.uk

🚃 **Train** Cutty Sark (DLR) or Maze Hill (5-minute walk). **Bus** Cutty Sark. **River bus** Greenwich Pier

🕐 **Open** 10am–5pm daily (last admission 4:30pm)

💲 **Price** Free

🏴 **Guided tours** Free themed talks in Maritime Galleries daily (times vary). Queen's House offers tours weekdays only (11:30am, 2pm) and free audio guide.

👫 **Age range** All

🧍 **Activities** Young Explorers' trails downloadable online only. Play Tuesdays for under-5s at 10:30am–12:30pm and 1–3pm weekly (free tickets at welcome desk). Explore Saturdays for over-5s and Discover Sundays for all ages, 11am–4pm. Programme runs daily in school holidays

🕐 **Allow** 2 hours

♿ **Wheelchair access** Yes

🍴 **Eat and drink** *Snacks* Galley Café (Level G) serves soup and sandwiches; Paul (Level 2) has cakes and sandwiches.

🛍️ **Shop** Level G, to right of entrance

🚻 **Toilets** Level G and Level 1

from five centuries of nautical history are here, including Prince Frederick's gilded barge, which once propelled Georgian monarchs along the Thames. Upstairs are galleries devoted to explorers, cruise travel and the slave trade, while it's all hands on deck on Level 2, where kids aged 5 to 85 get to hoist flags, load a cargo ship and even fire a cannon. Older children will love the simulation of a sea captain's bridge, which challenges them to steer boats into port. The sea-themed family events schedule divides into sessions for under-5s (Tue) and

Playing on one of the huge anchors outside the National Maritime Museum

over-5s (Sat) – both are catered for on Sundays. The museum's new Sammy Ofer wing hosts temporary exhibitions and is also home to a new café and shop, along with a more upmarket restaurant serving contemporary British cuisine.

It is the museum's artifacts that most capture the imagination, though: Admiral Nelson's bloodstained breeches, cut from his body after Trafalgar; and the snow boots, part-chewed in hunger, from Sir John Franklin's Northwest Passage expedition, lost in the ice in 1847. The adjoining Queen's House, a pearlescent Palladian villa from 1614, shows off the museum's nautical art collection, including Canaletto's celebrated view of Greenwich from across the Thames.

Letting off steam

There is plenty of space to run around in **Greenwich Park** (see p198).

④ Royal Observatory Greenwich

The world's timekeeper

Dominating Greenwich Park's skyline, the Royal Observatory is a Willy Wonka affair, with green onion domes and a red gobstopper on the roof. The gobstopper is actually the "time ball", which drops daily at 1pm to signal the hour to passing ships. The world has been setting its clocks by Greenwich Mean Time since an international conference fixed the

A favourite photo opportunity – astride the Prime Meridian

line of zero longitude here in 1884, making this the official starting point for each new day and year. Today, visitors queue to have a photo taken astride the Prime Meridian.

The observatory hosts a galaxy of exhibitions, from the intricate to the interplanetary. Watchmaker John Harrison's grapplings with the longitude conundrum will confuse most adults, but the astronomy galleries are much more friendly to children, with a film evocation of the Big Bang and a 4.5 billion-year-old meteorite. In the Astronomy Explorers room kids can man the flight deck and send a virtual space probe to Venus. The most memorable part of the visit, though, is the Peter Harrison Planetarium: tilt back in an armchair and watch as worlds appear, stars detonate and universes collapse on the big screen above.

Letting off steam

Head to **Greenwich Park** (see p198).

The Lowdown

🌐 **Map ref** 18 H4
Address Blackheath Avenue, Greenwich, SE10 8XJ; 020 8858 4422; www.nmm.ac.uk/places/royal-observatory

🚆 **Train** Greenwich or Maze Hill, both a 15-minute walk. **Bus stop** Romney Road. **River bus** Greenwich Pier

🕐 **Open** 10am–5pm daily

💷 **Price** £20–30, under-15s free (astronomy galleries free); Planetarium £22–32

👫 **Skipping the queue** Book ahead for Planetarium shows (020 8312 6608; www.nmm.ac.uk/tickets)

🚩 **Guided tours** Most weekdays (free, times vary); audio guide (£3.50)

👫 **Age range** 6 plus

🏃 **Activities** Kids' trail downloadable from website only. Free monthly Space Explorers workshops (Sat, age 6-plus). Planetarium shows include Space Safari (under-7s) and Sky Tonight Live (5-plus), both daily (check website for schedule).

🕐 **Allow** 2–3 hours

♿ **Wheelchair access** Yes, but slightly restricted in some buildings

🍴 **Eat and drink** *Snacks* Astronomy Café overlooking Greenwich Park. *Real Meal* The Pavilion Tea House serves hot and cold meals.

🛍 **Shop** In Astronomy Centre and near Meridian Line

🚻 **Toilets** In Astronomy Centre and Flamsteed House

Picnic under £20; **Snacks** £20–40; **Real meal** £40–60; **Family treat** £60 or more (based on a family of four)

⑤ Museum of London Docklands

Sailors, slaves and swashbucklers

London's best museum for children? Step forward the Museum of London Docklands which, not content with offering a terrific soft-play area for toddlers, runs weekly Mini Mudlarks sessions for gallery-goers under the age of 2. It shows just how hard the museum tries to engage families.

The museum is set within a Georgian sugar warehouse, built with the profits of the slave trade, and tells the 2,000-year story of wharfside London. Thanks to a series of galleries packed with models, movie clips and touch-screen fun, the place is surprisingly rewarding for children. They will be fascinated by a gibbet cage that was once used to dangle dead pirates above the Thames, and can explore the atmospheric alleyways of Sailortown, a realistic reconstruction of Victorian Wapping, complete with a noisy alehouse and a smelly wild animal emporium.

However, the dedicated children's gallery, Mudlarks, is best saved till last, otherwise it will be impossible to get the children away from its banks of bashing, flashing gadgets and games. Here, they get to hoist cargoes, delve for archaeological finds and even build a scale model of Canary Wharf.

Visit on a Saturday, or during school holidays, when the museum's family events programme shifts into top gear with a tumult of Caribbean dancing, cookery demonstrations and computer animation workshops.

The Lowdown

🌐 **Address** West India Quay, Canary Wharf, E14 4AL; 020 7001 9844; www.museumoflondon.org.uk/docklands

🚂 **Train** West India Quay (DLR). **Tube** Canary Wharf. **Bus** Westferry Circus. **River bus** Canary Wharf Pier, on London Eye–Woolwich Arsenal route (www.thamesclippers.com)

🕐 **Open** 10am–6pm daily

🏷 **Price** Free

🚩 **Guided tours** Free highlight tours: ask on arrival

👫 **Age range** All

🧒 **Activities** Mudlarks gallery open 2–5:30pm weekdays; 10am–5:30pm weekends and school holidays. Free Explorer Backpacks for ages 2–5. Download activity sheets from website. Mini

Mudlarks sessions (6 months–walking) 12:45–1:45pm Mon. Little Mudlarks (walking–age 5) 10:15am–noon Mon. Under-5s storytime 3–3:30pm Thu. Family events Sat and school holidays (check website for full programme).

⏱ **Allow** Half a day

♿ **Wheelchair access** Yes

🍴 **Eat and drink** Picnic Museum café-bar (11am–11pm weekdays, 10am–6pm Sat & Sun) serves sandwiches and kids' lunch boxes. Snacks The museum's Rum & Sugar restaurant serves heartier fare and often has special kids' offers.

🛍 **Shop** To left of entrance

🚻 **Toilets** Ground and third floors

Letting off steam

Millwall Park (Manchester Road, E14) has a lovely children's playground suitable for all ages.

⑥ Mudchute Park and Farm

Dally with Dalai the llama

It is one of the more surreal sights in London: a llama called Dalai trotting around his paddock, with the Canary Wharf skyscrapers behind. Mudchute is one of Europe's largest city farms, home to every bleating, braying animal from a child's colouring book – plus three llamas and a few rare breeds, too.

Arrive on the Docklands Light Railway (DLR) for a truly space-age journey along elevated tracks in driverless trains – it's best experienced in the front carriage. The farm's noisy donkeys, Dizzy and Snowflake, send a rallying call to visitors walking in from Mudchute or Crossharbour stations, and once inside, there are pastures and parkland to explore, riding stables and a courtyard with exotic aviaries and cuddly rabbits and guinea pigs. Stroking is actively encouraged, just ask a friendly farmhand.

The Lowdown

🌐 **Address** Pier Street, Isle of Dogs, E14 3HP; 020 7515 901; www.mudchute.org

🚂 **Train** Crossharbour or Mudchute (both DLR). **Bus stop** Crossharbour, Pier Street

🕐 **Open** Farm: 9am–5pm Tue–Sun; park: open daily

🏷 **Price** Free

👫 **Age range** All

🧒 **Activities** Duck walk (9am) and animal round-up (4pm). Drop-in sessions Mon–Wed in school holidays; plus seasonal fundays. Riding lessons available (charged).

⏱ **Allow** 2 hours

♿ **Wheelchair access** Yes, but can be difficult if wet

🍴 **Eat and drink** Snacks Mudchute Kitchen, beside the farmyard, serves hot food and snacks. Or take a picnic.

🛍 **Shop** Selling animal feed and sometimes eggs from the hens

🚻 **Toilets** In the courtyard

Checking out the nautical displays at the Museum of London Docklands

Prices given are for a family of four

Friendly goats lining up for petting at Mudchute Park and Farm

Take cover

The multiscreen **Cineworld Cinema** (0871 200 2000; www.cineworld.co.uk/cinemas/66), on West India Quay, has afternoon shows daily and is the perfect place to sit out the rain. Or head to the lively and engaging **Museum of London Docklands** (see left) for some indoors fun.

⑦ British Music Experience

Pop star for a day

This tribute to British pop has a suitably rock'n'roll setting, under the huge white dome of the O2. To kids, it looks like a flying saucer parked beside the Thames, and skimming there by riverbus from the centre of town is a thrill in itself.

Taking its place in the O2's "entertainment avenue", alongside concert halls, a multiplex cinema and restaurants, the Music Experience spins through 60 years of pop history with the aid of video screens, sound stations and memorabilia. Younger children won't be hugely impressed by Noel Gallagher's guitar or the Spice Girls' stage gear, but all the digital wizardry keeps it

One of the many hi-tech exhibitions at the British Music Experience

The Lowdown

🌐 **Address** O2, Peninsula Square, SE10 0DX; 020 8463 2000; www.britishmusicexperience.com

🚇 **Tube** North Greenwich (Jubilee line). **Bus stop** North Greenwich Station. **River bus** North Greenwich Pier, on London Eye–Woolwich Arsenal route (www.thamesclippers.com)

🕐 **Open** 11am–7:30pm daily (last admission 6:30pm)

💷 **Price** £32–42

👫 **Age range** 7 plus

👨‍👧 **Activities** Family activities (free with admission) in school holidays: check website

⏱ **Allow** Up to 2 hours

♿ **Wheelchair access** Yes

🍽 **Eat and drink** *Snacks* Wasabi in the O2 offers Japanese cuisine (www.wasabi.uk.com; noon –11pm). *Real meal* Las Iguanas, also in the O2 (020 8312 8680; www.iguanas.co.uk; noon–11pm), serves child-size portions of its Latin American favourites.

🛍 **Shop** Selling music-themed goods

🚻 **Toilets** By entrance

interesting – including "Smartickets" that allow visitors to tag film and audio clips to replay online at home. Giggles are guaranteed in the Dance the Decades booth, offering dance-floor favourites for kids (and adults) to groove along with, while the Gibson Interactive Studio has video guitar lessons from rock legends and the chance to belt out tracks by Girls Aloud and Leona Lewis.

Do investigate the temporary exhibitions elsewhere in the complex. Previously they have included an animatronic dinosaur show with life-size monsters and a CGI aquarium.

Letting off steam

It's a short bus ride (129, 188) to **Greenwich Park** (see pp198), with its playground and picnic lawns.

The iconic white dome of London's O2, viewed from the river

Picnic under £20; **Snacks** £20–40; **Real meal** £40–60; **Family treat** £60 or more (based on a family of four)

⑧ Eltham Palace
Art Deco dream house

With its gold-plated bathroom, self-vacuuming floors and lemur's bedroom, a tour of Eltham Palace is anything but humdrum. Squatting improbably in one of South London's suburbs, the royal palace began life in 1305 as the grand, moated manor of King Edward II, and its 15th-century Great Hall and Tudor bridge look much as they did when the young Henry VIII played in the grounds. Step inside the adjoining house, though, and there's an even bigger surprise – a decadent Art Deco interior from the 1930s, put together with enormous panache by society high-rollers Stephen and Virginia Courtauld.

The Courtaulds lavished their textile fortune on the house, and the whole place screams glamour: the dining room has a shimmering aluminium ceiling and pink leather chairs; Virginia's vaulted bathroom has an onyx tub and gold taps. A built-in "hi-fi" supplied the jazz

The impressive Art Deco interior of Eltham Palace

The Lowdown

- 🌐 **Address** Court Yard, Eltham, SE9 5QE; 020 8294 2548; www.english-heritage.org.uk/elthampalace
- 🚆 **Train** Eltham or Mottingham, then 15-minute walk. **Bus stop** Court Road; Eltham High Street. **Car** Free car park off Court Road
- 🕐 **Open** 10am–5pm Sun–Wed, Apr–Oct; 10am–4pm Sun–Wed, Nov–Mar; closed Jan
- 💷 **Price** £30–40
- 🚩 **Guided tours** Free audio guide with admission
- 👫 **Age range** 5 plus
- 🏃 **Activities** Children's activity sheets, frequent Time Traveller family days with historical themes, plus Easter Egg Hunt and Tudor Jousting weekend (Jun)
- 🕐 **Allow** 2–3 hours
- ♿ **Wheelchair access** Yes, but parts of garden are uneven
- 🍴 **Eat and drink** *Snacks* The palace tearoom (10am–4:30pm) serves light lunches and snacks.
- 🛍 **Shop** Selling gifts and souvenirs
- 🚻 **Toilets** On the ground floor

The Lowdown

- 🌐 **Address** Royal Artillery Museum, Royal Arsenal, Woolwich, SE18 6ST; 020 8855 7755; www.firepower.org.uk
- 🚆 **Train** Woolwich Arsenal (mainline and DLR), 5-minute walk. **Bus stop** Plumstead Road; Woolwich town centre. **River bus** Woolwich Arsenal Pier, services from Embankment (www.thamesclippers.com). **Car** Pay-and-display car park at Plumstead Road entrance
- 🕐 **Open** 10:30am–5pm Wed–Sun, plus bank holidays and 7 days a week during school holidays (last admission 4pm)
- 💷 **Price** £16–26
- 👫 **Age range** 7 plus
- 🏃 **Activities** Camo Zone activities cost extra (£1.50 each). There is a busy school holiday events programme – mostly free (check website)
- 🕐 **Allow** 2 hours
- ♿ **Wheelchair access** Yes
- 🍴 **Eat and drink** *Snacks* The Museum Café (020 8312 7138; 9:30am–5pm) has an appealing bistro vibe and a menu to match.
- 🛍 **Shop** Selling gifts, souvenirs, books, militaria, models and music
- 🚻 **Toilets** Ground and first floors

soundtrack for their Hollywood-style house parties. Children will be especially captivated by the deluxe living quarters of Mah-Jongg, the couple's pet lemur, who enjoyed such luxuries as central heating and hand-painted wallpaper. Mah-Jongg features heavily in Eltham's activity sheets for kids, and the palace's events programme typically includes Tudor jousting and Art Deco fairs.

Letting off steam
The palace's grounds are a delight, with views over London and lots of places to enjoy a picnic.

⑨ Firepower Museum
Battle stations everyone!

If only all wars were fought with sponge balls. Hopefully, that's the message kids will take away from Firepower, aka the Royal Artillery

Museum. Housed in warehouses at Woolwich Arsenal, once England's largest ordnance factory, this is a full-bore celebration of military weaponry, and its interactive Camo Zone squarely targets young children. Prepare to do battle on the sponge-ball firing range, chase along the bungee run and fight it out with radio-controlled tanks – it's great fun for all. Soldiers in combat gear are on hand to supervise.

Elsewhere, the Gunnery Hall bristles with vintage anti-aircraft guns and missile launchers, and visitors can attempt touch-screen missions – shoot down a bomber, or destroy a tank. The History Gallery takes visitors through the story of armaments, all the way "from catapult to rocket", while Fields of Fire is hopefully the closest kids will ever come to being in battle – four big-screens flash archive footage of artillery in action, while smoke fills the room, searchlights beam overhead, there's the sound of anti-aircraft guns, and bombs shake the floor. It's a sobering experience.

There are monthly toy soldier war-game weekends and the

Explore military weaponry throughout history at the Firepower Museum

school holiday programme might involve taking part in simulated army drill, peeking into ration packs, or dressing up in uniform.

Letting off steam

There is space to run around by the riverside. Alternatively, walk west for 10 minutes to the **Waterfront Leisure Centre** in Woolwich High Street *(020 8317 5010; www.gll.org/centre/waterfront-leisure-centre.asp)*, which runs Wild 'n' Wet family swimming sessions every afternoon.

10 Thames Barrier

The "sharks" that saved London

London has long been vulnerable to flooding: in 1236 the Thames rose so high that people were able to go boating across Westminster Hall, now part of the Houses of Parliament. But with sea levels inching upwards and tectonic movements tilting the south of England slowly into the sea, something had to be done. The crunch year was 1953, when more than 300 people drowned in floods around the Thames Estuary.

The 520-m- (1,706-ft-) long Thames Barrier became operational in 1982, adding a futuristic new landmark to the riverscape in the form of its seven curvy piers, which line up like shiny steel shark fins advancing on London. The barrier is effectively a tilting dam, swinging up from the riverbed in 10 circular sections whenever surge tides threaten.

The visitor experience is divided by the river. An information centre on the south bank has working models of the barrier in action. To the north, the Thames Barrier Park is a curious landscape of shaped hedgerows, honeysuckle and aerial walkways, perfect for hide-and-seek. Both sides of the river have cafés, playgrounds, and scintillating views,

Above The gleaming Thames Barrier protects London from flooding
Below Among the wavelike manicured hedges at the Thames Barrier Park

but in summer, the fountain plaza tempts most families northwards with its 32 jets of splashing fun.

Letting off steam

There are children's playgrounds on both sides of the river.

The Lowdown

🌐 **Address** Information Centre, 1 Unity Way, Woolwich SE18 5NJ; 020 8305 4188; www.environment-agency.gov.uk/thamesbarrier. Thames Barrier Park, North Woolwich Road, E16 2HP; www.thamesbarrierpark.org.uk

�train **Train** Charlton, then 15-minute walk (south side). **DLR** Pontoon Dock (north side). **Bus stop** Holborn College Park; North Woolwich Road; Connaught Bridge

🕐 **Open** Information Centre: 10:30am–5pm Thu–Sun) Park: 7am–dusk daily

💷 **Price** £11–21; under-5s free

🤸 **Activities** To see the barrier closed, visit on a maintenance day (dates listed on website).

⏱ **Allow** 1 hour

♿ **Wheelchair access** Information Centre: largely accessible but lift not working at date of publication, so no access to river front. Park: yes

🍽 **Eat and drink** Cafés and picnicking at both sites

🚻 **Toilets** Both sides of river

V&A Museum of Childhood and around

The Cinderella borough of Hackney is finally having a ball, as young professionals move in prompting the opening of hip shopping and dining venues. Especially vibrant are London Fields, home to a lido, and über-trendy Broadway Market. Families will love the V&A Museum of Childhood in nearby Bethnal Green, offering a full day of play for free – and the Central line brings visitors virtually to the door. Visit on the first Sunday of the month, when the Ragged School Museum, one Tube stop further, stages Victorian lessons.

Places of interest

SIGHTS
1. V&A Museum of Childhood
2. Geffrye Museum
3. Hackney City Farm
4. Hackney Museum
5. Sutton House
6. Discover
7. Ragged School Museum

● **EAT AND DRINK**
1. Broadway Market
2. L'Eau à la Bouche
3. The Gallery Café
4. E Pellici
5. Frizzante
6. The Grocery
7. Treacle
8. Caffè Theatro
9. Tre Viet
10. Railroad
11. Café Mondo
12. The Palm Tree

See also V&A Museum of Childhood (p208), Geffrye Museum (p210), Sutton House (p212), Discover (p212) and Ragged School Museum (p213)

● **WHERE TO STAY**
1. Boundary Rooms
2. Crowne Plaza Shoreditch
3. Town Hall Apartments

Feeding the ducks in a peaceful corner of Victoria Park

Fashion dolls on display at the V&A Museum of Childhood

Playing on the brightly coloured equipment in Haggerston Park playground

The Lowdown

🚆 **Train** Bethnal Green, Cambridge Heath, London Fields or Hackney Downs (all from Liverpool Street); Stratford.
Tube Bethnal Green, Mile End, Stratford (all Central line).
Bus number 388 runs to Bethnal Green from Embankment via Liverpool Street; number 254 to Bethnal Green and Hackney from Aldgate

ℹ️ **Visitor information** 0208 356 3500, *www.hackney.gov.uk/leisure-culture*

🛒 **Supermarkets** Tesco, 55 Morning Lane, Hackney, E9 6ND.
Markets Broadway Market (food, fashion, crafts), 9am–5pm Sat; Columbia Road Flower Market, 8am–2pm Sun; Brick Lane Market (vintage fashion, bric-a-brac), 8am–2pm Sun

🎊 **Festivals** Great Spitalfields Pancake Race, Brick Lane (Shrove Tuesday); Big Write, Stratford, children's books (Mar); Spitalfields Show & Green Fair, Allen Gardens (Sep); Bonfire Night, Victoria Park (Nov)

➕ **Pharmacies** Boots, 426 Bethnal Green Road, E2 0DJ (9am–6pm, closed Sun). For 24-hour pharmacies search at *www.nhs.uk/servicedirectories*

🛝 **Nearest playgrounds** Weavers Fields Adventure Playground (*Mape St, E2*); London Fields (*West Side, E8 3EU*); Mile End Park (*Grove Rd, E3 5BH*); Victoria Park playground (*Grove Rd, E3 5SN*)

One of the many exhibits packed into the Hackney Museum

Playing games at the interactive Discover Children's Story Centre

The mid-20th-century room at the Geffrye Museum

① V&A Museum of Childhood
The grandest playroom in London

Children want to play with toys, not just look at them, and that's tricky when the toys include a queen's doll's house, an 18th-century puppet theatre and the very first Mickey Mouse doll. The Museum of Childhood solves the problem by creating "activity stations" between its display cases, where kids can ride a rocking horse, jump in a sandpit or put together a robot. The impressive building – a huge Victorian pavilion with plenty of space and pink iron balconies – helps set the tone.

Classic Barbie with matching luggage

Key features

■ **First floor** This houses the Childhood galleries, which explore the social history of childhood.

■ **Ground floor** This floor is divided into two galleries – Moving Toys and Creativity.

① **Queen Mary's Doll's House** Part of a large collection, this was furnished personally by Queen Mary. Look for the tiny telephone – ultra-modern in 1910!

② **Vintage pedal car** A perfect replica of an open tourer, this has working lights, a horn and a turning starter handle. It would have cost a fortune in the 1920s.

⑤ **Venetian Puppet Theatre** This huge 18th-century theatre provided entertainment for an aristocratic Venetian family.

⑥ **Victorian seaside** This gallery has a sandpit for toddlers, overlooked by a 100-year-old Punch & Judy theatre and a booth for kids to stage their own shows.

③ **Game Boy** Hand-held games took off in 1989 with the Nintendo Game Boy, which sold 118 million. The Moving Toys gallery looksat toy technology from zoetropes onwards.

④ **Tiny Tears** Winner of the "UK Toy of the Year" in 1966, Tiny Tears was designed to behave like a baby – feed her, then put in her dummy, and she'll cry and wet her nappy.

⑦ **Early Lego** Invented by a Danish carpenter in 1949, these colourful bricks have since conquered the world. In May 2011, the Space Shuttle Endeavour took 13 Lego kits into space.

The Lowdown

🌐 **Address** Cambridge Heath Road, E2 9PA; 020 8983 5200; www.museumofchildhood.org.uk

🚗 **Train** Cambridge Heath (five-minute walk) or Bethnal Green (10-minute walk). **Tube** Bethnal Green (Central line). **Bus stop** Cambridge Heath Road

🕐 **Open** 10am–5:45pm daily (last admission 5:30pm)

💲 **Price** Free

👪 **Skipping the queue** Major events bookable up to two weeks in advance (check website)

🚩 **Guided tours** Free 30-minute family tour (11:15am) and I-Spy hunt (10:30am), weekends and school holidays

👫 **Age range** 3 plus

👫 **Activities** Kids' trails themed on toy vehicles, dolls and teddy bears; daily drop-in storytelling and Art Smarts sessions. Montessori Family Packs for under-5s, plus toddler sessions (usually Fri). Workshops on occasional Saturdays and daily in school holidays. "Making SENse" resource packs for children with autism.

⏱ **Allow** Half a day

♿ **Wheelchair access** Yes

☕ **Café** Benugo Café, in the main hall, serves simple hot lunches and salads. There are also picnic tables indoors and outside.

🛍 **Shop** Ground floor, selling books, stationery, gifts and pocket money toys

👫 **Toilets** Ground floor

Good family value?
Excellent – even the temporary exhibitions are free. Bring some change though, as some toys can be set in motion with a 20p coin.

Picnic area within the grounds of the V&A Museum of Childhood

Letting off steam

Museum Gardens, right next door, has lawns but no playground. For a playground, you need **Weavers Fields** *(Mape St, E2 6HW),* a 10-minute walk away off Bethnal Green Road, where a terrific staffed adventure playground has climbing frames, rope swings, an indoor playroom and tuck shop (3:30–6:30pm Tue–Fri on school days, 11am–6pm Mon–Fri during holidays; plus noon–5pm Sat, noon–3pm Sun). To the east, **Victoria Park** *(Grove Rd, E3)* is in easy striking range, with its scrumptious lakeside café *(www. towerhamlets.gov.uk/victoriapark).*

Eat and drink

Picnic: under £20; Snacks: £20–40; Real meal: £40–60; Family treat: £60 or more (based on a family of four)

PICNIC Broadway Market *(south of London Fields, E8 4QL; www.broadwaymarket.co.uk; 9am–5pm Sat),* a 15-minute walk or a short bus ride north of the museum, is an excellent source of provisions, with over 80 stalls, a cosmopolitan restaurant scene and the French deli **L'Eau à la Bouche** *(www.labouche.co.uk; open daily)* selling delicious continental classics.
SNACKS The Gallery Café *(21 Old Ford Road, E2 9PL; 020 8983 3624; http:// thegallerycafe.wordpress.com; open daily)* is a buzzing,

super-cheap veggie and vegan café with good chips and even better cakes.
REAL MEAL Grandest of all the East End "greasy spoon" cafes, **E Pellici** *(332 Bethnal Green Road, E2 0AG; 020 7739 4873; 6:15am–5pm Mon–Sat)* has been run by the same Italian family for a century, and is still serving good-value English and Italian dishes. The breakfasts here are deservedly renowned.
FAMILY TREAT Frizzante *(1a Goldsmiths Row, E2 8QA; 020 7739 2266; www.frizzanteltd.co.uk; 10am–4:30pm Tue–Sun plus occasional Thu evenings)* is a fashionable diner at Hackney City Farm *(see p210),* with gorgeous rustic Italian cuisine and hip toddlers scurrying underfoot. Its Thursday dinners are extra special.

Shopping for sweet picnic treats at a stall in Borough Market.

Find out more

DIGITAL The museum's kids' pages are busy with kaleidoscopes to make, jigsaws to solve, even a Victorian village to cut out and construct. Play the Build a Toy video game at home – it's also available on screens at the museum: *www. vam.ac.uk/moc/kids_pages.*

Next stop...

POLLOCK'S TOY MUSEUM

Unlock another trove of toys from yesteryear at Pollock's Toy Museum in Bloomsbury *(see p104).*

Enjoying the Italian dishes on offer at Frizzante, Hackney City Farm.

An elegant drawing room at the Geffrye Museum

Bella, a British saddleback pig, at the Hackney City Farm

② Geffrye Museum

The ghosts of London past

On paper, it sounds like the dullest family day out in London: a procession of roped-off living rooms revealing how carpets, sideboards and wallpaper have evolved from 1600 to the present day. But the Geffrye Museum has one of the hardest-working children's programmes anywhere, from its monthly Saturday Specials with activities such as portrait painting, spider handling and animation workshops, to its five-week Christmas Past season, when the halls are well and truly decked with historical holly. Family audio guides, quiz trails and activity packs are available every weekend, and there's a refreshing commitment to all age groups, from toddlers to teens. Choose a day when there is lots happening, tell the kids they're going to be travelling back in time to Tudor England, and they'll be gripped.

The museum is set in a cute quadrangle of 18th-century almshouses, its front pathway lit by ghostly furniture, the work of installation artist Kei Ito. Indoors, 11 set-dressed rooms chart the changing face of middle-class décor, from a 1630 merchant's parlour to a 1998 loft apartment. From April till October, the museum's immaculate period gardens host picnic parties, steel bands and other festivities.

Letting off steam

The Apples & Pears Adventure Playground (28 Pearson Street, London E2 8EL; school days: 3–6pm Tue–Fri; holidays: 9:30am–4pm Mon–Fri; 10am–4pm every Sat; 020 7729 6062) is a supervised play area just a 5-minute walk away.

③ Hackney City Farm

Meet Larry the showbiz donkey

One field does not a farm make, but hats off to the enterprising band of locals who transformed this postage stamp-sized piece of land in one of London's most congested boroughs. Created in 1984 on the site of a derelict lorry park, the farm now has calves, goats, sheep, pigs, rabbits, geese and chickens (not forgetting Larry the donkey, star of the small screen), plus a thriving crafts studio and a cottage garden growing seasonal vegetables.

Feeding time is at 4pm and there's a clutch of courses for all ages, from felt-making and yoga to beekeeping and green living, plus regular afternoon pottery sessions for children. It's worth visiting just for lunch at the sparkling Frizzante café, whose zesty Italian food has made it a dining destination in its own right.

Letting off steam

Haggerston Park (Audrey Street, London, E2 8QH) is on the doorstep, with its pond, ping-pong, BMX track, sports areas and playground.

Enjoying the children's playground at Haggerston Park, Hackney

The Lowdown

- 🌐 **Map ref** 6 G4
  Address 136 Kingsland Road, E2 8EA; 020 7739 9893; www.geffrye-museum.org.uk
- 🚆 **Train** Hoxton, 5-minute walk. **Tube** Old Street (Northern line), then number 243 bus or 15-minute walk. **Bus stop** Kingsland Road; Hackney Road
- 🕐 **Open** 10am–5pm Tue–Sat; noon–5pm Sun
- 💲 **Price** Free; £5–10 for special exhibitions, under-16s free
- 👫 **Skipping the queue** For Saturday Special family activities at 10:30am and 2pm, arrive 30 minutes early to secure a place
- 🚩 **Guided tours** Audio guide (£2), children free
- 👫 **Age range** 3 plus

- **Activities** Free family audio guide (ages 5–11) and activity backpacks (ages 3–5), weekends and holidays only. Free family days first Sat of month (ages 5–16), plus full school holiday programme. Website has recipes and garden design games
- ⏱ **Allow** 1–2 hours
- ♿ **Wheelchair access** Yes, except for Restored Almshouses Exhibition
- 🍴 **Eat and drink** Picnic The Grocery (54 Kingsland Road, E2 8DP) offers upmarket picnic fare. Snacks The museum's restaurant serves half-price, home-cooked children's dishes.
- 🛍 **Shop** Selling high-quality gifts and books relating to interiors
- 👫 **Toilets** On all floors

The Lowdown

🌐 **Address** 1a Goldsmiths Row, E2 8QA; 020 7729 6381; www.hackneycityfarm.co.uk

� **Train** Cambridge Heath, 10-minute walk. **Tube** Bethnal Green (Central line), 15-minute walk. **Bus stop** Hackney Road

🕐 **Open** 10am–4:30pm Tue–Sun, plus bank holidays

💲 **Price** Free

🧍 **Age range** All

🤾 **Activities** Self-guided tour leaflet has animal information and activities (£1). Feeding time 4pm; drop-in pottery twice weekly (£5, 2–4pm or 4–6pm). Summer holiday workshops might include rapping or puppet-making.

⏱ **Allow** 1 hour

♿ **Wheelchair access** Yes; contact Farm Manager beforehand

🍴 **Eat and drink** Snacks Treacle (020 7729 0538; www.treacleworld.com; Sun only 9am–3pm), part of Columbia Road flower market, recreates bygone British baking. Real meal Frizzante cafe (see p209) serves tasty children's dishes.

🚻 **Toilets** On ground floor

④ Hackney Museum

The world on your doorstep

Crime-troubled and cash-deprived, or the hippest place in London? Hackney is both, partly thanks to its rich stew of cultural influences, and this bright and breezy local museum does a tasty job of stirring the pot, especially for families.

The Lowdown

🌐 **Address** 1 Reading Lane, E8 1GQ; 020 8356 3500; www.hackney.gov.uk/cm-museum

� **Train** Hackney Central, five-minute walk; Hackney Downs (10 minutes). **Bus stop** Mare Street

🕐 **Open** 9:30am–5:30pm Tue–Fri (Thu till 8pm); 10am–5pm Sat

💲 **Price** Free

🏴 **Guided tours** Free Tea and Tour 3pm Wed. Occasional local history walks (call to check)

🧍 **Age range** 3 plus

🤾 **Activities** Interactive exhibits, dressing-up and toddler reading corner. Free drop-in crafts and storytelling events in school holidays, 2–4pm Wed–Thu

⏱ **Allow** 1 hour

♿ **Wheelchair access** Yes

🍴 **Eat and drink** Snacks Caffè Theatro (316 Mare Street, E8 1HY) has cool décor and great cakes. Real meal Tre Viet (251a Mare Street, E8 3NS; 020 8533 7390; www.treviet.co.uk; noon–11pm) is a good-value Vietnamese eatery.

🛍 **Shop** Selling books, souvenirs and pocket-money toys

🚻 **Toilets** On ground floor

Hands-on exhibits captivate at the Hackney Museum

The overarching theme of the museum is the 1,000-year history of people who have settled here, and the touchy-feely tone begins with the very first exhibit – a replica Saxon boat that kids can load up with goods. Elsewhere, they get to step into an East End pie-and-mash shop, play conductor on a vintage London bus, and race against the clock to make matchboxes – just as hundreds of poverty-stricken children did in 19th-century Hackney. There are drop-in dance, storytelling and art workshops in school holidays, often coinciding with a temporary show – the summer exhibition is always a hive of hands-on interactivity.

If it's sunny, combine a snoop around the museum with a splash at London Fields Lido, a short walk away via Richmond Road. Open every day, this is the city's only Olympic-size heated outdoor pool.

Letting off steam

As well as the Lido (020 7254 9038; www.gll.org), **London Fields** has tennis courts, ping-pong, a paddling pool and two playgrounds. Also nearby is St John at Hackney Churchyard (Lower Clapton Road, E5 0PD), with its neat play area.

⑤ Sutton House

A Tudor manor in 21st-century London

Oak panelling, echoing flagstones, roaring fires… Sutton House couldn't look more Tudor if Henry VIII himself was at the banqueting table, tossing chicken legs over his shoulder. Built in 1535 by Sir Ralph Sadler, Henry's Secretary of State, it's the last relic of the once-rural Hackney village.

There is plenty to engage kids, including the 16th-century kitchen, with food to handle and smells to sniff, and three "treasure chests" full of hands-on historical goodies – they include Elizabethan codes to crack, Jacobean jigsaws, and even a "dance mat" on which to perfect your 17th-century moves. The Sutton House stewards are ever ready to share a spine-tingling ghost story, while the mechanic's yard is being transformed into an imaginative outdoor play space, with an old Hackney cab and ice-cream van.

Atmospheric 16th-century room at Sutton House

Admission is cheap by National Trust standards, and free altogether on the last Sunday of the month, when there's a family day themed on music or meals, spooks or squatters (a room of "squatter art" has been preserved from the 1980s). In the summer holidays, there might even be a jousting tournament in the courtyard.

Letting off steam

The house's play area (with picnic tables) is free to all; or head to nearby St John's Churchyard, which has a tots' playground.

⑥ Discover

A stroll in storyland

Shock! Crisis! Emergency! The planet Squiggly Diggly is running out of stories, and a friendly alien named Hootah has been sent to Earth to gather some. That's the backstory for the Discover Children's Story Centre, a one-of-a-kind walk-through wonderland of enchanted towers, secret caves and wishing trees, with lashings of dressing-up and acting-out to help ensure a happy ending.

On the Story Trail, children wander wide-eyed among £6 million-worth of multi-sensory play gear designed to spark the imagination: they might bump into

The Lowdown

🌐 **Address** 2–4 Homerton High Street, Hackney, E9 6JQ; 020 8986 2264; www.nationaltrust.org.uk/suttonhouse

🚆 **Train** Hackney Central, 10-minute walk; Hackney Downs, 15-minute walk. **Bus stop** Homerton High Street; Lower Clapton Road; Morning Lane

🕙 **Open** 10am–4:30pm Thu–Fri; noon–4:30pm weekends early Feb–mid-Dec. Also open 10am–4.30pm Mon–Wed in school summer holidays

💲 **Price** £8–14

🚩 **Guided tours** First Sun of month, 3pm (free)

👫 **Age range** 5 plus

🏃 **Activities** Free family days last Sun of month; plus drop-in kids' activities Thu & Fri in school holidays, most days in summer

⏱ **Allow** 2 hours

♿ **Wheelchair access** No; ground floor is level, stairs to other floors

🍵 **Eat and drink** *Snacks* Tearoom serves hot snacks and cakes. *Real meal* Railroad (120–122 Morning Lane, E9 6LH; 020 8985 2858; www.railroadhackney.co.uk; 9am–11pm Wed–Sat; till 5pm Sun–Mon) is a café-bar nearby.

🛍 **Shop** Selling gifts and Trust goods; also secondhand books

🚻 **Toilets** Close to entrance

The Lowdown

🌐 **Address** 383–387 High Street, Stratford, E15 4QZ; 020 8536 5555; www.discover.org.uk

🚆 **Train** Stratford (DLR and mainline trains), 5-minute walk. **Tube** Stratford (Central and Jubilee lines), 5-minute walk. **Bus stop** Stratford Bus Station; High Street; Stratford Centre

🕙 **Open** 10am–5pm weekdays (closed Mon during school term); 11am–5pm weekends

💲 **Price** £18–28

🚩 **Skipping the queue** Book ahead for the frequent literature and art events

👫 **Age range** 3–11

🏃 **Activities** Free storytelling sessions every weekend (11:30am, 2:30pm), and in school holidays (11:30am, 1pm, 2:30pm), plus programme of workshops (see website)

⏱ **Allow** 2 hours

♿ **Wheelchair access** Yes

🍵 **Eat and drink** *Snacks* The centre's café has organic snacks and home-made cupcakes. *Real meal* Café Mondo (3 The Grove, E15 1EL; 020 8555 1319; www.mondocafe.aboriginalarts.co.uk; 8:30am–5pm Mon–Sat) offers fine focaccia toasties.

🛍 **Shop** Selling pocket-money toys, gifts and classic picture books

🚻 **Toilets** On the ground floor

Getting hands-on and stirring imaginations at the Discover Centre

Learning the Victorian way at the Ragged School Museum

a giant, dress up as a princess, sit down for a tea party, or make a spoon puppet and put on a show. Friendly "story builders" are on hand to help them compose their own tall tales; and in case they can't quite believe it themselves, a bank of TV screens shows their progress in storyland.

There is more make-believe in the Story Garden outside, with its pirate ship, space craft, trick mirrors and giant musical instruments; while interactive shows in the Story Studio profile popular kids' characters. Weekend storytelling sessions culminate in the Big Write festival each March, which throngs with well-known writers and illustrators.

Letting off steam
The garden is one big energetic adventure, with a slide and activities.

⑦ Ragged School Museum

Back to school, Victorian style

In Victorian London, children didn't just do without toys and books, they often lacked shoes and a shirt. More than half were illiterate, and one in three funerals were for children under five. A young Dubliner, Thomas Barnardo, was so shocked by the poverty he saw in the East End, he set about rescuing orphans and setting up "ragged schools" to educate them – including this one, in a canalside warehouse in Mile End.

Today, a Victorian education is delivered there again by strict-but-fair Miss Perkins, in full 1870s garb, who scratches the alphabet on her blackboard for pupils aged five to 85. The monthly lessons are a real eye-opener for kids – especially those with poor handwriting, who

may end up standing in the corner wearing a dunce's hat.

The school has also re-created an East End kitchen from 1900, with a mangle, a tin bath and other hands-on hardware. Top marks for interactivity, but the museum must do better on opening times.

Letting off steam
Just along Rhodeswell Road lies **Mile End Park playground** (*Locksley St, Limehouse E14 7EJ*), with its castle to conquer and "riverbed" sandpit. Older kids might favour the swimming pool at Mile End Leisure Centre (*190 Burdett Rd, E3 4HL; 020 8709 4420*), just opposite.

The Lowdown

🌐 **Address** 46–50 Copperfield Rd, E3 4RR; 020 8980 6405; www.raggedschoolmuseum.org.uk

🚆 **Train** Limehouse (DLR), 10-minute walk. **Tube** Mile End (Central, Hammersmith & City, District lines), 10-minute walk. **Bus stop** Ben Jonson Road; Burdett Road; Mile End Road

🕐 **Open** 10am–5pm Wed–Thu, plus 2–5pm first Sun of month

💲 **Price** Free

👫 **Age range** 5 plus

🎭 **Activities** Free 45-minute history lessons (all ages), 2:15pm and 3:30pm first Sun of month. Free themed activities for under-13s, usually led by eminent Victorians, Wed–Thu in school holidays.

⏱ **Allow** 1 hour

♿ **Wheelchair access** Yes

🍽 **Eat and drink** *Snacks* Museum café has decent snacks. *Real meal* The Palm Tree (*Haverfield Road, Bow, E3 5BH; 0871 223 8000*) is a good pub for a canal-side lunch.

🛍 **Shop** Selling vintage toys

🚻 **Toilets** No

Picnic under £20; **Snacks** £20–40; **Real meal** £40–60; **Family treat** £60 or more (based on a family of four)

Kenwood House and around

Aside from its Georgian mansion, Kenwood House, this locale is light on visitor attractions. But there's one compelling reason to make the train ride north: Hampstead Heath, a world of playgrounds, pools and woodland. Kenwood combines well with Golders Hill Park and lunch at The Spaniards Inn (Northern Line to Golders Green, then bus number 210). Or alight at Hampstead, pick up a picnic and hike to the Heath. Consider, too, a visit to Wembley Stadium (Jubilee Line) or the RAF Museum (Northern Line), a little further out of town.

Places of interest

0 kilometres   1

0 miles   1

SIGHTS
1. Kenwood House
2. Lauderdale House
3. RAF Museum
4. Wembley Stadium

EAT AND DRINK
1. The Hampstead Butcher
2. Golders Hill Park Refreshment House
3. The Spaniards Inn
4. Gaucho

See also Kenwood House (p216), Lauderdale House (p218), RAF Museum (p218), Wembley Stadium (p219)

WHERE TO STAY
1. Premier Inn, Hampstead
2. Quality Hotel Hampstead
3. La Gaffe

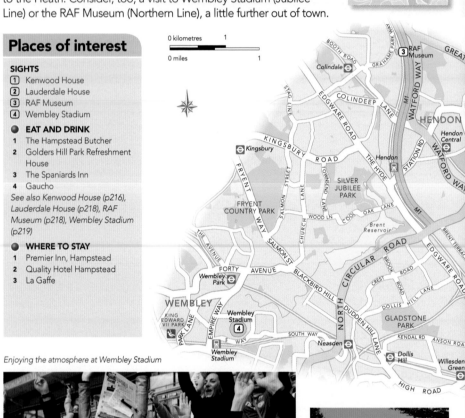

Enjoying the atmosphere at Wembley Stadium

Playing on the landscaped lawns around Georgian Kenwood House

Getting hands-on with the inmates of the Butterfly House, Golders Hill Park

The RAF Museum has dozens of historic aircraft, including the legendary Battle of Britain Spitfire and Hawker Hurricane

The Lowdown

🚗 **Train** For Hampstead Village and Parliament Hill (southern side of the Heath), take mainline trains to Gospel Oak and Hampstead Heath from Camden Road station. **Tube** For Kenwood House and Highgate, take the Northern Line (High Barnet branch) to Archway, Highgate or Golders Green stations

ℹ️ **Visitor information** www.lovecamden.org

🛒 **Supermarkets** Tesco Express, 27 Heath Street, Hampstead, NW3 6TR; Sainsbury's, 614 Finchley Road, Golders Green, NW11 7RX **Markets** Hampstead Community Market, Hampstead High Street, 10am–6pm Tue–Sat; Parliament Hill Farmers' Market, Highgate Road, 10am–2pm Sat; Archway Market, Holloway Road (crafts), 10am–5pm Sat

🎪 **Festivals** Hampstead Heath Easter Fair (also at Whitsun & August Bank Holiday); Proms at St Jude's (Jun); Kenwood Picnic Concerts (Jun–Aug); Hampstead & Highgate Literary Festival (Sep); Hampstead Heath Conker Championships (Oct)

➕ **Pharmacies** Boots, 40 Hampstead High Street, NW3 1QE (9am–6:30pm Mon–Sat, 11am–6pm Sun), or see www.nhs.uk/servicedirectories.

🧸 **Nearest playgrounds** Parliament Hill (Hampstead Heath); Golders Hill Park (West Heath Avenue, NW11 7QP or North End Road, NW3 7HA); King Edward VIII Park; Waterlow Park

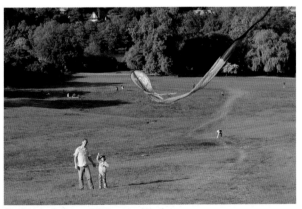

Kite-flying on Parliament Hill, Hampstead Heath

① Kenwood House
The big house on the Heath

With its manicured lawns, ornamental lakes, stables and kitchen garden, Kenwood is a gentleman's country estate, 6 km (4 miles) from London's West End. It's an authentic slice of Georgian England, where Robert Adam's Neo-Classical interiors and Humphrey Repton's picturesque park survive more or less intact from the late 1700s. Immediately to the south stretches Hampstead Heath, a hinterland frequented by wild swimmers, kite-fliers, Frisbee-throwers and tree-climbers. It is a big blast of freedom for families.

Picnicking outside Kenwood House

Key Features

The Orangery · Dressing room · The library

The Library, with its ostentatious painted ceiling, colourful friezes and colonnades, is one of Robert Adam's masterpieces.

Picnic concerts are staged in Kenwood's grounds on Saturday evenings in summer. In recent years the bill has featured Blondie and music by Vivaldi, usually with a fireworks finale.

Rembrandt self-portrait (1661) This picture is a highlight of Kenwood's collection of old masters, which also includes Vermeer's *The Guitar Player* and paintings by Hals, Turner and Gainsborough.

The park was remodelled in the 1790s under the guidance of Humphrey Repton. Its meandering lakeside walks are designed to spring picturesque "surprises".

The Lowdown

Address Hampstead Lane, NW3 7JR; 020 8348 1286; www.english-heritage.org.uk/kenwoodhouse

Train Gospel Oak or Hampstead Heath. **Tube** Golders Green (Northern line), then bus 210 or H3; or Archway (Northern line), then bus 210. **Bus stop** Hampstead Lane. **Car** West Lodge car park (pay-and-display); free parking on Hampstead Lane

Open House: 11:30am–4pm daily; Estate: from 8am (closing time varies with season)

Price Free; some temporary exhibitions charge

Guided tours Yes, times vary (small charge applies)

Age range 6 plus

Activities Occasional holiday crafts sessions; Easter Egg trails; bat-spotting walks on summer evenings. Picnic concerts programme Jun–Aug (www.picnicconcerts.com)

Allow Up to 2 hours

Wheelchair access Ground floor and toilets only

Café Set in Kenwood's servants' wing, the Brew House Cafe (020 8341 5384; 9am–4pm) serves breakfasts and lunches on the terrace; the Steward's Room serves home-baked bites.

Shop On the ground floor

Toilets On the ground floor

Good family value?
It's free, and so is the Heath

Hampstead Heath

First recorded in Saxon times and once the stalking ground of highwaymen, "The Heath" still has a wild streak. A swathe of sandstone hills and wooded glades, it runs from Kenwood House in the north to Parliament Hill, its view of London protected by law. Summer kite-fliers and winter sledgers gather here, at the bottom (near Gospel Oak station), there are playgrounds, a paddling pool and a lido.

Sampling the wares at Parliament Hill Farmers' Market

Letting off steam

Kenwood's own grounds have grass to sprawl on and trees to scramble up. Hampstead Heath's best playground (9am–dusk; 020 7433 1917) is in the far south, near the Nassington Road entrance, with a sandpit and paddling pool. There is an adventure playground for older children nearby, plus the lido swimming pool – unheated (open 7am–6pm May–Sep, 7am–noon Sep–Apr). Accompanied children aged eight and over can also swim in the reedy bathing ponds on the eastern fringe of Hampstead Heath. From Kenwood House, a handy playtime option is **Golders Hill Park** (West Heath Avenue, NW11 7QP; 020 7332 3511; 7:30am–dusk), with its petting zoo, deer, butterfly house and playground. Get there via a short bus ride from Kenwood towards Golders Green Station.

Eat and drink

Picnic: under £20; Snacks: £20–40; Real meal: £40–60; Family treat: £60 or more (based on a family of four)

PICNIC The Hampstead Butcher (56 Rosslyn Hill, NW3 1ND; 020 7794 9210; www.hampsteadbutcher.com) does good cold cuts, cheeses and ready-to-eat picnic hampers.
SNACKS Golders Hill Park Refreshment House (020 8455 8010; open from 9am, closing time varies) has a terrace, good cakes and home-made ice cream. For a

café on Hampstead Heath, try the one at Parliament Hill Fields (off Highgate Road; 020 7485 6606; 9am–dusk).
REAL MEAL The Spaniards Inn (Spaniards Road, NW3 7JJ; 020 8731 8406, www. thespaniardshampstead.co.uk; food daily from noon) has a large and splendid garden, a traditional British menu and barbecues and hog roasts sizzling away on summer weekends.
FAMILY TREAT Gaucho (64 Heath Street, NW3 1DN; 020 7431 8222; www.gauchorestaurants.co.uk; noon–11pm), between Hampstead Tube station and the Heath, has funky cowhide decor and specializes in Argentine steaks.

Find out more

DIGITAL A leaflet with three walking trails on the Heath is downloadable from www. cityoflondon.gov.uk: click on "Forests, Parks & Gardens"; "Hampstead Heath"; "Visitor information and map", then "Download the trail leaflet".
FILM Kenwood House features prominently in the 1999 romantic comedy *Notting Hill*, starring Julia Roberts and Hugh Grant.

Next stop...

POETS' CORNER Two tiny museums south of the Heath add weight to Hampstead's reputation as a hotbed of literature and the arts. Burgh House (New End Square, NW3 1LT; 020 7431 0144; www.burghhouse. org.uk) is a Queen Anne mansion once frequented by Rudyard Kipling; while Keats House (Keats Grove, NW3 2RR; 020 7332 3868; www.keatshouse.cityoflondon.gov. uk) is where the eponymous poet wrote *Ode to a Nightingale*. Both run occasional family events.

Hampstead's 400-year-old, oak-panelled tavern, The Spaniards Inn

② Lauderdale House

Poets and puppetry in the park

Lording it over Waterlow Park, with its flower-filled terraces, ponds and playgrounds, Lauderdale House has more than 400 years of history behind it. Built by Lord Mayor Sir Richard Martin in 1582, it was visited by Samuel Pepys and Charles II, lived in by the orange-selling royal mistress Nell Gwynne, and preached in by John Wesley.

Today, it is a hard-working arts centre, run by locals and alive with childish diversions: puppetry, poetry or clowns every Saturday morning; family-friendly classical music concerts most Sundays; and exciting Bizzy Kidz art and drama workshops in the school holidays. There are free art exhibitions, and cabaret, jazz and poetry sessions, too. But the big draw is the parkside setting, with bags of room to run around, a grand tearoom terrace and views of the City's skyscrapers above the trees.

The Lowdown

⊕ **Address** Waterlow Park, Highgate Hill, N6 5HG; 020 8348 8716; www.lauderdalehouse.org.uk

🚗 **Train** Upper Holloway, 15-minute walk. **Tube** Archway (Northern line), 10-minute walk. **Bus stop** Waterlow Park; Archway Station

⊙ **Open** House:11am–4pm Tue–Fri; 1:30–5pm Sat; noon–5pm Sun. Waterlow Park open 7:30am–dusk; www.waterlowpark.org.uk

🏷 **Price** Exhibitions free; shows and special events individually priced

👪 **Age range** Saturday morning kids' shows target ages 2–8

🏃 **Activities** Walk-up Sat morning children's shows; check website for holiday events and music and drama programme. Waterlow Park offers bat-spotting walks and "green" gardening sessions

⏱ **Allow** 2 hours for house and park

♿ **Wheelchair access** Limited. Ground floor only (no lift)

🍴 **Eat and drink** *Snacks* Lauderdale House (020 8341 4807; 10am–dusk Tue–Sun; plus spring and summer bank holidays) has a good café-cum-restaurant, with terrace tables for cake and ice cream guzzling.

🚻 **Toilets** At house and in the park

Swinging among the autumn foliage in a playground at Waterlow Park

Just to the north, smart Highgate Village is strong on atmospheric pubs and speciality shopping, while Highgate Cemetery (Swains Lane, N6; www.highgate-cemetery.org), resting place of Karl Marx, George Eliot and Michael Faraday, is next door, with daily tours (over-7s only).

Letting off steam

Waterlow Park *(Dartmouth Park Hill, N19 5JF)* has two playgrounds for children under 6, a terrace café and tennis courts.

③ RAF Museum

Fighter pilot playtime

Many kids want to be a fighter pilot when they grow up. Few actually make it, so here's the next best thing: a whole hangar full of interactive flying games and challenges at the Royal Air Force Museum in Hendon. Its Aeronauts Centre has 40 hands-on experiments that cunningly disguise principles of science as play: climb into a helicopter cockpit and take the controls; grab a hang-glider bar and manoeuvre through the air; or grapple with pilot aptitude tests.

The museum is spread across the former Hendon Aerodrome, the century-old birthplace of British aviation. Giant hangars house more than 100 full-size flying machines, from Sopwith Camels to cruise missiles, many suspended

The Lowdown

⊕ **Address** Grahame Park Way, NW9 5LL; 020 8205 2266; www.rafmuseum.org.uk/london

🚗 **Train** Mill Hill Broadway, 15-minute walk. **Tube** Colindale (Northern line), 10-minute walk. **Bus stop** Grahame Park Way; Lanacre Avenue. **Car** Parking on site (from £2.50)

⊙ **Open** 10am–6pm. Our Finest Hour show runs hourly, 1–5pm

🏷 **Price** Free, except flight simulator (£2.75) and 4-D theatre (£4).

🎗 **Guided tours** Free volunteer-led tours, times vary. Audio guide to selected galleries available by download only

👪 **Age range** 6 plus; Eurofighter simulator min height 107 cm (3 ft 6 in)

🏃 **Activities** Some activity sheets and audio guides available from website, plus worksheets. Family activity programme focuses on Commonwealth Day (Mar), Armed Forces Day (Jun) and the Battle of Britain (Sep), plus half-term holiday workshops.

⏱ **Allow** Half a day

♿ **Wheelchair access** Yes, although getting in aircraft will be difficult

🍴 **Eat and drink** *Snacks* Wessex Café has helicopters and home-made snacks; *Real meal* Wings Restaurant serves a health-conscious kids' menu.

🛍 **Shop** Selling a variety of aviation-themed gifts

🚻 **Toilets** By the entrance

Getting up close to one of the many planes on display at the RAF Museum

dogfight-style from the rafters. The Milestones of Flight gallery gives a literal overview of aircraft history from its "control tower" balcony, and other highlights include a sound and light show – Our Finest Hour – bringing alive the Battle of Britain, a new "4-D" theatre experience aboard an American B-17 bomber, and a Eurofighter Typhoon flight simulator, soaring at twice the speed of sound.

Letting off steam
There are lots of grassy picnic grounds at the museum.

④ Wembley Stadium
Ninety minutes of glory
After a controversial £750 million rebuilding, the "new" Wembley Stadium has resumed its mantle as the spiritual home of football, with 90,000 seats and a 133-m (436-ft) arch that curves like a rainbow above the North London skyline. As well as the FA Cup final each May, Wembley hosts international rugby, American football, rock concerts and the 2012 Olympic football finals.

For footie-mad kids (and adults), a trip here is akin to a pilgrimage, and the 90-minute guided tours won't let them down. They get to follow in the footsteps of their heroes on matchday – from the England team's dressing-room and warm-up area, through the tunnel to pitch-side, where they'll be greeted by the cacophonous roar of a piped-in crowd. After a sit down in the manager's dugout, it's up the famous steps to the Royal Box for a feel of a replica FA Cup. For the adults, there's also a video of historic highlights and a look at some

Going behind the scenes at Wembley Stadium

famous Wembley relics, including the crossbar that helped England win the 1966 World Cup.

Letting off steam
Brought your own ball along? For a good kick-about, head west via Dagmar Avenue to **King Edward VII Park** *(Park Lane, Wembley, HA9 7RX)* which has grassy space, football pitches and a playground.

Out and about on the pathways of King Edward VII Park

The Lowdown

🌐 **Address** Wembley National Stadium, HA9 0WS; 0844 980 8001 (booking line: 0844 800 2755); *www.wembleystadium.com/Wembley-Tours.aspx*

🚆 **Train** Wembley Stadium station. **Tube** Wembley Park (Metropolitan and Jubilee lines). **Bus stop** Olympic Way, Empire Way, Wembley Park Station. **Car** Green Car Park, Engineers Way

🕐 **Open** Tours run most days (check website), departing 10am–4pm. Sometimes only a 60-minute "mini tour" is offered, missing out dressing rooms and pitch-side.

💷 **Price** £46–56

🏃 **Skipping the queue** Advance booking strongly advised; arrive 30 minutes before tour

👫 **Age range** 6 plus

🏃 **Activities** Quiz sheets can be downloaded from the website's Groups and School Visits page

⏱ **Allow** 2 hours

♿ **Wheelchair access** Yes

🍴 **Eat and drink** Snacks A café at the entrance serves sandwiches and snacks

🛍 **Shop** Selling football and Wembley souvenirs

🚻 **Toilets** At start of tour

Horniman Museum and around

If the Horniman Museum was in Central London, it would be on every family's must-see itinerary. A treasure chest of strange marvels, it has everything from voodoo charms to mummy cases, live bees to stuffed apes and a skull-covered hat. The museum is near Forest Hill, a 15-minute train ride from London Bridge station. The P4 bus route runs from the Horniman to South London's other star attraction: Dulwich Picture Gallery, whose old masters come to life at ArtPlay family workshops. Better still, walk there across Dulwich Park, where the Pavilion Café is a super sunny-day lunch option.

Picnicking on the lawns surrounding the ornate Victorian conservatory at the Horniman Museum

Enjoying a ride through Dulwich Park on the recumbent bicycles available for hire

Places of interest

SIGHTS
1. Horniman Museum
2. Dulwich Picture Gallery
3. Crystal Palace Park

● EAT AND DRINK
1. The Teapot
2. The Pavilion Café
3. The Dartmouth Arms
4. The Herne

See also Horniman Museum (p222), Dulwich Picture Gallery (p224) and Crystal Palace Park (p225)

Getting up close to one of the many life-size dinosaurs that lurk at Crystal Palace Park

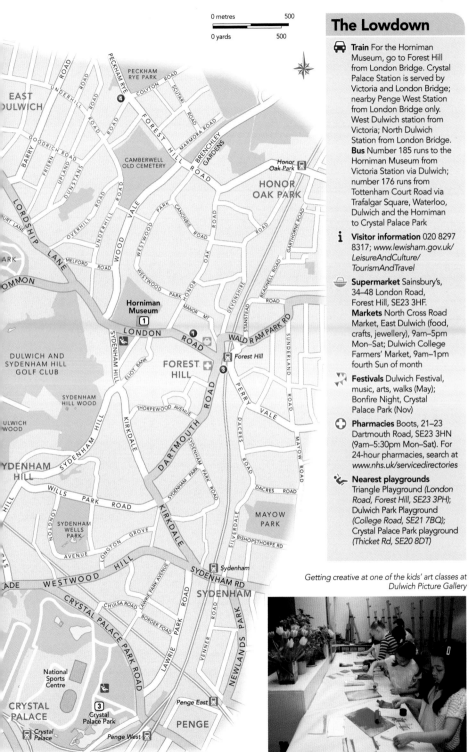

0 metres 500
0 yards 500

The Lowdown

🚗 **Train** For the Horniman Museum, go to Forest Hill from London Bridge. Crystal Palace Station is served by Victoria and London Bridge; nearby Penge West Station from London Bridge only. West Dulwich station from Victoria; North Dulwich Station from London Bridge. **Bus** Number 185 runs to the Horniman Museum from Victoria Station via Dulwich; number 176 runs from Tottenham Court Road via Trafalgar Square, Waterloo, Dulwich and the Horniman to Crystal Palace Park

ℹ **Visitor information** 020 8297 8317; www.lewisham.gov.uk/ LeisureAndCulture/ TourismAndTravel

🛒 **Supermarket** Sainsbury's, 34–48 London Road, Forest Hill, SE23 3HF. **Markets** North Cross Road Market, East Dulwich (food, crafts, jewellery), 9am–5pm Mon–Sat; Dulwich College Farmers' Market, 9am–1pm fourth Sun of month

🎉 **Festivals** Dulwich Festival, music, arts, walks (May); Bonfire Night, Crystal Palace Park (Nov)

➕ **Pharmacies** Boots, 21–23 Dartmouth Road, SE23 3HN (9am–5:30pm Mon–Sat). For 24-hour pharmacies, search at www.nhs.uk/servicedirectories

🛝 **Nearest playgrounds** Triangle Playground (London Road, Forest Hill, SE23 3PH); Dulwich Park Playground (College Road, SE21 7BQ); Crystal Palace Park playground (Thicket Rd, SE20 8DT)

Getting creative at one of the kids' art classes at Dulwich Picture Gallery

① Horniman Museum
Mummies, mermaids and magic amulets

A Victorian tea trader, Frederick Horniman gathered his eccentric stash of objects from across the British Empire. His museum bursts with artefacts from the wildest childhood imagination: a totem pole, a torture chair, magic amulets, mummies, even a mermaid. After a £13 million refit, the museum is fanatical about welcoming families. It hosts some of London's most exotic "Busy Bee" play sessions, which could involve sharks' teeth, ritual masks or thumb pianos.

Goliath Beetle in the Nature Base

Key Features

▓ **First Floor** Gallery overlooking the Ground Floor

▓ **Ground Floor** Natural History Gallery, Hands On Base, Textile Display, Education Centre and café

▓ **Lower Ground Floor** Music Gallery, African Worlds Gallery and Centenary Gallery

▓ **Basement** An aquarium reveals what lives in ponds, in coral reefs and the Amazon rainforest.

Entrance

① **Haitian voodoo shrine** This gloriously gaudy altar is loaded with strange offerings: make-up, dolls, posters, perfume, skulls. Haitians believe spirits are everywhere, even in discarded objects.

② **Igbo Ijele mask** Piled with figurines and feathers in fantastic colours, this towering mask is Africa's largest. It is worn at the lively ijele ceremony in Nigeria.

③ **Music Gallery** Touch the tabletops to hear sound clips from the dazzling instruments collection.

④ **Tlingit totem pole** Carved in cedar, the Horniman totem pole guards the entrance. It depicts the Alaskan legend of a girl who married a bear.

⑤ **Nature Base** Here you can observe a live honey bee colony, watch the scampering harvest mice and scrutinize beetles under a microscope.

⑥ **Aquarium** Small but sunny, the basement aquarium devotes tanks to seven habitats, from a British pond to a Fijian coral reef. For kids, the seahorses are the stars.

Letting off steam

Draped across the summit of Forest Hill, with panoramic views over London, the museum's grassy grounds include a nature trail, a bandstand and a small animal enclosure with alpacas and rabbits.

The vast sandpit at the Triangle, opposite the Horniman Museum

Prices given are for a family of four

In summer there are picnic tables and a new "musical play area" is on the way. For a traditional playground, cross London Road to the **Triangle**, which has a sandpit, a climbing wall and a tea kiosk.

Eat and drink

Picnic: under £20; Snacks: £20–40; Real meal: £40–60; Family treat: £60 or more (based on a family of four)

PICNIC The Teapot (56 London Road, SE23 3HF; 020 8699 2829) is a dapper little tearoom and deli, handily placed halfway between Forest Hill station and the museum.

SNACKS The Pavilion Café in Dulwich Park (College Road, SE21 7BQ; 020 8299 1383; 8:30am–5:30pm; weekends from 9am) is a lovely spot for coffee and home-baked cakes, and their lunchtime specials have an Italian flavour.

REAL MEAL The Dartmouth Arms (7 Dartmouth Road, SE23 3HN; 020 8488 3117; www.thedartmoutharms.com; food served noon–3:30pm, 6:30pm–10pm Sun–Fri; noon–10pm Sat) is a friendly gastro-pub with several dishes available in smaller portions, ideal for kids. It is near Forest Hill station.

The Lowdown

Address 100 London Road, Forest Hill, SE23 3PQ; 020 8699 1872; www.horniman.ac.uk

Train Forest Hill, 10-minute walk. **Bus stop** London Road; Sydenham Hill

Open 10:30am–5:30pm daily; gardens 7:15am–sunset Mon–Sat, from 8am Sun

Price Free. Aquarium £6–10; some temporary exhibitions charge

Skipping the queue Busy Bee tickets available on the day at 10:30am, 11:30am; and at 11:15am, 12:30pm at weekends

Age range 3 plus

Activities Free family activities every weekend afternoon: mix of drop-in "discovery for all" sessions (2–3:30pm) and ticketed art workshops and object-handling (11:45am–12:30pm, 1–1:45pm, 1:30–2:15pm, 2:45–3:30pm). Plus Sat morning Dads' Club (10:30am–12:30pm) and free family storytelling every Sun (2:15–3pm, 3:30–4:15pm).

Frequent sessions on school holiday weekdays, too (check website). Half-hour Busy Bee crafts and story sessions for under-5s every Wed and Fri (10:30am, 11:15am, noon). Download age-graded activity sheets and learning packs before visiting at: www.horniman.ac.uk/exhibitions/trails.php.

Allow At least half a day

Wheelchair access Yes, both museum and gardens

Café The museum's café has excellent variety for kids; on a sunny day, eat in the ornate Victorian conservatory.

Shop Selling toys, musical instruments and books inspired by the museum's collection.

Toilets In café and on Lower Ground Floor

Good family value?

Absolutely tremendous. Unlike many London museums, even the café is affordable.

This stuffed walrus dominates the Natural History Gallery

FAMILY TREAT The Herne (2 Forest Hill Road, SE22 0RR; 020 8299 9521; www.theherne.net; noon–2:30pm, 6:30–9:45pm) is more restaurant than pub, with a children's menu of grilled chicken, linguine, sausages or scampi. There's also a climbing frame out the back to help the kids run off lunch. It's at East Dulwich: take the 363 bus from the Horniman.

and insects, plus the Batsense game: steer a pipistrelle bat away from predators while hunting for insects. Tough task: pipistrelles use their echolocator radar to gobble up to 3,000 bugs in a single night!

For behind-the-scenes footage from the Horniman, including an X-ray view of its famous "mermaid", visit the museum's Youtube channel: www.youtube.com/user/Horniman.

Find out more

DIGITAL The museum website's Nature Base zone (www.horniman.ac.uk/naturebase) has facts and quizzes about native birds, animals

Next stop...

CRYSTAL PALACE PARK Head here for an afternoon of fun among the dinosaurs and playgrounds, or visit the Sports Centre in wet weather.

② Dulwich Picture Gallery

Old masters and leafy grounds

With its cloistered gardens, chapel and mausoleum, this looks precisely the kind of place that wouldn't welcome children, but appearances can be deceptive. London's oldest public gallery is crammed with priceless portraits – from 17th-century saints to 18th-century courtesans – which were gathered in the 1790s for the King of Poland, who was promptly overthrown, leaving his new collection homeless. Architect Sir John Soane (see p94) stepped in, and with his interlinked halls lit by skylights, created the template for art galleries the world over. There are works by Canaletto, Constable, Raphael and Rubens here – and free drawing trails help visitors to unpick their secrets.

The real joy for families, though, is the inspiring array of hands-on art classes that are offered here. On the first and last Sundays of the

The Lowdown

🌐 **Address** Gallery Road, SE21 7AD; 020 8693 5254; www.dulwichpicturegallery.org.uk

🚗 **Train** North Dulwich or West Dulwich, both a 10-minute walk away. **Bus stop** College Road; Dulwich College

🕐 **Open** 10am–5pm Tue–Fri, 11am– 5pm Sat–Sun (last admission 4:30pm)

💲 **Price** £10–15, under-18s free; temporary exhibitions extra

👫 **Skipping the queue** Book half-term and after-school courses in advance: 020 8299 8732

🚩 **Guided tours** 3pm Sat and Sun (free); multimedia iGuide (£3)

👫 **Age range** 8 plus

👫 **Activities** Free quiz and drawing trails (ages 4–12). Family ArtPlay drop-in, 2–3:30pm first and last Sun of month (free with entry, or £2); also Wed in school holidays. Half-term workshops (ages 6–8 and 9–11, charges apply). Jazz evenings and films in summer.

⏱ **Allow** 1–2 hours

♿ **Wheelchair access** Yes

🍴 **Eat and drink** Real meal The Café opens one hour earlier than the gallery and has £5 children's menu and celebrated afternoon teas. Snacks The Pavilion Café in Dulwich Park (see p222) is also a good bet.

🛍 **Shop** Selling art-related gifts, books and toys

🚻 **Toilets** On the ground floor

Left Hanging out paintings to dry at Dulwich Picture Gallery
Below Enjoying the playground in Dulwich Park

month, drop-in ArtPlay sessions encourage grown-ups and their children to work creatively together – drawing cartoons, making bunting or block-printing, perhaps. There is more of the same every Wednesday afternoon in summer, when the gallery gardens are transformed into a giant arty picnic. There are also half-term workshops for ages 6–11, and after-school art clubs for 7–18s.

The 15-minute zip out of town to leafy Dulwich Village feels like a magical journey into the heart of the countryside, and once sated with old masters, children get to cross the road into attractive Dulwich Park, with its boating lake, bike hire and adventure playground.

Letting off steam

The civilized gallery gardens are open for picnics and playtime – no "keep off the grass signs" here. **Dulwich Park** (020 8693 8635; www.southwark.gov.uk/info/461/a_to_z_of_parks/1296/dulwich_park/) has a playground, cycle hire (020 8299 6636; www.londonrecumbents.com; 8am–dusk) and turn-up-and-play tennis.

③ Crystal Palace Park

The land that time forgot

Television, theme parks and the Girl Guides – a fine trio of inventions, especially if you happen to be a child, and all were hatched here in one of London's most history-packed parks. So it's great that Crystal Palace is finally getting a new lease of life after years in the doldrums, with plans afoot for a multi-million pound makeover that will restore it to something like the popular pomp of its Victorian heyday.

The park was created by master gardener Joseph Paxton (1803–65) to house his mammoth Crystal Palace, which was moved here pane by pane from Hyde Park after hosting the 1851 Great Exhibition. Perched on a ridge overlooking the city, it had extensive pleasure grounds and fountains higher than Nelson's Column, and thousands flocked to visit. However, the Crystal Palace burnt down in 1936: look out for its ghostly terraces, and the odd statue of a sultan or sphinx. But one

Dinosaur-spotting in the Dinosaur Park at Crystal Palace Park

of the park's original wonders is still a huge draw for families – its Dinosaur Court, an army of 30 life-size prehistoric monsters that stalk the boating lake. Installed in 1853 by the sculptor Benjamin Waterhouse Hawkins and the pioneering palaeontologist Richard Owen, these models were a sensation in their day, prefiguring Darwin's *Origin of the Species* and staking a claim for Crystal Palace as the world's first "theme park".

Pick up a guide from the park information centre and go hunting for iguanodons and pterodactyls – dino-mad kids will enjoy pointing out the anatomical errors exposed by 150 years of science. The nearby children's playground boasts a dinosaur climbing frame, and the park also has a small farmyard with alpacas and a reptile room, plus one of the biggest hedge mazes in the country. Add the indoor facilities at the sports centre, the spiritual home of British athletics, and there's easily enough to warrant a train ride out from the city centre. Soon, there should be more entertainment, too – the Crystal Palace masterplan promises tropical glasshouses, a treetop walkway, even a revival for one of Paxton's 1850s fountains.

Take cover
The park is dominated by the **National Sports Centre** *(Ledrington Road, SE19 2BB; 020 8778 0131; www.gll.org/centre/crystal-palace-national-sports-centre.asp)*, which has an Olympic-size indoor swimming pool, tennis courts and a climbing wall. The centre's training pool is reserved for 2-hour family-only swimming most days.

Alternatively, visit the museum that tells the story of Paxton's original Crystal Palace *(020 8676 0700; www.crystalpalacemuseum.org.uk; open 11am–4:30pm, weekends and bank holidays only)*.

The Lowdown

🌐 **Address** Crystal Palace Park, Thicket Road, SE20 8DT; 020 8778 9496; www.bromley.gov.uk. Access via Thicket Rd, Crystal Palace Park Rd and Ledrington Rd

🚃 **Train** Crystal Palace, 2-minute walk; Penge West, 5-minute walk. **Bus stop** Crystal Palace Station; Penge West Station

🕐 **Open** 7:30am–dusk. Park information centre (near Thicket Road entrance) open from 9am

💲 **Price** Free

🚩 **Guided tours** Dinosaur trail leaflet from information centre, which has a small history display

👫 **Age range** All

🤸 **Activities** Playground and dinosaur area near Thicket Road gate, plus hedge maze (free). Most weekends, keepers at Crystal Palace Park Farm (noon–4pm Thu–Tue; 0208 778 5572) give talks at 2pm and 2:30pm. Occasional ranger-led pond-dipping and Easter egg hunts in school holidays (call to check). National Sports Centre hosts school holiday activity or sports schools (ages 6–15; www.gll.org/holidayactivities).

⏱ **Allow** Up to half a day

♿ **Wheelchair access** Yes

🍴 **Eat and drink** Snacks Park café (Thicket Road entrance; 020 8778 5422; 9am–5pm) offers fast food, snacks and drinks.

🚻 **Toilets** Near Thicket Road entrance

Picnic under £20; **Snacks** £20–40; **Real meal** £40–60; **Family treat** £60 or more (based on a family of four)

Kew Gardens and around

Glossy, well-groomed and handily located at the end of the District line, Richmond and Kew offer a breath of fresh air for families overcome by the pace of the city. Kids will delight in the gardens' attractions and they will love Richmond Park – especially its deer. For Kew, alight at the tube station, pick up a picnic and tour the gardens on the Explorer Bus. For Richmond Park, take bus number 65 or 371 from Richmond station. Several stately homes are close, too: try the riverside walk from Richmond to haunted Ham House.

Places of Interest

SIGHTS
1. Kew Gardens
2. WWT London Wetland Centre
3. Syon House
4. Osterley Park
5. Richmond Park
6. Ham House

● EAT AND DRINK
1. The Original Maids of Honour
2. The Kew Greenhouse Café
3. Bell & Crown
4. Ma Cuisine

See also WWT London Wetland Centre (p230), Syon House (p230), Osterley Park (p231), Richmond Park (p232) and Ham House (p233).

● WHERE TO STAY
1. Richmond Gate
2. Richmond Inn

0 kilometres 1

0 miles 1

Above *The Great Conservatory at Syon House*
Right *Delicious treats on display at The Original Maids of Honour*

The Lowdown

🚗 **Train** Kew Bridge and Richmond, both served by trains from Waterloo (via Barnes). Richmond and Kew Gardens (North London line). **Tube** Kew Gardens, Richmond (both District line)

ℹ️ **Visitor information** 08456 122 660; *www.visitrichmond. co.uk*

🛒 **Supermarkets** Waitrose, 4 Sheen Road, Richmond, TW9 1AE. **Markets** Richmond Farmers' Market, Heron Square, 11am–3pm Sat

🎭 **Festivals** Tropical Extravaganza, Kew Gardens (Feb); Holi Hindu Festival of Colour (Mar); Kew Summer Swing picnic concerts (Aug); Richmond Riverside Festival, world music and dance (Aug); Great River Race, finish point (Sep); Richmond Literature Festival (Nov)

➕ **Pharmacies** Lloyds, 19–21 Station Parade, Kew, TW9 3PS (9am–7pm Mon–Sat, 10am–4pm Sun). For 24-hour pharmacies, search at *www. nhs.uk/servicedirectories.*

👟 **Nearest playgrounds** Climbers and Creepers, Kew Gardens (*near Brentford Gate*); Petersham Gate, Richmond Park (*Petersham Rd, TW10 5HS*)

Above *Interactive play area, Climbers and Creepers, at Kew Gardens*
Right *Wildfowl at the London Wetland Centre*

Youngsters riding ponies through Richmond Park

① Kew Gardens
The world's most famous garden

Founded more than 250 years ago, the Royal Botanic Gardens – a treasure trove of lakes, mini-temples, nature trails and playgrounds – is a delightful place to spend time. Kew's Victorian glasshouses offer a botanical world tour, but even better is just dawdling in the dappled glades around Queen Charlotte's Cottage, or admiring the peacocks at the Waterlily Pond. Little visitors can burrow in a badger sett and climb into the treetops – and if that doesn't tire them out, there's an exhilarating plant-themed playhouse.

Oriental Pagoda

Key Features

① Treetop Walkway Clamber into the branches of Kew's arboretum for giddying views. The walkway is designed to sway in the wind.

② Palm House The tropical plants here drip and steam. In the basement aquarium, don 3-D glasses and go "swimming with plankton".

③ Temperate House The world's biggest Victorian glasshouse is also home to the world's tallest "house plant", reached via ornate iron balconies.

④ Climbers and Creepers Fall prey to the slippery pitcher plant or wriggle into a field-mouse nest in this ingenious indoor playground. Outside, the Treehouse Towers park has a zipwire and rope bridges.

⑦ Badger Sett Expect muddy kneecaps after a crawl inside this child-size badgers' home. Nearby, the Nature Hide and Stag Beetle Loggery explore more native wildlife.

⑤ Evolution House Waterfalls crash and insects hum on this trip through primordial swamps back to the age of the dinosaurs. Watch out for monster millipedes!

⑥ Princess of Wales Conservatory Look out for Venus flytraps and the world's largest flower in one of 10 climatic zones. Portholes give a close-up view of the fishponds.

Brentford Gate · Main Gate · Victoria Gate · Lion Gate · Queen Charlotte's Cottage · Waterlily Pond

---

Take cover

Kew's glasshouses, aquariums and indoor playroom offer rainy-day diversions all year round – plus there's a toddler corner in the White Peaks Shop. On nearby Kew Green, the Ceramics Café offers drop-in pottery painting (1a Mortlake Terrace, TW9 3DT; 020 8332 6661; 10am–6pm), while just north of Kew Bridge, Brentford Fountain Leisure Centre (658 Chiswick High Road, TW8 0HJ; 0845 456 6675) has a family pool (weekends 9am–5:30pm, weekdays vary) and a soft-play centre for under-12s (10am–6pm Mon–Fri, 9am–11:15am weekends).

Prices given are for a family of four

Eat and drink

Picnic: under £20; Snacks: £20–40; Real meal: £40–60; Family treat: £60 or more (based on a family of four)

PICNIC The Original Maids of Honour (288 Kew Road, Kew, TW9 3DU; 020 8940 2752; www.

"Maids of Honour" pastries, which gave the popular Kew bakery its name

theoriginalmaidsofhonour.co.uk; 9am–6pm) is a Kew institution, said to date back to Tudor times. It offers tearoom treats, smart lunches and pre-packed picnics of varying extravagance.

SNACKS The Kew Greenhouse Café (1 Station Parade, Richmond TW9 3PS; 020 8940 0183; 8am–dusk) is a traditional English café, between the Tube and Victoria Gate, serving pasta, quiches, eggs on toast and home-made cakes.

REAL MEAL Bell & Crown (11–13 Thames Road, W4 3PL; 020 8994 4164; www.fullers.co.uk; food: noon–3pm, 6:30–10pm, plus

The Lowdown

🌐 **Address** Royal Botanic Gardens, Kew, Richmond, Surrey, TW9 3AB; 020 8332 5000; www.kew. org

🚆 **Train** Kew Gardens, 5-minute walk; or Kew Bridge, 10 minutes. **Tube** Kew Gardens (District line). **Bus stop** Kew Gardens, Kew Bridge Station. **Car** Parking at Brentford Gate (£5 per day). **River bus** Kew Pier, Apr–Sep, four services daily to and from Westminster (020 7930 2062; www.wpsa.co.uk)

🕐 **Open** 9:30am–6:30pm, Apr–Aug; 9:30am–6pm Sep–Oct; 9:30am–4:15pm Oct–Jan; 9:30am–5:30pm Feb–Mar. Last admission 30 minutes earlier, weekends close an hour later

💷 **Price** £28–38 (free admission for under-17s)

🚩 **Guided tours** Explorer Bus tours the gardens hourly, half-hourly in high season (£10–15). Free walking tours daily from Victoria Plaza, 11am and 2pm; plus themed tours

👫 **Age range** All

👪 **Activities** Cimbers and Creepers (ages 3–9); Treetop Towers park

(up to 11). School holiday craft activities for ages 3–9. Kids' Kew guidebook (£5) has stickers and garden trails. Tropical Extravaganza festival in February (orchids etc); Kew the Music picnic concerts in July

⏱ **Allow** Up to a day

♿ **Wheelchair access** Mostly. Aquarium and top-level galleries not accessible, but garden paths and most buildings are. Explorer Bus can take one wheelchair.

☕ **Café** The Orangery is waiter service, with children's portions and afternoon teas; White Peaks Café serves simpler family fare and ice cream next to the play area; Victoria Plaza Café sells sandwiches and snacks. In summer, Pavilion Restaurant has outdoor BBQ and salad buffet. All offer a kids' lunchbox.

🏷 **Shop** Selling plant-related and cookery items; children's toy/gift shop near play area

🚻 **Toilets** At main attractions

Good family value?
Free admission for under-17s, and there's almost nothing to pay for once inside.

weekend afternoons) is one of a pleasant strip of popular riverside pubs just across Kew Bridge that boast good pub grub for families. **FAMILY TREAT** Ma Cuisine *(The Old Post Office, 9 Station Approach, TW9 3QB; 020 8332 1923, www.macuisinebistrot.co.uk; 10am–11.30pm)* is a neat French bistro with a very relaxed and welcoming atmosphere, as well as a Michelin Bib Gourmand for its authentic French food; one child under 12 eats free from noon–6pm Mon–Sat and all day Sun.

The "Flying fox" zipwire at Treetop Towers, outside Climbers and Creepers

Find out more

DIGITAL On the Kew Gardens website, the Climbers and Creepers zone has colouring, stories and virtual plant-growing games for ages 3–6: www.kew. org/climbersandcreepers. Older kids can learn how to grow mango plants and make smoothies, at www.plantcultures.org/activities.

Next stop...

KEW PALACE Inside the Royal Botanic Gardens is a playhouse of princesses. Kew Palace *(0844 482 7777; www.hrp.org.uk/kewpalace; 10am–5pm, from11am Mon, Apr–Sep)* looks like an overgrown doll's house – which is apt, since it was bought by King George III as a nursery for his children. It is the smallest surviving royal palace, and its highlights include a 200-year-old "baby house" built by the Georgian princesses themselves. Admission costs extra (£5.30), though accompanied under-16s get in free of charge.

② WWT London Wetland Centre

London's best duck pond

Opened in 2000, London Wetland Centre has been a conservation triumph – an ugly-duckling reservoir site transformed into a beautiful wilderness of lagoons and pasture just 6 km (4 miles) from Westminster. Thousands of waterbirds live here, including exotic duck species such as grey-and-gold feathered wigeons, which graze the fields like sheep; and shovelers, which swim in manic circles to create a vortex to bring their food to the surface.

The indoor Discovery Centre is all about engaging children, with its underwater pond camera and poo-shooting exhibit, demonstrating how reed beds filter dirty water. The all-action adventure playground has frogs to bounce on and rubber ducks to race, and kids can wander out into the wetlands to watch for

Whistling ducks by the water at the London Wetland Centre

water voles and admire the reserve's eco-friendly lawnmowers – a trio of cute frizzy-wigged highland cattle. There is warden-led bird feeding each afternoon, while the family events programme fills every weekend and school holiday with nestbox-building, pond safaris and (at Easter) egg candling – a fascinating glimpse inside a duck egg as it develops. But what young ones will appreciate most, perhaps, is the immense feeling of space, and the glorious London skyline stretched across a far horizon.

Take cover
The interactive Discovery Centre, pond zone and "bird airport" observatory offer at least an hour's weatherproof entertainment.

Little dippers looking for waterborne wildlife at the London Wetland Centre

The Lowdown

🌐 **Address** Queen Elizabeth's Walk, Barnes, SW13 9WT; 020 8409 4400; www.wwt.org.uk/visit-us/london

🚃 **Train** Barnes or Barnes Bridge, 15-minute walk. **Tube** Hammersmith, then number 283 bus. **Bus stop** Wetland Centre or Red Lion. **Car** Free parking on site

🕙 **Open** 9:30am–6pm Apr–Oct; 9:30am–5pm Oct–Mar (last admission 1 hour earlier)

💲 **Price** £30–40

🚩 **Guided tours** 11am, 2pm (free), plus noon at weekends

👫 **Age range** All

👫 **Activities** Bird feeding 3pm daily. Free family activities (30–60 mins) weekends and holidays, plus Animal Discovery weekends. Occasional evening bat walks (age 8 plus, £10).

🕐 **Allow** Half a day

♿ **Wheelchair access** Yes, apart from Wildside Hide (steps)

🍴 **Eat and drink** *Snacks* Water's Edge Café sells cakes and hot lunches from 11am–3pm

🛍 **Shop** Selling books, eco items, bird feeders/boxes and souvenirs

🚻 **Toilets** Ground floor near café and in the car park

The Lowdown

🌐 **Address** Brentford, Middlesex, TW8 8JF; 020 8560 0882; www.syonpark.co.uk

🚃 **Train** Kew Bridge, then bus 237 or 267; or Brentford, then 15-minute walk. **Tube** Gunnersbury (District line) then bus 237 or 267. **Bus stop** Brent Lea. **Car** Free car park

🕙 **Open** House: 11am–5pm Wed, Thu, Sun mid-Mar–Oct; (last admission 4pm); Gardens: 10:30am–5pm daily and winter weekends

💲 **Price** £28–38

🚩 **Guided tours** Occasional guided garden walks

👫 **Age range** 8 plus

👫 **Activities** Garden cinema, Aug; Enchanted Woodland evening openings, Nov; craft fairs

🕐 **Allow** Up to 2 hours

♿ **Wheelchair access** Garden paths are accessible, as is ground floor of the house (via chair lift)

🍴 **Eat and drink** *Snacks* Refectory Café sells a range of snacks and light lunches.

🛍 **Shop** Small gift shop and garden centre

🚻 **Toilets** On the ground floor

③ Syon House

Costume drama heaven

Gleaming like a gold ingot beside the Thames, this is outer London's last bastion of aristocratic England – still home to the Dukes of Northumberland after more than 400 years. It's easy to imagine the house as a stage set, and on the big screen it has starred in both *Gosford Park* and *The Madness of King George*. Meanwhile, its stellar cast of real-life characters includes Henry VIII and Sir Walter Raleigh, Indian chiefs and Gunpowder Plotters.

Explore the epic suite of rooms designed for the first duke by Robert Adam (1728–92), who gave him the gilded gods, silk hangings and wedding-cake ceilings he had seen in Neo-Classical Italy. There is also the domed Great Conservatory – so grand it inspired Joseph Paxton's Crystal Palace (*see pp224–5*) – and the extensive grounds modelled by "Capability" Brown (1716–83). For kids, the ornamental arboretum is especially bewitching during Syon's

The Neo-Classical Northumberland family dining room at Syon House

The Great Conservatory at Syon House, built of gunmetal, Bath stone and glass

"Enchanted Woodland" season, when it twinkles with more than 1,000 lights. Younger children can be humoured with the promise of a romp at Snakes and Ladders, a soft-play centre in the grounds.

Letting off steam

Snakes and Ladders (020 8847 0946; www.snakes-and-ladders. co.uk; 10am–6pm daily) has a three-storey play-frame, a toddler area, electric bikes and an outdoor assault course. Separate admission charges apply (children over 5, £7.30; ages 2–4, £6.30; under-2s £5.30).

④ Osterley Park
A very big banker's bonus

In 1761, when wealthy banker Sir Francis Child wanted a flashy new look for his family pile at Osterley Park, there was only one man to call – the style guru extraordinaire, Robert Adam. He didn't just add a Roman portico, stuccoed stairways and the 40-m (131-ft) Long Gallery to the Elizabethan mansion, he

designed new carpets, new furniture, fireplaces and ceilings. The result is a "palace of palaces", a glimpse of how Britain's super-rich bankers lived 250 years ago.

What's great for children is that the rooms "below stairs" at Osterley remain pretty intact, too: in the vaulted servants' hall, they can get to grips with antique kitchen gear, don servants' mob caps and aprons, and watch spooky film projections of Georgian maids and footmen at work. A hand-held audio-visual guide just for kids stars Tweeny the serving girl, who leads the way from room to room, filling fireplaces and fetching water. Osterley's panoramic parkland is open daily all year round – but aim to visit on one of the monthly family discovery days, when it's busy with history trails, crafts and stories.

Letting off steam
The beautiful lake-filled park is prime picnic country: pick up a walks leaflet from the house.

The magnificent mansion at Osterley Park, seen from across the Garden Lake

The Lowdown

- 🌐 **Address** Jersey Road, Isleworth, Middlesex TW7 4RB; 020 8232 5050; www.nationaltrust.org.uk/osterley
- 🚗 **Train** Isleworth, 30-minute walk. **Tube** Osterley (Piccadilly line), 15-minute walk. **Bus stop** Jersey Road (number H28); Hammersmith (H91, 15-minute walk). **Car** Parking £3.50
- 🕐 **Open** House: noon– 4:30pm; Wed–Sun (till 3:30pm Mar) Mar–Oct; noon–3:30pm, Sat & Sun Nov–mid-Dec. Garden: 11am–5pm Wed–Sun Mar–Oct; noon–3:30pm, Sat & Sun Nov. Park: 8am–7:30pm daily.
- 💲 **Price** House and garden: £25–35; garden only, £11–15; park free

- 🚩 **Guided tours** Audiovisual guide includes family trail; occasional themed tours and parkland walks (charges apply, see website).
- 🧍 **Age range** 6 plus
- 🧍 **Activities** Family Discovery Days last Sun of month, noon–4pm; children's activities on Thu pm in school holidays, 1–4pm; both free with admission
- ⏱ **Allow** 2 hours
- ♿ **Wheelchair access** No
- 🍴 **Eat and drink** Snacks Stables Café (11am–5pm Wed–Sun; noon–4pm Nov) serves home-cooked lunches and teas
- 🛍 **Shop** Selling gifts; also a farm shop selling flowers and vegetables
- 🚻 **Toilets** Close to stableyard

Picnic under £20; **Snacks** £20–40; **Real meal** £40–60; **Family treat** £60 or more (based on a family of four)

⑤ Richmond Park

Hills, hinds and Henry VIII

Gibbet Wood, Bone Copse, Leg of Mutton Pond... the names of the natural features in this park are rich with romance and they describe the place well: it is the wildest tract of country in London. Richmond is the largest royal park and remains much the same as when Charles I put a 13-km (8-mile) wall around it in 1637 and 2,000 deer were released for him to hunt. Some of the oak trees the king knew are here still, and so are the deer: 650 reds and fallows, a great draw for children – though it's best not to get too close, especially during the autumn rut, when they spar for supremacy.

The best way in for families is from Richmond, for the playground at Petersham Gate and Pembroke Lodge Café, set in a Georgian mansion. Walk off the cakes with a hike up Henry VIII's Mound to take in the view to St Paul's Cathedral: some say the king stood watch here for the signal that his marriage to Anne Boleyn had been terminally severed.

A colourful performance at the Polka Theatre in Wimbledon

There is year-round cycle hire inside Roehampton Gate, on the east side, and the park's other sporting options include power-kiting, horse riding and fishing in Pen Ponds. Isabella Plantation, with its azaleas and maze of streams and bridges, looks sensational in spring and autumn, and the hide-and-seek potential goes on for miles.

Take cover

Take the 493 bus from Richmond or Roehampton to the **Wimbledon Lawn Tennis Museum** *(Church Rd, SW19 5AE; 020 8946 6131; www. wimbledon.com/visiting/museum; 10am–5pm daily; £35–45, stadium tours extra)*, which appeals to all the family with its interactive exhibits, including the "ghost" of John McEnroe. Or stay on the bus and visit the **Polka Theatre** *(240 The Broadway, Wimbledon SW19 1SB; 020 8543 4888; www.polkatheatre. com; 10am–4:30pm daily)* for under-14s, with a busy roster of live drama (twice daily Tue–Sat), a playground and a dressing-up corner with rocking horses and storybooks.

Above Children's playground near Petersham Gate, Richmond Park
Below Magnificent male red deer under the trees at Richmond Park

The Lowdown

🌐 **Address** Holly Lodge, Richmond Park, Richmond, TW10 5HS; 0300 061 2201; www.royalparks. gov.uk/richmond-park

🚗 **Train** Richmond, then bus 65 or 371; or Norbiton, then 15-minute walk to Kingston Gate. **Tube** Richmond (District line), then bus. **Bus stop** North side: 33, 190, 337, 391, 419, 485, R68. South: 85, 263, K3. East: 72, 493. West: 65, 371. **Car** Six free car parks

🕐 **Open** Park: from 7am Mar–Sep; from 7:30am Oct–Feb (closes half an hour before dusk). Park office: open weekdays 8:30am–4pm. Visitor centre: Pembroke Lodge (Richmond Gate) open 10am–4pm Fri–Sun (till 3pm Nov–Feb)

💲 **Price** Free

🚩 **Guided tours** Free garden walks and history rambles most months (dates vary, check website)

👫 **Age range** All

👫 **Activities** Playgrounds at Petersham and Kingston Gates. Cycle hire at Roehampton Gate (10am–5pm Mon–Fri, till 7pm weekends and school holidays; from £4 per hour; 0705 020 9249; www.parkcycle.co.uk). Power-kiting lessons (020 7870 7700; www.kitevibe.com); fishing permits (Jun–Mar; 020 8940 3209); pay-and-play golf (020 8876 1795); for riding stables, see park website.

⏱ **Allow** Up to a day

🍴 **Eat and drink** *Snacks* The park's Roehampton Café *(9am–5pm daily)* sells snacks and ices. Plus kiosks at Broomfield Hill and Pen Ponds. *Real meal* Pembroke Lodge Café in the park *(020 8940 8207; summer: 10am–5:30pm; winter till dusk)* has a full restaurant menu, with children's dishes, and outdoor seating.

🚻 **Toilets** All main gates

⑥ Ham House

The most haunted house in London?

With its riverside gardens, children's treasure map and gaggle of ghosts, it's hard to think of a more appetizing stately home for families than Ham House. The main draw is its dreamy setting, with lawns running down to an especially bucolic stretch of the Thames. The house itself is a time capsule, little changed since the 1670s, when the ruthless and beautiful Duchess of Lauderdale schemed her way to the top of Stuart society. A prime mover in the secret Sealed Knot society, which restored Charles II to the throne, the duchess filled Ham's halls with exuberant furniture and art.

What will interest kids, though, is not the duchess's legacy, but the fact she may still be in residence. Staff and visitors sometimes hear the tap-tap-tap of her silver cane and glimpse her King Charles spaniel scampering along the corridors. Regular ghost tours complement an imaginative spread of children's stuff here: a dedicated Discovery Room, complete with treasure map for investigating the house; garden trails; and al fresco storytelling, cinema and theatre every summer.

On sunny days, walk to Ham from Richmond station along the Thames Path (download the route at *www.nationaltrust.org.uk/ hamhouse*) or hop on the historic foot-ferry across to the north bank, where Marble Hill House *(Richmond Rd, Twickenham, TW1 2NL; 020 8892 5115; www.english-heritage. org.uk)* shimmers like a mirage above the water. A masterpiece Palladian mansion, Marble Hill has a weekend programme for families.

Letting off steam

Children can run wild in the garden's labyrinthine wilderness of hedges and summerhouses.

The Lowdown

- 🌐 **Address** Ham Street, Richmond, TW10 7RS; 020 8940 1950; *www. nationaltrust.org.uk/hamhouse*
- 🚗 **Train** St Margarets or Twickenham, then 10-minute walk and foot ferry (10am–6pm or dusk, Feb–Oct, plus winter weekends); Richmond, then 30-minute riverside walk, or bus 65 or 371. **Tube** Richmond (District line). **Bus stop** Ham Street, Sandpits Road. **Car** Free parking nearby
- 🕐 **Open** Noon–4pm Sat–Thu, Apr–Oct; Feb, Mar and Nov: guided tours only, 11:30am–3:30pm. Garden, shop and café: 11am–5pm daily
- 💷 **Price** House and garden: £25–35. Garden only, £12.50–17.50
- 🚩 **Guided tours** Feb, Mar and Nov only: 30-minute tours of selected rooms. Garden tours all year round (call for times). "Servants' Tours", Apr–Oct, Tue (charged)
- 👫 **Age range** All
- 🧒 **Activities** Interactive Discovery Room, quiz trail and garden trails. Art Cart craft activities Apr–Oct, Sun. Occasional family ghost tours (ages 5 plus; book ahead). Easter egg hunts; summer cinema and theatre in the gardens; Christmas events for families
- ⏱ **Allow** 2 hours
- ♿ **Wheelchair access** Limited: steps and narrow doorways inside – lift available; gravel paths outside
- 🍴 **Eat and drink** *Snacks* The luscious Orangery Café does its own baking, and has a kids' corner.
- 🛍 **Shop** Selling local and unusual gifts and souvenirs
- 🚻 **Toilets** In courtyard

The beautifully kept kitchen garden at Ham House

Picnic under £20; **Snacks** £20–40; **Real meal** £40–60; **Family treat** £60 or more (based on a family of four)

Day Trips

London packs in enough history for several cities – but to really breathe the atmosphere of Henry VIII's England, nowhere beats Hampton Court Palace. Families get to dress, act and even eat and drink the period. Windsor, by contrast, is all about the modern monarchy, with a majestic castle, parkland, a school for princes and one of Britain's best theme parks. Do what the Queen does and come for the whole weekend.

Highlights

Play the king
Hampton Court's live history experience includes free cloaks, so kids can dress up and explore Henry VIII's magnificent home (see p236–7).

Eat like a Tudor
The palace kitchens regularly re-create dishes from 500 years ago – sometimes available to try at the Tiltyard Café (see p237).

Get lost!
People have been losing themselves in Hampton Court Maze for 300 years, and three new forks have made it more fiendish than ever (see p236).

See monarchy in miniature
Displayed at Windsor Castle, Queen Mary's Dolls' House is an exquisite creation and the world's most opulent – a snapshot of royal life in the 1920s (see p238).

Ride with the royals
The royal family love riding in Windsor Great Park. In the absence of horses, saddle up and explore by hiring bicycles from Windsor (see p239).

Visit toyland
Windsor's Legoland is totally geared for pre-teens, with its "pink-knuckle" roller coasters and splashing water rides (see p241).

Left As well as thrilling rides, there are tamer entertainments at Legoland, such as Miniland, a Lego reconstruction of landmarks from around the world
Above A collection of sporting caps in the museum at Eton College

① Hampton Court Palace
Where Henry VIII still rules

Children need to be on their best behaviour at Hampton Court, in case they run into its former owner in one of his tempers. Henry VIII, everyone's favourite bad-boy monarch, caroused here with his 1,000-strong court and his six wives, and still roars through the Great Hall most days, as part of an interactive history experience. As the aroma of roasting meat wafts from the kitchens, families get to dress as 16th-century courtiers in miniature costume dramas – velvet cloaks are available from the Information Centre.

Falconry display in the grounds

Key features

The maze The world's most famous maze was planted for William III in 1690. But don't follow the map at the entrance – it's wrong!

Young Henry VIII Exhibition Sporting hero, musician, dancer... before becoming a bloated tyrant, Henry was a "lusty and brave prince". These hands-on displays trace his early years.

Wine Fountain This was re-created by studying archaeological remains found in Base Court in 2008. As in Henry VIII's day, it can serve wine.

Haunted Gallery It's said Queen Catherine Howard still wails in the corridor through which she was dragged by Henry's guards in 1541.

Great Vine Planted by "Capability" Brown in 1768, this vine produced an amazing 383 kg (745 lb) of sweet black grapes in 2001.

Tudor Kitchens The kitchens had 55 rooms and 200 kitchen hands. On certain weekends, costumed "food archaeologists" re-create banquets based on 500-year-old recipes.

Fountain Court In 1689, William and Mary hired Christopher Wren to execute a Baroque makeover here, in a bid to outdazzle Versailles.

Great Hall Shakespeare's company performed here for James I in 1603. The walls are hung with splendid tapestries of *The Story of Abraham*.

Letting off steam

The grounds go on forever, with the maze, formal gardens and the 20th Century Garden, great for hide-and-seek. For under-5s, there's a soft-play room off Base Court. To the north and within walking distance, **Bushy Park** (Hampton Court Road, Hampton, TW12 2EJ) has a playground, while to the west lies the open-air

Deer in Bushy Park, within walking distance of Hampton Court

Prices given are for a family of four

Hampton Swimming Pool *(High Street, Hampton, TW12 2ST; www. hamptonpool.co.uk; open daily).*

Eat and drink

Picnic: under £20; Snacks: £20–40; Real meal: £40–60; Family treat: £60 or more (based on a family of four)

PICNIC There are picnic tables in the 20th-Century Garden, or else spread a rug in the Tiltyard or Wilderness gardens. **Mada Deli** *(11 Bridge Road, East Molesey, KT8 9EU; 020 8979 7553; 9am–5:30pm)*, close to Hampton Court train station, is a great place to pick up supplies.
SNACKS In an area originally used for jousting by Henry VIII, Hampton Court's **Tiltyard Café** has meal deals

on its home-made children's food and serves Tudor dishes on the first weekend of the month. There's also a playroom for younger kids.
REAL MEAL Jamie's Italian *(19–23 High Street, Kingston, KT1 1LL; 020 3326 4300; www.jamieoliver. com/italian/kingston; noon– 10:30pm)*, stands out among the chain restaurants across the river in Kingston upon Thames, for atmosphere. Kids dine free from the children's menu on weekdays.
FAMILY TREAT Cammasan *(8 Charter Quay, Kingston, KT1 1HR; 020 8549 3510; www.cammasan.co. uk; noon–3pm, 6pm–11pm Mon– Fri; noon–11pm weekends)* offers flavourful Asian food: the downstairs noodle bar is best for families.

The Lowdown

🌐 **Address** East Molesey, Surrey, KT8 9AU; 0844 482 7777; www.hrp.org.uk/hamptoncourtpalace

🚗 **Train** Hampton Court Station (trains from London Waterloo). **Bus stop** Trophy Gate, Hampton Court Station. **River bus** Services run Apr–Oct from Westminster, Kew and Richmond (www.wpsa.co.uk or www.turks.co.uk). **Car** Park at Hampton Court Palace, Hampton Court Green or Hampton Court Station

🕐 **Open** Apr–Oct: 10am–6pm; Nov–Mar: 10am–4:30pm (last admission one hour earlier). Gardens open one hour later.

💲 **Price** £44–54; maze only: £11–16; gardens only: £11–16, under 15s free

👪 **Skipping the queue** Book ahead online to skip the ticket queue – it's a little cheaper, too.

🚩 **Guided tours** Costumed tours and dramatic vignettes daily (free, times vary). Four themed audio tours for adults, plus four for children. Occasional evening ghosts tours on Fri and Sun (ages 12 plus).

👫 **Age range** 3 plus

👫 **Activities** Range of age-graded children's trails, with prizes; plus audio tours for ages 6 plus (all free). Tudor cloaks in all sizes available from Information

Centre. Cookery weekends in Henry VIII's kitchens (see website for dates), plus additional live interpretations in school holidays, which might include Tudor etiquette, falconry displays, jester shows and jousting. Chapel Royal open for services daily. Hampton Court Music Festival (Jun) and Flower Show (Jul).

⏱ **Allow** A full day

♿ **Wheelchair access** Most of the routes are accessible via a lift. There are some shallow stairs, but doorways are wide. There are scooters for the gardens.

🍽 **Café** Both Tiltyard Café (see left), in grounds, and Privy Kitchen Coffee Shop, inside the Palace, offer light lunches and a children's menu.

🛍 **Shop** Four – Barracks, Tudor Kitchens, Garden and Henry – selling a vast array of themed gifts, books and toys

🚻 **Toilets** Main car park, Tiltyard Café, Base Court, Fountain Court

Good family value?
It's quite expensive, but apart from the Tower of London, no heritage attraction in Britain does a better job of keeping families entertained all day.

Find out more

DIGITAL The Palace's website has Tudor crafts and recipes to try, plus interviews with expert curators. Learn how tapestries are conserved, make your own Henry VIII bonnet, or take on the king himself in virtual combat: www.hrp.org.uk/HamptonCourt Palace/educationandcommunity/learning/funandgames.aspx.

Next stop. . .

THEME PARKS AND THEATRE
With a car, two top theme parks are in striking distance. **Thorpe Park** (Staines Rd, Chertsey, Surrey KT16 8PN; 0871 663 1673; www.thorpe park.com), 16 km (10 miles) west, has white-knuckle roller-coasters. **Chessington World of Adventures** (Leatherhead Rd, Chessington, Surrey, KT9 2NE; 0871 663 4473; www.chessington.com), 10 km

(6 miles) to the south, is better for younger children. They're big parks, though: don't try to combine either with Hampton Court in a single day. **The Rose Theatre** (24–26 High St, Kingston, KT1 1HL; 0871 230 1552; www.rosetheatrekingston.org) puts on classy children's shows in school holidays, and has storytelling (under 5s) most Fridays at 11:15am.

The Tiltyard Café sometimes serves Tudor dishes, and has a playroom

② Windsor Castle
Her Majesty's fairytale fortress

Bristling with turrets and suits of armour, the world's oldest occupied castle stands theatrically on a hilltop by the River Thames. The Queen stays here regularly – though presumably she doesn't use all 1,000 rooms. Non-royal visitors should pick up a free audio guide (a kids' version is available too) and tour the State Apartments, Chapel and Art Gallery. Children also enjoy the marching guardsmen, carriage rides and all-round holiday atmosphere of the little riverside town of Windsor, below the castle.

Royal Standard

Key Features

Round Tower The oldest part of the castle, this was built of wood in the 1070s by William the Conqueror. A guided tour climbs 200 steps to the top (over-10s only).

Royal Standard When the Queen's flag flies from the Round Tower, Her Majesty is at home.

① **Queen Mary's Dolls' House** The world's most luxurious doll's house was designed by architect Sir Edwin Lutyens in the 1920s, and took 1,500 artists and craftsmen three years to complete.

St George's Chapel This is a Gothic wonder from the 15th century. Light from the stained-glass windows illuminates the tombs of Henry VIII and Charles I.

Changing the Guard Everything stops in Windsor High Street when the castle guard marches through at 10.45am most mornings. The ceremony happens in the castle's Lower Ward.

State Apartments Furnished with gilt, crystal, antiques and armour, these rooms also have priceless art: look out for works by Rembrandt, Rubens, Canaletto and Gainsborough.

② **Long Walk** If the weather is dry, horse-drawn carriages trot along the Long Walk, which leads down to Windsor Great Park (from 12:30pm; Easter–Oct: daily; Nov–Easter: Sat & Sun).

The Lowdown

🌐 **Address** Castle Hill, Windsor, SL4 1NJ; 020 7766 7304; *www.royalcollection.org.uk/windsorcastle*

🚗 **Train** Windsor & Eton Central, served by trains from Paddington via Slough; or Windsor & Eton Riverside, direct from Waterloo (journey time: 40 minutes–1 hour). **Coach** Green Line daily from London's Victoria Coach Station (*www.greenline.co.uk*). **Car** Use long-stay parking in Windsor town centre (charged)

🕐 **Open** Mar–Oct: 9:45am–5:15pm; Nov–Feb: 9:45am–4:15pm (last admission 75 minutes earlier). State Apartments closed very occasionally (check ahead). St

George's Chapel open Mon–Sat, and for services only on Sun

💷 **Price** £53–63 (less when State Apartments are closed). Plus £1.25 per ticket booking fee

🚻 **Skipping the queue** Buy tickets direct from the Royal Collection (online or from castle ticket office) for one year's free re-admission

🎧 **Guided tours** Free 2-hour audio-tour, plus children's version (ages 7–11). Frequent 30-minute tours of Castle Precincts daily (free with admission). Aug–Sep only: 45-minute Conquer the Tower Tour for ages 11 plus (£22–32); 30-minute Great Kitchen Tour (£17–22), check website for dates, pre-booking essential.

👫 **Age range** 5 plus

🧒 **Activities** Free kids' audio-guide plus activity sheets for ages 5–7 and 7–11 (also downloadable from website). Art activities in Moat Room, first Sat every month. School-holiday programme may include special children's tours, storytelling, object-handling and armour design (check website). Changing the Guard ceremony: Apr–Jul: 11am daily; Aug–Mar: alternate days; no ceremony on Sun

⏱ **Allow** 2–3 hours

♿ **Wheelchair access** Yes, but there are steps to the main entrance and to St Georges Chapel. There is a lift inside the castle. The outside areas can be uneven.

Letting off steam

Playtime and picnicking are not smiled upon inside the castle grounds, through there are endless lawns and trees to run among along the Long Walk, south of the castle. The nearest playground is at **Bachelors Acre**, off Victoria Street.

Eat and drink

Picnic: under £20; Snacks: £20–40; Real meal: £40–60; Family treat: £60 or more (based on a family of four)

PICNIC Café 78 *(8 George V Place, SL4 1QP; 01753 858338; www. cafe78.co.uk; 7:30am–5pm)*, handily located on the way from the train station to the castle, sells lovely baguettes and pastries.
SNACKS Extreme Motion and Windsor Skate Park Café *(Alexandra Gardens, Alma Rd, Windsor, SL4 5HZ; 01753 830220)* serves sandwiches and pizza. It also has rails and ramps for all ages, mini-golf, a bungee trampoline and bike hire – a good option if exploring Windsor Great Park *(see p240)*.
REAL MEAL Gastro-pub the **Riverhouse** *(10 Thames Street,*

Playing cricket on the Long Walk, which runs south from Windsor Castle

☕ **Café** None on site; ice cream and water available from North Terrace
🛍 **Shop** There are three shops, all selling Royal- and castle-themed souvenirs and gifts
🚻 **Toilets** Via security area

Good family value?

Far from cheap, but just about worth it when combined with the town and Windsor Great Park *(see p240)*. Aim to visit when children's activities are scheduled, and avoid Sundays, when there's no Changing the Guard and St George's Chapel is closed to visitors. Visit again within 12 months for free.

Bouncing around on a trampoline in Alexandra Gardens, Windsor

Windsor, SL4 1QN; 01753 620010; www.windsorpubco.co.uk/ riverhouse; food: noon–10pm) is a child-friendly option with a lovely Thames-side terrace and a special £7 menu for under-10s.
FAMILY TREAT Gilbey's *(82 High Street, Eton, Windsor SL4 6AF; 01753 854921; www.gilbeygroup. com; noon–10pm)* serves smart modern-British fare with an emphasis on seasonal ingredients. It also has delicious afternoon teas in not-too-formal surroundings.

Find out more

DIGITAL Explore Queen Mary's Dolls' House in every tiny detail at this interactive mini-site: *www. royalcollection.org.uk/ queenmarysdollshouse.*

Next stop...
BOAT TRIPS
Among the raft of River Thames cruises offered from Windsor Promenade, 5 minutes from the castle, are 40-minute return trips with **French Brothers** to Boveney Lock, with views of Eton College *(daily Mar–Oct, plus some winter weekends; 01753 851900; www. boat-trips.co.uk).* Or try **Salters Steamers** *(01753 865832, www. salterssteamers.co.uk).*

A leisurely tour down the Thames aboard the French Brothers' boat

③ Windsor Great Park

Where the royals ride out

He gallops across the Great Park at midnight on a black stallion, wearing a ghoulish antler headdress and with a pack of hell-hounds in his wake. No, it's not the Duke of Edinburgh, but Herne the Hunter, a legendary ghost from Windsor folklore – and he is not the only exotic apparition in this 13th-century hunting park, which stretches south of the castle. There's also a Canadian totem pole to discover, rising incongruously beside Virginia Water, the park's large ornamental lake. The nearby "Roman temple" was picturesquely assembled in 1818 by George IV, with columns taken from Leptis Magna, a major city of the Roman Empire in what is now Libya.

Windsor Great Park is a vast expanse of woods, ponds and pasture, with deer, formal gardens, the royal polo club and more. The

The Deer Park, just one area of the vast Windsor Great Park

The Lowdown

🌐 **Address** The Savill Garden, Wick Road, Englefield Green, Surrey TW20 0UU; 01784 435544; www. theroyallandscape.co.uk

🚃 **Train** Windsor & Eton Central. Egham or Virginia Water for Savill Garden. **Car** Free parking on A332 south of Windsor. Pay car parks at Savill Garden (free with garden admission), Valley Gardens, Wick Road, Virginia Water Gate and Blacknest Gate

🕐 **Open** Park: 7am–dusk. Savill Garden: Mar–Oct: 10am–6pm; Nov–Feb: 10am–4:30pm (last admission 30 minutes earlier)

💷 **Price** Windsor Great Park free. Savill Garden: summer £21–31; winter £15–25

🚩 **Guided tours** Groups only

👫 **Age range** All

👨‍👩‍👧 **Activities** Seasonal treasure trails and activities for families in some school holidays. Open-air theatre

and opera (Jun–Aug); carriage rides from Savill Garden on selected spring and summer weekends (check website for details).

🕐 **Allow** Half a day

🍴 **Eat and drink**
Snacks Refreshments at Windsor Great Park post office and (seasonal) kiosks at Obelisk Lawn, Blacknest Gate, Totem Pole and Virginia Water car park. *Real meal* Savill Garden Restaurant (01784 485 402; Mar–Oct: 10am–5:30pm; Nov–Feb till 4pm) has home-made kids' meals and lunchboxes.

🛍 **Shop** Savill Garden visitor centre, selling gifts, toys, books, garden items, wildlife and eco products, and the Duchy Original range

🚻 **Toilets** Savill Garden, Valley Gardens, Virginia Water car park

Long Walk stretches south into the park from Windsor Castle – but it's a 1- or 2-hour walk to reach the Savill Garden, where, a visitor centre offers a good café, carriage rides and occasional holiday activities for children. A better bet is to hire bikes from Windsor and cycle here on National Cycle Route 4, which largely avoids busy roads. Or go by car, parking either at the Savill Garden or Virginia Water.

Letting off steam

The park's playground is at **Obelisk Lawn**, near the Savill Garden car park, with a shipwreck to scramble on and a sandpit to jump around in.

④ Eton college

Classes for the upper classes

"Etonians should not be approached, shouted at or photographed", says the Eton College website – though children can be forgiven one small giggle at the tail-coated young gentlemen who promenade like penguins around the School Yard. Founded in 1440 by King Henry VI, Eton is the world's most prestigious boys' school, having produced 19 British prime ministers, including David Cameron. Princes William and Harry also studied here – the fees are close to £30,000 per year.

The college is best approached on foot across the river from Windsor

The Lowdown

🌐 **Address** Windsor, SL4 6DW; 01753 671177; www.etoncollege. com

🚃 **Train** Windsor & Eton Riverside, then 15-minute walk. **Car** Arrive from north via Slough Road, or (preferably) walk from Windsor

🕐 **Open** Apr–mid-Oct by guided tour only; see website for details

💷 **Price** £24–34

🚩 **Guided tours** 1-hour tours at 2pm and 3:15pm

👫 **Age range** 8 plus

🕐 **Allow** 1–2 hours

♿ **Wheelchair access** Mostly – there is a chairlift to the chapel and cobbled surfaces outside

🍴 **Eat and drink** *Picnic* Tastes (92 High St, Eton, SL4 6AF; 01753 641 557; www.tastesdeli.co.uk; 10:30am–6pm Tue–Sat) is a super deli; eat your picnic in Windsor Park. *Snacks* Zero 3 (21 High St, Eton, SL4 6BL; 01753 864725) serves good-value food to eat in.

🛍 **Shop** In Eton High Street, selling school-related items

🚻 **Toilets** Brewhouse Yard

and through Eton village. Tours are offered twice daily in season, covering the school's stately main quadrangle, cloisters and 15th-century chapel. The highlight is the very first schoolroom, preserved from the 1400s and carved with the graffiti of later students Robert Walpole, Percy Shelley and others. The guides happily field questions about the quirks of college life past and present – and children who fail to pay attention can be pointed towards the little museum at the end of the tour. It displays the cane and "swishing block" employed by infamous headmaster Dr Keate, who once flogged almost the entire school.

Eton students in tail-coats relaxing in between lessons

Prices given are for a family of four

Viking River Splash ride, one of many attractions at Legoland

Letting off steam

Home Park playground (*Romney Lock Road, off King Edward VII Avenue*), just across the footbridge in Windsor, was given to the public by Queen Victoria.

⑤ Legoland
Tiny-brick wonderland

Pack swimsuits and sunglasses before heading for Windsor's super-popular brick-themed fun park. The swimsuits are for the assorted splash rides, which include simulated jet skis and a super-fast water slide. The shades are for the sheer multi-coloured intensity of it all: Legoland packs in 10 zones of stunt shows, children's theatre, roller-coasters and model-building, all loosely inspired by the classic toy box building blocks.

The focus is on pre-teens, especially ages 5–10, with a handful of mildly thrilling rides plus lots of junior race-car driving, balloon races and submarine adventures (among real-life sharks). Purists will enjoy Miniland, with its intricate Lego landmarks. The whole thing is fiendishly expensive: seek out online ticket deals, and try not to visit at holiday times, when the queues stretch almost to Denmark.

The Pirates' Training Camp playground at Legoland

Letting off steam

Kids with any energy left should head for the climbing apparatus at Pirates' Training Camp or DUPLO Playtown, both in Legoland.

The Lowdown

🌐 **Address** Winkfield Road, Windsor, SL4 4AY; 0871 2222 001; www.legoland.co.uk

🚗 **Train** Windsor & Eton Central or Windsor & Eton Riverside, then shuttle bus (charged; from 10am till 30 minutes after park closes). **Coach** Green Line service daily from London Victoria (www.greenline.co.uk). **Car** 3 km (2 miles) from Windsor on B3022; parking fee

🕐 **Open** Apr–Oct: call for details (closing time varies with season)

💲 **Price** £146–76; 10 per cent saving for booking online

👫 **Skipping the queue** Book online to skip the ticket queue. Ride queues peak noon–3pm; for a hefty extra charge, Q-Bot devices enable visitors to reserve time slots on selected rides.

👪 **Age range** 3–12 years

🎭 **Activities** Stunt performances, puppet plays and 4-D cinema shows in Imagination Theatre. Programme might include events with kids' TV characters, laser spectaculars and Hallowe'en fun and fireworks.

⏱ **Allow** A full day

♿ **Wheelchair access** Yes

🍴 **Eat and drink** More than a dozen outlets in park, such as Mexican Cantina and Pirate's BBQ, many offering healthy meal deals for kids.

🛍 **Shop** Throughout the park; the Big Shop is at the entrance, selling Lego® products.

🚻 **Toilets** In car park and throughout the park

Where to Stay in London

London's hotels are much more child friendly than they used to be. Today, even the grandest have family rooms and restaurants with children's menus. As alternatives to traditional hotels, B&Bs or small hotels offer more informal accommodation and apartments can make a flexible and good-value option.

AGENCIES

At Home in London
020 8748 1943; www.
athomeinlondon.co.uk
This agency specializes in B&B accommodation in private homes in central and suburban London. It has more than 80 homes on its books, all carefully chosen and regularly inspected. The website search engine is organized according to London Transport zones 1 (very central) and zones 2/3 (further out).

London Bed & Breakfast Agency
020 7586 2768;
www.londonbb.com
An agency offering B&B in private houses, and some apartments, covering central, north (a particularly good selection here), south and west London. It prides itself on paying attention to visitors' individual requirements. Hosts welcome families with children aged five and over.

London Home to Home
020 8769 3500; www.
londonhometohome.com
This friendly B&B agency offers good quality family accommodation in private houses in central, north and west London. Rooms are comfortable and well maintained, and rates include a generous breakfast. The usual minimum stay is two nights.

London House
0845 834 0244;
www.london-house.com
Gold-standard service, a wide choice and value for money are at the heart of this online business's success. It has made finding family-friendly accommodation across the city one of its specialities, with apartments, B&Bs and hotels on its books.

Westminster and the West End

HOTELS

Brown's
Map 9 D4
33 Albemarle Street, W1S 4BP; 020 7493 6020; www.brownshotel.com
The kindly staff at London's oldest hotel go out of their way to make children feel at home. Afternoon tea is a must in the iconic English Tea Room, where Rudyard Kipling wrote *The Jungle Book*. Kids' treats include a Brown's bear to snuggle up with and DVDs to watch.

£££

Stylish bedroom in London' oldest hotel, Brown's

Duke's
Map 9 D5
35–36 St James's Place, SW1A 1NY; 020 7491 4840; www.dukeshotel.com
This traditional Mayfair hotel offers plenty to keep boredom at bay, from story books to designated TV channels and PlayStation games. The special menus are always popular and usually rounded off with Duke's signature Knickerbocker Glory ice cream. Delicious picnic boxes can be supplied for lunch on the move.

£££

The Goring
Map 15 C2
15 Beeston Place, SW1W 0JW; 020 7396 9000; www.thegoring.com
Owned and run by the Goring family for four generations, this London institution prides itself on giving a warm welcome to its "VI (little) Ps". Treats include a bedtime story library, a gift bag and a visit to the kitchen, where children get to don aprons and chef's hats and decorate cakes.

£££

The Langham
Map 9 D2
1C Portland Place, W1B 1JA; 020 7636 1000; www.london.langhamhotels.co.uk
This luxurious West End hotel offers family packages, including a shopping expedition to Hamleys toy store or a day at London Zoo, plus a complimentary family movie to watch on your return. If your kids are picky eaters, the one-bedroom apartment has its own kitchenette.

£££

Renaissance London Chancery Court
Map 10 H2
252 High Holborn, WC1V 7EN; 020 7829 9888; www.marriott.com/hotels/travel/loncc-renaissance-london-chancery-court-hotel
This impressive hotel is approached through an imposing arch to a Neo-Classical courtyard. It is well placed for Covent Garden and West End theatre trips. A fun family package includes a city "Duck Tour" on land and water in an amphibious vehicle.

££

The entrance of The Goring hotel, a short walk from Buckingham Palace

BED & BREAKFAST
B&B Belgravia and Studios@82
Map 15 C3

64–66 Ebury Street, SW1W 9QD;
020 7259 8570 www.bb-belgravia.com
Handy for Victoria Station, this
popular B&B is conspicuous for its
fresh appearance and laid-back
approach. Bedrooms are decorated
in earthy tones, with small but smart
glass-partitioned bathrooms.
Studios@82 next door provides
good family accommodation. Hot
drinks (including great cappuccinos),
fruit and shortbread are on tap.

 ££

A modern kitchen in the Athenaeum Apartments

Fleet River Bakery Rooms
Map 10 H2

71 Lincoln's Inn Fields, WC2A 3JF;
020 7691 1457; www.
fleetriverbakery.com
At the eastern edge of bustling
Covent Garden, and above the
elegant arched windows of a
popular bakery, these are quietly
stylish, well-equipped studios with
their own kitchen areas. Good,
fresh breakfasts are served every
day by friendly staff in the bakery
– except for Sundays, when
hampers are provided.

 £

Lime Tree
Map 15 C3

135–7 Ebury Street, SW1W 9QU; 020
7730 8191; www.limetreehotel.co.uk
With the same postcode as the
Queen (well, Buckingham Palace),
this is a brilliantly located, simply
furnished and comfortable island of
good value. Rooms are bigger than
prices suggest and the welcoming
staff give sound advice on travel,
dining and making the most of what
London has to offer. Please note, it
is not suitable for under-fives.

 ££

Luna Simone
Map 16 E3

47–49 Belgrave Road, SW1V 2BB;
020 7834 5897; www.
lunasimonehotel.com
Fresh looking and contemporary,
this hotel was established in 1970
and is now run by the original
owner's sons. Rooms are
comfortable – there is just enough
space for the family to sprawl –
and there are shiny bathrooms
with power showers. It's a friendly
place and a cooked breakfast is
included in the price of the room.

 **££**

Vandon House
Map 16 E1

1 Vandon Street, SW1H 0AH; 020
7799 6780; www.vandonhouse.com
Owned by a private US university,
Vandon House operates both as
guesthouse and residence for the
college's London-based students.
In the heart of Westminster, where
there's a dearth of hotels, this
house provides cheap and safe
accommodation – there's a 24-hour
manned reception. The rooms are
fairly basic with bunks for the kids.

 ££

SELF-CATERING
Athenaeum Apartments
Map 9 C6

116 Piccadilly, W1J 7BJ; 020 7499
3464; www.athenaeumhotel.com/
apartments.aspx
They come at a bit of a price,
but these roomy apartments
benefit from the facilities of the
nearby luxurious Athenaeum
Hotel, while allowing families a bit
of space and total independence.
The resident Kids' Concierge will
keep your apartment stocked with
children's essentials from soft drinks

*Comfortable, contemporary rooms in
the Luna Simone hotel*

to DVDs. Check out the half-term
and holiday offers.

£££

Citadines Prestige Holborn-Covent Garden
Map 10 H2

94–99 High Holborn, WC1V 6LF;
020 7395 8800; www.citadines.com/
*en/uk/london/holborn_covent_*
garden.html
What these apartments lack in
space, they make up for in quality
furnishings (everything sparkles
following a comprehensive
refurbishment) and a handy
location (on the borders of Holborn
and Covent Garden). Pleasant
touches include a welcome tray,
mineral water, tissues and bedroom
slippers. Air conditioning makes
summer stays more comfortable.

£££

Flemings Apartments
Map 9 C5

7–12 Half Moon Street, W1J 7BH;
020 7499 0000; www.flemings-
mayfair.co.uk
Attached to Flemings Hotel but with
their own entrance in Clarges Street,
these ten serviced apartments in the
heart of Mayfair are smart without
being too precious. Helpful hotel
staff are happy to arrange outings,
from picnics and cycle rides in
Green Park to tickets for Premier
League football matches.

£££

> **Price Guide**
> The following price ranges are based on
> one night's accommodation in high
> season for a family of four, inclusive of
> service charges and any additional taxes.
> **£** Under £90 **££** £90–140 **£££** £140–200

Key to symbols *see back cover flap*

The kitchen and sitting area of one of the SACO – Holborn apartments

SACO – Holborn
Map 10 H1

*Lamb's Conduit Street, WC1N 3LT;
117 970 6999; london.www.
sacoapartments.co.uk*

Exceptionally comfortable and with all mod cons, these award-winning apartments are in a vibrant part of the city. Eclectic boutiques, restaurants, delicatessens and cafés characterize the area, and children can scamper around Coram's Fields, a playground with slides, a flying fox and pets' corner. Not for very light sleepers.

£££

44 Curzon Street Apartments
Map 9 C5

44 Curzon Street, W1J 7RF; 020 7373 6265; www.44curzonstreet.co.uk

Built in 1908 as a gentlemen's pied-à-terre, this is one of three salubrious apartment buildings in the vicinity under the same ownership. Their style is traditional English and cosy. Kitchens are extremely well equipped, though there's no shortage of local restaurants.

£££

In the heart of Mayfair, 44 Curzon Street Apartments offer traditional decor

Bloomsbury & Regent's Park

HOTELS

Bedford
Map 10 G1

83–95 Southampton Row, WC1B 4HD; 020 7636 7822; www.imperialhotels.co.uk/bedford

If one visit to the British Museum isn't enough, the pick of the Imperial group's six Bloomsbury hotels is just around the corner. Interesting local walks are featured on its website, and sightseeing tours further afield leave from the nearby Royal National Hotel. The on-site Café London offers a child-friendly menu.

££

The Landmark
Map 8 H1

222 Marylebone Road, NW1 6JQ; 020 7631 8000; www.landmarklondon.co.uk

Well placed for an early start at Madame Tussauds, the Planetarium or Sherlock Holmes Museum, this red-brick Victorian building was originally a railway hotel. It now boasts a stunning atrium with towering palm trees, where afternoon tea is served. Families won't feel cramped because the bedrooms are huge.

£££

Marriott Regent's Park
Map 2 G1

128 King Henry's Road, NW3 3ST; 020 7722 7711; www.marriott.com/hotels/travel/lonrp-london-marriott-hotel-regents-park

In leafy north London, within striking distance of Regent's Park, London Zoo, Primrose Hill and Camden Lock Market, this Marriott is perennially popular with families. Reasons include the large, airy bedrooms with sliding patio doors on to small balconies, lovely indoor pool, helpful concierges, and excellent weekend rates.

££

BED & BREAKFAST

Alhambra
Map 4 G5

17–19 Argyle Street, WC1H 8EJ; 020 7837 9575; www.alhambrahotel.com

An affordable, hospitable base in the King's Cross area, particularly useful for Eurostar travellers. In an 1840s building with a modern interior, it is a family-run affair and has been for 50 years. Rooms are on the small side, but squeaky clean. The owner cooks irresistible full English breakfasts.

££

Arosfa
Map 10 F1

83 Gower Street, WC1E 6HJ; 020 7636 2115 www.arosfalondon.com

Guests are made to feel like part of the family at this simple Bloomsbury B&B, where the genial staff keep the rooms spotlessly cleans and tidy. Be aware that some bedrooms have minuscule bathrooms. Four nearby Tube stations bring the whole city conveniently within reach.

£

The Arosfa has neat, if compact, bedrooms

Arran House
Map 10 F1

77–9 Gower Street, WC1E 6HJ; 020 7636 2186; www.arranhotel-london.com

People fall so comprehensively for this family-run B&B that they just keep coming back. The 200-year-old house has kept its original features intact and exudes old-fashioned charm. There's a sitting room with TV and leather sofas, seating in the garden for

The attractive Georgian façade of Arran House

summer picnics, plus a fridge and laundry for guests' use.

🐾 🛏 🔥   ££

Blandford   Map 9 B1
80 Chiltern Street, W1U 5AF; 020 7486 3103; www.capricornhotels. co.uk/hotel_blandford/index.php
The most charming in the small Capricorn chain is perfectly placed for the shops and a visit to Madame Tussauds. Family rooms are snug for four, but clean and well appointed. It's worth staying here just for the English breakfast, guaranteed to get you through the day.

🐾   ££

Euro   Map 4 G5
53 Cartwright Gardens, WC1H 9EL; 020 7387 4321; www.eurohotel.co.uk
This is a good hotel to choose if you have a budding tennis star in the family – guests can use the courts in Cartwright Gardens (reservations at reception). Of the clutch of modest hotels that occupy the fine former merchants' houses in this Georgian crescent, the Euro stands out for its service and competitive rates.

🐾   ££

Hart House   Map 9 A2
51 Gloucester Place, W1U 8JF; 020 7935 2288; www.harthouse.co.uk
For families seeking fair prices but more character than a chain, this B&B provides plain, reliable accommodation in a Georgian house that once sheltered French nobility during the Revolution. The staff are attentive, and the rooms spotless. If you tire of the shops, the Wallace Collection is nearby.

🐾   ££

Jesmond Dene   Map 4 G5
27 Argyle Street, WC1H 8EP; 020 7837 4654; www.jesmonddenehotel. co.uk
Mostly small rooms, even smaller bathrooms (some microscopic, some shared) and a few steep stairs to

negotiate, but (and it's a big but) the friendly, thoughtful staff, the cleanliness, the breakfasts, the free Wi-Fi and, above all, the price for this central, King's Cross location keep families coming back.

🐾   ££

Lincoln House   Map 9 A2
33 Gloucester Place, W1U 8HY; 020 7486 7630; www.lincoln-house-hotel. co.uk
A trustworthy alternative to Hart House – in the same road but closer to Oxford Street. Bedrooms are modest, with tiny bathrooms, but have a number of treats, including five-star Hypnos mattresses, satellite TV, unlimited tea and coffee and free Wi-Fi. Air conditioning has been fitted in two-thirds of the rooms.

🐾   ££

PUB WITH ROOMS
New Inn   Map 2 G3
2 Allitsen Road, NW8 6LA; 020 7722 0726; www.newinnlondon.co.uk
Close to Regent's Park and the canal, the price, the good-natured welcome and the spotless, ample rooms above this pub are hard to beat. If sleep before midnight is vital, though, check the live music forecast before booking (usually at weekends). The pub serves Thai and traditional English specialities.

    ££

The New Inn pub, just steps from Regent's Park

SELF-CATERING
Europa House   Map 2 E5
79A Randolph Avenue, W9 1DW; 020 7724 5924; www. europahouseapartments.co.uk
With children in tow, Little Venice has great appeal – it's away from the hurly-burly and has a colourful canal and pretty bridges. Europa House has 13 comfortable, airy apartments, large, leafy communal gardens and a children's playground. Frazzled parents can order groceries, take-aways or an in-house massage.

🛏 🔥   £££

23 Greengarden House   Map 9 C3
St Christopher's Place, W1U 1NL; 020 7935 9191; www. greengardenhouse.com
One of London's secret alleys, St Christopher's Place is distinctive and lined with fashionable shops, restaurants and cafés (many with outdoor tables and chairs). These apartments are in pleasant, modern surroundings, with weekday maid service, double glazing and a first-day survival kit for families.

🛏   £££

The City & the East End
HOTELS
Apex City of London   Map 12 G4
1 Seething Lane, EC3N 4AX; 020 7702 2020; www.apexhotels.co.uk/ hotels/city-of-london
Early birds can get to the Tower as soon as the gates open from this modern hotel situated just minutes away. There are complimentary kids' menus for under-13s and under-18s can stay free in their parents' room. The pristine rooms have comfortable beds and plenty of storage for the family paraphernalia.

🐾   ££

Grange City   Map 12 G4
8–14 Cooper's Row, EC3N 2BQ; 020 7863 3700; www.grangehotels. com/hotels-london/grange-city-hotel/grange-city-hotel.aspx
The greatest draw of this hotel is the fabulous 25-m (82-ft) swimming pool, something of a rarity in London, with generous children's hours, particularly at weekends (7am–9pm). It is also close to the Tower, with splendid views of it from some of the rooms.

🐾 🛏   ££

The Hoxton   Map 6 F6
81 Great Eastern Street, EC2A 3HU; 020 7550 1000; www.hoxtonhotels. com
The huge ground-floor space here incorporates a reception, shop, sitting room, bar, the Hoxton Grill restaurant, Internet café and two blazing fires. The place has a real buzz that characterizes the local area. Working on budget airline principles, the earlier you book, the less you pay. There are occasional sales, when rooms are offered for just £1.

🔥   ££

Key to symbols *see back cover flap*

SELF-CATERING

Cheval Calico House   Map 12 E3

42 Bow Lane, EC4M 9DT; 020 7489 2500; www.chevalresidences.com/ CalicoHouse.asp

Cheval Residences have several apartment buildings in London; Calico House offers the best value for money. Flats are attractive yet practical, with little luxuries such as goose-down duvets and Frette linen. Close to St Paul's Cathedral, the location is hectic and bustling during the week and quite peaceful at weekends.

🦯 £££

Close to the Tower of London, Hamlet (UK) offers basic accommodation

Hamlet (UK)   Map 12 H5

Nightingale House, 50 Thomas More Street, E1W 1UA & Burr Close, E1W 1ND; 01462 678037; www.hamletuk. com

Arriving at the Tower early to avoid the crowds is painless for guests staying at these modest one- and two-bedroom apartments in St Katharine's Dock. The area was redeveloped in the 1970s and is now surrounded by shops and restaurants. Kids will love the activity of the marina as the pleasure boats come and go.

££

Market View by BridgeStreet   Map 11 C2

15 West Smithfield, EC1A 9HY; 020 7792 2222; www.bridgestreet.com/ Market_View_by_Bridgestreet_ Worldwide.htm

Of BridgeStreet's City apartment buildings, this restored Victorian red-brick block provides the best family accommodation. Ranging from studios to three bedrooms, all have sensible hardwood floors and furniture, and superb views of the still working Smithfield Meat Market. Lots of restaurants in this lively area.

🦯 ££

MiNC Eagle Court   Map 11 C1

10–11 Britton Street, EC1M 5QD; 020 7397 1325; www. mincapartments.com/london/ eaglecourt_apartments/details.php

Clerkenwell is a reinvigorated district that is fun for families, with child -oriented restaurants and the Little Angel (puppet) Theatre in nearby Islington. Eagle Court provides clean, modern accommodation at excellent rates if booked some time in advance. Weekly maid service and 24-hour phone support.

££

Southwark & the South Bank

HOTELS

All Seasons Southwark Rose   Map 11 D5

43–47 Southwark Bridge Road, SE1 9HH; 020 7015 1480; www. all-seasons-hotels.com/gb/ hotel-7465-all-seasons-london- southwark-rose/index.shtml

A shiny new budget hotel, the UK's first All Seasons includes all the latest technology in its bargain-priced rooms, such as Wi-Fi and flat-screen TVs. With the Globe, the National Theatre and Tate Modern only minutes away, it is a perfect choice for families of culture vultures.

🦯 £

London Bridge   Map 12 E6

8–18 London Bridge Street, SE1 9SG; 020 7855 2200; www. londonbridgehotel.com

If the London Dungeon features on your "to do" list, this welcoming and intimate hotel in an interesting

The elegant exterior of the London Bridge hotel

central area could hardly be better located. The enticing lobby sets the scene, while rooms are restful with neat black-and-white bathrooms. The hotel is much larger than it appears from the outside and contains three restaurant/bars.

🦯 🦯 £££

Park Plaza County Hall   Map 10 H6

1 Addington Street, SE1 7RY; 020 7021 1810; www.parkplaza.com/ london-hotel-gb-se1-7ry/gbcounty

This vast 398-room high-rise giant is handily located for such must-visit sights as the London Eye and Aquarium. Its smart Spectrum restaurant boasts a breathtaking setting below a 14-storey glass atrium. Studios, ideal for families, have a living area with plasma TV (movies on demand) and kitchenette. Useful extras include a free laundry service.

🦯 🦯 ££

Comfortable sitting area in one of Market View by BridgeStreet's apartments

Key to Price Guide see p243

Premier Inn London County Hall
Map 10 H6

Belvedere Road, SE1 7PB; 0871 527 8648; www.premierinn.com/en/ hotel/LONCOU/london-county-hall

Two under-16s stay for free when sharing with their parents in this well-kept hotel. Geared to family life, this reasonably priced hotel offers high chairs, additive-free kids' meals and activity packs. It also has an enviable location opposite Westminster.

£

BED & BREAKFAST
Kennington B&B
Map 17 B4

103 Kennington Park Road, SE11 4JJ; 020 7735 7669; www. kenningtonbandb.com

This B&B in an impeccably renovated Georgian townhouse is a standard setter: it scores top marks for location, price, welcome and comfort. It has adjoining rooms, perfect for families with young children, and is virtually on the doorstep of Kennington Tube station, giving easy access to the rest of London. Babysitting and English courses are available.

££

SELF-CATERING
London Tower Bridge
Map 12 H6

Queen Elizabeth Circle, PO Box 36608, SE1 2WN; 020 8679 6485; www.londontowerbridgeapartments. co.uk

It may be tricky to find, but once you're here, this building offers an agreeable refuge from the bustle. Hard-to-match prices, colourful furnishings and plenty of space for lounging add to the all-round appeal of these apartments. Patronize the local deli, bakery and Borough Market (Thu–Sat), then cook up a feast in the well-kitted-out kitchen.

££

Kensington, Chelsea & Battersea

HOTELS
Crowne Plaza Kensington
Map 14 E2

100 Cromwell Road, SW7 4ER; 020 7373 2222; www.ichotelsgroup. com/h/d/cp/1/en/hotel/lonke

Probably the best-value hotel in Kensington, this is just a short stroll from the Science and Natural History museums and a favourite with families. Although the Cromwell Road is a busy thoroughfare, once inside, or in the large garden, all is calm. Guests who decide to eat out are spoiled for choice.

££

Mandarin Oriental Hyde Park
Map 9 A6

66 Knightsbridge, SW1X 7LA; 020 7235 2000; www.mandarinoriental. com/london

From mini bathrobes, books and crayons to popcorn on demand, children want for nothing at this luxurious Edwardian pile on the edge of Hyde Park and bang opposite Harvey Nichols. The smart interior is part contemporary, part traditional, with a stunning ballroom where in the 1930s, the Queen learned to dance.

£££

Rafayel on the Left Bank

34 Lombard Road, SW11 3RF; 020 7801 3600; www.hotelrafayel.com

You'll find large rooms with remarkably comfortable beds in this glossy, eco-friendly hotel. If the kids wake up hungry in the night, there's 24-hour room service. There's also pampering for parents

Smart lobby of the Crowne Plaza Kensington

in the spa and gym; a free shuttle bus to and from Clapham Junction; and the kind staff will organize cycling and boating trips.

££

Royal Garden
Map 7 D6

2–24 Kensington High Street, W8 4PT; 020 7937 8000; www. royalgardenhotel.co.uk

Favoured by footballers and rock bands, this is a hotel for celebrity spotting. However, the attraction for families is having Kensington Gardens, with the Diana Memorial Playground, Peter Pan statue and Round Pond, as their backyard. The hotel provides bread for feeding the ducks.

£££

BED & BREAKFAST
Amsterdam
Map 13 C3

7 Trebovir Road, SW5 9LS; 020 7370 5084; www.amsterdam-hotel.com

In a quiet street around the corner from Earl's Court Road Tube station, this prize-winning townhouse B&B has decent-sized and reasonably priced family rooms – these are at a premium in this area, so book early. Breakfast is served by smiling staff in a bright, pretty room with crisp tablecloths. The garden is especially lovely in summer.

££

Base2Stay
Map 13 D3

25 Courtfield Gardens, SW5 0PG; 020 7244 2255; www.base2stay.com

What you see is what you get in this smart, stuccoed townhouse in a rather salubrious corner of Earl's Court: spotless, functional accommodation with no hidden extras on the bill when you check out. Family rooms are a squeeze for four, but there are fun bunk rooms, too. Make your own breakfast in the well-equipped kitchenette or have it delivered to your room in a box.

£££

Key to symbols *see back cover flap*

The luxurious Mandarin Oriental, near Hyde Park and Sloane Street

The elegant interior of The Beaufort hotel

The Beaufort
Map 14 H1

33 Beaufort Gardens, SW3 1PP; 020
7584 5252; www.thebeaufort.co.uk
This privately owned hotel offers
29 comfortable, tastefully
decorated bedrooms, a relaxed
atmosphere and a very classy
Knightsbridge address. Be sure
to return from shopping or
sightseeing in time for tea and
mouth-watering home-made
scones, served from 3–5pm
and included in the room price.
There's also a great choice of
excellent restaurants nearby.

£££

The Cranley
Map 14 E3

10 Bina Gardens, SW5 0LA; 020
7373 0123; www.thecranley.com
A night spent here feels more like
staying with friends than in a hotel:
it's a traditional, luxurious home-
from-home with plenty of personal
touches, such as an honesty bar
and turn-down service. A highlight
of the day is afternoon tea, served
on the front terrace in summer and
by the fire in winter. There are
family offers from time to time.

£££

Darlington
Hyde Park
Map 8 G2

111–117 Sussex Gardens, W2 2RU;
020 7460 8800; www.
darlingtonhotel.com
The area around Paddington is
full of B&Bs, many of them rather
dubious. However, here is a
superior one, well located for the
train station and Heathrow Express,
as well as Oxford Street's shops.
Although some family rooms are
on the lower-ground floor, they still
feel bright and breezy. Fridges in
the rooms are a bonus.

££

Hyde Park Rooms
Map 8 G2

137 Sussex Gardens, W2 2RX; 020
7723 0225; www.
hydeparkrooms.com
In business for more than 30 years,
this modest family-run B&B offers
no-frills accommodation plus a
generous breakfast at unbeatable
prices for central London. Guests
are guaranteed a warm welcome
from the owner and staff, and
although rooms are simple and not
all have en-suite facilities, they are
certainly spick and span.

£

Lavender Guesthouse

18 Lavender Sweep, SW11 1HA;
020 7585 2767; www.
thelavenderguesthouse.com
Simply decorated and equipped,
but squeaky clean and very friendly,
this guesthouse is in a quiet suburban
area but is only a short walk from
Clapham Junction (7 minutes by
train from Victoria). Rooms are small
(but prices are smaller) and those
without bathrooms mostly have
their own WC. The sunny garden
is filled with flowers and shrubs.

££

New Linden
Map 7 C3

59 Leinster Square, W2 4PS; 020
7221 4321; www.newlinden.co.uk/
IndexMain.htm
Not far from Portobello Road,
this converted townhouse has
51 pristine and carefully designed
rooms. Floors are wooden; walls,
plain with the occasional modern
painting; and beds have distinctive
headboards and colourful covers.
The staff couldn't be friendlier, and
rooms are good value, especially,
as the excellent buffet breakfast
is included in the price.

££

Number Sixteen
Map 14 F3

16 Sumner Place, SW7 3EG; 020
7589 5232; www.firmdale.com
Tim and Kit Kemp, who own
Firmdale Hotels, have the knack
of creating places to stay that
not only look stunning but are
easy going and smooth running.
Number Sixteen is no exception.
Extras include 24-hour room
service, a DVD library, honesty
bar and freshly-squeezed orange
juice for breakfast.

£££

Park City
Map 13 D2

18–30 Lexham Gardens, W8 5JE;
020 7341 7090; www.theparkcity.
com
Tucked away behind busy
Cromwell Road, which runs in an
almost straight line from
Hammersmith to Harrods,
the award-winning Park City
spreads itself through seven
substantial houses. Once the little
ones are in bed, the grown-ups
can enjoy a nightcap in Ruby's
Cocktail Bar (which also serves
lunchtime snacks).

£££

The Parkwood
at Marble Arch
Map 8 H3

4 Stanhope Place, W2 2HB; 020
7402 2241; www.parkwoodhotel.
com
This is a tranquil oasis close to,
but a world apart from, the
frenzy of Marble Arch. Tasteful prints hang
on the walls of the spacious,
cheerfully decorated bedrooms,
some of which have handsome iron
bedsteads. There are no hidden
costs, and the price, which includes
a full English breakfast, represents
terrific value for money.

££

Rhodes
Map 8 F3

195 Sussex Gardens, W2 2RJ; 020
7262 0537; www.rhodeshotel.com
The current owners of the Rhodes
have been at the helm since 1978
and take great pride in their friendly,
eclectic B&B in an elegant Georgian
house, which was first opened
before World War II. Double glazing
keeps the rooms beautifully quiet;
the ones at the top are a fairly steep
climb, but there are willing
members of staff to help
with luggage.

££

Key to Price Guide *see p243*

Royal Park
Map 8 F3
3 Westbourne Terrace, W2 3UL;
020 7479 6600; www.theroyalpark.
com
The name is apt: Hyde Park is only
a few minutes' walk south from this
smart, traditional little hotel. Families
can arrange to have interconnecting
rooms, where breakfast is served in
bed each morning. It may be pricey,
but extras, such as Wi-Fi, use of
a guest computer and champagne
at 7pm, are included.

£££

Sydney House
Map 14 G3
9–11 Sydney Street, SW3 6PU;
020 7376 7711; www.
sydneyhousechelsea.com
Plumb between the shops of the
King's Road and the museums
of South Kensington, this is a cool
but cosy Georgian townhouse that
has undergone a chic makeover.
Rooms have pale walls, blonde-
wood floors, flat-screen TVs and
deliciously comfy beds. It has
charming staff and fair prices (look
out for special offers).

£££

Trebovir
Map 13 C3
18–20 Trebovir Road, SW5 9NH; 020
7373 6625; www.trebovirhotel.com
In the same street as the
Amsterdam and occupying two
19th-century white stucco houses,
this revamped small hotel has
some double-height windows,
which make the interior feel light
and airy. A number of rooms have
traditional bathrooms, while others

have tiny pods, so be sure to check
first. The best rates just drop it into
the inexpensive bracket.

£

Apartment in Allen House, off
Kensington High Street

SELF-CATERING
Allen House
Map 13 C1
8 Allen Street, W8 6BH; 020 7938
1191; www.allenhouse.co.uk
Families who like to shop need look
no further than these traditional,
roomy apartments in an Edwardian
mansion block off Kensington High
Street, one of London's most vibrant
shopping streets. Communal
gardens and Holland Park (within
strolling distance) will stop the
children from feeling cooped up.
There is first-rate service too.

£££

Beaufort House
Map 14 H1
45 Beaufort Gardens, SW3 1PN;
020 7584 2600; www.
beauforthouse.co.uk
Just a 5-minute hop from Harrods
toy department, these exclusive
one- to four-bedroom apartments
overlook a quiet Knightsbridge
cul-de-sac. Each one is handsomely

furnished and boasts a top-of-the-
range kitchen and bathroom.
Facilities include iPod docking
stations and an extensive DVD
collection.

£££

Castletown House
Map 13 A4
11 Castletown Road, W14 9HE; 020
7386 9423; www.castletownhouse.
co.uk
If these were a short distance east,
inside the Royal Borough of
Kensington and Chelsea, prices
could be double. Choose between
studios (a tight fit) and one- or
two- bedroom apartments with
delightful courtyards. The owners
are on hand to welcome and help.

£

Dolphin House
Map 16 E5
Dolphin Square, SW1V 3LX; 020
7798 8000; www.dolphinsquare.co.
uk/house
Part of the 1930s Dolphin Square
development by the river in Pimlico,
this offers a good choice of
apartments. Among the main selling
points are the 18-m (59-ft) indoor
pool and extensive grounds, which
include a tennis court – ideal for
little ones to let off steam.

££

Fraser Place
Queens Gate
Map 14 E2
39B Queens Gate Gardens, SW7
5RR; 020 7969 3555; london-
queensgate.frasershospitality.com
Ideal for families planning a visit
to the dinosaurs at the Natural
History Museum, these apartments
are well designed, and with
wipeable surfaces, they are available
per night. Home entertainment
includes cable TV and DVD and
CD players. Daily maid service and
24-hour reception.

££

Royal Court
Apartments
Map 8 F3
51 Gloucester Terrace, W2 3DQ; 020
7402 5077; www.
royalcourtapartments.co.uk
Managed by the Paddington Hotel
opposite, these apartments range
from the modest and old-fashioned
to the sleek and refurbished
(reflected in the price). Families will
be comfortable with two bedrooms,
a sitting room and kitchen.

££

Sydney House, located between the King's Road and the Natural History Museum

Key to symbols *see back cover flap*

SACO @ St George Wharf
Map 16 G5

St George Wharf, SW8 2LE; 0117 970 6999; london.sacoapartments. co.uk/destinations/uk/London-South_of_the_River/SACO-St-George-Wharf

The great advantage of staying here is the spectacular riverside setting: the best apartments have uninterrupted views. Set in the sprouting towers of a glass village in the sky, there are shops and a pay-per-use gym, and the look is uncluttered, with no-nonsense wooden floors and pretty indestructible furniture. A short walk across Vauxhall Bridge and you're in Westminster in minutes.

£££

Space Apart Hotel
Map 7 D3

36–37 Kensington Gardens Square, W2 4BQ; 020 7908 1340; www. aparthotel-london.co.uk

These are an outstanding choice for families, with everything on demand, from Wii games to potties. The excellent management are hands-on and the wide-open spaces of Hyde Park are on the doorstep. The apartments (some duplex) are enlivened by quirky details (such as zebra-print carpets) and have the latest Bosch appliances, practical but attractive furniture and clever storage.

££

Beyond the Centre

HOTELS

Boundary Rooms
Map 6 G5

2–4 Boundary Street, E2 7DD; 020 7729 1051; www.theboundary.co.uk

There is plenty of space to spread out in the bedrooms at Terence Conran's typically stylish converted Victorian printworks in buzzy Shoreditch. Have breakfast and snacks in the congenial Albion, a café-cum-bakery (open 8am–midnight) and, in summer, eat on the rooftop (which hums at weekends) with the whole City on display.

£££

Church Street
29–33 Camberwell Church Street, SE5 8TR; 020 7703 5984; www. churchstreethotel.com

A lively one-off, this Latin American-inspired sanctuary in multi-ethnic Camberwell is owned and was designed by two artistic

brothers. It has an informal tapas restaurant and large colourful rooms, furnished with wrought-iron beds and Mexican art. Buses 176 and 185 go from here to the excellent Horniman Museum.

£££

Crowne Plaza Shoreditch
Map 6 G6

100 Shoreditch High Street, E1 6JR; 020 7613 9800; www.ichotelsgroup. com/h/d/cp/925/en/hd/lonsd

Handy for east visiting families, who can eat breakfast with a view in the top-floor Globe restaurant, or nip around the corner to Leila's Shop (15 Calvert Avenue), a Spitalfields' institution. With Brick Lane, Columbia Road and Spitalfields all within striking distance, this is a recommended option for market enthusiasts. Rooms are bland, but spacious.

£££

Hilton London Docklands
265 Rotherhithe Street, SE16 5HW; 020 7231 1001; www.hilton.co.uk/ docklands

With a complimentary ferry service to and from Canary Wharf Tube station, getting around from this riverside hotel could hardly be easier. The rather utilitarian family rooms are a decent size, but if you need two because of your children, the second room will be half price. There is also a small pool.

££

Novotel Greenwich
Map 18 E4

173–85 Greenwich High Road, SE10 8JA; 020 8312 6800; www.novotel. com/gb/hotel-3476-novotel-london-greenwich/index.shtml

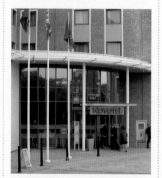

Novotel Greenwich, close to the Old Royal Naval College

This branch of the ubiquitous hotel chain stands out for the warmth of its staff and the comfort and cleanliness of its rooms. The company aims to make families a priority, and this hotel comes equipped with a PlayStation 3 and two Apple computers. The splendid breakfast will set you and the family up for a day of sightseeing in Greenwich.

£

The Premier Inn, Hampstead has on-site parking

Premier Inn, Hampstead
215 Haverstock Hill, NW3 4RB; 0871 527 8662; www.premierinn. com/en/checkHotel/LONHMP/london-hampstead

Fairly convenient for the sights of the West End (via the Northern Line from Belsize Park tube) and close to the attractive outdoor spaces of Hampstead Heath and Kenwood House, this Premier Inn has smart, contemporary public areas and an on-site Chez Gérard restaurant. Bedrooms are quiet, if slightly smaller than average for this chain. It looks a bit dull on the outside, but is made more cosy by attentive service at reception.

£

Ramada London Docklands
ExCeL, 2 Festoon Way, Royal Victoria Dock, E16 1RH; 020 7540 4820; www.ramadadocklands.co.uk

A cut above the usual chain hotels and handy for City Airport and the DLR, which zooms into the heart of the City in minutes. The best suites overlook Victoria Dock and have their own kitchenettes. Alternatively, forget cooking and try the tasty Italian dishes on offer at the hotel's Stresa restaurant. Free parking.

££

69 The Grove enjoys a quiet location in a leafy Victorian square

Richmond Gate
152–58 Richmond Hill, TW10 6RP; 0844 855 9121; www.akkeronhotels. com/Hotels/Southern-England/ The-Richmond-Gate-Hotel
A hotel with a country-house feel, steps from London's largest park, the river and the centre of Richmond, with its shops and theatres. A cottage in the grounds provides good family accommodation, and guests can use the pool at the health club next door. Highly-rated food.

🛏️🚼🖊️ £££

69 The Grove   Map 16 H5
69 Vauxhall Grove, SW8 1TA; 07796 874 677; www.69thegrove.com
Set in a quiet Victorian square close to Vauxhall tube station and several main bus routes into the West End, this townhouse has excellent travel connections. The building has been elegantly remodelled by its helpful owner/managers to offer a choice of smart rooms at different prices. Free Wi-Fi, toiletries and an iPod dock/alarm clock all add to the comfort. Breakfast (can be taken outside in summer) is hearty, healthy, or both.

🛏️🚼🖊️ £££

BED & BREAKFAST
Number 42
42 Daybrook Road, SW19 3DH; 020 8543 8709; www.bedandbreakfast-wimbledon.com
A truly warm welcome, faultless hospitality, impeccable light and airy bedrooms with proper furniture and comfortable beds are all gathered together in this home-from-home in leafy Wimbledon. The owners are also parents, so there's no shortage of toys, equipment and safe places to play. Good transport into town.

🛏️🚼🖊️🚫🏷️ £

Quality Hotel Hampstead   Map
5 Frognal, NW3 6AL; 020 7794 0101; www.qualityhampstead.com
"Olde worlde" it is not, but it does have proper bathrooms, decent-sized, comfortable bedrooms, lifts to every floor and free parking. It is also close to Finchley Road tube and bus routes into the centre. Staff are knowledgeable and helpful; breakfasts are generous. A variety of tempting local restaurants nearby.

£££

Richmond Inn
50–56 Sheen Road, TW9 1UG; 020 8940 0171; www.richmondinnhotel.com
Aspiring botanists and their parents will enjoy being so close to Kew Gardens, while theatre buffs should know that many West End productions try out in Richmond first. The clean, well-equipped bedrooms may be slightly suburban for some but there are elegant marble-covered bathrooms, which are something of a treat. Helpful 24-hour staff, a good choice of local restaurants and free parking.

🛏️ ££

SELF-CATERING
Fox Apartments
Warehouse K, Western Gateway, ExCeL Centre, E16 1DR; 020 7558 8859; www.foxapartments.com
A superb conversion of a 170-year-old warehouse next to an official Olympic venue and handy for the DLR. Exposed brickwork, warm neutral colours, two bathrooms, small patios and simple stylish fixtures and fittings make these duplexes a great find in Docklands. There is some airport noise, but it's not a huge problem.

££

Glenthurston
30 Bromley Road, SE6 2TP & 27 Canadian Ave, SE6 3AU; 020 8690 3092; www.londonselfcatering.co.uk
For energy-filled young ones, there are swings, a trampoline and grass to run around on in the gardens of these neighbouring Victorian houses, as well as a pool table and an indoor swimming pool. These simple, cheerful apartments are perfect for families. There are direct buses to Greenwich and the Horniman Museum, and a good

train service into town. Only week-long lets are available.

🚼 £

Sanctum   Map 1 C3
1 Greville Road, NW6 5HA; 020 7644 2100; www.sanctum-international.com
There is little doubt that you get more space for your money even a short distance out of the centre. A three-minute walk from Kilburn Park Tube station (and a direct route to Oxford Circus), this circular space-age building houses 43 light, handsomely furnished apartments, with well-appointed kitchens and first-class management.

🚼 £££

Town Hall Apartments
8 Patriot Square, E2 9NF; 020 7871 0460; www.townhallhotel.com
Just a five-minute walk from the V&A Museum of Childhood, the Town Hall Apartments are a happy combination of imposing Edwardian architecture and striking contemporary furnishings. The beautifully designed apartments have state-of-the-art facilities, such as wet rooms, and enjoy those of the hotel, including pool and gym. Hotel staff are obliging.

🚼 £££

RESTAURANT WITH ROOMS
La Gaffe
107–111 Heath Street, NW3 6SS; 020 7435 8965; www.lagaffe.co.uk
Above its own cheerful family-run Italian restaurant in Hampstead's village atmosphere, near the Heath and Kenwood House, La Gaffe has cosy, pleasing rooms with serviceable bathrooms. There are very friendly, hospitable staff, who are prepared to go the extra mile to help, and, of course, wonderful home-cooked Italian food.

🛏️🖊️ ££

La Gaffe restaurant and rooms in the centre of Hampstead village

Key to symbols *see back cover flap*

The distinctive "Gherkin" building towering over the City of London

London
MAPS

London City Maps

The map below shows the divison of the 18 pages
of maps in this section, as well as the main areas
covered in the sightseeing section of this book.
The smaller inset map shows Greater London
and the areas covered in Beyond the City Centre.

BELSIZE PARK

HIGHBURY

1

QUEEN'S
PARK

ST. JOHN'S
WOOD

MAIDA
VALE

2 **3**

CAMDEN

REGENT'S
PARK

KING'S
CROSS

4 **5**

ISLINGTON

FINSBURY

7

PADDINGTON

NOTTING
HILL

HYDE
PARK

8 **9** MARYLEBONE

MAYFAIR

SOHO

ST JAMES'S

BLOOMSBURY **10** **11**

HOLBORN

COVENT
GARDEN

SOUTH
BANK

13 KENSINGTON

EARLS
COURT

HAMMERSMITH

14 **15**

CHELSEA

Thames

WESTMINSTER

PIMLICO

Thames

VAUXHALL

16 **17**

LAMBETH

KENNINGTON

BATTERSEA

STOCKWELL

0 kilometres 1

0 miles 1

Beyond the City Centre
pp192–233

Walthamstow
Highgate
Hampstead
Wembley
Ilford
Greenford
Bow West Ham
Acton **Central London**
Chiswick Docklands
Brentford Charlton
Thames
Putney Clapham Peckham
Richmond Eltham
Twickenham Dulwich Catford
Wimbledon Streatham
Kingston Beckenham
Mitcham

0 kilometres 5

0 miles 5

DALSTON HACKNEY

6

SHOREDITCH

BETHNAL GREEN

12

CITY WHITECHAPEL

Thames

UTHWARK

BERMONDSEY

WALWORTH SOUTH BERMONDSEY

DEPTFORD

Thames

18

GREENWICH

NEW CROSS

CAMBERWELL PECKHAM

LEWISHAM

KEY TO MAPS 1–18

- Major sight
- Place of interest
- Other building
- Train station
- Tube station
- Riverboat stop
- Parking
- Visitor information
- Police station
- Playground
- Public toilets
- Motorway
- Pedestrian road
- Railway

0 metres 200

0 yards 200

London Maps Index

Index

Page numbers in **bold** type refer to main entries.

Acknowledgments

Dorling Kindersley would like to thank the following people whose help and assistance contributed to the preparation of this book.

Main Contributor
Journalist Vincent Crump, an Oxford English graduate, has worked widely across most spheres of written journalism: on staff for trade magazines, regional newspapers and consumer magazines, and latterly as a freelance writer and editor, principally on travel. Most of his recent work has been as resident UK travel specialist for the *Sunday Times Travel* section and *Sunday Times Travel Magazine*, for whom Vincent has been writing and editing for 10 years. This is his first book.

Introducing London & Where to Stay
Written by Leonie Glass.

Additional Photography
Demetrio Carrasco, Tim Draper, Steve Gorton, Dave King, Stephen Oliver, Rough Guides/Victor Borg, Chris Stowers.

Cartography
Maps on pages 196–7, 206–7, 214–15, 220–21, 226–7 are derived from © www.openstreetmap.org and contributors, licensed under CC–BY–SA; see creativecommons.org for further details.

Additional Design and Editorial Assistance
ASSISTANT EDITOR Claire Bush
JACKET DESIGN Tessa Blindoss, Louise Dick
ICON DESIGN Claire-Louise Armitt
READERS Scarlett O'Hara, Anna Streiffert
FACT CHECKER Karen Villabona
PROOFREADER Huw Hennessy
INDEXER Helen Peters

Photography Permissions
Dorling Kindersley would like to thank all the museums, galleries, churches and other sights that allowed us to photograph at their establishments.

Terri and Sir Richard Raleigh at 44 Curzon Street Apartments, Apple UK Press Office, Nicolas at Arosfa B&B, Hélène Muron for Barbican Film Sunday, Finoa Vella at Battersea Park Children's Zoo and Lemon Tree Café, Benjamin Pollock's Toyshop, Britain at War, British Music Experience, Paul and Sarah at Brown's Brasserie, Sophie Darley at Browns Hotel, Brunel Museum, Burgh House, Camden Arts Centre, Cartoon Museum, Shannon Hermes at Charles Dickens Museum, Jess Walker at Davis Tanner for Chelsea Football Club and all at the club, The Clink Museum, Crystal Palace Museum, Crystal Palace Sports Center, DR Johnson's House, Lettie McKie at Dulwich Picture Gallery, Farady Museum and the Royal Institution, Fire Brigade Museum, Florence Knightingale Museum, Gemma Colgan at the Foundling Museum, Lorenzo & Giuseppe at La Gaffe, Garden Museum, Guards Museum, Nancy Loader at Geffyre Museum, Vikki at Giraffe, Golders Hill Butterfly House, Amelia Atkinson at The Goring, Hany Kirollos at Gourmet Burger Kitchen Windsor, Guildhall Art Gallery, Jo Wilkinson and Madeleine McClure at Hamleys, Richard Brindley at Hard Rock Café, Harrods, Tim Powell at Historic Royal Palaces, Sarah Beckett at the Horniman Museum, Household Cavalry Museum, Hunterain Museum, Imperial War Museums, Alison Bledge at Legoland®, Sophie Lilley at The London Eye, London Film Museum, Wendy Neville at London Transport Museum, Nicola Kalimeris at Museum of London, Becca Hubbard at National Army Museum, Claire Gilbey at Natural History Museum, Old Operating Theatre Museum and Herb Garret, Malida at Original Maids of Honour, Gren Middleton at Puppet Theatre Barge, Royal Air Force Museum, Bryony Phillips at Royal Botanic Gardens Kew, Royal Observatory Greenwich, SACO – Holborn, St Paul's Cathedral, Nicola Osmond-Evans at Science Museum, Serpentine Gallery, Snook's Fun Store, Syon House, Theatre Royal Drury Lane, Unicorn Theatre, Joanna Bolitho at V&A Museum of Childhood, Amy Randall at the Wallace Collection, Dean and Chapter of the Collegiate Church of St Peter Westminster, WWT London Wetland Centre, Zoological Society of London (ZSL).

Picture Credits
a = above; b = below/bottom; c = centre; f = far; l = left; r = right; t = top.

The publisher would like to thank the following for their kind permission to reproduce their photographs:

ALAMY IMAGES: The Art Gallery Collection/*The Execution of Lady Jane Grey* 1833 Hippolyte (Paul) Delaroche 80cra; Robert Bird 80tr; Mike Booth 184br; Greg Balfour Evans 20bl; John Warburton-Lee Photography 178cl.

BATTERSEA PARK CHILDREN'S ZOO: 187tl.

THE BRIDGEMAN ART LIBRARY: Index/Bymuseum, Oslo, Norway 54cra.

BRITISH AIRWAYS: Newscast 20–1.

THE TRUSTEES OF THE BRITISH MUSEUM: 103tc, 103cla; Alan Hills 103ca.

CHESSINGTON WORLD OF ADVENTURES/MERLIN ENTERTAINMENTS GROUP: 49bl.

CORBIS: Demotix/David Mbiyu 46br, /James Gourley 18bl, /P Nutt 18br; EPA/Frantzesco Kangaris 11t; Eurasia Press/Steven Vidler 55cb; Jason Hawkes

252–3; Heritage Images 78bl; Robbie Jack 91tl; Pawel Libera 58–9; Reuters/A.J. Sisco 17bl; SuperStock/Clive Sawyer PCL 8–9.

DESIGN MUSEUM: 157tc.

DORLING KINDERSLEY: Jamie Marshall Collection 30bl; Courtesy of The Science Museum 180tr; Park Lane Group Young Artists' Concert 164bl.

DREAMSTIME.COM: Padmayogini 16br, 17br.

EDF ENERGY LONDON EYE: 160bc.

© ENGLISH HERITAGE PHOTO LIBRARY: 204clb, 216cl, 216c, 216cr.

EUROLINES: 21bc.

GAMBADO CHELSEA: 48br.

GETTY IMAGES: 19br; AFP 62br, /Carl de Souza 19bl; Express/Stan Meagher 57crb; Imagno 80cr; Chris Jackson 72c; Christopher Lee 16bl; Clive Rose 63t; Oli Scarff 15bl; SuperStock 80c; Time & Life Pictures/Mansell 56tr.

THE GOLDEN TREASURY BOOKSHOP: 43bl.

THE GOVERNOR & COMPANY OF THE BANK OF ENGLAND: 129cr.

WWW.KIDSROLLERBLADINGLESSONS.CO.UK: 13b.

THE KOBAL COLLECTION: Walt Disney Pictures 131bc.

LONDON BOROUGH OF CAMDEN: 48bl.

LONDON CITY AIRPORT: Andrew Baker 20bc.

LONDON RECUMBENTS: 188cl.

THE LONDON DUNGEON/MERLIN ENTERTAINMENTS GROUP: 153cla, 156tc.

MADAME TUSSAUDS/MERLIN ENTERTAINMENT GROUP: 114tc.

THE MAYOR'S THAMES FESTIVAL: Barry Lewis 15br.

NATIONAL PORTRAIT GALLERY, LONDON: 79tl.

THE NATIONAL TRUST PHOTO LIBRARY ©NTPL: Arcaid/Richard Bryant 233bl; Andrew Butler 231cb; Geoffrey Frosh 212tc; David Levenson 44br.

POLKA THEATRE: © Robert Workman 47br, 232tr.

REGENT'S PARK OPEN AIR THEATRE: Tristram Kenton 14bl.

RIPLEY'S BELIEVE IT OR NOT: 85tl.

ROYAL ALBERT HALL: © Marcus Ginns 2009 185tl.

ROYAL NATIONAL THEATRE: Simon Annand 162tr.

ROYAL OPERA HOUSE: Sim Canetty–Clarke 45br.

THE ROYAL COLLECTION © 2011 HER MAJESTY QUEEN ELIZABETH II: 238cr; John Freeman 74crb; Derry Moore 74cla, 74clb.

SHAKESPEARE GLOBE TRUST: Pawel Libera 146cl, Rocco Redondo 146cr.

SIR JOHN SOANES MUSEUM: 94tc.

SOMERSET HOUSE: © Gideon Mendel 13tr, 93t.

THORPE PARK/MERLIN ENTERTAINEMENTS GROUP: 49tl.

TRAVEL PICTURES: Charles Bowman 27clb.

WESTFIELD LONDON: 41bl.

Jacket images: Front: ALAMY IMAGES: Jon Arnold Images Ltd tc; AWL IMAGES: Travel Pix Collection tr; PHOTOLIBRARY: Age fotostock/North Light Images tl; Mike McQueen b; Back: ALAMY IMAGES: Veryan Dale tr; AWL IMAGES: Alan Copson tl, Julian Love tc; Spine: CORBIS: Sylvain Sonnet t.

All other images © Dorling Kindersley
For further information see: www.dkimages.com

SPECIAL EDITIONS OF DK TRAVEL GUIDES

DK Travel Guides can be purchased in bulk quantities at discounted prices for use in promotions or as premiums.

We are also able to offer special editions and personalized jackets, corporate imprints, and excerpts from all of our books, tailored specifically to meet your own needs.

To find out more, please contact:
(in the United States) **SpecialSales@dk.com**
(in the UK) **TravelSpecialSales@uk.dk.com**
(in Canada) DK Special Sales at
general@tourmaline.ca
(in Australia) **business.development@pearson.com.au**